Habsburg Lemberg

Architecture, Public Space, and Politics
in the Galician Capital, 1772-1914

Markian Prokopovych

Purdue University Press
West Lafayette, Indiana

Library of Congress Cataloging-in-Publication Data

Prokopovych, Markian, 1972-
  Habsburg Lemberg : architecture, public space, and politics in the Galician
capital,1772-1914 / by Markian Prokopovych.
      p. cm. -- (Central European studies)
  Includes bibliographical references.
  ISBN 978-1-55753-510-8
  1. Nationalism and architecture--Ukraine--L'viv. 2. Architecture--Political
aspects--Ukraine--L'viv. 3. Architecture and society--Ukraine--L'viv. 4.
City planning--Ukraine--L'viv. 5. L'viv (Ukraine)--Buildings, structures,
etc. I. Title.
  NA1455.U472L897 2008
  701'.03094779--dc22
                                    2008012779

To the memory of Volodymyr Vujcyk

Contents

Illustrations

Acknowledgments

I would like to express my gratitude to all those who have read and commented on this text – or fragments of it – in both its earlier and later incarnations: Susan Zimmermann, Maciej Janowski, Yaroslav Hrytsak, Michael Miller, and Ilona Sármány-Parsons at the Central European University, Budapest; Kati Vörös at the University of Chicago; Philipp Ther at the European University Institute, Florence; Daniel Unowsky at the University of Memphis; and Viktor Hugo Lane at the New York City Department of Education. I would also like to thank Robert Evans at Oxford, who channeled my easily distracted mind toward concrete issues of historical research and analysis, and Heinz Reif at the Technical University of Berlin, who carefully and patiently followed the progress of my slowly maturing project. My very special thanks are to Harald Binder at the Center for Urban History of East Central Europe for all his help and support.

I owe a debt of thanks to the staff of the Central State Historical Archive of Ukraine (CDIAU) and to the staff of the Arts Division of the L'viv Scientific Stefanyk Library for making my research rewarding, efficient, and enjoyable. I would like to acknowledge the assistance of the Stefanyk Library, the L'viv Historical Museum, Iryna and Ihor Kotlobulatov, the Center for Urban History of East Central Europe, and the Foundation for the Preservation of the Historical-Architectural Heritage of L'viv in giving their gracious permission to reproduce visual materials without which this book would not make very meaningful reading.

My thanks are also due to the editorial board of *East Central Europe - l'Europe du centre-est - eine wissenschaftliche Zeutschrift*, to Peter Stachel at the Austrian Academy of Sciences, and to Serhiy Tereščenko at the Center for Urban History of East Central Europe in L'viv. Because of their good assistance, some of the outcomes of the research conducted for this book have already been published or are forthcoming.

My parents, Mykola and Anita Prokopovych, were of immeasurable help to me during my research in L'viv. And Ágnes and Mia were my best companions during this long saga, though I'm sure they were sometimes unaware of how much their patience and always being there meant to me. I apologize for sometimes failing to express how much I appreciated them and their encouragement.

Budapest, 27 November 2007

Foreword

Markian Prokopovych offers here a fresh and original history of architecture, public celebrations, and public space in Lemberg/Lwów/L'viv, the capital of Austrian Galicia from the late eighteenth century to World War I. This book can serve as a model for writing the history of modern urban design in Central European cities with ethnically mixed populations and competing nationalist political movements. The study focuses on the interaction of politicians, cultural leaders, and architects and engineers in Lemberg with the Habsburg imperial center and its various provincial and local agents. During the late nineteenth century the competing Polish and Ruthenian nationalist forces in the city struggled to capture public space and celebrations for their respective causes and to impose their own nationalist narratives on urban design, but Prokopovych's thorough and scrupulous research demonstrates that the nationalist interests achieved few sweeping, unalloyed victories in shaping public space in Lemberg. The Habsburg state and those who worked on its behalf or remained loyal to it continued to play important roles in determining the physical framework in which modern urban culture developed in the city.

This book convincingly demonstrates how the Habsburg imperial authorities, provincial and municipal officials, local architects and engineers, and regional or local political interests all participated in shaping the major public buildings, monuments, parks, and other public spaces of the city. All these forces influenced the face of the city, despite the efforts of particular groups such as Polish and Ruthenian nationalists to impose their own stamps on architecture and public spaces in the city. Throughout, the study effectively contrasts the multilayered and composite reality of the city's public spaces with the efforts of various political forces to try to capture public architecture and urban design for their own causes. The resulting hybrid character of the city's public architecture and public spaces bears witness to the multiple and overlapping loyalties of the inhabitants throughout the nineteenth century and to the reality of their living there simultaneously as citizens of the Habsburg monarchy, inhabitants of the multicultural city of Lemberg, and members of particular national and/or religious communities.

This book shows that the public audiences which attended imperial, local, religious, and ethnic or nationalist celebrations in the new or renovated streets and parks of an expanding Lemberg were not as nationalized, in fact, as the conventional nationalist historiography has often assumed. The nationalist parties of educated Poles and Ruthenians could not overcome the deep social divides which separated them from important segments of the population. Loyalties to class, neighborhood, the city community, Austrian Galicia, and the Habsburg monarchy remained strong for many in Lemberg. Nationalist loyalties during the late nineteenth century were new for many in the general population and for some remained weaker than the older solidarities. Many of Lemberg's inhabitants continued to share much with each other in habits, values, and culture despite differences in language, religion, or national loyalties. Prokopovych argues that the Habsburg context allowed many of the inhabitants to avoid making a final decision on their national loyalties. The book shows that in many ways, then, Lemberg remained a Habsburg city until World War I.

These conclusions and the fascinating illustrative material which the author has gleaned from a wide variety of source material in German, Czech, Polish, and Ukrainian make a significant contribution to the historiography of recent years which is moving away from the old view which saw late nineteenth-century society and popular culture in the Habsburg monarchy as dominated overwhelmingly by the various nationalist interests. More than a quarter century ago, Carl Schorske produced a brilliant micro-study of the social, cultural, and political dynamics of the building of Vienna's Ringstrasse in his prize-winning *Fin-de-siecle Vienna*, but no one, to my knowledge, has examined with similar insight the development of the public architecture and public spaces for a whole city in nineteenth-century Central Europe. Prokopovych's work on Lemberg offers important new understandings of the relationship between public architecture and public space on the one hand and loyalties to the imperial state, province, city, and nationalist causes on the other. He persuasively challenges Polish and Ukrainian national narratives about the development of Lemberg by showing that overlapping identities and loyalties continued to characterize this Habsburg provincial capital until the final collapse of the Habsburg state. This advances greatly our understanding of urban development in Habsburg Central Europe during the nineteenth century and offers important new insights about society and culture in Galicia.

—Gary B. Cohen
Series Editor

INTRODUCTION

The Other
Lemberg

On 11 August 1869, members of the Polish Democratic Party – Franciszek Smolka, former revolutionary, later provincial Diet (*Sejm*) and Austrian parliament (*Reichsrat*) deputy and an honorary citizen of Lemberg,[1] together with a small group of his followers from the National-Democratic Society – assembled at the top of *Franz-Joseph-Berg*, the highest of the hills surrounding the Galician capital. There they laid the foundation for a memorial, planned as a mound that would commemorate the 300th anniversary of the Union of Lublin's establishment of the Polish-Lithuanian Commonwealth. To arrive at the hill, known to everyone by its medieval Slavic name *Wysoki zamek* (Castle Hill), the participants had passed through the city center in small groups so as not to disturb "the public peace" among other Lemberg inhabitants. These "others" were the Ruthenians and the German speakers, notably officials that had arrived in Galicia in the early nineteenth century as a result of Josephinian administrative reforms.[2] At about the same time, the representatives of the "Ukrainian and Galician-Ruthenian Party" – an even smaller group of largely Greek Catholic clerics that had openly stated its opposition to Smolka's initiative – began to distribute printed brochures of protest in the major streets and squares.

At first blush, this event might appear to mark a metaphorical attempt to vanquish Habsburg Lemberg and transform it into Polish Lwów, a common desire of the time that reflected the expectation that Galicia would soon gain special constitutional status, similar to that of Hungary. Indeed, the Ruthenian leaders protested the event on these grounds, and, not surprisingly, a police informer called the event a "national manifestation."[3] An appeal to a historical precedent of the Polish-Lithuanian Commonwealth, if taken seriously, would challenge the legitimacy of the Habsburg state altogether. Yet a closer look reveals that such an interpretation is overly simplistic. Unlike the Polish conservatives headed by

1

Count Agenor Gołuchowski, Smolka and his supporters were against pursuing a special status for Galicia to the extent that they supported street protests against the 1867 Compromise.[4] Instead, they wanted the establishment of a federal structure for all of Cisleithania that would take into account the distinct political heritage of all nations in the Austrian half of the Dual Monarchy. Thus although the celebration of the Union of Lublin played on Polish patriotism, the event's real point was to highlight the federalism of the Polish Commonwealth as an alternative to a centralized model.[5]

The event Smolka and his party staged that day did not lead the way to political victory. The National Democrats eventually lost out in the struggle to transform the Austrian half of the new Dual Monarchy into a federal state, though most of Lemberg's inhabitants remained loyal – or *kaisertreu*, a German word that needed no translation at the time – despite this and other national projects. Nevertheless, the episode illustrates two issues that lie at the heart of this book. The first stems from the historical fact that irrespective of his political agenda and its eventual failure, Smolka launched the construction of what was to become one of Lemberg's future main landmarks, as well as a major annual commemoration held in the Vormärz-era park and beside the ruins of the medieval castle. Therefore the rich history and architectural heritage of Lemberg offers an especially tangible means of exploring the political and cultural issues that shaped the inhabitants' views of their city, its place within Austria, and the invention of new traditions in this historic setting. Second, although appeals to nationality were employed as a frequent means of initiating discussion on the city's appearance and its public space, the actual meaning of this rhetoric needs careful consideration. This meaning reflected the complex political and social arrangements of the fin-de-siècle Habsburg Monarchy, in which ideas about nationality and political identity differed significantly from what twentieth-century national historians often assumed them to be. Several simultaneous yet conflicting nationalizing projects existed side by side in the public space of the city, the space hitherto dominated by imperial symbolism. Yet while these projects did attempt to reclaim some of this space for themselves, they seldom aimed at any radical questioning of the legitimacy of imperial rule. Moreover, the effect various nationalist celebrations had on the wider public can often be overestimated in the face of evidence that even the most radical intellectuals – such as the former revolutionary and later parliamentary deputy Smolka – shared multiple loyalties and involved themselves in several projects simultaneously.

The goal of this book then is to examine these issues through a consideration of Lemberg's changing appearance and Municipal celebrations by exploring its remarkable development from a baroque and almost medieval town – as it was when Austria annexed it during the first partition of Poland in 1772 – to a booming provincial capital that Poles and Ukrainians would fight over with the outbreak of World War I in 1914. In so doing, the work will reveal that behind a variety of national and positivist historical narratives of Lemberg – and of its architecture – there always existed a city that was labeled "cosmopolitan" yet "provincial," and "Vienna" yet "of the East." Buildings, streets, parks, and monuments – in short, architecture – became part and parcel of a complex set of culturally driven politics. Established during the Vormärz period by the Austrian political elite, these politics were continued by a variety of agents in the period of nationalism. Architecture, imagined and real, shaped the broader, illiterate Lemberg public into an "imagined community" to a much greater extent than one would have thought.

This book is a contribution to the recently booming field of urban history, the subdiscipline that despite its relatively recent institutionalization[6] claims descendance from fundamental scholarly works of the twentieth century.[7] Out of the large list of relevant literature that would be redundant here, I would like to single out two essential works that directly influenced this book. First, twenty-five years ago, in his groundbreaking study on the emergence of modernism in Vienna, *Fin-de-Siècle Vienna: Politics and Culture,* Carl Schorske demonstrated how historians can use architecture and the changing cityscape as sources.[8] His work continues to resonate and shape the way scholars of Central Europe look at cities, as demonstrated by Péter Hanák's valuable comparative study of Vienna and Budapest and Ihor Žuk's work on Lemberg.[9] On the other hand, Ákos Moravánszky's path-breaking architectural historian's work, *Competing Visions: Aesthetic Invention and Social Imagination in Central European Architecture, 1867-1918,* compared Vienna with other urban centers of the Dual Monarchy and drew a picture of various "competing visions" – sometimes several in one city – of how modernity was conceptualized in architecture.[10] What follows is the text in urban biography currently undergoing revival in East Central Europe,[11] and it is informed by recent scholarship on urban culture, perceptions of urban experience, and various images and representations of the city in the press, in art, architecture, music, and literary criticism,[12] and in research on the culture of celebrations in the Habsburg Monarchy.[13]

Although the present work would have been impossible without these scholars' writings, the story it tells has rather different concerns, resulting from Lemberg appearing to be fundamentally different from the two capitals of the Dual Monarchy. Yet this difference brings its story into line with the other "provincial" ethnically mixed Habsburg cities of a similar size – far from the imperial center, yet administratively important – such as Prague and Trieste, and other, smaller towns.[14] Lemberg's development followed broader Austrian and European architectural trends, but it nevertheless failed to achieve the modernization envisioned by Viennese or other theorists and planners. More precisely, the city underwent a modernization different from that of the largest cities of the Dual Monarchy, Vienna and Budapest, but similar to those in Prague, Budweis, and Trieste, because instead of becoming a center of political unity, Lemberg evolved into a center of political conflict. Its public spaces became contested sites in the struggles between various organizations and individuals for prestigious locations for cultural institutions, central locations for monuments, "historically appropriate" restorations, and favorable representation at provincial exhibitions or upon a visit by the emperor. When Jürgen Habermas's concept of public sphere was applied to the analyses of urban spaces, political manipulation with the city's architecture and space in general resulted in the emergence of several parallel and overlapping public spaces or spheres.[15] Thus the story in this book is an invitation to explore what may be a general pattern that could elucidate the processes of modernization in the Habsburg Monarchy and in East Central Europe generally.

On the other hand, Lemberg also had its own peculiarities in the monarchy, stemming from the specifics of the Habsburgs' incorporation of Galicia at a later stage than "older" territories such as Bohemia or Moravia, and even the Littoral, and this incorporation thus coincided with the Josephinian reforms. Similar to how the rule of Maria Theresia had marked the beginning of a flourishing era for Trieste, Joseph II's keen interest in the Galician capital provided for the economic and urban development that would outlive the years of reaction following his death.[16] Another distinction is that even though Lemberg's "German" urban element played a decisive role in local politics only until about 1848, bitter late-nineteenth-century struggles evolved there between what we would imagine to be "brotherly" Slavic nations, the Poles and the Ruthenians. This is an important difference that highlights aspects of the growth of nationalism in Central Europe further than those already researched by the scholars of other ethnically mixed Habsburg cities.

Although these conflicts may have had their victors, with Poles among victorious national groups at the fin de siècle, not every triumphant nationalist had as his primary goal the establishment of a nation-state. While "Habsburg Lemberg" was increasingly becoming "Polish Lwów," it was far from obvious to the groups that eventually lost out – these primarily being Ruthenians, Jews, and German speakers – let alone to those that were ostensibly victorious, that the urbanization processes or new political arrangements would not reverse in favor of a theretofore marginalized group. Moreover, despite being dominated by Polish architectural projects, Lemberg's landscape continued to be a contested space until World War I. With the fall of the monarchy and the power transfer to Warsaw during the interwar period, the battle was won – or lost, depending on perspective.[17]

This story roughly begins with Austria's acquisition of Lemberg as part of the first partition of Poland in 1772, and it closes with World War I. Founded as a *metropolia* (capital) by a Ruthenian prince in the mid-thirteenth century on the site of a much older settlement[18] that had been under the Polish crown since 1340, Lemberg became the capital of Galicia and Lodomeria in 1772. This run-down baroque town had lived through difficult times, often called "the times of ruin," before its acquisition by Austria. Prior to this, Lemberg's economic and political influence had been in decline because of changes in trade routes that had previously been its major source of prosperity, and also because of numerous sieges it had suffered in the seventeenth and eighteenth centuries.[19] Under Austria, Lemberg once again lived through yet another period of difficulties – as in 1809 when it was taken over by Napoleonic Polish troops and the Russian army, only to fall back to Austria just a few months later, and in 1848 when it became a center of turbulent revolutionary events. As a consequence of continual political and cultural influence from Vienna, Lemberg in some respects was transformed into a Habsburg city. Yet from the late 1860s on, this administrative capital of economically backward Galicia also became an open battleground for contests of representation between its major ethnic groups in the reformed Dual Monarchy, the Poles and the Ruthenians: Jews essentially did not participate in these struggles.[20] It must then be asked, had Lemberg become truly Habsburg – or Austrian – from its forceful incorporation into Austria in 1772 until the fin de siècle? Or, alternatively, if to some the city had remained *semper fidelis* (always loyal) throughout its history to whatever national "bastion," what account can be given for those far-from-marginal facts in its history that revealed it as "European," "*kaisertreu,*" or simply something else?

The turn-of-the-century contests over space drew on long-standing ethnic and religious divisions in Lemberg that any map of the city would have revealed, though such a map would have also betrayed surprising combinations of dissonant forces that continue to exist today. Most of the buildings in the well-preserved Renaissance core were built on older medieval foundations, and the facades of some have since undergone renovation in the baroque and neoclassical styles. The names of the streets adjacent to Renaissance Market Square (in Polish, *Rynek*; in German, *Ringplatz*) reflect the ethnic groups that historically inhabited the city: Ruthenian, Armenian, Serbian, and Jewish, and most of the historic churches – Roman and Greek Catholic – possess imposing baroque towers that impart to Lemberg its distinctive cityscape. Major public buildings and the earliest cultural institutions, including the new building of the Town Hall and the Polish *Ossolineum* Library, were erected under early Austrian rule and boast a distinctive touch of "German" – meaning Viennese – neoclassicism. The road encircling the historic city center is highly reminiscent of the *Ringstrasse*'s historicism, though its creation dates back earlier. Many fin-de-siècle ethnic institutions, such as the Ruthenian "Dnister" joint stock company building, were designed in the local, folkloristic variant of Art Nouveau, known as the Carpathian style and Ruthenian Sezession, whose Viennese origins are obvious even to the untrained eye. In fact Lemberg may offer an even more diverse and intriguing picture of "competing visions" in architecture or, as Antony Alofsin recently described it, the "language of hybridity" imprinted on the urban landscape.[21] It is precisely its multilayered, complex history, shaped by its multiethnic and multireligious character, that is most apparent to the architectural historian and that makes the city a fitting focus for historical research into issues beyond the evolution of architectural styles.

Although "Habsburg town" would be problematic as an analytic category – unless one uses a purely geographical determinant and lumps together most of the Central European cities that for a certain period were under Habsburg rule – there are several linguistic, symbolic, and landscape elements that reveal astonishing similarities between nineteenth-century cities as divergent and different in function as the provincial capital of Lemberg and the free port of Trieste. Until 1867, Lemberg's official language – and thus the language of the official culture, theater, and entertainment – was German, and so was that of its street signs and city

Figure 1. Café "Central." Unknown photographer, 1904. Private collection of Ihor Kotlobuvatov.

maps, yet most of the urban population spoke a mixture of Slavic and German. Its café culture was vivid, and the "Viennese Café" was one of the most popular (Fig. 1. This could be anywhere in Central Europe). Its new buildings were marked with that particular kind of style that Polish and subsequently Soviet and Ukrainian scholars would call "Viennese barrack classicism,"[22] with public buildings painted "Habsburg yellow," and its historic center was surrounded by broad boulevards that had replaced the derelict city walls.

This was a similar yet much more far-reaching project than the ones initiated by Vienna in the late eighteenth and early nineteenth centuries in some other cities, notably Trieste and Prague, particularly so if the economic situation in Galicia is taken into account. In mid-eighteenth-century Trieste, Vienna managed the urban planning of the city even more directly, independent of the Municipal administration, with the port being a separate administrative entity. The creation of the wide and straight-lined *Distretto Camerale*, later renamed *Borgo Theresiano*, the demolition of the fortification walls as early as 1749,[23] and the erection of San Antonio Nuovo by Pietro Nobile in 1842 all marked the beginning of a grand planning project that continued even after the abolition of the free port status in 1867, turning fin de siècle Trieste into a real metropolis.[24] What makes the Lemberg project evermore striking in comparison with Trieste is that the main driving force behind the modern urban landscape of the latter, the wealthy commercial bourgeoisie, was a far smaller and less significant actor in the Galician capital. Conversely, when Lemberg is compared with much larger Prague, where no significant urban restructuring was undertaken during or shortly after Joseph's life, except for the filling in of a moat between the Old Town and New Town of Prague, thereby creating Na Příkopě Boulevard, and where until the 1870s various new fortification buildings were designed to replace the older ones, Lemberg stands out as a particularly radical planning achievement.[25]

Although some of the historical details listed above reflect the ways in which Lemberg differed from other Habsburg towns, other facts point to certain general tendencies. First, like Prague and Trieste, but unlike Vienna and Budapest, Lemberg was historically a provincial trade city, rather than an imperial capital, and it came under Habsburg influence relatively late. The time of Galicia's incorporation into Austria coincided with the period of Josephinian reforms that Lemberg's residents viewed favorably in comparison with the earlier years of what they termed "ruin." Second, the city's Habsburg era is marked by long-standing imperial rule in the absence of a significant German population, something that distinguishes Lemberg from other provincial cities in the monarchy, most notably Prague. Third, unlike most of the larger cities in the monarchy, Lemberg developed as an administrative provincial capital where urban growth was often characterized as "urbanization without industrialization"; that is, development largely occurred through the revenues generated by the city's administrative functions.[26] Fourth, the processes of urbanization and political modernization led ethnic diversity to become more contentious over time, rather than less so: this fact led to comparisons with Sarajevo.[27] And fifth, it is precisely this multiethnic dimension – a source of recent nostalgia for Habsburg times in many places of the former monarchy, yet the one that deserves further critical assessment – that allows for a better understanding of how Lemberg's architectural landscape evolved both under and after Austrian rule.

Competition among Lemberg's various groups for national representation in urban public space often overrode these groups' other values and loyalties but rarely led to immediate results because official cultural policies were largely concerned with promoting imperial loyalty rather than ethnic sentiment. The nature of public space was restrictive, yet this space was also contested. Although by the late nineteenth century a small independent body of Polish intellectuals had emerged that found willing partners in the Polish-dominated Municipality for symbolically charged architectural projects, the city's Ruthenians and Jews neither espoused nor desired to espouse such a strategy in their search for public representation. In short, Lemberg presents yet another version of how modernity was experienced than that found in Vienna, Budapest, or Prague. To grasp the full complexity of this particular experience, we need to look closely at unrealized ambitions within both the dominant Polish national project and the marginalized Ruthenian one, and also at the way proposals were transformed over time to fit into the official understandings of public space.

For this to be a meaningful intellectual enterprise, its temporal span must extend beyond the fin-de-siècle to capture the intertwining of politics and culture throughout all of Habsburg rule.[28] By the early nineteenth century, architecture had become an attractive tool used by diverse individuals and institutions to justify certain political endeavors and aspirations that appealed not only to a select political elite, but also to the broader public. Following the arrival of the Austrian administration in Lemberg, the new buildings and streets it developed became metaphors of the newly established Habsburg rule and of an entire set of values it claimed to bring into Galicia through the Crown Land's incorporation into the Habsburg Empire.[29] Galvanized into action by this imperial Municipal project, local Polish and Ruthenian intellectuals chose these and yet other buildings to symbolize the national revivals of their respective nationalities several decades later.

An examination of the invention of national and imperial projects[30] in the specific urban environment of nineteenth-century Lemberg is complicated because the conceptions of identity then were themselves in flux and were transformed to fit given political settings. Nineteenth-century "nations" included loyal

Habsburg subjects who occupied a diverse array of local governmental positions as professionals of different ethnic backgrounds. Together with other, freelance professionals of diverse ethnic backgrounds, these individuals alternatingly placed higher priority on the values of their professions or on those of their national affiliation, depending on the situation, and similarly affiliated themselves – or not – with activist organizations that pursued political change. Each of these urban elite groups had its own changing understanding of the link between ethnicity, political loyalty, and cultural identity. Moreover, the very understanding of what constituted public space was also in constant flux. Therefore a study of the invention of new traditions and practices in the construction, interpretation, and use of architecture in the spirit of Hobsbawm needed to tackle the concept of public space.

Discussions of the Habsburg period, both academic and popular, on occasion tend to portray Ľviv – or, alternatively, Lwów, Lvov, Leopolis, or Lemberg – in terms of whose city it was and subsequently to which national group it belongs today. Rather than draw historical lines and construct continuities to support the thesis of a "Polish bastion," the "Ukrainian Piedmont," a "Mother of Israel," or some other one,[31] this book focuses instead on a historical period when the city was both all of these as well as something more. In the light of recent scholarship on multiethnic cities in Central and Eastern Europe,[32] it becomes clear that urban societies with multicultural characters, located "at the crossroads of cultures," were not limited to Central Europe alone. Although Lemberg may have differed from other Polish cities at the fin-de-siècle in the strong presence of three ethnic and religious groups and in the specific interplay of several nationalisms with imperial loyalties, these very same qualities make it representative of the multinational character of the monarchy.

In recent years, several collective volumes have appeared in Ukrainian, Polish, and German that attempt to integrate Lemberg's architecture into broader discourse on nineteenth-century European culture and politics,[33] but none is a monograph-length study that establishes a relationship between architectural practices and between general urban strategies and symbolic representation.[34] Such a historical study will construct continuity differently, not emphasizing ethnic difference as a constant, and it will encompass both smooth transitions and sudden change. This "other" Lemberg – one of the most *kaisertreu* cities in the monarchy and the birthplace of several modern nationalisms, yet it was also a place of diverse unnoted practices occurring both indoors and outdoors – figures as the focus of my attention. In so doing, I aim to answer this question: If the standard assumptions on what constitutes architecture, urban development, nationalism, and the public sphere hold true, how was fin-de-siècle Lemberg possible?

Chapter four deals with three specific uses of architecture, notably public celebrations, restoration practices, and industrial/architectural exhibitions. Imperial celebrations, which remained largely unchanged throughout the period, attracted large crowds that could enjoy public spaces to a greater degree on these occasions than they could otherwise. Conversely, medieval traditions declined because of the Vormärz-era official restrictions of public space to imperial celebrations. The local Polish political elite aimed to insert its own "national" symbols into imperial visits, though these symbols were of a Galician variant, thus legitimizing the presence of Polish cultural nationalism at official events. During the same time, alternate visions of Polish Lwów were also staged. Restoration practices reflected a radicalization of Lemberg's contested public space as motivated by the desire to create national heritage, that is, Polish and Ruthenian, and what was termed civilizational heritage, meaning European, Western or Eastern. These practices imparted to individual historical spaces an ostensibly Polish character, rather than providing a universally relevant approach to Lemberg's architectural heritage. Lastly, from a modest beginning as unsuccessful displays of industrial achievement, Lemberg's industrial exhibitions turned into sites that promoted a cultural, rather than a technical, nationalism.

In a situation of contested spaces, such as that of nineteenth-century Habsburg Lemberg, conflicting – and competing – views on the meaning and uses of architecture unavoidably existed among the various ethnic, social, and professional groups that made up the city's population. Traditional street ceremonies were adapted to fit imperial *and* national purposes, and historic buildings were fashioned to accommodate both a Western appearance *and* a national pantheon. Provincial exhibitions evoked the message of technical *and* national progress. Nationalist architectural histories were written on the basis of universalistic architectural ideologies such as neoclassicism, historicism, and Art Nouveau. The diverse individuals who engaged in reshaping Lemberg and its architecture to suit modern visions each embraced a unique combination of ethnic sentiment, nationalist politics, imperial loyalty, and social or professional affiliation. Ideas on how to beautify the city were transmitted from generation to generation and from camp to camp. Fin-de-siècle nationalists invented multiple histories for Lemberg, yet remained loyal to the Dual Monarchy even after Franz Joseph's death in 1916. The city's architecture, deeply rooted in a neoclassical philosophy, closely followed European fashions, but was judged according to its alleged national value and was invoked as an argument for Lemberg's being, and remaining, a bastion of national cultures.

Notes

1   Franciszek Smolka (1810-99), by education a lawyer, was a Polish revolutionary and a liberal politician in Galicia. Arrested in 1841 for his membership in the secret, separatist Society of the Polish Nation (*Stowarzyszenie Ludu Polskiego*), he was sentenced to death in 1845, though later released. He was active during the events of 1848 and in the Slavic Congress in Prague of the same year. In 1848-49 he served as Vice President and President of the Austrian parliament in Vienna. He was elected a deputy to the Galician Diet (Sejm) in 1861 and to the Viennese parliament in 1862. See Józef Białynia Chołodecki, *Franciszek Smolka* (Lemberg: Komitet budowy pomnika Franciszka Smolki, 1913). Here and further in the text, the official Habsburg name "Lemberg" is used, unless in quotations from sources in Polish or Ukrainian, where the names Lwów and L'viv are used, respectively. As a place of publication, the name "Lemberg" is used for the Habsburg period (1772-1918), "Lwów" for the interwar period, and "L'viv" for the period from 1939 until today. Official names of streets, squares, and other places within the city (German for the 1770s to the 1860s and Polish for the 1870s to the 1910s) are provided with English translations in brackets and with Ruthenian equivalents when relevant.

2   One way to achieve Joseph II's aim of centralizing and homogenizing the empire was to foster the circulation of administration functionaries into the newly acquired territories, which in Galicia resulted in a heavy predominance of German-speaking Bohemians in the Crown Land and the municipal government. On early Josephinian reforms in Galicia, see especially Paul P. Bernard, *From the Enlightenment to the Police State: The Public Life of Johann Anton Pergen* (Urbana and Chicago: University of Illinois Press, 1991), 91-112. Also see Larry Wolff, "Inventing Galicia: Messianic Josephinism and the Recasting of Partitioned Poland," *Slavic Review* 63 (Winter, 2004) 4, 818-40; T.C.W. Blanning, *Joseph II* (London: Longman, 1994); Derek Beales, *Joseph II* (Cambridge: Cambridge University Press, 1987), 359-66; Saul K. Padover, *The Revolutionary Emperor: Joseph II of Austria* (London: Eyre and Spottiswoode, 1934, 1967); Karl Gutkas et al., *Osterreich zur Zeit Kaiser Josephs II: Mitregent Kaiserin Maria Theresias, Kaiser und Landesfürst* (Vienna: Amt der Niederösterreichichen Landesregierung, 1980).

3   Central'nyj Deržavnyj Istoryčnyj Archiv Ukraïny, [Central State Historical Archive of Ukraine, further CDIAU], F. 165, Op. 5, Sp. 110, L. 6, 20.

4   Daniel Unowsky, *The Pomp and Politics of Patriotism: Imperial Celebrations in Habsburg Austria, 1848-1916* (West Lafayette, Indiana: Purdue University Press, 2005), 47.

5   Although the conflicts between various factions of the Galician Polish political elite are well known, only recently has the centrality of the Austrian context in this debate been highlighted. See Hugo Lane, *Nationalizing Identity: Culture and Politics in Austrian Galicia, 1772-1918* (unpublished book manuscript), 161-65.

6   Urban history was institutionalized in the U.K. during the 1960s largely because of the works by H. J. Dyos. See David Cannadine and David Reeder, eds., *Exploring the Urban Past, Essays in Urban History by H. J. Dyos* (Cambridge: Cambridge University Press, 1982). For a brief analysis of the relevant scholarship on urban history in general and on East Central Europe in particular, see Markian Prokopovych, Maciej Janowski, Constantin Iordachi, and Balázs Trencsényi, "Editorial Introduction," in *East Central Europe/l'Europe du Centre-Est: Eine wissenschaftliche Zeitschrift 33* (2006) 1–2, spe-

cial issue, "Urban History in East Central Europe," 1-4 (http://www.ece.ceu.hu/files/pdf/volumes/33/introduction.pdf).

7   These include, among others, the early twentieth-century works by Max Weber and Walter Benjamin, as well as fundamental works from the 1960s by Lewis Mumford, Spiro Kostof, and Donald Olsen. See Max Weber, *The City*, (New York: Free Press, 1966); Walter Benjamin, *The Arcades Project*, translated by Howard Eiland and Kevin McLaughlin (Cambridge, MA, Belknap Press of Harvard University Press, 1999); Lewis Mumford, *The City in History* (New York: Harvest and HBJ, 1961); Spiro Kostof, *The City Shaped: Urban Patterns and Meanings Through History* (London: Thames and Hudson, 1991); Donald Olsen, *The Growth of Victorian London* (New York: Holmes & Meier, 1979); idem, *The City as a Work of Art: London, Paris, Vienna* (New Haven: Yale University Press, 1986).

8   Carl E. Schorske, *Fin-de-siècle Vienna: Politics and Culture* (N.Y.: Vintage Books, 1981).

9   Péter Hanák, *The Garden and the Workshop: Essays on the Cultural History of Vienna and Budapest* (Princeton, NJ: Princeton University Press, 1998); Ihor Žuk, "Budynky Halyćkoï Oščadnoï Kasy ta Zemeľnoho Kredytnoho Tovarystva" [The Buildings of the Galician Savings Bank and The Land Credit Union], *HB* 2: 38 (1998), 8-9. In transliteration of Ruthenian and Ukrainian sources and names, Czech letters were applied, as generally accepted in recent international editions on Central European architecture. See, for example, Eve Blau and Monika Platzer, eds., *Shaping the Great City: Modern Architecture in Central Europe, 1890 – 1937* (Munich, London, and New York: Prestel, 1999). Polish spelling for Ruthenian names was also provided, when relevant. The exceptions are names of scholars whose names already have an established transliteration, such as Yaroslav Hrytsak and Bohdan Tscherkes. The attempt was made to keep the translations as close to the original as possible (for example, *Narodnyj Dom* and not *Narodnyj Dim*).

10   Ákos Moravánszky, *Competing Visions: Aesthetic Invention and Social Imagination in Central European Architecture, 1867-1918* (Cambridge, MA: MIT Press, 1998); also see idem, *Die Architektur der Donaumonarchie, trans. from the Hungarian by Marina Annus* (Berlin: Ernst, 1988). Several recent comparative architectural surveys attempted to integrate other fin-de-siècle Habsburg cities into wider discourse on nationalism and modernity (Blau and Platzer, *Shaping the Great City*). Also see Anthony Alofsin, *When Buildings Speak: Architecture as Language in the Habsburg Empire and Its Aftermath, 1867-1933* (Chicago: The University of Chicago Press, 2006).

11   See especially Norman Davies and Roger Moorhouse, *Microcosm: Portrait of a Central European City* (London: Jonathan Cape, 2002); Mark Mazower, *Salonica, City of Ghosts: Christians, Muslims, and Jews, 1430–1950* (New York: Alfred A. Knopf, 2005).

12   Alan Mayne, *The Imagined Slum: Newspaper Representation in Three Cities, 1870–1914* (Leicester: Leicester University Press, 1993); Peter Fritzsche, *Reading Berlin 1900* (Cambridge, MA: 1996); James H. Johnson, *Listening in Paris: A Cultural History* (Berkeley: University of California Press, 1995).

13   Maria Bucur and Nancy M. Wingfield, eds., *Staging the Past: The Politics of Commemoration in Habsburg Central Europe, 1848 to the present* (West Lafayette, IN : Purdue University Press, 2001); Unowsky, *The Pomp and Politics*; Patrice M. Dabrowski, *Commemorations and the shaping of modern Poland* (Bloomington: Indiana University Press, 2004); Keely Stauter-Halsted, *The Nation in the Village: The Genesis*

of Rural National Identity in Austrian Poland, 1848-1900 (Cornell University Press, 2001).

14   In 1800, Trieste had 25,000 inhabitants; this total rose to 64,000 in 1850. Lemberg had 42,000 in 1800 and 68,000 in 1850. Prague remained almost two times larger than Trieste or Lemberg during the nineteenth century: 76,000 in 1800 and 118,000 in 1850. Paul Bairoch, Jean Batou and Pierre Chevre, *La population des villes europeennes, 800 -1850: banque de donnees et analyse sommaire des resultats* (Geneve: Droz, 1988), 49, 62, 68. According to the preliminary results of the census taken on 31 December 1910, the size of the three cities became much more comparable: Trieste had a population of 229,475, Prague 224,721, followed by Lemberg with 206,574 (Henry Wickham Steed, et al., *A Short History of Austria-Hungary and Poland* [London: Encyclopedia Britannica, 1914]). Although the literature on nineteenth-century Trieste is thriving, it exists mostly in Italian and thus remains inaccessible to the English reader. On a brief overview of relevant scholarship, see Pamela Ballinger, "Imperial nostalgia: mythologizing Habsburg Trieste," *Journal of Modern Italian Studies* 8 (2003) 1: 84–101. On eighteenth-century Trieste, see especially Lois C. Dubin, *The Port Jews of Habsburg Trieste: Absolutist Politics and Enlightenment Culture* (Stanford: Stanford University Press, 1999). On twentieth-century nation making, see Maura Hametz, *Making Trieste Italian, 1918-1954* (Woodbridge: Boydell Press, 2005). Although Prague's ethnic troubles have been researched at length (see Gary B. Cohen, *The Politics of Ethnic Survival: Germans in Prague, 1861-1914* [Princeton: Princeton University Press, 1981]), only recently was an attempt made to incorporate the Schorkean legacy. See Cathleen M. Giustino, *Tearing down Prague's Jewish town: Ghetto Clearance and the Legacy of Middle-class Ethnic Politics around 1900* (Boulder: East European Monographs, 2003); Scott Spector, *Prague Territories: National Conflict and Cultural Innovation in Kafka's Fin de Siècle* (Berkeley: University of California Press, 2000). On Budweis, see Jeremy King, *Budweisers into Czechs and Germans: A Local History of Bohemian Politics, 1848-1948* (Princeton, NJ: Princeton University Press, 2003). On Pressburg/Pozsony, see Eleonora Babejova, *Fin-de-siècle Pressburg: Conflict and Cultural Coexistence in Bratislava 1897-1914* (Boulder: East European Monographs, 2003).

15   Jürgen Habermas, *Structural Transformation of the Public Sphere* (Cambridge, Mass: MIT Press, 1989). Also see Steven Seidman, ed., *Jürgen Habermas on Society and Politics: A Reader* (Boston, 1989) 231-236. Few concepts apart from "public sphere" have been applied so extensively to and, at the same time, critiqued in the scholarly literature: a space of negotiated political decision-making that is neither private, professional, nor state-controlled, but one that ultimately shapes state policies. Several recent studies have aimed at combining Hobsbawm's notion of the invention of tradition with Habermas' concept of the public sphere. See, for example, Stauter-Halsted, *The Nation in the Village*. To the best of my knowledge, an analysis of urban public spaces in a multi-ethnic environment in which several parallel public spheres emerged has remained yet to be explored in the scholarly literature.

16   Joseph II demonstrated great interest in both Lemberg and Trieste during his travels to Galicia in 1773 and Littoral in 1775. See Wolff, "Inventing Galicia," 819-22; Beales, *Joseph II*, 359-67. By the end of Joseph II's reign, Galicia's signs of modernization became obvious: the urban population grew, factories were erected, and roads were built; the 1786 Lemberg fair, practically stagnant before, had more than a thousand visitors. See Padover, *The Revolutionary Emperor*, 223; also see Blanning, *Joseph II*, 79-80. On an alternative interpretation, see Blanning, *Joseph II*, 130.

17   On the Interwar period see Christoph Mick, "War and Conflicting Memories – Poles, Ukrainians and Jews in Lvov 1914–1939," *Simon Dubnow Institute Yearbook*, 4 (2005), 257-78; idem, "Ethnische Gewalt und Pogrome in Lemberg 1914–1941," Osteuropa, 53 (2003), 1810-29; idem, "Wer verteidigte Lemberg? Totengedenken, Kriegsdeutungen und nationale Identität in einer multiethnischen Stadt," in Dietrich Beyrau, ed., *Der Krieg in religiösen und nationalen Deutungen der Neuzeit* (Tübingen: 2000), 189-216; idem, "Nationalisierung in einer multiethnischen Stadt. Interethnische Konflikte in Lemberg 1890–1920," *Archiv für Sozialgeschichte*, 40 (2000), 113-46; on the ethnic divisions in Galicia, especially among the Ruthenians, with a focus on Russophiles, see Anna Veronika Wendland, *Die Russophilen in Galizien: ukrainische Konservativen zwischen Österreich und Russland, 1848-1915* (Vienna: Verlag der Österreichischen Akademie der Wissenschaften, 2001), also see idem, "Russophilie: Auch ein ukrainisches Projekt?" *Ï* 18 (2000).

18   Recent archaeological excavations have revealed that urban settlement in Lemberg is actually much older, dating to at least as early as the end of the fifth century, and one of the oldest in Central and Eastern Europe. See Volodymyr Patehyryč, Vasyľ Ivanovśkyj, "Seredňovična archeolohgija Ľvova: pidsumky i perspektyvy" [Medieval archeology in Ľviv: conclusions and perspectives] in *Halyćko-Volynśka deržava: peredumovy, vynyknennia, istorija, kuľtura, tradyciï* [Halyč-Volyń State: Preconditions, Origins, History, Culture, and Traditions] (Ľviv, 1993), 41-43; also see Yaroslav Hrytsak, "Constructing a National City: The Case of Ľviv," in John J. Czaplicka, Blair A. Ruble, and Lauren Crabtree (eds.,) *Composing Urban History and the Constitution of Civic Identities* (Woodrow Wilson Press, Johns Hopkins University Press, 2003).

19   Joseph II received a shock when he visited Galicia in 1773. Galicia was unlike anything he had seen before: stagnant and delapidating towns, roadless countryside, and an incompetent and confused administration made him conclude that it was "incredible how much [had] to be done here." Wolff, "Inventing Galicia," 820-22; Padover, *The Revolutionary Emperor*, 73; Blanning, *Joseph II*, 263.

20   In the nineteenth and early twentieth centuries, Lemberg's major ethnic groups fell into a stable, tripartite division: Poles (50%-55%), Jews (30%-35%), and Ruthenians (15%-20%) (Maria Kłańska, *Daleko od Wiednia. Galicja w oczach pisarzy niemieckojęzycznych 1772-1918* [Far from Vienna: Galicia in the Eyes of Authors Writing in German 1772-1918] (Cracow: Universitas, 1991). 1991: 7-23).

21   Alofsin, *When Buildings Speak*, 177-229.

22   On a similar lack of appreciation for Trieste's Borgo Theresiano, and generally also of the legacy of the monarchy in architecture, see Hametz, *Making Trieste Italian*, 150.

23   Dubin, *The Port Jews of Habsburg Trieste*, 12.

24   On the demographic boom and dwelling patterns of fin-de-siècle Trieste, see Sabine Rutar, "Wohnen in Triest um die Jahrhundertwende," in Alena Janatková and Hanna Kozińska-Witt, eds., *Wohnen in der Großstadt 1900-1939: Wohnsituation und Modernisierung im europäischen Vergleich* (Stuttgart: Franz Steiner Verlag, 2006), 55-75; esp. 56-57.

25   The four independent urban areas of Prague (Old Town, Malá Strana, Hradčany, and New Town) were united by Joseph II in 1784. Josefov (named after the emperor) was added to Prague's historical center only in 1850. The 1873 plan to create a circular street around the old center, similar to the Viennese Ringstrasse, was never realized in full. See Jiří Hrůza, *Město Praha* [The City of Prague] (Prague: Odeon, 1989), 143-49, 219-23; Jiří Kohout and Jiří Vancura, *Praha 19. a 20. stoleti: technicke promeny*

[Prague of the 19th and 20th centuries: technological changes] (Prague: SNTL-Nakl. technicke literatury, 1986), 15-145.

26   Patricia Herlihy, "Cities: Nineteenth Century," in Ivan Rudnytsky (ed.), *Rethinking Ukrainian History* (Edmonton: CIUS Press, 1981).

27   On a comparison of various radical secret societies and individual terrorism in the 1900s in the Habsburg Monarchy, with a particular emphasis on the politically, socially, and culturally marginalized nationalities such as the Ruthenians, the Romanians, and the Southern Slavs, see Vladimir Dedijer, *The road to Sarajevo* (New York: Macgibbon and Kee, 1967), 173-74. On the ethnic divisions and conflict in Galicia and specifically in Lemberg, see Wendland, *Die Russophilen in Galizien*; Andrei S. Markovits and Frank E. Sysyn, eds., *Nationbuilding and the Politics of Nationalism: Essays on Austrian Galicia* (Cambridge, MA: Harvard University Press, 1982); also see Liliana Hentosh, "Rites and Religions: Pages from the History of Inter-denominational and Inter-ethnic Relations in Twentieth-Century Lviv," in Czaplicka, Lviv: *The City in the Crosscurrents of Culture*, 171-203. On religious and political divide among the Galician Ruthenians, see John-Paul Himka, "The Greek Catholic Church in Nineteenth-Century Galicia," in Geoffrey Hosking, ed., *Church, Nation and State in Russia and Ukraine* (London: Macmillan, 1991), 52-64; idem, *Religion and Nationality in Western Ukraine: The Greek Catholic Church and the Ruthenian National Movement in Galicia, 1867-1900* (Montreal and Kingston, London, Ithaka: McGill-Queen's University Press, 1999), 8-12, 138-58; idem, "German Culture and National Awakening in Western Ukraine before the Revolution of 1848," in Hans-Joachim Torke and John-Paul Himka, eds., *German-Ukrainian Relations in Historical Perspective* (Edmonton and Toronto: Canadian Institute of Ukrainian Studies Press, 1994), 29-44; idem, "The Construction of Nationality in Galician Ruś: Icarian Flights in Almost All Directions," in Ronald Grigor Suny and Michael D. Kennedy, eds., *Intellectuals and the Articulation of the Nation* (Ann Arbor: University of Michigan Press, 1999); 109-64; Jan Kozik, *The Ukrainian national movement in Galicia, 1815-1849* (Edmonton: Canadian Institute of Ukrainian Studies Press, 1986).

28   Others have also seen the value of looking at the whole period of the Austrian rule in Galicia as a way to investigate changing ideas of identity. Hugo Lane's dissertation examining the importance of high cultural institutions for the emergence of mutually exclusive Polish and Ukrainian identities likewise takes the long view. See Lane, *State Culture and National Identity in a Multi-ethnic Context: Lemberg 1772-1914* (PhD Dissertation, University of Michigan, 1999).

29   Franz Kratter, *Briefe über die itzigen Zustand von Galizien, Ein Beytrag zur Statistik und Menschenkenntniss*. 2 vols. (Leipzig, 1786), p. 153.

30   Eric Hobsbawm and Terence Ranger, eds., *The Invention of Tradition* (Cambridge: Cambridge University Press 1992). On a remarkable discussion following Hobsbawm and Ranger's lines within Habsburg history, see Bucur and Wingfield, eds., *Staging the past*, Unowsky, *The Pomp and Politics of Patriotism*; Dabrowski, *Commemorations*; Stauter-Halsted, *The Nation in the Village*.

31   Representative of national narratives are, to name a few, Leszek Podhorodecki, *Dzieje Lwowa* [History of Lwów] (Warsaw, 1993) 162–73; Ivan Krypjiakevyč, *Istoryčni próhody po Ľvovi* [Historical walks through Ľviv] (Lwów: 1932, reprinted Ľviv, 1991); Majer Bałaban, *Żydzi Lwowscy na przelomie XVI i XVII wieku* [Lwów Jews at the turn of the 16th to the 17th century], (Lemberg, 1909). See Hrytsak, "Constructing a National City."

32   Babejová, *Fin-de-Siècle Pressburg*; Mazower, *Salonica, The City of Ghosts*, 173-271.
33   Jaroslav Isajevyč et al., ed., *Istorija Lvova v trioch tomach* [History of Lviv in three volumes], vol. 2, "1772-1918" (Lviv: Centr Jevropy, 2007); John J. Czaplicka (ed.) *Lviv: a City in the Crosscurrents of Culture* (Cambridge, MA: Distributed by Harvard University Press for the Harvard Ukrainian Research Institute, 2005); Czaplicka, Ruble, and Crabtree eds., *Composing Urban History and the Constitution of Civic Identities*; Marjan Mudryj, ed., *L'viv: misto-suspiľstvo-kultura: Zbirnyk naukovych praċ* [L'viv: city, society, culture], 3 vols. (Ľviv: Vydavnyctvo Ľvivśkoho Universytetu, Serija Istoryčna, Specialnyj vypusk, 1999). See also Henryk W. Walicki and Kazimierz Karolczak, eds., *Lwów. Miasto, Spoleczeństwo. Kultura* [Lwów: city, society, culture], 2 vols. (Cracow: Studia z dziejów Lwowa, 1998); Hans Bisanz, ed., *Lemberg/Ľviv 1772-1918. Wiederbegegnung mit einer Landeshaupstadt der Donaumonarchie*. exh. cat. (Vienna: Museum of History of Vienna, 1993).
34   On a recent architectural historical study of Lemberg's late nineteenth-century architecture, see Jakub Lewicki, *Między tradycyją a nowoczesnością: architektura Lwowa lat 1893-1918* [Between tradition and modernity: Lwów architecture in 1893-1918] (Warsaw: Nevison, 2005).

CHAPTER ONE

Architecture, Public Space, and Politics Revisited

The last decade of the eighteenth century following Joseph II's death and the rise of Klemens Metternich's police state in the early nineteenth century was marked by the termination, and even reversal, of many Josephinian reforms in politics and social affairs.[1] In Galicia and elsewhere in the empire, many scholars have assumed that the multifaceted everyday activities of provincial and local governments followed the change of, and worked fully in accord with, the political climate then current in the Viennese Court. They therefore expected that during the first decades of the nineteenth century, and especially after 1815, the Crown Land administration's architectural and planning efforts would be marked by a break with the earlier Josephinian programs.[2] Although such a view would seem logical in the light of far-reaching capacities of control that Metternich's police apparatus exercised over the vast spectrum of society, it stands in sharp contrast to the early Austrian architectural and planning achievement in Lemberg, which was steady, continuous, and uninterrupted throughout the entire nineteenth century. Even in the turbulent year of 1809, when Lemberg was temporarily captured by the Polish troops from the Duchy of Warsaw, by the Russian army, and later recaptured back by the Austrian troops, the authorities continually and seriously concerned themselves with Lemberg's urban sanitary conditions and general urban "beautification."[3] Throughout the whole preautonomy period (1772-1870), political and military turmoil notwithstanding, these issues were a matter of concern. We may speculate as to how much of this activity would have occurred in the absence of Crown Land policies made by a new class of officials, the Austrian bureaucrats, who arrived in Lemberg in the late eighteenth century as part of the Josephinian policy of centralization and regular transfers of bureaucracy. This aspect of policy reforms – architectural and urban planning combined with the establishment of sanitary and humanitarian institutions – far outlived other Josephinian reforms, and even fin-de-siècle planning methods can be partly seen as its transformed continuation.

In terms of the governing provincial office Gubernium's priorities, in their scale and unusually early timing these architectural and planning initiatives appear unusual. How are we to reconcile them with the same government's constant suspicion and policing of the local population, its restrictions on public societies, and its censorship of literature and the press? Are we to assume that for Lemberg's new rulers in the early nineteenth century and during the Vormärz, architecture was simply an expression of their curious affection for the city, connected only with their genuine wish to improve the dilapidated city's everyday practical measures?

Clearly, before addressing the specific issues related to the imagining, building, and uses of architecture for diverse political purposes, the role of the Habsburg administration in both initiating comprehensive urban planning policies and utilizing them for particular political use needs to be carefully rethought. This first chapter addresses the role of the Habsburg administration, setting in a sense a general framework for the interpretation of issues more specifically related to architecture that will be elaborated on in the following chapters. I argue that although being a matter of everyday practice that was motivated by the Enlightened "Reason," architectural and planning initiatives also served a deeply symbolic purpose: as much to the new rulers as to the local population, architecture and planning visually imprinted the government's beliefs on the local environment. Thus in regard to key governmental buildings, matters of symbolic representation dictated much stylistic upgrading, without which the government's notoriously wretched financial situation would have been much more manageable. Urban planning strategies, established by the Josephinian late eighteenth-century administration and carried further during the Vormärz, established a framework for further actions in the second half of the nineteenth century when the methods of governmental rule – as well as of the rulers themselves – changed. From the 1850s on, sanitary improvements and especially the drastic and irregular interventions in the Jewish neighborhoods were linked to the elimination of beggars from public spaces. These measures in turn demonstrated that there was a greater agenda supporting official architectural projects that reached beyond mere sanitary improvements. Architecture – just as the press, literature, theater, and social life – was a matter of cultural politics in which Lemberg was to become a homogeneous, rational, and planned provincial Habsburg capital. In such public spaces, there was no place for suspicious ethnic-topographical clusters, romantic fortifications, medieval ceremonies, or street beggars. The success of these policies, as we shall shortly see, was dubious, this due on one hand to the Gubernium's and Municipality's consistent lack of financial and human resources, and on the other to nationalism's strengthening both the ties and the divisions within Lemberg's diverse groups. However, neither should we overestimate the mobilizatory power of nationalism. In effect, the main reason that in Lemberg neither the imperial project nor the national project was successfully accomplished was because in the process of a gradual redefinition of public space from an entirely state-controlled area into one where no public actors would acquire hegemonic roles, street events became primary occasions to enjoy the city's public space irrespective of their underlining political narrative. Although the ethnically and socially marginalized urban groups were further excluded *en masse* from the main celebratory street narrative, an otherwise very similar crowd would follow a very similar collection of "masters of ceremonies" in celebrating the monarchy, the Polish nation, or, as happened most often, both.

Vormärz to Fin de Siècle: Disorder, Cultural Politics, Beautification

The significance that the new rulers of the early nineteenth century and the Vormärz period saw in the city's urban restructuring should not be taken for granted, precisely because other political and social matters also needed urgent attention. Other more pressing issues clearly existed throughout the entire early nineteenth century period: revolutionary upheavals, economic underdevelopment, and criminality, to name the most pressing ones. In these circumstances, the Gubernium's treating of Lemberg's urban planning as a complex issue that encompassed social, engineering, and architectural issues – an approach being attempted in urban planning today – fell within the realities of a local context. Within the new government's agenda, architecture played only a contributing role: rather than figuring as the central focus, architecture was conceptualized in connection with the regulation of urban criminality and sanitary conditions.[4]

Yet as partial as the role of architecture was in urban planning measures, it nevertheless enjoyed a proportionately large presence within the Gubernium's policies. With the exception of 1848, when because of military operations and street fights more damage than improvement was done to the city's existing urban landscape, the population witnessed a gradual improving of the city's public spaces, in which the role of state administration was decisive. In these ameliorations, the central focus was routinely put on rationalizing space. Such measures included regulating the width and straightness of streets, demolishing the outdated fortification walls, putting underground the city's river Pełtew (*Poltva*) to be used as a conduit for sewage, cleaning public spaces, relocating graveyards to outside the city limits, managing greenery, and establishing sanitary and humanitarian institutions. The government used such initiatives to foster Lemberg's steady but gradual physical (and economic) growth, to improve its existing urban environment, and subsequently to make its most symbolically charged public places inhabitable and aesthetically pleasing.

Vormärz, *Verschönerungsplan* and its Restrictions

When Austria acquired Galicia in 1772, Lemberg's medieval and Renaissance historic core was surrounded with a system of outdated fortification walls and moats, as in other cities of late eighteenth- and early nineteenth-century Central Europe (Fig. 2). In Lemberg, these walls and moats were particularly run down. By that time the Municipality had neither the money, nor the intention, to

Figure 2. View of Lemberg, the capital of Galicia and Lodomeria. Lithograph by Francois Perner, 1772. L'viv Stefanyk Scientific Library. (Fragment)

Figure 3. View of the Bernardine Cloister before Noon in Morning Light, painted Anno 1795. Gouache by Jan Wenig. L'viv Stefanyk Scientific Library.

keep and maintain the fortifications, and the new government rationalized this into a coherent urban planning strategy. Thus the first comprehensive attempts were made to reshape the historic core and to replace the old city walls with recreational promenades in the early nineteenth century, quite earlier than in Vienna, the Habsburg capital.[5] Ecclesiastical buildings and estates that had come into public possession through Josephinian policies on church ownership were also in a sorry state, as was much of Lemberg's urban structure, a situation that brought the term "*ruina*" (ruin)[6] into local use (Fig. 3). The new rulers inherited centuries-old files on the dilapidated houses in the historic center known as *rudera* houses.[7] Because of the extremely poor condition of Lemberg's existing environment, which had emerged as a result of the loss of the city's importance as a trade center and the numerous sieges of the eighteenth century, the new state administration's early efforts in urban planning stand as reasonable and appropriate to its physical condition.

From 1785 onward, Josephinian legal reform had as its goal the harmonization of the legal system in all Habsburg territories and the centralization of government. Strict administrative hierarchies were established, and German became the sole language of communication in Galicia. Joseph II abolished Magdeburg law in 1793, and the Lemberg Municipality was subordinated to the Galician Gubernium. The staff of the Municipality was also reduced, and the position of the mayor was routinely left unoccupied during the Vormärz.[8] The Municipal Construction Department (*Lemberger Oberbau-Direction*) was incorporated into the Crown Land administration[9] as *Vereinte Galizische Provinzialbaudirection* the same year (later renamed *Landesbaudirecion*). With Lemberg reclassified as a royal city, important Municipal affairs were subject directly to the Court Chancellery.[10] The reduced city construction bureau was kept within the Municipality (*Städtisches Bauamt*), and it concerned itself with meeting the Crown Land Building Department's orders (*Berichten*) and projects, and with monitoring the construction of private buildings with its construction inspectors (*Bauinspektor*). The head of the office was also a member of the Crown Land Building Department.[11] So from the late 1780s on, the erection of every new building in the city was monitored by the Gubernium, which reported on major planning initiatives to the Court Chancellery. With the establishment of the *Hofbaurat*, the central advisory body at the Viennese Court in 1809, the Lemberg Crown Land Building Department was rendered subordinate to this body and required to answer to it.

Archival sources provide scattered evidence of these early planning efforts in Lemberg. However, it is clear from them that as early as 1774, city plans had already been commissioned. A certain architect and engineer (*geschworner Ingenieur, Architekt*) Defilles was only one of several who drew up a new city plan, and Galicia's new governor, Count Johann Anton Pergen, was uncertain about showing the Defilles plan to the emperror for approval.[12] By 1784, an approved detailed plan for city enlargement and beautification, known as the *Verschönerungsplan,* which had been designed by Crown Land Building Director (*Baudirektor*) Mörz and Head Engineer (*Ingenieur-Hauptmann*) Pintershofen, already existed. Sanitary issues, greenery, and especially the regulation of the Pełtew played a crucial role in this document.[13]

As in 1783, Joseph II forbade burials in city centers, four cemeteries were set up outside the city in 1786. As early as starting in 1777, the fortification walls were pulled down and new planning methods (taking into account both the social and physical aspects of urban planning and considering the city as a unity consisting of the historic center and the outlying districts) were being applied.[14] The Gubernium introduced the ring project for the "Vienna of the East," apparently not without causing some tension with the Viennese Court, which was much more cautious, yet not negative, about such radical planning initiatives. As reported by the Court Chancellery on 10 May 1787:

> The Gubernium created a joint Crown Land–Municipal commission to deal with the question [whether the costs of the ring walls renovation (*Herstellung*) could be covered by the city alone]. There a suggestion was made that provided that the highest [imperial] approval [be received], it would perhaps be much more appropriate (*übereinstimmender*) for the entire ring walls to be demolished,...the moats filled, and meanwhile permission to build houses in their place [would be sought...,] and in the end, the gates to the ring [road] would be moved across the [present] moat closer to the outlying neighborhoods so that, for greater public security considerations, the streets and exits leading into the outer districts would be made narrower.[15]

After all, Vienna, which was the most densely populated and the second largest city in Europe after Paris, still remained within its Renaissance fortification system. In response to the Crown Land administration's suggestion, the Court Chancellery presented the emperor's opinion:

> Lemberg is not to remain a fortress, but to remain a city, it should remain within its walls (*müsse sie gesperrt verbleiben*), and the gates should be preserved (*beibehalten*). At the same time, it is indisputable that the entrance [to the city] should be moved to the outlying districts and the gates moved along with it, while the city walls [should be] totally removed and the moats properly filled, on the condition that all these changes be made through the purchase of building plots and that the materials from the city walls and similar are covered by the Municipality (*aus der städtischen Kassa bestritten werden könne*).[16]

Figure 4. Herrngasse. Lithograph by Karol Auer. Ľviv Stefanyk Scientific Library. This lithograph shows Herrngasse Boulevard, later renamed Reitzenheimówka, and the governor's palace in the early 19th century.

The architectural bureaucracy – meaning the employees of the Gubernium's Building Department[17] – was decisive in Lemberg's physical reconstruction of the late eighteenth and early nineteenth centuries. Together with these planning initiatives for the historic center, here for the first time the Municipal employees saw Lemberg as an urban conglomerate that included both the historic center *and* the outlying districts. At first, streets and boulevards took priority over individual buildings – the latter could be adapted for governmental needs from the abolished cloisters[18] – and the historic center took priority over the outer districts. The city was to be brought into physical accordance with the new "beautification" plan, and all the urban planning arrangements were to correspond to it.[19] All the enterprises that engaged professionally in "plastering, restoration, and street cleaning work that would be connected with the beautification of the city of Lemberg" were required to obtain requisite governmental approvals.[20]

Almost from the start of this undertaking, the application of the idea of a modern ring boulevard to replace the city walls and that would have an administrative and also a cultural function was pursued. By the late 1820s, most of the fortifications had been demolished.[21] Simultaneously, the historic center acquired major additions, such as the governor's palace (Fig. 4), and private houses rose by one or even two stories.[22] Lemberg witnessed an attempt to reshape its historic core in conjunction with the introduction of a comprehensive system of new insertions along the ring – in fact, an entire modern center outside the historic core in place of the demolished fortifications.

Political and military turmoil of the time notwithstanding, sanitary and humanitarian issues were a matter of common concern throughout the entire pre-autonomy period in Lemberg and seem not to have been influenced by the change of the political climate after 1815. And although the post-1815 Austrian regime is viewed as conservative and reactionary, it is quite likely that the bureaucratic system in fact continued many of the rationalizing policies established under Joseph II in the late eighteenth century. These concerns were among the most enduring legacies of the Josephinian administration.[23] The establishment of educational, welfare, and mercenary institutions figured as one of Joseph II's major humanitarian policies, which in Vienna materialized in several major buildings.[24] Although in Lemberg the first public hospital (*Allgemeines Krankenhaus*) was established during Joseph II's lifetime, in 1784 several similar humanitarian institutions were established in the 1830s (the hospitals in former Carmelite and Magdalene Cloisters) and subsequently in the 1850s.

Yet from the very beginning, issues other than a purely practical or humanitarian nature were present in the new government's architectural and planning policies. The principle of a "rational" city, mathematically planned, cleaned, and ordered and filled with neoclassical architecture and architect-designed greenery, was implemented solely for the historic center and to the degree, or at times beyond the degree, that Municipal finances allowed. The grandeur of the ring project did not match the condition of Lemberg's urban fabric in the late eighteenth century, as evidenced in a pragmatic suggestion by the Gubernium's Accounts Office (*Buchhalterei*) of 18 April 1783:

> The suggested sum of 36,000 Florins for the city enlargement...is too great for the city community to be able to cover....But one could much easier avoid such a costly suggestion, since the urgency for the city enlargement is not yet so pressing: There are many empty, unbuilt places, and per the suggestion of the Military to demolish the historic fortification walls, 132 new building places will yet appear. In the light of the slow pace by which the number of houses has increased in the past 10 years, one may speculate that one will not feel a shortage of building plots in the nearest future. [25]

The ordering and urbanizing of the Galician capital city that was soon to come in effect was largely dependent on government revenues and figured as a political as well as an economic issue. Specifically, the Gubernium and central administration aimed to create a Crown Land-wide market for Galician agricultural production and even for export.[26] As decreed by the Court Chancellery in 1783 and 1785 regarding the development and classification of Galician cities (*urbs*) and towns (*oppidum*), Lemberg's change of status into a royal city was done "to create middle class (*Bürgertum*) in the Crown Land."[27]

In 1823, for example, the statistical report on Galician cities regretted that "it is a pity that the professional and cultural level of our population, exempting Lemberg, to a large extent remains far from truly urban. The physical layout in most of the cities is in exceptionally inadequate condition in terms of the materials with which buildings are being erected and also of the building techniques being used."[28]

Notwithstanding the overall concern of the plans with "technical" issues – introducing greater physical functionality and sanitary improvement – actual planning actions differed by city section and, in at least one instance, contradicted the overall homogenizing planning policies. Instead, from 1772 onward the Gubernium concentrated on the removal of Jewish tenants residing in areas outside the limits of the ghetto, continuing a policy introduced by the previous Polish rulers.[29] The two imperial decrees from 1793 and 1795 finalized the restriction of Jewish settlement on Żydowska (*Judengasse*), Zarwańska (*Boimow*), and Ruśka (Ruthenian) Streets in the historic center, and in the Cracow and Żółkiew outer districts.[30] In the latter districts, the widening of streets as part of the demolition of the old fortifications and the creation of the ring road was raised as an issue within the context of the city's "beautification plan" as early as 1801-5.[31] In this

Figure 5. View of Lemberg in the direction of Cracow district. Lithograph by Karol Auer, 1830. Hausner and Violand house is on the foreground, left.

situation, Jewish residents from the areas subject to demolition were forced to move into already highly populated, physically small, and economically poor areas.[32] The numerous appeals of the Jewish community to the Viennese Court Chancellery were unsuccessful, and it was only in 1867 that the residential restrictions were finally lifted. Even after this date the historic Jewish ghetto barely received attention, resulting in its exceptionally dilapidated condition as recorded at the fin de siècle.[33]

Neither were matters of symbolic representation left out of the enlightened government's introduction of public order and city beautification.[34] These were often met with great financial challenges; just how poor and ruined the city's urban landscape was – and how limited Municipal funds for symbolic representation were – can be illustrated by a complaint expressed by Ludwig Taaffe ("Salomon"), Galician governor of that time (1823-26), in a letter he wrote to Count Nadazdy as late as 1824. Taaffe claimed that there was "no *aerarial*[35] house that would qualify to host Our Majesty or a prince. The Kratter house, presently rented to the governor, is the only one that qualifies for this purpose."[36] The new government thus had great financial difficulties; therefore at least a single state residence would serve both as the governor's dwelling and for imperial visits, and the government maintained that the desired enlargement of the governor's residence to enclose the house in back would entail serious expenses.[37] Indeed, in 1824 there existed no other house in the city – apart from the aforementioned house owned by the theater director, Franz Kratter, and a second one owned by the rich entrepreneurial family Hausner & Violand (Fig. 5) – that would suit the requirements of the governor's household, and especially the needs of state functions.[38] Prior to that date, the Greek Catholic archbishop routinely hosted the emperor at his residence next to St. George's cathedral.[39] The Gubernium was short of finances[40] and, as it happened, qualified workers.[41] Moreover, the financial standing of the local gentry had fallen, and relations between the authorities and the gentry become hostile, which meant that renting from local house owners at special prices was not an option.[42]

Yet all the difficulties of a financial nature notwithstanding, the government succeeded in giving the city – at least in its most symbolically significant inner areas – its "German character," as recorded by travelers, and a likeness to Magdeburg and Frankfurt am Main. This similarity stemmed not only from the use of new, contemporary planning, physically suggesting rule by an enlightened government, but also from the availability of modern cultural entertainment, notably cafés. Modernity, new urban planning, rational government, and a neoclassical style went hand in hand (Fig 6).

Such early, comprehensive and efficient planning initiatives are a historical curiosity. The reasons for their use might have been trivial, yet they were

Figure 6. View on Lemberg from Wronowski Hill, 1840. Gouache by Teofil Czyszkowski. Ľviv Stefanyk Scientific Library.

Figure 7. Ferdinand Square. Gouache by August Gatton, 1847. Ľviv Stefanyk Scientific Library.

rarely purely practical. Just as later, during Georges-Eugène Hausmann's famous reshaping of Paris in the 1850s to 1870s, the new, broad, and straight Lemberg promenades not only made the city's public space easier to clean and navigate in peaceful moments, but also allowed for easier control in the times of trouble. The Vormärz functionaries' writings show that they had not grown to fully trust the city's inhabitants after the events of 1809, when popular sympathies with Polish

Napoleonic troops had been clearly expressed.[43] Thus when General Wilhelm Hammerstein's army bombarded Lemberg on 2 November 1848, his divisions took up strategic positions: near the palace of the Roman-Catholic archbishops, on the promenade across *Ruśka* Street, on *Castrum* Square, Ferdinand Square (Marian Square), across from the Bernardine Cloister, and at the beginning of Halicka Street. In short, the army surrounded the revolutionary city by locating its regiments on the ring. The battery itself stood on the terrace on Castle Hill, another "healthy" green project finalized in the Vormärz.[44]

An additional explanation for Lemberg's early planning initiatives can be found in the negative preconception of Galicia in general and its capital in partic- ular, a notion rooted in the Austrian government's belief in its cultural superiority. The influence of this preconception on the way leading Municipal and viceroy functionaries viewed contemporary events and personalities helps to explain their urge to reform Galicia and its capital. Contrary to Governor Gołuchowski and his later Polish followers within the Crown Land administration of the Autonomy era, who were interested in maintaining a positive impression of Galicia and its capital at the Royal Court, high-ranking bureaucrats of the Austrian Vormärz had neither an incentive nor a true desire to do the same.[45] "Far from Vienna,"[46] they instead wanted to compensate for this "misfortune" by creating the new, modern "Vienna of the East" by restricting the Polish gentry and by relying largely on the new German-speaking population in the city and the Ruthenian peasants in the countryside. Practicality and concern for sanitary improvement were cultural codes that referred to the allegedly superior (German) culture of the new rulers, in contrast to a previous "baroque" Polish rule that many newly arrived imperial state officials viewed as notorious for its disregard of such issues in urban affairs. The renaming of the streets and institutions into German-language equivalents – a deeply symbolic activity that cemented the new rule and its official represen- tatives – also took place along with these seemingly purely practical planning interventions.[47] Although imperial symbolism in architecture was not insignifi- cant, the new Austrian rulers chose not to see such symbolism as an end in itself, but preferred to commemorate practical architectural innovations with symbolic imperial celebrations, as will be demonstrated in the last chapter of this book.

By the late Vormärz the authorities had gradually conceded cultural repre- sentation in the city center to the adherents of another "high" culture, meaning the Polish, the *Ossolineum* and the Skarbek Theater, but this did not signal a change in the general principles driving governmental cultural politics. None of these Polish institutions challenged the idea of the Germanic cultural superiority, and when the Polish institutions did so – as with *Ossolineum*'s illegal printing activ- ity – the government used all available means to annihilate the perceived threat.[48] Shortly after 1848, feeling shaken, aware of its weakness, and wishing to counter the recent Polish revolutionary upheaval, the provincial authorities granted to the major Ruthenian institution the Ruthenian National Institute (*Narodnyj Dom*), an appropriately statelike and central building. The institute, deeply conservative and loyal to the throne, was to become the core of the first secular Ruthenian cluster of cultural institutions in the city, within which loyal Ruthenian subjects would later voice and take to the street ethnic arguments that would be severely repressed by a very different Municipal government in 1905.

Neoabsolutism: Disorder and Representation

When news of the outbreak of the revolution in Vienna and of Metternich's resignation arrived in Lemberg on 18 March, 1848, a group of Polish politicians initiated the signing of a petition to the emperor demanding the introduction of civic freedoms and a local language – meaning Polish – into the public realm. The following day, the mass signing of the petition became a public demonstration of popular political participation, including all major religious and ethnic urban groups, that culminated in the solemn procession through the city to deliver the manifesto to the governor, Count Franz Stadion. The governor's famous speech from the balcony of his palace, which granted the founding of a national guard and political amnesty, as well as the collective experience of the short-lived

Figure 8. House of the Invalids. Photograph by Józef Eder, 1860-70. Ĺviv Historical Museum.

revolution, has been analyzed in great detail by Harald Binder in his "Making and Defending a Polish Town: Lwow (Lemberg), 1848-1914."[49] The barricade fights were followed by heavy bombardment by the Austrian army under General Wilhelm Hammerstein and the reinstitution of the Habsburg rule on 2 November 1848. With more than 50 dead among the civilian population and major buildings such as the Town Hall and the University burned down, the Gubernium's Construction Department did not withdraw from implementing its architectural and planning ideas in the years of political reaction that followed the events of 1848. The city, devastated by General Hammerstein's bombardment, needed urgent measures to combat health conditions and to ensure a sensible flow of traffic.[50] Just as in the Vormärz, medical and humanitarian institutions were erected to demonstrate the Austrian state's commitment to humanitarian causes. Notable examples include the Institute of the Blind, built in 1848-49; the hospital of the Sisters of Mercy, founded 1849; and the House of the Invalids, built 1855-63 (Fig. 8).[51] Yet despite the general population's extreme poverty, issues of architectural symbolism were not forgotten by the city architects and planners. Although the Neoabsolutist administration would have needed no justification to prove its loyalty to the court, it greatly concerned itself with ornamenting the public buildings' interiors and facades.[52] Matters of symbolic representation now dictated not only minor decorative work on existing structures, but also insisted on the purchase of new buildings. The previous Vormärz policy of locating administrative institutions inside formerly ecclesiastical buildings was no longer considered adequate for the state's needs.[53]

The Municipality remained a strictly executive body, yet its cadre of staff was enlarged.[54] The Crown Land Building Department, similarly expanded, began to concern itself with public greenery and public space planning for the historic center and the ring, while also managing larger projects throughout the Crown Land financed by the Austrian Ministries of Trade, Industry, and Public Works.[55] It continued the ring project begun in the Vormärz, but now on a greater scale,[56] equally assuming the project's direct connection to the city's "beautification," amelioration of sanitary conditions, criminality issues, and dealing with the Jewish quarters. On 25 October 1854, for example, the Gubernium's Presidium issued a regulation concerning "public establishments that disturb general communal safety" (*öffentliche, die gemeinschaftliche Sicherheit berührende Anstalten und Verkehrungen*) as those related to the city's expansion, a matter that also concerned public works. In responding to this regulation, the Municipality complained of the great difficulty it experienced in maintaining order as a result of Lemberg's peculiar public "misconception of order."[57] Later in this book, we shall encounter a very similar image of the local Lemberg public in Vormärz German writings on the city. The Gubernium thus incorporated the previous Vormärz policies into practice: police control and the threat of legal measures. But the latter was difficult to implement legally with private establishments, and the former was impossible to achieve because of the lack of a police force in the slowly expanding city.[58] The official Municipal note (*Kundmachung/obwieszczenie*) of 28 December 1854 informs us of how unmatched the success of architectural planning was with general city management:

> It has been noticed with regret that in this city diverse actions, punishable both through the penal code and the police regulations, still take place, such as
>
> 1. That public roads (*öffentliche Strassen/publiczne drogi*) are blocked with carriages, cases, barrels, and wood, and thus free transportation (*Verkehr*) is also blocked.
> 2. That diverse substances are being thrown out of windows.
> 5. That street lights (*öffentliche Beleuchtung/publiczne oświetlenie*) are in many ways damaged; and that notices about buildings and building repairs, especially of roofs, are not being posted.
> 6. That flammable materials are stored in nonfireproof places.
> 10. That houses, passageways, and street routes are not maintained in a clean manner.
> 12. That snow from courtyards is being thrown out onto the streets.
> 14. That draught cattle are being fed on the street.
> 15. That carriages with firewood are driven into the streets and left standing outside the assigned places.
> 16. That public parks (*öffentliche Gartenanlagen*) are in diverse ways damaged.
> Since such actions endanger personal security in public places (*öffentliche Privatsicherheit* [sic]) and clearly jeopardize municipal order as regards fire, cleanliness, and general danger..., they should be brought to the greatest attention, and the guilty persons should be fined as strictly as possible, while with the issue of this note the claim of unawareness will no longer be possible.

The text clearly shows the failure to establish an ordered and neatly regulated capital city – a "Vienna of the East" – out of a provincial town by simple "ordering" its physical urban fabric and implementing legal measures against its lawbreakers. Legal irregularities of these kinds were usual in Lemberg prior to the reordering of the city. As the 1854 note describes, the "actions *still* took place." Although blockage of the streets may have resulted because the streets in the historic center were inadequately wide for modern transportation, especially in poor and densely populated areas such as inner Lemberg, most remaining items speak of the population's disrespect of order and, consequently, of public space. The Austrian planners put much effort into improving the physical structure of

Figure 9. Upper Lyczaków. Unknown photographer, 1900s. L'viv Historical Museum.

the city's prestigious central areas. Yet out of their suspicion and dislike of the local population, and also the lack of finances for purely practical improvements, the Habsburg planners failed to create a wealthy and orderly town that would have corresponded to the beautification plan. Lemberg's ring road might have resembled its equivalents in Magdeburg or Frankfurt am Main, but despite all the efforts of the Vormärz administration and the strict policing of the post-1848 city, much of its public space outside the central areas was still "disorderly" – or even commonly rural – in the 1850s and 1860s, remaining so even at the century's turn (Fig. 9).[60]

Under the conditions of high inflation and subsequent extreme poverty among the population in the 1850s, the poor emerged as a potentially explosive urban element.[61] The predominantly Jewish areas,[62] the Cracow and Żółkiew districts, were a matter of constant concern,[63] yet also subject to rather unsystematic and scattered planning during the Vormärz. But they remained one of the most disorderly and dirty areas into which the Gubernium continued to intervene rather unsystematically. From the 1850s on, Jews, beggars, and unsanitary conditions were grouped together as factors that disturbed the city's "beautification" in the minds of city planners. However, as resources had already been put into areas of significance to the state, the realization of these policies fell short in everyday, poor, and non-Christian areas. In January 1855, the Municipality noted an unusual blockage of streetways in the Żółkiew district.[64] On 25 May 1855, a police report added the issue of urban filth to the matter and asserted the following:

> One finds streets dirty to the highest degree in all parts of the city[.] Especially [unclean], however, are the districts populated by the Jews, such as Cracow Square and the entire Żółkiew Street, in the neighborhood of the synagogue, the main Jewish street leading to the market and selected side streets in the neighborhood containing Jewish butcheries....Most courtyards of Jewish houses have not been cleaned in years.[65]

The Municipal report of 17 July 1855 on the cleaning of public spaces stated that the Municipality suffered from an extreme shortage of funds, employees, and tools to fulfill the Gubernium's request. Yet the extreme overpopulation of the Jewish districts seems to have been a matter of concern only to the autonomous Jewish commune, represented by the committee of elders, the *kahal*, which continuously appealed to Vienna to enlarge the highly restricted residential area. Vienna was reluctant to issue a definitive decision, and the Municipality fiercely opposed the idea of the ghetto's enlargement.[66] Finally, the Ministry of the Interior gave a decision on the matter to the viceroy administration in 1858; the decision of Agenor Gołuchowski, then Galician governor, was negative.[67]

Fin de Siècle: *Upiększenie*, Renaming and Memorializing

The establishment of Galician autonomy in 1867 and Municipal self-government in 1870 led to major changes in the hierarchy of actors in Lemberg's rebuilding. The Municipal Council became the official elected city body, headed by the mayor, elected from the members of the council for three years. The mayor and the entire Municipal administration were made an executive body that was to carry out the council's decisions.[68] The Crown Land administration's Construction Department was incorporated into the Technical Department (known from 1874 as the Technical and Road Department – *Oddział techniczno-drogowy*).[69] The enlarged Municipal Construction Department became responsible for architectural planning, such as creating and implementing building policies.

Just as in the 1850s and 1860s, most of the urban-built environment outside the historic center remained "disorderly" in the 1870s and 1880s. When Juliusz Hochberger, the Berlin-trained Polish architect from Poznań, came to occupy his position as the Municipal Building Department's director in 1872, his task was difficult. As reported by the Polytechnic Society's journal *Dźwignia* in its characteristic bias against the Vormärz planning, much of Lemberg was still "a memorial from the times of pre-Partition, enlarged only by military barracks and government buildings."[70] This implied that apart from the city center and the surrounding ring project, public institutions were located in inadequate buildings, streets and roads were in a sorry condition, the sewer system was in disarray, and the water pipes sometimes dated from the pre-Austrian period.[71]

The history of late nineteenth- and early twentieth-century urban planning and architectural innovations in Lemberg does not need to be told here in full, given its excellent treatment in recent local scholarship.[72] In brief, at the fin de siècle the city's image changed radically. By the 1890s the ring project was finalized,[73] and all new buildings were to correspond to established building regulations.[74] The city possessed a comprehensive system of streets, transport, water pipes, and sewer systems extending into the outlying districts,[75] and it had its own central electric station as well as a butchery. That the pattern of growth resulted from administrative rather than economic reasons may or may not have had advantages for the city's overall character,[76] yet Lemberg had become an undoubtedly modern city in terms of its public institutions, transportation capacity, sanitary characteristics, and architectural style.[77]

Modeled on the Viennese *Ringstrasse* as in many other provincial capitals of the monarchy, Lemberg's ring project adopted similar planning and aesthetics to its Viennese counterpart. The fin-de-siècle Municipal administration continued to legitimize its power through modern planning and historicist architecture in the city center. As in previous periods, greenery was planted and hospitals were established.[78] In line with a coherent planning policy, the rechanneling of the city's river underground, street regulations, new green plantings, and the erection of hospitals and penal establishments were still at the fin de siècle a part of a greater project of city beautification and sanitary improvement. Indeed, the term "*Verschönerung*" was translated literally as "*upiększenie*." Concurrently, the construction of state buildings on the ring road – notably, the Opera House, the Galician Savings Bank, and the Museum of Industry – served as further legitimization of the "good rule," even if not all were built on Municipal initiative.[79] Yet as recorded by Polish writers in the last decades of the nineteenth century, the Jewish districts remained dirty and run down.[80]

Just as in the Vormärz and the period of Neoabsolutism, matters of symbolic significance also meant cultural politics. Each decade the idea emerged of the need for a new edition of the city guidebook. The city was growing: new streets emerged, new districts needed to be included, and the streets were regularly renamed. The increasingly Polish administration placed great emphasis on the renaming of streets, making the use of Polish names. At each renaming, this required large sums of money for printing documents, making new maps, and creating new street signs.[81] Yet being stimulated by the activity of several independent organizations and societies, the Municipality paid much greater attention to symbolic architecture and monuments than in the previous period. To use Alice

Freifeld's term, Lemberg's public space was becoming increasingly "memorialized."[82]

Imperial Loyalty and Nationalism: Convergence versus Divergence

Since the Middle Ages, Lemberg's population had been characterized by its ethnic-religious diversity, even within the vernacularly accepted definitions of its "nations" (*nationes*).[83] The medieval "Polish nation," for example, was equivalent to the ruling Roman Catholic community, and therefore by definition included also the German, the Italian, and the Scottish populations.[84] As late as the eighteenth century, however, the local Polish nobles (*szlachta*) in the countryside considered themselves a different "nation of gentry" and for that purpose invented a myth of unique "Sarmatian" origins.[85] It is in this sense of a distinct, "genteel nation" that the Polish aristocrats phrased their demands to the Viennese Court in their *Magna Charta* in 1790, fiercely criticized by a Galician councilor, Ernst Kortum.[86] Yet even this "nation" originally had a Ruthenian element, besides the dominant Polish one, and it constructed for itself a separate identity known as *Gentre Rutheni Natione Poloni.*[87]

Lemberg's medieval "nations" were divided not only by confessional boundaries, but also by residential requirements that physically clustered them around their religious and governing institutions. The "Ruthenian nation" included other groups that practiced the Eastern Christian rite, such as the Greeks, the Serbs, the Wallachians, and the Moldavians, and this population clustered around Ruthenian (Ruśka) Street and its church. Medieval Armenian and Jewish communities were each split according to their "Eastern" or "Western" origins. Both Armenian groups resided around the Armenian Cathedral; the Jewish community was split into the ghetto in the historic center (*Communitas Judaeorum intra moenia habitantium*) and the Żółkiew and Cracow outlying neighborhoods.[88] This physical separation roughly corresponded to a religious-ideological divide within the Jewish community: the historic center figured as the center of Orthodoxy, and the Żółkiew and Cracow districts boasted an impressive reform synagogue at the fin de siècle (Figure 10 shows the Ruthenian Church in the background, and Fig. 11 pictures the reform synagogue).[89]

The German-speaking group, the "nation of bureaucrats" that came to the city during Joseph II's politics of enlightened Absolutism, was also heterogeneous. Although a modern arrival among the city's traditional ethnic divisions,[90] the cultural significance of this population was crucial during the Vormärz. Yet this group, the identity of which was cemented in deep imperial loyalty and a belief in German cultural superiority, also contained a significant non-German

Figure 10. Podwale Street. Unknown photographer, 1905. Ľviv Historical Museum. The Ruthenian Church is in the background.

Figure 11. Reform synagogue. Photograph by Józef Eder, 1863. Ľviv Historical Museum.

element – Bohemian and Moravian Czechs – and thus it showed divergent trajectories in its identity formation.[91] Germans from core-German lands, such as the Crown Land administration's employee and theater director, Franz Kratter, and Crown Land Councilor Koffler – notorious for calling local gentry "Sarmatian beasts,"[92] – tended to be much more explicit in their belief in German cultural superiority. Therefore this group's decreasing presence in Lemberg in the mid-nineteenth century was marked by a deep mistrust in local affairs and, later, by German nationalism. Regardless of their ethnic origin, newcomers from multiethnic Bohemia and Moravia, such as Police Director Rohrer and the architect Ignac Chambrez, conversely, were characterized by imperial loyalty, cultural mission (with German as the *lingua franca*), and multiple loyalties rather than by diverse nationalisms. In the era of late nineteenth-century nationalism, this population ceased to exist as a coherent group.[93]

Alongside Lemberg's considerable growth under Habsburg rule, there remained a stable, proportionate division between the three major ethnic groups: Poles, Jews, and Ruthenians.[94] The major religious denominations traditionally associated with the "West" (Roman Catholicism) and with both the "West" *and* the "East" (Greek Catholics, Armenian Catholics, and Jews) also survived. These religious divisions were preserved until the fin de siècle, a situation that made the appeals of nationalist intellectuals to the "wider public" highly inefficient. This characteristic mosaic of loyalties and myths of origin that survived throughout the nineteenth century, however, signified neither the absence of nationalism as a deeply emotional, potentially explosive bond to an imagined "nation" during Vormärz, nor the mutation of this bond into a predominant political ideology in the fin de siècle. However, a central point that emerges is that the working of nationalism in the times of peace has until now been greatly exaggerated.

Vormärz: Taming Polish Nationalism?

The Vormärz administration put great efforts into restricting the public reach of Polish nationalism, which was largely an import from abroad.[95] One example of such efforts to contain it may be found in a case from 1813, when the Lemberg bookkeepers Kuhn and Milikowski acquired a series of color lithograph portraits of great Poles from a Poznań-based entrepreneur. Among the thirteen portraits of individuals who later would be repeatedly recalled as national icons, there were lithographs of Tadeusz Kościuszko and Jan Kiliński.[96] The advertisement booklet that accompanied the portraits spoke of "major events in national history" (*głowniejsze zdażenia dziejów narodowych*) beneficial not only to historians and art collectors, but also to the general public.[97]

In the same year of 1813, the Lemberg Municipality expressed the wish to be honored with a portrait of the emperor "in the name of the local citizens (*im Namen der hiesigen Bürgerschaft*)." The Municipal letter to the Gubernium on this matter implied the Municipality's and the population's loyalty during the events of 1809:

> Under the best government, a small provincial town was turned into a capital of a great Crown Land (*aus einem kleinen Landstädchen die Hauptstadt eines grossen Königreiches geschaf*) [and now] belongs to the greatest Austrian cities. This favorable state attitude influenced the spirit of its inhabitants.... During the last war [1809] and foreign invasion, loyalty to and dependency on our Motherland was strongly marked. [...We thus hope that] Our Majesty will give a sign of gratitude to its Galician capital that will remain for future generations. Millions of inhabitants would celebrate such a present with a great feast, and it would help to maintain love for our Motherland.[98]

However, the events of 1809 left a bitter taste in the mouth of an everyday Austrian clerk in Galicia. When Polish Napoleonic troops from the Duchy of Warsaw arrived in Lemberg, major street celebrations were staged, and many among the local Polish gentry were reported to have supported the troops' arrival. Thus the statement in the Municipality's request on "loyalty and dependency to our Motherland" that "strongly marked" the local population's attitude during the "foreign invasion" seems inaccurate at first blush. Hugo Lane's research on the events of 1809 makes it reasonable to assume that popular support for the Polish troops was quickly overshadowed by the following Russian occupation, which made the Austrian rule appear in a much more favorable light.[99] So the government's fears might well have been unjustified, and its exaggerated statements on local loyalty somewhat unnecessary. As a consequence of the bitter events of 1809, a Crown Land administration's inquiry was made in 1812 that aimed to determine what the predominant mood of the population had actually been during the years of "occupation" in 1809. The result was the following report:

> I have to ensure Your Excellency that the local citizens in general (*hiesige Bürgerschaft im Allgemeinen*) behaved in a troublesome, rather than supportive manner during the aforementioned epoch....From the functioning of the Municipality in that period, it became evident that selected individuals within the Municipality, but not the Municipality taken as a whole (*wohl einzelnen Individuen aber nicht der Magistrat im Ganzen genommen*), demonstrated loyalty to and dependency on Our Majesty's throne.... Yet as concerns the novelties that the foreign authorities introduced, their very short presence...caused...mistrust in them [by the local population], and the wish for the Austrian govern-

ment's return became predominant among the local population. Similarly, the expressions of joy at the Austrian troops' return in June and December 1809 looked no less truthful than they were resounding and commonly shared (*nicht minder wahrhaft gewesen zu seyn, als es laut und allgemein war*).[100]

Thus although the report commented on the explicit anti-Habsburg statements by the "two-thirds of the local [Lemberg's] population [that] consisted of Polish nobles," at the same time it confessed that in the local city the *Bürger* actually wished for the Austrian return.[101] The 1813 war ultimatum by Austria against Napoleon, despite the disapproval by the Polish gentry, "was a true celebratory feast for all well-disposed Austrian citizens (*gutgesinnte österreichische Staatsbürger*)."[102]

The belief common in Polish national historiography that 1809 provides early evidence of Polish political nationalism in Galicia and that the entire Vormärz was marked with "passive resistance" against the Habsburgs has already been adequately challenged.[103] The evidence provided here is to support this challenge; most of Lemberg's – and generally Galicia's – inhabitants demonstrated Habsburg loyalty throughout the entire nineteenth century. True, Polish nationalism, often imported into Galicia, acquired explicit anti-Habsburg connotations during the events of 1809 and 1848. Moreover, the brochures of Polish democratic societies, appealing to national sentiment, were repeatedly confiscated by the authorities throughout the Vormärz, the revolutionary years, and their aftermath.[104] Yet it is doubtful that these brochures had seriously influenced the thinking of most of the population during the Vormärz period. Police Director Sacher-Masoch's 1846 reports on the general mood of the Lemberg population clarify that extreme inflation and the subsequent increases in food prices, rather than nationalism of any kind, created the explosive situation in the city.[105] While acknowledging the "revolutionary outcry" (*Revolutions-Geschrei*) among particular urban groups, mostly among the richer Poles, Sacher-Masoch stated the following:

> I would not acknowledge that the present revolutionary outcry in the [Galician] capital stands on a well-calculated and grounded plan. It is a loud expression of a particular emotion, which has existed since 1831, and was in great effort tamed by the alertness of the authorities and legal fines, and it found a new impetus at the last closing of the Diet.[106] Yet according to my most exact, prolonged observations (*nach den genauesten, auf langjährige Beobachtungen gegründeten Wahrnehmungen*), I confirm that, in general, the inhabitants of this capital city rely on the government in times of danger even if they are not properly Austrian-spirited (*wenn sie nicht gut österreichich sind*), because their material situation depends on its existence.[107]

Moreover, discontent in the times of trouble may not have necessarily been caused by nationalism. In 1809, the reasons for demonstrations of disloyalty by some Polish noblemen – and noblewomen – might have been many. These possible reasons include political sentiment, a fading yet still present belief in the revival of the Commonwealth, personal frustration from the loss of privileges, and loyalty to one's social group.[108] However, even though the term "Polish nation" was used and abused at the time, all these actions of the period rarely suggested a political system alternative to the Habsburg Empire. The short-lived events of 1848 had already showed that backed by centuries-old ethnic and religious divisions and recent economic misfortune, radical political doctrines had already mobilized larger groups of populations. Yet nationalist historiography all too easily disregards the fact that even the most radical revolutionaries recognized the legitimacy of the Habsburg rule in Galicia as the lesser evil, compared to the Russian and Prussian administrations over other parts of partitioned Poland. Furthermore, this historiography all too easily assumed that the population's efforts were aimed at the political restoration of the Commonwealth. In reality, a strong Galician identity, promoted by the Habsburgs, was already in place.[109] Moreover, the state – working in the name of the governor of Galicia, Franz Stadion – learned to manipulate the ethnic issues too by taming Polish nationalism during the Vormärz and having "invented the Ruthenians" in 1848.[110] Because ethnic bonds did not supersede imperial and class loyalties, such policies remained in effect until the Autonomy era.

Neoabsolutism to Autonomy: *Parteien* into Nations and the Survival of Habsburg Loyalty

While revolutionary Polish brochures spoke confidently of a Polish "nation" and its "Slavic brothers," but derivatively of the Austrian "hierarchy" that was refused by its own "nation" – meaning, the Germans – in 1848,[111] the Crown Land documents of the late nineteenth century still used the terms *Parteien* and *Nationen* interchangeably.[112] For most functionaries, there existed only *one* nation, just as there existed only *one* public culture: the people of the monarchy and the imperial culture. The activity of independent social organizations based on the principle of nationalism and committed to a national cause in the Autonomy era put an end to such a uniform vision. Activist societies and committees, which helped to shape the public sphere, including its existing architectural heritage, appear with the establishment of Galician Autonomy in 1867. They were different from government-supported humanitarian societies, which enjoyed only a minor presence in the public sphere.[113]

Their coming to existence did not signal the demise of great loyalty to the empire. In fin de siècle Galicia, many speak of Habsburg loyalty and concurrently express clear national aspirations, whether based on ethnicity or a liberal concept. One of the most illustrative of these cases was the appeal for private support by the Memorial Foundation for Youth in the name of Franz Joseph on 13 October 1873, which was written by, among others, Franciszek Smolka,[114] with whom we shall meet extensively in the following chapters as a national activist. Full of loyal rhetoric and the glorification of the "national freedoms," it read as follows:

> On 2 December comes the twenty-fifth anniversary of the Emperor and King Franz Joseph I's dear rule at the Austrian throne....He has given us...proofs of His personal favor by supporting us in the sense of our national existence (*w poczuciu naszego narodowego istnienia*), by recognizing the work of our scholars and artists, and by suggesting the creation of the Cracow Academy of the Arts and offering His highest patronage to the latter.... Thanks to his Monarchic will, family hearths are not the only salvation of our mother language; we can express to Him our true gratitude in our own language at school and in the state administration, from the academic seat and from the public tribune.[115]

The emperor was therefore supposed to have played a decisive role in the Polish national renaissance and thus become if not a catalyst, at least a fervent supporter of the Polish national cause and a reason for this cause's privileged treatment in Galicia. Statements of further imperial loyalty were repeatedly made in the later nineteenth century at imperial celebrations, and not only by bureaucrats out of office. Although many adhered to the tenets of nationalism, very few went so far as to allow their imperial loyalty to be superseded by an agenda of political independence. In the fin de siècle, fundamental problems with the restricted franchise that favored the wealthy combined with the constant presence of the three proportionately large and stable ethnic groups to result in profound conflicts in political representation[116] and the contest for cultural and political presence in Lemberg. However, the city remained a cultural environment where large – and politically organized – ethnic groups coexisted on the basis of a shared, deep loyalty to the Habsburg Court.

Public Space, Nationalism, Construction

The reasons for the initial state restriction of non-German urban cultures from the public sphere in the late eighteenth and early nineteenth century lie at the core of a Josephinian vision of unified, vast Habsburg lands under an enlightened "high" German – and therefore initially only *public (öffentliche)* – culture; the

Figure 12. View of Lemberg. Lithograph by Anton Lange, 1826. Ľviv Stefanyka Scientific Library.

Figure 13. Kortum's House. Tadeusz Mańkowski, *Początki nowożytnego Lwowa w architekturze* (Lwów: Drukarnia Uniwersytetu Jagiellońskiego w Krakowie, 1923).

public realm, both physical and conceptual, was to be shaped and dominated by the official imperial culture. This political belief explains, in part, why the many Austrian Vormärz functionaries initially refused to acknowledge the existence of a separate, local "high" and at times equally enlightened culture of the Galician Polish gentry. For those clerks, given that the "Sarmatian beasts" required reeducation to be men,[117] they could have possessed no aesthetic taste or erudition worthy of note.

A shift in these views occurred after the Congress of Vienna, when the Austrian central administration and, along with it, the Galician provincial bureaucracy, came to the realization that the concessions of representation to local gentry were necessary to ensure its loyalty.[118] From complete isolation, through gradual concessions to a representation of Poles after 1815 and of Ruthenians after 1848, public policy arrived at the deliberate Municipal promotion of the Polish national cause after 1870. Although these concessions did not suggest the reconceptualization of the notion of German cultural superiority, they signaled the beginning of a long process of transformation of the meaning of the German term "*Öffentlichkeit*," diversely defined in English as "publicity," "public realm," "public space," and "the public," and usually rendered in Polish as "*publiczność.*"

The Official Concept of Public Space

The Vormärz official concept of public space (*Öffentlichkeit*) was that of imperial symbolic representation and the restriction of everything else, a move that was justified as the preservation of "public peace and order." Habermasian "public sphere" – a space of negotiated political decisions that is not private, professional, or state-controlled, but that ultimately influences state policies[119] – has no place in this definition. The establishment of Lemberg's first *public* library (*Ossolineum*), a Polish institution, in 1817 was a matter for the highest imperial approval, to which its aristocratic founder subscribed fully.[120] For a Vormärz functionary such as Governor Ludwig Taaffe in 1824, public space *was* the state: he saw the need to satisfy his dwelling's "purposes of public representation" (*des Bedürfnisses der öffentlichen Repräsentation*) from precisely this perspective.[121]

For "greater public security considerations," the Gubernium first envisioned the demolition of the city fortifications and the ring project in the late 1780s[122] and concerned itself with criminal offenses and sanitary regulations throughout the Vormärz. In the late 1840s, its functionaries wrote about "preserving/disturbing public peace and order" (*öffentliche/gemeinschaftliche Sicherheit und Ordnung zu erhalten/stören*) as concerned revolutionary demonstrations. From the 1850s on, they concerned themselves with beggars and with "public establishments disturbing general communal safety" on the city streets.[123]

Because the public space figured as the state's exclusive domain, the use of streets and building facades also fell exclusively to the state and its agents. This position implied the right to the physical restructuring of the historic center, but it also implied the prohibition of using public buildings for purposes other than those intended, such as street celebrations and ceremonies, and, in the second half of the nineteenth century, pronational demonstrations. The need to restrict public space from national political expressions in favor of imperial ones, made in the name of "public peace," survived in official documents until late in the nineteenth century. It is exactly in this sense that reports by Police Directors Sacher-Masoch in the 1840s and Chomiński in the 1860s through the 1880s speak of "revolutionary/national demonstrations" that threaten the "general public peace."[124] In 1888 a "national demonstration" was still found outrageous by the Gubernium precisely because it took place in a public space.[125]

Yet even though the official definition of the public realm did not allow for even the mere existence of a public sphere outside the government's immediate monitoring and control, it did not mean that such a realm did not emerge under even the most restrictive of policies. Despite severe censorship, the Vormärz times saw the emergence of a press that by 1848 had gradually challenged the government's monopoly on cultural and political affairs.[126] More important, in parallel with the official public space of the street and with the halls of the institutions of power[127] restricted to imperial self-representation, several other public realms emerged. These realms functioned at some times in accord with the authorities, and at others – and from the 1800s on increasingly – as alternative spaces for debate where discussions on culture and politics could flourish uncontrolled. Physically, these spaces existed either outside, or on the margins, of the official *Öffentlichkeit* and thus were considered by the authorities as either nonpublic or simply private: they included professional clubs, salons, public assemblies, pubs, coffee houses, meeting halls, and public parks. Individuals who partook in the goings-on in such spaces were often segregated by ethnicity and class, as seen in the following organizations: the Riflemen's club, the Polish private aristocratic theater, the Polish café, the low-class Ruthenian pub or hotel, and public parks restricted to upper-class Christians. Yet many participated in several such alternative spaces, and nearly everyone engaged in the official one.

Privacy as a realm from which the authorities officially constrained themselves was also a legacy of *Biedermeier*. This epoch, characterized by its retreat into solitude, privacy, and Nature, introduced an understanding of enlightened living that was underscored by modesty, civic commitment, and, notably, a house with a decorum-free façade set in a complex of ordered greenery. Restricted public access and the possibility for solitude were such houses' crucial elements (Fig. 13). Although the ideal of good architecture for public buildings was embodied in Lemberg Town Hall, Crown Land Councilor Ernst Kortum's[128] private estate, known as *Kortumówka,* served as a good example of an "ideal" private house, a result of its neoclassicism and being restricted to upper-class Christians.[129]

The *Biedermeier* administration was deeply respectful of privacy and solitude, though it also disliked public socializing in cafés and pubs. Later in the century, the authorities' suspicions were increasingly directed toward ethnic-based socializing, yet the authorities let this flourish if it occurred *indoors*. By definition – perhaps by the coincidence of "publicity" (*Öffentlichkeit*) stemming from "open space" – anything that was happening *indoors* seemed to possess a sense of *privacy*. As such, these events were given more tolerance and were policed only secretly. This policy would become a crucial issue when the public would begin expressing its political sentiments, first in open meetings held inside ethnic societies' public buildings, in public parks, and, eventually, on the street in the form of demonstrations.

Public Representation and Segregated Socializing: Vormärz to Constitutionalism

During the Vormärz, places of a public nature existed within the city where different social groups socialized separately. For the gentry and government officials, such places included balls and exclusive evenings. Historians have often had trouble integrating this evidence into their analyses because it stood in sharp contrast with statements on the profound "Germanization" of Lemberg's Vormärz public life and also with the Polish gentry's exclusion from – and its willing ignoring of – official German culture (Fig. 14).[130] Lemberg's highbrow social life was unusually active in the 1820s-30s.[131] In June through November of 1823, for example, strict restrictions needed to be put in order to stop marriages, balls, masquerades, and dances from being held during the major Christian feasts, as well as to assign specific places for public celebrations and for holiday illumination (the latter being accomplished with the use of military cannons).[132] These diverse uses demonstrate the possibility of *public* enjoyment of public space by the diverse social strata then present in the city.

A second category of places for socialization – with socially segregated clientele – were Lemberg's cafés and pubs. As early as 1802, Police Director Joseph Rohrer had commented in his *Bemerkungen* on the great popularity of Lewandowski's café on the *Ringplatz*, apparently the earliest in the city.[133] Another high-class establishment carrying the telling name "Viennese Café" had operated in Lemberg since 1829, as had Höcht's Casino in the former Jesuit Garden. The city's lower classes also had their own places of socialization, such as the "Pekelko" pub, which functioned from 1843 to 1900, and the Theater Café in the building of the Skarbek Theater, which chronically failed to attract a wealthy clientele. The history of Vormärz Lemberg speaks of a gradual mixing of the local inhabitants in the government-produced imperial culture and public space, albeit in the form of socially and ethnically segregated groups and not precisely in the way that officials such as Rohrer would have wished. In this process of mixing, the exclusive German architectural cluster previously centered on the German Theater and the university was on the loss in the long run. The understanding of this high culture – just as the understanding of public space, political and symbolic representation, and nation – changed as a result of the events of 1848 and the imperial liberalization of domestic affairs after the *Ausgleich*.

A rather different understanding of the public was represented by activist societies of the Autonomy era, the forerunner of which was Franciszek Smolka with his idea of the Union of Lublin anniversary celebration, whom we shall meet several times throughout this book. Here it will suffice to say that Smolka was the first to use the notion of the public in the terms of "citizen rights/freedoms" (*prawa/wolności obywatelskie*) and skillfully manipulated the interpretation of

Figure 14. Redoute in the German Theater, 1806. Gouache by Franz Gerstenberger. Mieczysław Opałek, *Obrazki z przesłości Lwowa* (Lwów: Towarzystwo Miłośników Przeszłości Lwowa, 1931).

Figure 15. Wały Hetmańskie around 1888. Drawing by Karol Mlodnicki. Franciszek Jaworski, *Lwów stary i wczorajszy: Szkice i opowiadania z illustracyami* (Lemberg: Nakl. Tow. Wydawniczego, 1911).

outdoor celebrations as ones of *private* character that the authorities could not prohibit.[134] Over time, the Polish-dominated Municipality inverted this argument by viewing every building project as a one of *public* works and thus marginalized independent organizations from participating in nationalist architectural projects, such as the Lublin Union Mound, and consequently mitigated the initial radical political messages of such organizations. The viceroy administration, conversely, remained hostile to nationally inspired architecture projects.

Lemberg *Parteien* exercised national sentiment *indoors*, always couched in statements of imperial loyalty. Polish aristocrats' palaces and ethnocultural public institutions (*Ossolineum*) were centers of such activities for the Polish "party" in the Vormärz. They enabled the Polish activists to gradually establish sites of what had long been traditional Polish commemoration practices in indoor spaces – such as the Roman Catholic Cathedral, the City Casino, and the Skarbek Theater – in outdoor locations in a traditional route of their processions through the city and in institutions of power, such as the Town Hall.[135] In contrast, the Ruthenians, who were divided, deeply loyal to the Habsburg Court, and increasingly hostile to the Polish-dominated Municipality, continued to socialize indoors until the late 1900s.[136]

As we shall see in detail for the erection of the Union of Lublin Mound and its anniversary celebrations,[137] the city's wider public possessed a conception of public space that differed from both that of the Vormärz administration and that of the activist intellectuals. It rather saw urban greenery as public space, and was increasingly hungry for loud attractions and enthusiastic about every city's *public* novelty. The city's population at large loved pubs and cafés, and Municipal residents actively participated in diverse street ceremonies. Yet rather than challenge the right of political authorities to public space through "political demonstrations," as nationalist intellectuals did, they viewed these celebrations as an occasion to socialize. Not until the late 1900s did the "national crowd" become a threat to public space, with serious police effort needed to suppress it.

◆

Apart from mere financial difficulties, an array of restrictions prevented the authorities from maintaining a coherent urban planning strategy throughout the entire period of Habsburg rule in Galicia. One such restriction can be found in a contradictory understanding of public space by the authorities. On the one hand, they reserved it for sanitary improvement and imperial representation, and on the other they attempted to homogenize it by prohibiting national representation. However, public space was conceded to Polish cultural institutions during the Vormärz period and to Ruthenian ones after 1848; thus public space provided for the appearance of modern "national" clusters in the historic center was based on existing ethnic divisions and clustered residence patterns. The homogenizing policy of architectural urban planning, which was to render Lemberg a modern capital with regular streets and support the easy flow of traffic in its ring project, was until 1868 impeded by its own Jewish residential restrictions, which condensed the ghetto and turned it, together with Jewish outlying districts, into the city's most neglected and dilapidated areas.

These factors further strengthened the existing ethnic divisions in local social life and politics. Yet the ethnic, religious, and class tensions that found expression during the events of 1809 and 1848 have all too easily been taken as the evidence of nationalism. During Vormärz, even the most convinced adherents of nationalism could be counted on a single hand, but even they had no clear political agenda. The official homogenizing project in planning and architecture faced its first serious challenges only in the 1860s. At that time, several independent societies – often truly nationalist in the full sense of the word – instrumentalized ethnic bonds, historical frustrations, and political loyalties in order to lay claims to the city's public space. Initiated by a skillful lawyer, Franciszek Smolka, mentioned above, and based on a civic-liberal national principle, these societies demonstrated that public space could and would be used for pronational memorials and celebrations. In the era of late nineteenth century national revival and under conditions of Galician autonomy that favored Polish political representation, this move brought on a contest for public space between Polish and Ruthenian activist groups. The Ruthenians, however, were very late to engage in the endeavor and were thus disadvantaged from the start. Their claims for public space were indecisive and met with resistance from the Polish-dominated Municipality, which saw building projects, including Polish national memorials, as its own area of responsibility.

As clearly nationalist as many mass street celebrations were in the 1900s – and thus a serious issue for public order – for many these events were also simply occasions to enjoy the public space of the street. As such, they did not necessarily threaten the public order itself, because the latter's nature was redefined in the reformed monarchy: the state no longer perceived public space as an area where self-representation was restricted to imperial symbolism. The success of nationalist intellectuals in mobilizing the wider public seems questionable in the face of the same nationalists' multiple loyalties and recognition of the Habsburg rule's legitimacy. Diverse sources speak of the segregated public's enjoyment of imperial ceremonies and its gradual mixing in a public culture of the fin de siècle (Fig. 15). Yet this very culture was different from that of the Vormärz period. On the street and in the institutions of power, it spoke of imperial loyalty *in Polish*. No ethnic national groups – or the societies that claimed to represent them – could have completely fulfilled their aspirations. The only true loser in the long run was the culture that failed to incorporate nationalism: the Vormärz culture of enjoyable privacy, where public space was restricted to imperial representation and German was the *lingua franca*.

Notes

1   The best insight into the administrative practices in Galicia and the establishment of the police state in pre-Metternichian Austria remains Bernard, *From the Enlightenment to the Police State*. Much of the scholarship on Metternich remains on a breach of biographical and political historical study (see especially Alan Palmer, *Metternich* [London: History Book Club, 1972]). On an attempt to grasp cultural developments and regional differences under Metternich, see Mack Walker, ed., *Metternich's Europe* (New York: Harper & Row, 1968).

2   This is a common bias in Polish national scholarship that considered the entire period from 1772 to 1867 – i.e., the time preceding the Polish national revival in Galicia – as the "Austrian yoke." This bias was then picked up by Soviet scholars and has even survived in some of the current Ukrainian scholarship. Ihor Žuk, for example, provides a long list of Austrian architectural and planning achievements in Lemberg, rich in examples of particularly interesting and outstanding buildings. He then concludes that "during the first decades of Austrian administration the results of construction activity in Lviv were relatively modest...Building activity escalated after the Congress of Vienna. However, prior to the construction of the so-called "House of Invalids" in the

late 1850s, no architectural projects were carried out that equaled the scope of the Dominican Church or St. George's Cathedral [the city's largest baroque churches, M. P.]" (Ihor Zhuk, "The Architecture of Lviv from the Thirteenth to the Twentieth Century," in Czaplicka, *Lviv: A City in the Crosscurrents of Culture*, 112). For a detailed account of this literature, see Prokopovych, "Lemberg (Lwów, Lviv) Architecture."

3   On government correspondence between the Crown Land and the municipal authorities concerning Lemberg's urban planning (regulation of streets, land ownership, and food provision) in 1801-5, see CDIAU F. 146, Op. 85, Sp. 2492; between the Police Department and the Gubernium's Accounts' Office (*Buchhalterei*) in 1807-9, see CDIAU F. 146, Op. 7, Sp. 258; 300; On 1811-16, see CDIAU F. 146, Op. 7, Sp. 576.

4   During the early nineteenth century, the Crown Land administration's files on city planning issues of criminality and sanitary conditions predominate. See, for example, CDIAU F. 146, Op. 7, Sp. 512 (1810). To what degree the ideas about city planning and the control of crime were intertwined is evident from the fact that in the late 1820s and early 1830s, the Crown Land administration's correspondence with the Ministry of the Interior on issues of the illegal trade of poisons, public holiday organization, and the maintenance of general public order was grouped in its archive under one file (CDIAU F. 146, Op. 7, Sp. 1884).

5   In point of fact, the fortifications in Vienna survived well into the second half of the nineteenth century. While the new planners of Lemberg were demolishing fortification walls and planning new streets in their place, in Vienna, under Joseph II, the Glacis – the empty territory separating the fortified city's old town from the adjacent outer districts – was turned into a recreation area with the planting of trees there. Later in the 1780s, Josephinian planners concentrated on the development of the Leopoldstadt district, especially the area of the Prater recreational park. In the first decade of the nineteenth century, several major intrusions into the city center did take place – the construction of the Neustadt Canal, the opening of the Kärntnertor in the early 1800s, and the demolition of the Burgbastei and the planning of Volksgarten, Heldensplatz, and Burggarten in 1812 – but these were intrusions of a more modest scale than the ones undertaken in Lemberg. Only in the 1820s did the planners of Vienna cover the whole Glacis area with plantings and paths, and even then, some fortifications ruined by Napoleonic troops – especially the Burgbastei – were recovered and rebuilt rather than destroyed. On Vienna, see Robert Waissenberger, ed., *Vienna in the Biedermeier Era, 1815-1848* (London: Alpine Fine Arts Collection, 1986), 62-76, 139-59; idem, *Vienna, 1890-1920* (New York: Tabard Press, 1984), 9-29. Also see Reinhard Pohanka, *Eine kurze Geschichte der Stadt Wien* (Vienna, Cologne, and Weimar: Böhlau, 1998), 140, 142, 145, 148, 151, 155. On Budapest in the nineteenth century, see András Gerő and János Poór, eds., *Budapest: A History from Its Beginnings to 1996* (Boulder, Colo., New York: East European Monographs, 1997), 35-138.

6   "Ruina" (Ukr. *ruïna*) is a routine term in historiography concerning the times of war and stagnation in eighteenth-century Lemberg.

7   Under the Austrian rule, these included, among others, the following *Rudera Lapidea*: Dobieszowska, Serafińska, Bobrzecka, Waliszewska, Bernatowiczowska, Balzamowiczowska, Tobieszowska, and Grensowska (See CDIAU F. 52, Op. 1, Sp. 15).

8   As, for example, in the 1840s. See *Schematismus der Königreiche Galizien & Lodomerien für das Jahr 1842* (Lemberg: Galizische Aerarial Drükerei, 1842).

9   Tadeusz Mańkowski, *Początki nowożytnego Lwowa w architekturze* (Lwów: Drukarnia Uniwersytetu Jagiellońskiego w Krakowie, 1923), 10.

10   Iuliana Ivakočko, "Urbanizacijni procesy Halyčyny (1772-1914)" [Urbanization processes in Galicia, 1772-1914] *Architektura* 358 (1998), 216.

11   For the purposes of major projects such as the ring road, a special commission was often created that included members of both Municipal and Crown Land Building Departments (as *Stadtische Gubernial Commission* mentioned in government correspondence in 1782-83. See CDIAU F. 146, Op. 79, Sp. 210, L. 1-2).

12   CDIAU, F. 52, Op. 1, Sp. 17, L.1. On Pergen's governorship of Galicia, see Bernard, *From the Enlightenment to the Police State*, 91-112.

13   CDIAU, F. 52, Op. 1, Sp. 17, L. 2-6.

14   On more regarding the government's activities on filling in the moats in 1782-83, see CDIAU F. 146, Op. 79, Sp. 210. Also see Anonymous [von Mathes], "*Geschichtliches über Lemberg,* [Historically on Lemberg]," CDIAU F. 52, Op. 1, Sp. 953, L. 4-5.

15   On the discussion of the issue of this plan's expense – and who should cover it – and of the actual implementation of the project held between the Court Chancellery, the Gubernium, and the Municipality (1872-73), see CDIAU F. 146, Op. 79, Sp. 210, L. 1-10.

16   CDIAU F. 146, Op. 79, Sp. 210. L. 2.

17   Relevant personalities were the state-employed architects, primarily the directors of the Building Department of the Municipality (*Lemberger Oberbau-Direction*, later incorporated into the Viceroy's administration): Max von Kruz (since 1772), Mörz (1880s), Pierre Denis Gibeau (until 1800), Jerzy Glogowski (until 1838), and other architects working at the department, including Franz Trescher (father and son), Josip Wandruszka, Franz Onderka, and Alois Wondraczka.

18   On sanitary improvements and the general management of governmental institutions (1810), see CDIAU F. 146, Op. 7, Sp. 512; On information concerning the allocation of government offices in former ecclesiastical buildings and on plans of the *Kreisamtsgebäude* next to the former Jesuit cloister (1811-14), see CDIAU F. 146, Op. 7, L. 611. On a comprehensive strategy of renovating the post office and laying out a new street (1828), see CDIAU F. 146, Op. 7, Sp. 1577, L. 17.

19   The activities of the surviving masons' guild was also subordinated to the Crown Land Building Department (Mańkowski, *Początki Lwowa,* 11-12).

20   As stated in the Crown Land Presidium's reminder from 22 April 1826 (CDIAU F. 146, Op. 7, Sp. 1616, L. 3).

21   That in this fortification-demolition policy Lemberg was not an exceptional case in Galicia can be illustrated by the governor's administration deciding in the early 1810s to demolish the fortifications in Brody and Stanislau (CDIAU F. 146, Op. 7, Sp. 445).

22   Minor restoration of the Town Hall building occurred immediately after Galicia's acquisition, prior to the arrival of its first governor, Count Anton Pergen. See Michał Lityński, *Gmach Skarbkowski na tle architektury lwowskiej w pierwszej połowie XIX wieku* [Skarbek Building on the Background of Lwów Architecure in the First Half of the 19th century] (Lemberg: Nakl. Fundacyi Skarbkowskiej, 1912), 7.

23   On 1826, for example, see CDIAU F. 146, Op. 7, Sp. 1430. On the establishment of new hospitals in the former Carmelite and Magdalene cloisters, as connected to the establishment of walking paths around the city in 1836-45, see CDIAU F. 146, Op. 1, Sp. 1428, L. 30-33, 56. On the establishment of legal punitive mechanisms for the negligence of sanitary aspects and city planning in 1854-55, see CDIAU F. 146, Op. 7, Sp. 3365, L. 36-37. For a good summary see H. Pertyšyn and Uliana Ivanočko, "Terytorial'no-planuval'ni peretvorennia L'vova v avstrijkyj period (1772-1918)" [Ter-

ritorial and planning transformations of Ľviv in the Austrian period: 1772-1918], in Mudryj, 191-208.

24 *Allgemeines Krankenhaus, Invalidenhaus, Taubstummeninstitut, Anstalt der Geisten-kranken, Narrenturm, Waisen- und Armenhaus*, the Academy of Medicine and Surgery were all established during Joseph II's lifetime. For a good summary, see Echart Van-csa, "Die Wiener Architektur des 19. und der 1. Hälfte des 20. Jahrhunderts im Über-blick, in Bohdan Tscherkes, Martin Kubelik, and Elizabeth Hofer, eds., *Architektura Halyčyny XIX-XX st. Vybrani materialy mižnarodnoho sympoziumu 24-27 travnia 1994 r. prysviačenoho 150-ričča zasnuvannia Deržavnoho universytetu "Ľvivśka Politech-nika" – Baukunst in Galizien XIX-XX Jh.* (Ľviv: Ľvivśka Politechnika, 1996), 199-206.

25 CDIAU Fond 146, Op. 79, Sp. 210, L. 5-6. The Accounts Office therefore asked the highest permission to restore the ruined city walls for a much lesser sum (7996 florins), on the condition that it would be done in two stages, with a lesser burden on the munici-pal coffers.

26 Ivakočko, "Urbanizacijni procesy Halyčyny," 213. Also see idem, "Peredumovy urbanistyčnoho rozvytku Halyčyny naprykinci XVIII- po XX st." [Preconditions of Galicia's urbanization developmment from the late 18th century until the 20th century] *Architektura* 439 (2002), 211-16.

27 Ivakočko, "Urbanizacijni procesy Halyčyny," 5.

28 *Statistische Übersichten von Galizien und der Bukowina. Tabelle "Städte"* (Vienna, 1823, manuscript). Quoted in Ivakočko, "Urbanizacijni procesy Halyčyny," 217.

29 Although certain municipal laws theoretically benefited Jews, in practice they were seldom enforced, and for the Austrian authorities, the Jewish population often became the object of fiscal exploitation. In fear of an unwanted increase in the Jewish popula-tion as a result of migration, the Austrian state closed Lemberg to newcomers soon after the establishment of Habsburg rule in 1772. As previously, the Jews were allowed to dwell only in the districts of the inner-city ghetto and the Cracow and Żółkiew outer district: introduced first in 1798, this restriction was reissued in 1804 and again in 1811. Exceptions were made only for wealthy Jews on an individual basis by the Court Chan-cellery in Vienna, and only in 1867 were all the residential restrictions finally removed. See Wacław Wierzbieniec, "The Processes of Jewish Emancipation and Assimilation in the Multiethnic City of Lviv during the Nineteenth and Twentieth Centuries," in Czaplicka, *Lviv: A City in the Crosscurrents*, 226-44; Bałaban, *Dzielnica żydowska we Lwowie*; idem, *Historya lwowskiej synagogi postępowej* [The history of Lwów Reform Synagogue] (Lwów, 1937). Also see Raphael Mahler, *Hasidism and the Jewish Enlight-enment: Their Confrontation in Galicia and Poland in the First Half of the Nineteenth Century* Philadelphia: Jewish Publication Society of America, 1985; Ezra Mendelsohn, "Jewish Assimilation in L'viv: the Case of Wilhelm Feldman," in Markovits and Sysyn, *Nationbuilding and the Politics of Nationalism*, 94-110; Paul Robert Magocsi, *Gali-cia: a historical survey and bibliographic guide* (Toronto: University of Toronto Press, 1983), 228-31; L. Katzenelson and David Ginzburg., eds., *Evreiskaia entsiklopediia, Svod znanii o evreistvie i ego kulture v proshlom i nastoiashchem* [Jewish Encyclo-pedia. A Collection of Knowledge on Jews and their culture in the past and present] (St. Petersburg: Obshchestvo dlia nauchnykh evreiskikh izdanii and Brockhaus-Efron, 1906-1913), vol. 6, 87-98).

30 Already on 20 November 1772, the Gubernium ordered the Municipality to carry out the removal of six Jewish families per month into the ghetto from 1 December 1772.

The imperial decrees from 12 December 1793 and 12 December 1795 finalized the residence restriction. The decree was repeated in 1804 and 1811 (Wierzbieniec, "The Processes of Jewish Emancipation," 227).

31 On the street widening in 1801-5 in the inner city and the Żółkiew outer district, see CDIAU F. 146, Op. 85, Sp. 2492, L. 1, 4-13.

32 CDIAU F. 146, Op. 85, Sp. 2492, L. 1, 13; Wierzbieniec, "The Processes of Jewish Emancipation," 227.

33 As recorded, for example, by Stanisław Schnür-Pepłowski, *Obrazy z przeszłości Galicyi i Krakowa: 1772-1858* (Lemberg: Gubrynowicz & Schmidt, 1896), 169.

34 An illustrative case is the correspondence within the Gubernium concerning the building of the lodge in the Lemberg Theater for the arrival of the new governor, Count Würtemberg, in 1815. Provincial officials noted the close modeling of the Lemberg Theater on the Viennese *Burgtheater* (CDIAU F. 146, Op. 7, Sp. 706, L. 11-13).

35 The term used to distinguish the real estate in state ownership.

36 Taaffe thus suggested including the Kratter house's back building (*Nebengebäude*) into the *aerarial* rent (CDIAU F. 146, Op. 6, Sp. 322, L. 1731-35. On further suggestions concerning improvement of the state governor residence, see ibid., L. 1735-53).

37 CDIAU F. 146, Op. 6, Sp. 322, L. 1739-40. Only the first floor of the back house could be used for state functions (*gesellschaftliche Vereinigungen*) (ibid., L. 1745).

38 In 1817, when Emperor Franz visited Lemberg, Taaffe's predecessor, Count Franz Hauer, had to move into the "peasant hut" (*bauerisches Haus*) to host the emperor in the Kratter house (CDIAU F. 146, Op. 6, Sp. 322, L. 1742-45). In 1815 his predecessor, Duke Würtemberg, had lacked sufficient furniture in his residence, newly acquired from Kratter, and had to transport furniture from Vienna (CDIAU F. 146, Op. 7, Sp. 706, L. 7; 16; 22). On Kratter, see Wolff, "Inventing Galicia," 822-28.

39 CDIAU F. 146, Op. 7, Sp. 706, L. 23. On similar arrangements made for the arrival of Archduke Carl to Lemberg in 1809, see CDIAU F. 146, Op. 7, Sp. 436. In 1815, Municipal Building office employee (*Adjunkt*) Jerzy Głogowski was appointed to manage the furniture issue for Governor Würtemberg's residence (CDIAU F. 146, Op. 7, Sp. 706, L. 1-7).

40 The prices of wood rose drastically and unexpectedly in the early 1800s (CDIAU F. 146, Op. 85, Sp. 2492, L. 48-52, 68-96).

41 In 1834, the Gubernium's President Krieg ("Swoboda") mentioned in his letter to Governor Ferdinand d'Este that "there exists a great lack of building instructors (*verlässtigen Bauführer*) in Galicia" (CDIAU F. 146, Op. 1, Sv. 76, Sp. 1427, L. 6).

42 CDIAU F. 146, Op. 1, Sv. 76, Sp. 1427, L. 1749-52.

43 See Leopold Sacher-Masoch. "Memorien des k. k. Hofraths vs. Sacher-Masoch (1809-1874)," *Auf der Höhe* (1880-82).

44 Anonymous [von Mathes], "Geschichtliches," CDIAU F. 52, Op. 1, Sp. 953, L. 9.

45 In their regular reports to Vienna, significant Austrian bureaucrats such as Krieg and later Stadion, as well as military commanders such as Hammerstein, depicted the region as a backward eastern province, pregnant with eruptions and revolutionary upheavals, and later as a place of secret Polish revolutionary list makers (*spiskowców*) where the state could rely only on the German population in towns and on the Ruthenian peasants in the countryside.

46 Kłańska, *Daleko od Wiednia*, 229-45.

47 Titles such as *Kaiserwald* (1780), *Reitzenheim* Boulevard (*Reitzenheimówka*, 1816), and later *Franz-Joseph-Berg* (1851) came as a result of such renaming.

48 See Tadeusz Mańkowski, *Dzieje gmachu Zakladu Narodowego imienia Ossolińskich* [History of the Building of the National Ossoliński Institute] (Lwów, 1927). Also see chap. 3 of this book.

49 Harald Binder, "Making and Defending a Polish Town: Lwow (Lemberg), 1848-1914,"*Austrian History Yearbook*, 34 (2003): 57-82.

50 On 1847-50, see CDIAU F. 146, Op. 7, vol. II, Sp. 2633. On repairs of streets and roads (1857), see CDIAU F. 146, Op. 7, Sp. 3457, L. 31-45. Also see CDIAU F. 146, Op. 7, vol. II, Sp. 3212 (1852).

51 On the erection of the Institute of the Blind, see CDIAU F. 146, Op. 7, vol. II, Sp. 2788 (1848) and Sp. 2929 (1849), and Sisters of Mercy CDIAU F. 146, Op. 7, vol. II, Sp. 2933 (1849). On the erection of the Invalidenhaus, see CDIAU F. 52, Op. 1, Sp. 32 (1855-1857).

52 On the acquisition of the portrait of the emperor for the hall of the Crown Land Administration Building (1850), see CDIAU F. 146, Op. 7, vol. II, Sp. 3006. On the decoration of the halls of administrative buildings (1851-53) see CDIAU F. 146, Op. 7, vol. II, Sp. 3107; (1856) ibid., Sp. 3429; On the decoration of the governor's apartment (1856) See CDIAU F. 726, Op. 1, Sp. 1616.

53 On 1860, see CDIAU F. 146, Op. 7, vol. II, Sp. 3628; on 1862-64, see ibid., Sp. 3742; on the purchase of the building of the *Statthalterei* (1865-66), see CDIAU F. 146, Op. 7, vol. II, Sp. 3868, 3915; on the building of the *Statthalterei*, see CDIAU F. 146, Op. 31, Sp. 2; F. 726, Op. 1, Sp. 30, (1843-73), Sp. 31 (1878), Sp. 33 (1915); on the purchase of *Castrum* Square by the Municipality (1883), see CDIAU F. 146, Op. 7, vol. II, Sp. 4310, F. 165, Op. 5a, Sp. 47 (1881-85), 48 (1887-1910); on the Crown Land Court building, see CDIAU F. 146, Op. 31, Sp. 38 (1891), 49 (1893-99), 602 (1913-14); on the Finance Department building (1908-9), see CDIAU F. 146, Op. 31, Sp. 243, 248.

54 In 1859, for example, the Municipality is "not yet organized (*noch nicht organisirt*) and temporarily functions as[…]a communal administration and a political district office for the capital city of Lemberg," and in 1860 it was "organized provisorily" (*Handbuch Statthalterei-Gebietes in Galizien für das Jahr 1859*, (Lemberg: Galizische Aerarial Drückerei, 1859, 1860).

55 *Handbuch Statthalterei-Gebietes*, 1859, 157.

56 For work on the building plan for Lemberg (1836-47), see CDIAU F. 146, Op. 78, Sp. 7; for correspondence between the *General Commando* and the Gubernium on the building of private houses on the former fortifications (1860), see CDIAU F. 146, Op. 79, Sp. 219.

57 "Among the lowest strata of the population there exists a regrettable misconception of the idea of order and cleanliness, and [also] an unmatched indolence (*sehr bedaurelich … unrechtige Begriff von Ordnung und Reinlichkeit, und eine beispielslose Indolenz*), which works against [our] efforts. Teaching helps minimally, since long-time practice perverts it, or it does not take root at all" (CDIAU F. 146, Op. 7, Sp. 3365, L. 31-32).

58 The Municipality had difficulties putting such a regulation into force because "public establishments" were of two kinds: those directly controlled by the Municipality, to which legal measures applied, and private ones, which were much more difficult to regulate (ibid., L. 32-34).

59 Ibid., L. 37.

60 On repeated cases of violation of building regulation by the inhabitants of the outer districts – Zniesenie, Krywczyce, and Lysynycze (1826-50) – see CDIAU F. 146, Op. 78, Sp. 338-40.

61 A police report from 5 April 1855 mentions periodic attacks by the poor on the streets and blamed this on the lack of humanitarian institutions that could deal with the problem (CDIAU F. 146, Op. 7, Sp. 3365, L. 51). On the measures for the elimination of beggars (1857), see vol. II, Sp. 3455.

62 In 1865, Jews who would agree to dress in European styles and shave their beards were permitted to reside outside the ghetto, though only in the 1860s could they buy real estate property and freely reside within the city. Despite the regulations, the actual movement of richer Jews outside the ghetto limits, especially in the area west of the Pełtew's left bank, which was later one of Lemberg's largest areas of Jewish population, had already started in the 1830s-40s. See Vladimir Melamed, *Evrei vo Lvovie, XIII – pervaia polovina XX veka. Sobytia, obshchestvo, liudi* [Jews in Lvov, 13th – first half of the 20th century. Events, Society, Personalities] (L'viv: TEKOP 1994), 107-9).

63 As mentioned by Police Director Chomiński, poor clothing had become so commonplace – especially among the Jewish population – that one need not qualify every poorly dressed person as a beggar (CDIAU F. 146, Op. 7, Sp. 3365, L. 53).

64 Ibid., L. 42-47.

65 Ibid., L. 70-73.

66 Municipal letters to the Ministry of Home Affairs from December 1846 and 16 January 1855 (Wierzbieniec, "The processes of Jewish emancipation," 227; Bałaban, *Dzielnica żydowska*).

67 29 March 1858, l. 3295. The last appeal by the *kahal* on 11 January 1863 was unsuccessful. The final abolition of residential restriction was made in 1868 (ibid.).

68 *Szematyzm król. Galicyi i Lodomeryi z Wielkim Księżstwem Krakowskim na rok 1872* (Lemberg: Winiarz, 1872), 86. For an overview of the establishment of Austrian legislation on municipal self-government in relation to the Crown Land, see Wandruschka and Urbanitsch. *Die Habsburgermonarchie: 1848-1918*, vol. 2 (Vienna: Verlag der sterreichischen Akademie der Wissenschaften, 1975), 249-51; 270-305.

69 Ibid., 6.

70 "*Zabytek z czasów predrozbiorowych, powiększony tylko koszarami i koszarów stylem budowanymi gmachami publicznymi*" (S., "Nekrologia. Juliusz Hochberger," *CzT* 9 [1905], 171).

71 Ibid.

72 See Pavlo Grankin, "Dva stolittia holovnoï vulyci Lvova [Two centuries of L'viv's main street]," *HB* 2: 38 (1998); Oleksandr Šyška, "Ferdinand-Marijśka-Mickievyča: deščo pro topografiju, ikonografiju ta istoriju odnijeï lvivśkoï plošči [Ferdinandplatz – Marjacka – Mickewicza: some notes on the topography, iconography, and history of L'viv's streets]," *HB* 9: 33 (1997).

73 Mykola Bevz, "Urbanistychni transformaciji central'noji častyny mista Lvova u XIX-XX st." [Urbanistic transformations of L'viv inner city in 19th-20th centuries], Tscherkes, Kubelik, and Hofer, 52.

74 Although first introduced in the 1820s in Linz and Salzburg, building regulations for Galician towns date only to the 1880s (specifically, to 1883 in Cracow and 1885 in Lemberg). On the establishment of Lemberg's building regulation (1882-1909), see CDIAU F. 146, Op. 4, vol. I, Sp. 2505, 2507. 2508, 2510, and 2511-14. By 1900, the fortification walls remained only in those places where they did not obstruct traffic, such as at the backs of the Bernardine Cloister. The other remaining fortifications could still be observed in 1901 around St. George's Cathedral and around the Carmelite Cloister (CDIAU F. 52, Op. 1, Sp. 953, L. 5.).

75 On the obligatory regulations concerning the connection of city buildings with the municipal canalization sewer system (1903), see CDIAU F. 146, Op. 8, Sp. 205.

76 Lemberg's population passed 100,000 late in the 1870s. Ivanočko, "Urbanistyčni procesy Halyčyny," 219.

77 Krzysztof Pawłowski, "Miejsce Lwowa w rozwoju urbanistyki europejskej przełomu XIX i XX wieku" [Lwów's place in the development of European urbanization at the turn of the 19th to the 20th century], in Tscherkes, Kubelik, and Hofer, 125-31.

78 On the Zniesienie outer district, see CDIAU F. 146, Op. 8, Sp. 400. In 1910-11, the city built the Crown Land Hospital for Contagious Diseases (CDIAU F. 146, Op, 8, Sp. 1172). By the 1890s, the river had also been completely diverted underground in the city center. This widened a part of the ring above it, Wały Hetmanskie, and allowed for the relocation of the promenade into the center of the street, while its peripheral areas were used for traffic (Bevz, 53-54).

79 Galician Savings Bank, the Austrian-Hungarian Bank, Galician Lease Society, and hotels "Imperial," "George," "Grand," "Central," "English," and "French."

80 For example, Schnür-Pepłowski, *Obrazy z przeszłości*, 169.

81 Typical were the concerns of the Municipality in 1886-87, when debates on guidebooks engaged various strata of the society. A certain Pole, Michał Kowalczuk, even wrote his own individual version of the city guide and suggested that the city should publish it as an official one. The Municipality chose their own functionary to produce such a work instead. (CDIAU F. 55, Op. 1, Sp. 75).

82 On a summary of the construction of monuments in Lemberg, see Ihor Siomočkin, "Pamjatnyky" [Monuments], *HB* 2: 38 (1998), 14-15.

83 The medieval urban *"nationes"* were equivalent to countryside estates (*stany, Stände*).

84 Apparently, based on Magdeburg law, much of the "Polish nation" within Lemberg's governing institutions included Polonized Germans (Hrytsak and Susak, "Constructing a National City"), similar to other Polish towns.

85 Specifically, Royal Sarmatians, who allegedly descended from the Biblical Adam. (ibid.).

86 Calling themselves "the Galician nation," the Polish aristocrats demanded the restoration of their own feudal aristocratic privileges and the preservation of serfdom. See Schneider, *Das Kolonisationswerk Josefs II*, 35-36. On a thorough revisionist analysis of *Magna Charta*, see Hugo Lane, "Szlachta Outside the Commonwealth. The Case of Polish Nobles in Galicia," *Zeitschrift für Ostmitteleuropa-Forschung* 52/4 (2003), 526-42. Also see Wolff, "Inventing Galicia," 828-33.

87 See Andzej Walicki, *Poland Between East and West: the Controversies Over Self-Definition and Modernization in Partitioned Poland* (Cambridge, Harvard University Press, 1994).

88 Ibid. This split resulted from the historical specifics of the city's development; Jews were present in the city from its very origins. The early settlement founded by Ruthenian princes lay around Żółkiew Street and Old Market Square (*Stary Rynek*). On the medieval Jewish community in Lemberg, see Bałaban, *Dzielnica żydowska*.

89 Besides the divides noted above, one could also make a distinction between the Orthodox and liberal Jews. Although until now nobody has traced the residential patterns of richer, assimilated, and bourgeois Jewry, an educated guess suggests that its members did not reside in the ghetto in the historic center.

90 German tradesmen had resided in Lemberg since the Middle Ages. However, the German population as a coherent group dates back to the period following the incorporation

of Galicia into Austria and thus bears no continuity with the previous German presence whatsoever.

91 On the great proportion of Czechs and Bohemian Germans within the Crown Land and the municipal administration, see Jevhen Topinka et al., *Čechy v Halyčyni: Biograficnyj dovidnyk* [Czechs in Galicia: Bibliographical Guide] (L'viv: Centr Jevropy, 1998).

92 This phrase is attributed to Crown Land Councilor Koffler, who reported to have "worked for the House of Austria thirty-seven years to make these Sarmatian beasts into men" *(hat das Haus Österreich daran gearbeitet, aus diesen sarmatischen Bestien Menschen zu machen)*. Quoted from Bronislaw Pawłowski, *Lwów w 1809 r. z 20 rycinami w tekście* [Lwów in 1809 with 20 illustrations in the text] (Lemberg: Towarzystwo Miłośnikow Przeszłości Lwowa, 1909), 14.

93 Maria Kłańska, "Lemberg. Die 'Stadt der verwischten Grenzen'," in Bisanz, 10-16.

94 The proportion of ethnic groups was as follows: Poles (50%-55%), Jews (30%-35%), and Ruthenians (15%-20%). This division survived the monarchy's demise as well as the interwar period and ended only during and after World War II. The German population gradually decreased in number in the second half of the nineteenth century (ibid.; idem, *Daleko od Wiednia*, 7-23).

95 Lane, "Szlachta Outside the Commonwealth," 526-42.

96 A full list of the portraits includes Tadeusz Kościuszko and other military heroes: Jan Kiliński; Generals Jan Henryk Dąbrowski, Jakub Jasiński, and a certain S.K.B. Mokrowski [possibly Stanisław Mokronowski]; the aristocrats from the Czartoryski family; politicians Piotr Bieliński (president of the Diet Court of the Congress Kingdom), Jan Nepomucen Małachowski (Senate president of the Duchy of Warsaw), Julian Ursyn Niemcewicz (Senate secretary, president of the Academic Society); a certain Stanisław Kowalski; and religious leaders Hugo Kołłątaj and Archbishop Ignacy Krasicki.

97 CDIAU F. 146, Op. 7, Sp. 1950, L. 6.

98 Signed on 30 October 1812 by municipal representatives, among whom were also Poles (Lewandowski). CDIAU F. 146, Op. 7, Sv. 46, Sp. 661, L. 17-20. Municipal Councilor (*Magistratsrath*) Lewandowski was apparently the same person who in 1824 was accused of a misuse of his administrative position: as were several other municipal and provincial officials, he was allegedly also an owner of a pub (*Weinschänk*), which was against regulations for state employees (See CDIAU F. 146. Op. 6, Sp. 319, L. 1400-02.

99 Lane, "Szlachta Outside the Commonwealth," 526-42.

100 CDIAU F. 146, Op. 7, Sv. 46, Sp. 661, L. 8, 10-12.

101 On 24 May 1813, an even more curious opinion was reported in the Crown Land; although the Polish population was generally not happy with the Austrian troops' return, it thought that rather than return and stay in Galicia, the former should have united with the Polish troops from the Duchy of Warsaw in Cracow to make a great diversion against Russia (CDIAU F. 146, Op. 6, Sp. 218, L. 1021).

102 As reported by Crown Land Councilor (*Gubernialrath & Kreishauptmann*) Count Castiglioni. CDIAU F. 146, Op. 6, Sp. 223, L. 1796-98. Brezany reported on 10 September 1813 that even some Poles had become convinced by the War Manifest to stand against Napoleon (ibid., L. 1803-4).

103 Lane, "Szlachta Outside the Commonwealth."

104 For example, in 1849. CDIAU F. 146, Op. 7, Sv. 149, Sp. 2863, L. 2-4.

105 For Sacher-Masoch's report from 11 January 1846 to the Galician Governor, see CDIAU F. 146, Op. 6, Sp. 572-82. The police report also mentions a shortage of secret agents.

106 It was allegedly the cry of a Polish aristocrat at the meeting in 1846, "There is no Diet!" (*Niema Sejmu!*), that catalyzed further revolutionary upheaval in the city.

107 CDIAU F. 146, Op. 6, Sp. 573-75.

108 Lane, "Szlachta Outside the Commonwealth."

109 See Wolff, "Inventing Galicia"; Lane, "Szlachta Outside the Commonwealth."

110 The first Ruthenian political institution, known as the Ruthenian Council (*Holovna Ruśka Rada - Ruthenischer Hauptrat*), was established on Stadion's suggestion to counter the Polish revolutionary threat. See "Franz Graf Stadion (1806-1853)" *Neue österreichische Biografie ab 1815: grosse Österreicher* (Zurich, Leipzig, and Vienna: Amalthea-Verlag. vol. 14, 1960), 62-73.

111 CDIAU F. 146, Op. 7, Sv. 149, Sp. 2863, L. 2-4.

112 As in the police report on the erection of the Union of Lublin Mound in 1869: "*democratische Partei*" (the Polish Democrats) and "*ukrainische und galizisch-ruthen-ische Partei*" (CDIAU F. 165, Op. 5, Sp. 110, L. 6, 20).

113 Heavily subsidized by the state and protected personally either by the Monarch or by his Crown Land governor, such institutions largely served a state function. It is possibly about those institutions that an anonymous writer satirically remarked in 1852: "I would not write a book on the fear that someone might include me as an active member of some inactive society." (Anonymous [Dr. B], "Wzorki lwowskie" [Lwów ornaments], *Czas* [1852]; CDIAU F. 52, Op. 1, Sp. 950, L. 11).

114 See further discussion on Franciszek Smolka in chap. 4.

115 The appeal was also signed by Diet Speaker Leon Sapieha and Vice-Speaker Oktaw Pietruski (CDIAU F. 165, Op. 5, Sp. 230, L. 12).

116 The existing voting structure resulted in an overrepresentation of Polish landowners in both the Galician Diet (*Sejm*) and the Austrian parliament, an underrepresentation of other groups, and an almost total exclusion of the Ruthenian peasant population. For this reason, in turn-of-the-century Galicia the provincial voting rights movement was a national issue.

117 Bronislaw Pawłowski, *Lwow w 1809 r.*, 14.

118 See Lane, *State Culture and National Identity*.

119 Jürgen Habermas, *Structural Transformation of the Public Sphere* (Cambridge, Mass: MIT Press, 1989). Also see Steven Seidman, ed., *Jürgen Habermas on Society and Politics: A Reader* (Boston, 1989), 231-36.

120 "According to Imperial regulation (no. 508/1811), reading libraries can be organized only in capital cities as selected by Our Majesty. Lemberg belongs to such cities, while no other city in Galicia does" (CDIAU F. 146, Op. 7, Sp. 2293, L. 2, 7).

121 CDIAU F. 146, Op. 6, Sp. 322, L. 1742. The concept of "public responsibility," however, is a later one; on the level of the municipal government, one speaks of "public responsibility" only in the late 1840s (CDIAU F. 52, Op. 1, Sp. 30, L. 11).

122 See CDIAU F. 146, Op. 79, Sp. 210, L. 1-10.

123 CDIAU F. 146, Op. 7, Sp. 3365, L. 31-32.

124 In connection with the Union of Lublin celebration in 1869: "Bringing together (*Zusammenströmen*) foreign guests and certain familiar politically exalted [local] personalities...can give a pretext for demonstrations...and will also unavoidably threaten public peace and the general communal well-being. (CDIAU F. 165, Op. 5, Sp. 10, L. 20-25).

125 In connection with the Jan Kiliński monument (CDIAU F. 146, Op. 7, Sp. 4437, L.4).

126 Apart from the official municipal newspaper "Lemberger Zeitung" that had been coming out since 1811, a variety of other local informational, cultural, and professional

periodicals appeared in Lemberg in the nineteenth century: "Gazette de Leopol" in the 1870s; "Pismo Uwiadamiające Galiciji," "Lemberger Wöchenfliche Anzeigen," "Lemberger k. k. priviligirtes Intelligenz-Blatt," and "Dziennik patriotycznych polityków" in the 1880s and 1890s; "Pamiętnik Lwowski"(since 1816); "Pamiętnik Galicyjski" and "Mnemosyne" in the 1810s-20s; "Czasopism Naukowy Księgozbioru publicznego im. Ossolinskich" from 1828 to 1834; and "Lwowianin" since 1836. The first political journal that caused official outrage was "Dziennik mód paryżskich," which came out from 1840 on, later being renamed "Tygodnik polski." Nationalist literature from the Congress Kingdom was also successfully smuggled into Lemberg.

127 This space was itself not homogeneous: the rhetoric in the cabinets of the Gubernium may have been much more imperial than that in the Municipality, and even more so than in the Galician Diet. On the complexity of the Polish aristocracy's participation in the Diet, see Lane, "The Galician Nobility and the Border with the Congress Kingdom before, during, and after the November Uprising"; this was an unpublished paper presented at the workshop *Die galizische Grenze 1772-1867 – Kommunikation oder Isolation?*, Institut für Osteuropäische Geschichte der Universität Wien, 2005.

128 Ernst Bogumil Kortum came to Lemberg from Bielitz (Bielsko), Silezia, and before his employment by the Habsburg state had served in Teschen, Schleswig-Holstein, and as a personal secretary to the last Polish king Stanislaw August. He served as a Crownland Councilor in matters related to the university and education, while also directing the Galician salt mines and serving as a Privy Councilor (*Geheimer Rat*) to the Court. His major work was *Magna Charta von Galizien* (1790), in which he bitterly criticized the Polish gentry's conservatism and fiercely opposed the idea of Galician autonomy (Franciszek Jaworski, *Lwów stary i wczorajszy [szkice i opowiadania] z illustracyami, Wydanie drugie poprawione* [Old and yesterday's Lwów. Sketches and stories with illustrations] (Lemberg: Nakl. Tow. Wydawniczego, 1911), 328.

129 After having acquired it, the Crown Land Council (*Gubernialrat*) stripped the facade of its rococo decoration, inserted a marble plate with a quotation from Horace in its place, and added a few neoclassical structures to the garden (ibid.).

130 Most of the Galician governors were regularly inviting the gentry to such events. Baron Franz Krieg, the hated Crown Land president (1832-46), also held regular evening events at his house on *Szeroka* Street in the 1830s-40s, which the entire city's Polish aristocracy attended with very few exceptions (Schnür-Pepłowski, *Obrazy z przeszłości*, 372).

131 In 1823, a certain road specialist (*Wegmeister*) Radislaus Hodoly reported on the intense social life of the Lemberg gentry, full of luxurious balls and weddings: *"[Meine Gemahlin] erzählte, wie gut sie sich durch dieser Zeit auf Bällen, Hochzeiten und sonstigen Lustbarkeiten unterhalten hatte"* (CDIAU F. 146, Op. 6, Sp. 313, L. 546).

132 These sites were the Jabłonowski Park, and for a short time the hill of St. George Cathedral. The latter, however, proved inadequate in 1830. On intense correspondence between the Court Chancellery, the Gubernium, and the Municipality about the issues related to public celebrations, see CDIAU F. 146, Op. 85, Sp. 2768.

133 Joseph Rohrer, *Bemerkungen auf einer Reise von der türkischen Grenze über die Bukowina durch Ost- und Westgalizien, Schlesien und Mähren nach Wien* (Wien, 1804, Berlin, 1989), 141.

134 CDIAU F. 165, Op. 5, Sp. 110, L. 31-32, 46-47.

135 In 1867, Józef Ignacy Kraszewski (1812-87), the leading Polish playwright, held lectures in the Town Hall. Kraszewski's play was applauded at the Opera. Jan Matejko, the leading Polish national-academy-trained painter, spoke passionately upon receiv-

ing honorary citizen status at the Town Hall in 1869 (Schnür-Pepłowski, *Obrazy z przeszłości*, 222-23).

136 The Ruthenian National Institute became the recurrent place for the police secret informers' reports. See, for example, CDIAU F. 146, Op. 7, Sp. 4215; Sp. 3685; Sp. 4254.

137 For greater discussion, see chap. 4 of this book.

CHAPTER TWO

Writing the City: Bureaucrats, Historians, Technicians, and Nationals

The official architecture of the Austrian Vormärz, the neoclassicism of Pietro Nobile (1776-1854), the Royal Court architect and director of the Viennese Academy of Arts that was influential in Lemberg until the 1830s, has traditionally received little appreciation, even though leading Polish interwar scholars recognized Nobile as one of the most outstanding architects of the epoch.[1] Neither his figure nor his architectural school has been studied in any depth until recently, and his contributions to the architectural history of Central Europe,[2] as well as his involvement in the Galician capital,[3] still await revision. One of the reasons for the neglect of Vormärz architecture lies in the assumption of rupture, which has its roots in the Polish historiography of the early twentieth century and the interwar period, which traditionally emphasized the great difference between neoclassical architecture and later historicist styles, and interpreted this difference as a consequence of political modernization in Galicia. Similarly, this historiography distanced itself from the German writing of the Vormärz, inasmuch as the evaluation of buildings and styles was concerned.[4] This line of argument culminates in an emphasis, still current in the scholarship on Habsburg Lemberg, on a great change that occurred in architecture in the second half of the nineteenth century when Julian Zachariewicz established a historicist architectural school at the Lemberg Technical Academy.[5]

Following the lead of Maria Kłańska, who was the first to call for a rethinking of the Vormärz "German" written legacy in Galicia,[6] this chapter is meant to challenge the assumptions of early twentieth-century historiography. Closer examination reveals that it is inadequate to judge neoclassical architecture according to late nineteenth-century concepts of beauty as much as twentieth-century historiography did. Fin-de-siècle writing in both Polish and Ruthenian was profoundly influenced by authors of the Vormärz and appropriated, developed, and at times inverted the latter's normative judgments for its own purposes. Writings by several high-ranking clerks of the Vormärz, neoabsolutism, and Autonomy eras, and also architects' views, show lines of continuity as well as rupture. The continuity between the earlier texts in German and the later ones in Polish and Ruthenian can be especially traced in the interpretation of new architecture, planning, and greenery. The new urban planning was seen as both "beautifying" and "healing"; the quality of architecture – "baroque," "barrack," or "national" – was equated with the nature of government; and an intellectual arrogance vis-à-vis the "backward" local population, especially against the Jews, has survived.[7] In fact, great change took place only in the early twentieth century, when the discussions over Lemberg's new cultural institutions transformed from intellectual musings into a political issue with a clear national agenda.

Bureaucrats and Reason: Franz Kratter, Joseph Rohrer, and the Polish Context

Vormärz neoclassical architecture in Lemberg was most strongly informed by Johann Joachim Winckelmann's writings; Giovanni Battista Piranesi's drawings of Ancient Greek sites (notably Herculaneum and Paestum) and Roman buildings; English Palladianism; and the principles of antique architecture and planning as conceptualized by Giacomo Barozzi da Vignola and Francesco Milizia.[8] The Austrian Vormärz bureaucracy's arrogance notwithstanding, neoclassical views – including views on architectural beauty – were neither limited to nor introduced by the authors writing in German in Galicia. As pointed out by Tadeusz Mańkowski, contemporary Polish literature on the subject existed as early as the late eighteenth century: specifically, works by Kajetan Zdzański, Florian Strawiński, and Michał Szulz.[9] Architecture based on Vignola's principles had been taught in pre-partitioned Poland in Jesuit colleges since the early eighteenth century. Throughout the nineteenth century, local professionals in the lands of partitioned Poland knew Sebastian Sierakowski's theoretical writings on architecture, especially his *Architektura obejmująca wszelki gatunek budowania i murowania* [Architecture as Overarching All Kinds of Building and Mural Works] and Stanisław Potocki's *O sztuce u dawnych czyli Winkelman polski* [On the Art of the Ancients or Polish Winckelmann]. Both works were strongly Winckelmannian.[10] Local professionals were also aware of Alberti's writings on Vitruvius, and not only in German, but also in Polish translation.

Although major architectural trends did not pass Lemberg before the arrival of the Austrian architectural bureaucracy, the actual blossoming of neoclassicism in the city took place in the late Vormärz. Local Lemberg architects of the Vormärz have left us little written evidence of their personal aesthetic views.

With the exception of the life of Ignac Chambrez, whose writings will be treated at length in the following pages, we have only scattered knowledge about their professional lives and views. Austrian bureaucrats arrived in Lemberg during and after the Josephinian reforms of the late eighteenth and early nineteenth centuries, and they were Germans and Germanized Czechs. They were publicly employed, mainly educated in Vienna, and resided in Lemberg as long as required by their employment, which was often brief, by the Crown Land and Municipal administration or the college.

Because of the lack of writings by professional architects, memoirs by several Austrian officials who were concerned with or interested in culture in general and especially in architecture, are extremely valuable.[11] It is useful to compare their memoirs with accounts by professional architects. Such a comparison elucidates to what extent professional affiliations determined views on culture and art, and it also clarifies whether a difference existed between the two groups in their tendency to voice loyalties and sentiments, including national tendencies. Personalities that are considered here include Franz Kratter (1757-1837), a clerk of Bavarian origin and a director of the German theater; Joseph Rohrer (1769-1828), a Bohemian German and a long-term police director; and Ignac Chambrez (1758-1842), a Moravian Czech and one of the very few architects to leave a written account. Examinations of these individuals' beliefs reveals that a negative bias against the "baroque" – understood broadly as a moral imperative dividing virtue and vice and applied equally to the nature of government, architectural principles, and even the style of fashion – figured as a prevailing thought that was not limited to either architectural profession or to educated bureaucrats. This belief in the physical ugliness of baroque, versus the beauty of neoclassical architecture, planning, and other fields of art, as well as a characteristic admiration of the beauty of natural landscape as places of recollection and solitude, were in fact universal European trends. Locally, the Habsburg clerks associated the "baroque" with the "Poles" while reserving the Enlightenment, and thus neoclassicism, for themselves. The perception of Lemberg as aesthetically unappealing and dirty, and the related view of its population as being ignorant and stupid, stemmed from these administrators' negative perceptions of the local element.

As were most of the bureaucrats stationed in Lemberg in the early nineteenth century, Kratter and Rohrer were enlightened men who read Rousseau and Voltaire.[12] Kratter, a fervent Josephinian,[13] often compared Lemberg with his native Bavaria and metropolitan Vienna. His extremely bitter account of early nineteenth-century Lemberg life resulted in part from his deep belief in what he saw as the enlightened German culture's civilizing mission, of which both the local inhabitants and many Austrian bureaucrats were obviously ignorant. Rohrer, whose complex identity is much more difficult to fit into the straightjacket of

"German bureaucracy," was a Bohemian German.[14] By education a lawyer and by avocation an ethnographer, born and buried in Vienna, he maintained an attachment to Prague throughout his life, citing Prague, and occasionally other cities in Bohemia, as examples of good Municipal management.[15]

It is in this light that Kratter's and Rohrer's criticisms of Lemberg's local inhabitants should be seen: their critique was an integral part of their dislike of Galicia, and in their writings the new German-speaking bureaucracy also received its due.[16] As representatives of a new class of Josephinian bureaucrats sent to an "Austrian Siberia," they strongly criticized everything that reminded them of being away from "civilization"[17] and strictly differentiated between themselves and the local public:

> Perhaps very few Lembergers think at this very moment…the same as I do. They flee their homes. Eternal solitude would for them be a sin. They do not know in those [evening] hours how to use the good that exists in their hearts. They hurry into the cafés and the kiosks of the Mandoletti sellers and prefer to drink there rather than entertain themselves at home....This type of behavior has caused a peculiar Lemberg character, in which a German and a Polish café keeper and an Italian Mandoletti seller [compete] to rent the largest houses in the city center.[18]

In contrast to the Vienna of Mozart and German opera, the dirt of Lemberg's inner city appeared even more distasteful to these observers, and the well-known episode when Joseph II's carriage got stuck in mud in the middle of Lemberg in 1773 demonstrated how terribly backward this city was in comparison with Western capitals.[19]

During Vormärz, public green spaces fundamentally transformed the appearance of nineteenth-century Habsburg cities. István Széchenyi is largely responsible for the establishment of the new kind of garden culture in Hungary, while Adalbert Stifter's rhyme, "Oh happy we who have the Prater!" could be used to describe the Vienna culture of the Vormärz.[20] The importance of plantings in planning the Vormärz Lemberg was evident not only in German-written accounts such as those of Kratter and Rohrer, but the value of green spaces was also appreciated by the upper-class Polish public.[21] The admiration of the city's natural green surroundings figured as an integral part of the *Biedermeier* romantic admiration of Nature as "private" space, as compared with the public space of city streets. Greenery was connected with solitude, as opposed to public space in the city, its streets and its crowds, which were to be avoided.[22]

To make green spaces enjoyable, however, they needed to be ordered and simplified in the same manner in which many rococo houses were stripped of their rich decorations at the time. Only then could those "forests" – private and Municipal gardens with restricted public access – be cherished, once they were redesigned to offer a comfortable refuge from urban noise and dirt with footpaths, promenades, and vistas. Thus straight allées were created, along with simple and modestly decorated neoclassical buildings. From such sightseeing points, the beauty of the distant city's architecture could be admired, since the aesthetics of the time disliked the *decoration* of the "baroque" buildings, not the buildings themselves. Kratter captured the difference between the dilapidated houses of the outlying districts and their beautiful gardens in 1786.[23] His views on the topic are evident in his admiration of Castle Hill's green areas:

> All the beauty of Eden stands here in its full greatness: nature and [man-made] beautification, blessed cornfields, rich and colorful mead-ows, springs and lakes, forests and the wilderness, changing vistas, unmatched views. How often was I absorbed in the joyful, youthful mood of this hill! How I spent hours at its top and filled my spirit with pictures of omnipotence and thoughts of mankind, myself, salvation and savior, and all blessed things![24]

Greenery was thus seen by Kratter and Rohrer — and perhaps by the Austrian planning bureaucracy in general — not only as an integral element of the new city planning, but also as a beautifying factor. In their views, plantings figured as an integral part of architecture, as architecture itself. Just as in the Schönbrunn of Vienna, in Lemberg gardens, nature and art were to work together.[25] In combination, neoclassical buildings and ordered parks symbolized novelty, modernity, and beauty: the opposite of the inner city. Private gardens that were open to high society's leisure activities, such as the Jabłonowski Park, the Lonchamp Park (*Lonszanówka*),[26] and the former Jesuit Garden were especially valued.

In the rapidly urbanizing Lemberg of the Vormärz, the destruction of gardens was unthinkable.[27] On some occasions, however, change to a building's ornamentation was envisioned to fit into the garden arrangements. Such it was with the abandoned Jabłonowski palace built in the seventeenth century, the façade of which Rohrer wished to alter to create the harmonious, orderly impression of an English country house.[28] *Biedermeier* admiration of green spaces was soon followed by Polish authors, as evident from Antoni Schneyder's article in the local German-language newspaper *Mnemosyne* (1846):

> [Castle Hill] can stand in line with the most beautiful splenderous parks (*Prachtanlagen*) in this *genre* because of its excellent, majestic position near the city, its heavenly view, as well as its tender, virile, and stylish (*geschmackvollen*) greenery.[29]

One may find similar descriptions, accompanied with assumptions of intellectual superiority over the local population, in the Polish press in the 1850s. In accounts such as the following, the actual presence of a Western visitor is employed to support this belief:

> These are...splendid walks with miraculous views on Lwów, on the ring of its outlying parks[, and] on the distant fields and commons....The air is so clean and so refreshing that if one breathes it for just a minute, one immediately feels healthier, lighter, merrier, freer, and even more inclined to do good – and if one were still young and unspoiled – in love....It would be difficult to find a more suitable walking path [than the one to Castle Hill]. Only God knows what the inhabitants of the leading capitals would not give to have [such greenery] as close as almost one step away [from the city center]....Such an abundance in this most beautiful place has often spoiled my best moods, since how can it be reconciled, I thought, that [the local public] would have so little sense for...the beautiful outdoors![30]

While having a troubled relationship with his home city and being acutely caught up in comparing it with Western capitals, this anonymous Polish writer has attempted to convince both himself and the imagined foreign reader of the wonderful nature of the city's green spaces. Thus, dissatisfied with this place whose value locals do not see as a civilized Westerner would, such as the French novelist and enthusiast of Nature Charles Didier[31] or a contemporary, this Polish writer assumed the role of a Vormärz "German," guiding a Westerner through the city.

For authors writing in German, however, greenery also became symbolic of lofty thoughts and memories: above all, green spaces became associated with the mind of God and with recollections of the 1773 visit of the emperor. As a representation of the divine and associated with memories of the monarch, public green spaces occupied a disproportionately significant place in their writing. Joseph Rohrer gave particular value to the Lonchamp Park at the foot of Castle Hill shortly after Emperor Joseph II had visited it:

> I would like to show you Lemberg's beautiful surroundings, into which I sometimes flee from the city when the trees are green again. Unfortunately, I often feel so much out of place with people...that I prefer to conclude my reflections on my city's inhabitants in this letter....I cannot control myself and hide my feelings, which fill me through and through, when I look down the hill [from Lonchamp Park]. Little houses lie dispersed among the green areas, while at the same time, the fields are separated from the hills in the distance. The whole of Nature, when one goes there in the morning, it seems, wishes to quietly celebrate this

magnificent scene. This garden is basically nothing but a quiet forest (*Wäldchen*). I rarely, and only for a change, look toward the other side on the city, overwhelmed with the triumph of these heights where such different winds blow. [I have] escaped the city noise through a small footpath.[32]

The very fact of the emperor's visit meant to loyal Habsburg subjects such as Kratter and Rohrer that the site was beautiful and worthy of recognition. Monuments did not need to be physical in the Vormärz; the sites of imperial visits were just as beautiful, as was the emperor himself, and the erection of a statue to the emperor at such a site was not an absolute necessity. Rohrer's admiration of Lonchamp Park was partly due to, and resulted from, the emperor's presence there. When Rohrer spoke of the memorial plaque to mark Joseph II's visit as a "small monument in memory of the great monarch,"[33] the actual plaque was, for Rohrer, a mere extension of his memory.

Similarly, the state was viewed as an extension of the royal person that was undertaking beautiful acts for its citizenry. Planning actions on behalf of the Crown Land administration headed by Leopold Lazansky in the 1840s, for example, were a "monument" (*Denkmal*) to his own personality. A poetic German verse by Moritz Siegerist, titled "Total-Charade," recalled the transformation of Castle Hill with the following words:

I proudly bear the name of the noble count,
who had erected a monument to himself,
a monument of his charitableness and dignity,
... and a most beautiful decoration of Lemberg![34]

Just as German writing used "*Monument*" and "*Denkmal*" interchangeably in the middle of the century to signify both imaginary and "real" memorials, i.e., erected ones, the Polish word "*pamiatka*" came to assume the same two meanings. Yet the issue of memories and of a monument's beauty was a more complicated one for Polish writers, who needed to reconcile national memories with official Austrian history. As evident in Antoni Schneyder's account, written a year after his commentary on Castle Hill plantings in *Mnemosyne*, he needed to legitimize the preservation of the medieval ruins on the hill with the memory of the glorious Polish king, Casimir the Great:

It is generally known that our fathers' monuments [are] our greatest treasures, and that they [are] the most outspoken proof of their glorious deeds and virtues of yesteryear. The High Castle's ruins also belong among such monuments, the more so that we possess through them the last memory of King Casimir the Great, who, as [oral] tradition teaches us, personally laid bricks in the foundation of this castle – and later resided there several times.[35]

As regards buildings proper, the issue of style becomes even more acute in this period. In the early nineteenth century, "style" (*Styl*) was a concept referring to a certain building manner, used interchangeably with "type" (*Typ*), "taste" (*Geschmack* in German, *smak, gust* in Polish), and "manner" and "kind" (*Art* in German, *sposób* in Polish). The idea of universal beauty, rather than stylistic categorization, was applied to differentiate between "good" and "bad" architecture.[36] In writing, authors routinely concerned themselves with worthy architectural examples of "all kinds" (*aller Art*). In 1836, for example, Franz Tschischka wrote on the Dominican Church in Lemberg not as a rococo piece, but as one of the Viennese Karlskirche "type." At the same time, he grouped together Lemberg's Gothic Roman Catholic Cathedral, the baroque Jesuit monastery, the neoclassical governor's palace, and the neoclassical Town Hall as "exemplary beautiful works of *new* architecture."[37]

Instead of style strictly defined, architecture was judged according to "rational" criteria, such as simplicity, adequacy, and scale. Franz Kratter's calling the rococo St. George's Cathedral "a church built in an unusual neo-Gothic taste,"[38] has been easily picked up by Mańkowski and brought as evidence of the Austrian clerk's ignorance.[39] However, Kratter might have simply been judging buildings according to the prevailing criteria. Baroque - also rococo - was in bad taste, because this style did not and could not correspond to the neoclassical principles of architectural beauty, though selected medieval churches did meet these principles.

For the followers of architectural neoclassicism and Francesco Milizia's planning methods,[40] beauty was, above all, to be found in simplicity, symmetry, and clear geometrical shapes, "*der edlen Einfalt und stiller Grösse.*"[41] Anything that failed to correspond to this neoclassical ideal was in poor taste. For Franz Kratter, baroque was thus an architecture of senseless artistic ornamentation and exaggeration, of "petty-minded" (*kleinlich*) churches, excessively decorated altarpieces, and "grimacing" (*grimassierende*) sculptures. Baroque features thus understood could only have spoiled buildings with baroque's unnecessary ornaments and masonry, and the erection of an entire, aesthetically pleasing church according to its principles was simply unthinkable:

> The [Roman Catholic] cathedral [and] the Dominican church are beautiful buildings, yet inside decorated with wretched (*elenden*) statues ..and defaced with frequent depictions of highly superstitious nature (*häufigen Verzierereien einer höchst abergläubischen Undächterei ganz verunstaltet*). The taste of church decorations is in Galicia gener-

ally petty and mediocre (*kleinlich, unedel*), and mostly it constitutes discord between the building plan and jammed rows of altars; a few, grimacing statues; paintings of multicolored, foolish arrangement (*in buntem, kindischem Scheckwerk*); and a waste of clumsy, shapeless (*plumpen, ungestalten*) masses of gold.[42]

Insofar as Kratter's general judgment of building style went, his aesthetic eye disliked anything that did not refer to classical antiquity. In this, he simply followed the founders of theoretical classicism, notably Leon Battista Alberti, the Renaissance architect and translator of Vitruvius, and the French eighteenth-century theoretician Mark-Antoine Laugier. For Alberti, the key interpreter of Vitruvius, architecture was divided by its fundamental purpose rather than by its style, with the classical orders an unquestioned canon: between sacred and secular and between public and private. One was to build for solidity, for convenience, and adequately to the building's purpose. Beauty was to be seen in a building's whole, rather than in a combination of its parts, and would be as universal as the laws of Nature.[43] For Laugier in his "*Essai sur l'architecture*" (1753), architecture was to be "neither more nor less magnificent than is appropriate to its purpose," and hence ornamentation "must always be in relation to the rank and quality of those who live in the [buildings] and conform to the objective envisaged."[44]

◆

A true admirer of neoclassicism, Kratter was truly able to appreciate any building that was "tasteful, simple, and majestic in its splendor."[45] Although sometimes applied to historic architecture, such as the parish church in the town of Dukla, such a description also applied to what late nineteenth century writers labeled "dull, barrack classicism," i.e., simple architecture based on the principles of symmetry and classical proportions, often built after standard designs drawn in Vienna. For him, simple geometry was a synonym for good taste. Just as modesty in ornamentation and symmetry was admired in a building, thus order, straightness, and wide streets was appreciated in planning:

> Lemberg is relatively orderly and well planned, the streets follow straight lines, and some have a comfortable width. The city has four gates, with the Cracow and Halicz gates standing on direct axis from one another. The New Gate and Jesuit Gate could also be moved onto a straight axis at little costs, an idea that has already been suggested.[46]

Renaissance Market Square (then officially *Ringplatz*), similarly, was a "beautiful, large, correct geometrical square with beautiful large, four- and five-story houses built mostly in the best Italian taste (*nach dem besten italienischen Geschmacke*) [and] standing in straight lines. It is a great pity that its magnificent looks are spoiled by the Town Hall in the middle,...its tower unworthy of consideration (*sonst sehr unansehnliche*)."[47]

Importantly, Kratter saw everything that was negative in Lemberg not only as being in bad taste - that is, baroque - but also as distinctly *Polish*. For example, he explained his dissatisfaction with the adaptation of the Trinitary Cloister to a university for the following reasons:

> The former Trinitary Cloister...became the building of the university. The building has a shape of an approximate square... yet one sees at first glance that it was never...intended that...it would function as a temple and residence of ungodly [academic] muses...[The accommodation of university facilities is] ill-mannered and clumsy (*übel und ungemächtig*), made in the Polish manner (*nach polnischer Art*). The reading rooms were made up of two or three cells (*Zellen*) and therefore had to be very narrow, disproportionate, and unstylish (*unschicklich*).[48]

Just as the "Polish" methods of state rule were an anachronism to Lemberg newcomers, so were their building principles. The same ethnic connection Kratter applied to his judgment of the Lemberg buildings also made its way into his commentary on their interiors: "The art of Polish houses' interior arrangements was no less miserable (*elend*). Uncomfortable, elongated nooks (*Winkel*) replace spacious rooms by way of bad, unsymmetrical partitioning."[49]

Kratter's lament on the sorry condition of houses and streets at the moment of Austrian arrival implied a connection between the Polish "baroque" state rule and the physical appearance of pre-Austrian Lemberg.[50] Thus the connection between the nature of state rule and architecture – "baroque" Polish rule versus the neoclassical Austrian one – was cemented in writing. In practice, making street layout adequate became a sign of good government, while cleaning up and replanning the historic center remained one of the city's most pressing needs. The establishment of the Austrian rule in Galicia was associated with progress.[51] Rohrer followed Kratter's above statement a decade later with a commentary on this topic:

> As often as I see these new [two- and three-story] houses, I am pleased by the extraordinary progress that, for the first time in the past few years, the city of Lemberg has added to its numerous new houses in terms of elegance....This winter a great undertaking was accomplished on behalf of the government, namely, that in each of the four Lemberg outer areas – Cracow, Żolkiew, Halicz, and Litschakow districts – a refuge house (*Warmstube*) was erected for those in need.[52]

Such views were not limited to authors writing in German. An anonymous writer commenting on the replacement of the city fortifications in the Polish popular periodical *Przyjaciel domowy* [Home Companion], commended in 1857 that "on that spot, which today serves as a pleasant walk, the city's walls had been pulled down and replaced by shady green trees."[53] As the city's public enjoyed the new walking paths around Lemberg's historic core, the popular press recognized the Austrian planning achievement. Yet it saw public greenery primarily as a public attraction and a site of socializing, rather than as a place of intimate solitude and escape from public life into the natural realm, as did Kratter and Rohrer.

Vormärz Architects: Ignac Chambrez between Vienna and Prague

The new Austrian bureaucrats arrived with manifold identities in Lemberg, where professional affiliation, sense of national belonging, and dynastic loyalty coexisted. In the case of some authors writing in German, such as Kratter, ethnicity was as clear and unproblematic as loyalty to the Habsburg throne. This did not apply to the major Vormärz professional architect and art historian Ignac Chambrez, a university professor and designer of several major buildings in Lemberg. Tadeusz Mańkowski called him "a German whose name only sounded French" in the 1920s,[54] reflecting a generalization of Vormärz architects as "Germans," as was typical of Polish historiography. However, Chambrez was above all a Moravian, for whom German was not his mother tongue.[55]

Notably the only professional architect in Vormärz Lemberg to put down theoretical architectural premises on paper,[56] Chambrez learned German and French shortly before entering the secondary school *gymnasium* in Kremsier.[57] His travels westward through Prague, Upper Austria, and Munich to Paris and Rome turned him into a professional artist and architect. His architectural background stemmed from his studies at the Royal Academy of Arts and Architecture in Paris, which was strongly based on the theoretical works of Laugier.[58] Chambrez was, for his times, unusually well educated in the arts and architecture, as well as in general philosophical works from Vitruvius to Winckelmann, Lessing, and Falconet.[59] His public employment as an architect – from 1793 on in Teschen, from 1803 on in Cracow, and from 1815 on at the Lemberg Lyceum (which from 1817 on was known as *Universitas Franciscea*)[60] – made him a typical representative of the Austrian bureaucratic machine, outstanding perhaps only in terms of his superior education.

Chambrez was a university professor, a practicing architect,[61] an artist, and an art historian. His blurred idea as to where exactly "Austria" lay[62] was typical of the time. He was a loyal Habsburg subject, admired Vienna,[63] and yet his motherland was limited to Moravia and Bohemia:

> I saw the city of Prague in my mind...: you would see that city, about which you would read so much in the Bohemian chronicles, where there are so many works of art to see, the castle where Charles IV lived, and other buildings that he had erected during his rule. I wished I had wings of an angel to arrive there, in such a great city...[64]

In Lemberg, according to Finkel's history of Lemberg University, Chambrez taught architecture "after Vignola" and collected numerous architectural ornaments and technical instruments for his students.[65] His architectural and painting practice notwithstanding, Chambrez's most valuable contribution was in his architectural criticism, which revealed him as a convinced neoclassicist: "all antiquity stimulates imagination."[66]

From the 1800s on, Chambrez admired ancient Greece and Rome, disliked most Gothic buildings, and despised the baroque. In 1801, when he finalized his diary that compiled all his traveling and learning experiences, he believed that the Gothic (as he called it, "*gotisch maurische Styl*") was brought to Europe by the Arabs who with an unusual zeal destroyed all the most beautiful buildings in the "Greek and Roman style."[67] He despised the Gothic church of St. Vitus in Prague for its senseless decorative detail. In line with the Vitruvian differentiation between private and public, sacral and secular architecture,[68] he disapproved of the colonnade of the eighteenth-century Czernin palace because it did not correspond to the building's function. "The Greeks and the Romans," he insisted, "[indeed] used those [columns], but not in their dwellings. They rather decorated their temples with them, but there they rarely used windows."[69] Faithful to the classical canon of architectural beauty, Chambrez also disliked most of the recent architecture (i.e., the baroque), as in the case of the *Clam-Gallas* palace, built by the court architect Fischer von Erlach:

> The interior leaves nothing better to wish for, yet the decoration of its façade that, at one point, came into being through a search for a new [style] could be treated aesthetically as vices (*Sünden*). This [architect], admirable for his description of the antique author, whom I often heard quoted later at architectural lectures in Paris, followed the word of fashion and piled up (*überhäufte*) such decoration on his buildings. Since it shortly went out of fashion, [the building soon] acquired its amiss (*übel*) look.[70]

He appreciated in buildings of all periods their simplicity, "good" (meaning, neoclassical) proportions, symmetry, well-lighted interiors resulting from adequate windows, and ornamentation appropriate to the building's function.[71] His value of simplicity is evident in his admiration of Prague's medieval buildings,[72] though his admiration of provincial Gothic churches in Bohemia, such as in Chrudim[73] and Kuttenberg, derived from their "good plan, order, harmony, color scale, treatment of the whole, [and] light [character]."[74]

Chambrez's appreciation of simple, provincial churches is reminiscent of Kratter's admiration of the church of Dukla. He too appreciated the Renaissance and fiercely disliked the baroque. Like the entire generation of early nineteenth-century writers, Chambrez was influenced by the *Biedermeier* admiration of nature. He advised the study of Nature, which, he insisted, made one sensitive to "that which is splendorous, beautiful, and romantic" (*für das Prächtige, für das Schöne und Romantische*), and stressed the importance of harmonizing a building plan with its future natural surroundings where one could find refuge in one's own solitude.[75]

While Chambrez' views on architectural beauty were typical of his age, it would be wrong to group him with such great proponents of German culture as Kratter and Sacher-Masoch. He never lost contact with his Moravian origins and was a quiet advocate of national awakening, evident from his correspondence with his Moravian friends Tomáš Fryčaj, Josef H. A. Gallaš, and Josef Fiala.[76] Contrary to the stereotype that all Austrian functionaries were "Germans" and shared the same moral qualities, this major Vormärz writer on architecture was neither German nor playing a missionary's role for Germanic culture in Lemberg. Loyal to the Habsburg Court, just like Kratter and Rohrer, he combined this loyalty with a deep patriotism for Moravia and Bohemia. His description of Prague – similar to Kratter's and Rohrer's accounts of Vienna – shows the multiplicity of cultural centers in the Vormärz Habsburg Empire that architects and bureaucrats took as models for Lemberg's physical reshaping. His writing also illustrates to what a remarkable degree writings on architecture can elucidate personal affiliation. In Chambrez's account of Moravia and Bohemia, and especially in his admiration of Prague's Gothic architecture from the times of Charles IV – the Gothic he otherwise despised – his local patriotic sentiment becomes clearly pronounced.

The link generally made in Polish and Ukrainian historiography between Vormärz bureaucracy, with its "barrack-like" architecture, and the politics of Germanization needs to be reassessed in the light of historical evidence.[77] The Vormärz authors writing in German were true pioneers in aesthetic theory in assuming the existence of a direct link between the nature of state rule and its concomitant architecture, a link evident in their writing on baroque architecture. Several other concepts, expressed by these authors of the Vormärz, survived in later historiographies. This included, for example, an admiration of Lemberg's historic architecture, such as the Renaissance buildings on Market Square and the Greek Catholic St. George Cathedral. At the same time, the disapproval of the (Renaissance) Town Hall building outlived the building itself and was transformed into a dislike by late nineteenth-century Polish authors of the neoclassical Town Hall, erected by the Austrian architects in 1826. The dichotomy of beauty, privacy, and green spaces on the one hand, and ugliness, public space, and the deteriorating city center on the other was also introduced by "German" Vormärz writing. The belief in green spaces as beautifying factors and in the inner city as a place of filth and stench survived throughout the nineteenth century, as we shall shortly see, particularly in the writings on the Jewish quarter. Several other concepts, characteristic of their time, speak also through these writings: the belief that the linearity and width of streets was a symptom of health and that the large scale of houses figured as signs of beauty and prosperity. Yet the routine assumption of Western travelers of the local population's ignorance is not to be found in Chambrez. This is further evidence that Lemberg's Vormärz "Germans" were actually a more heterogeneous group than was previously assumed, and that it is problematic to treat them as a separate, homogeneous, and distinct group. Even if they shared certain aesthetic values and interpretations of beauty – and ugliness – in judging the baroque, in other instances, such as with Chambrez's multiple "homelands," his contradictory treatment of Prague Gothic, and his lack of an otherwise typical arrogance toward the locals, their views on building, beauty, and matters related to Municipal management were at times diverse and incongruent.

Bureaucrats and Nationalism

The establishment of the Polish-dominated administration over the Crown Land and its capital in the period of autonomy (1867-1918) is often linked to architectural development: thanks to the new ruler's "national" mission, the city was developed. The city's acquisition of numerous beautiful buildings, squares, monuments, and streets is used as an argument to support this interpretation of historical events in Polish national historiography. Yet the prevailing bias in this historiography on the comprehensive "national" architectural program that favorably portrays the work of the neoabsolutist governor, Agenor Gołuchowski Sr. (1846-66) and fin-de-siècle Lemberg mayors, such as Edmund Mochnacki

(1836-1902), needs to be challenged. A closer view reveals that the gradual shift to national architectural politics took place within the Municipality only in the twentieth century – in line with the general tendencies in the monarchy, when Karl Lueger radically transformed the Municipal politics of earlier Liberal mayors of Vienna in 1897 and of István Bárczy in Budapest in 1906[78] – specifically with the election of Tadeusz Rutowski (1852-1918) as Lemberg's vice mayor in 1905. Yet even Rutowski's actions are highly reminiscent of Vormärz beliefs in their viewing architecture as representative of ethical beliefs – such as public works being good, healthy, practical, and supportive of the poor – and of the presence of high culture.

Agenor Gołuchowski

Count Agenor Gołuchowski was one of Galicia's outstanding administrators who enjoyed appreciation by the Viennese Court and later by some Polish reformers. His main achievement was the diplomatic maneuvering that led to the 1860 October Diploma, which marked the end of neoabsolutism by establishing diets and transforming the empire along federal lines.[79] In 1849-59, 1866-68 and 1871-75, Gołuchowski served as the appointed governor of Galicia. At the time, supporting public foundations and institutes was, as it previously had been in the Vormärz, a matter of duty for great men of state. He supported the Institute of the Poor out of a sense of ethics and the Polish *Ossolineum* out of cultural concerns, and further concerned himself with city planning and green spaces.

As evident from the contemporary press, Gołuchowski's actions as governor had the desired effect on the city's public: in the middle 1850s, he was admired for his efforts on city beautification, as well as for his achievement of bureaucratic reform:

> Not less important is his [Gołuchowski's] concern for our Crown Land's charitable institutions, especially for the...*Ossolineum* [and] the Institute of the Poor. The establishment of the great botanical garden...in our capital city came about thanks to his effort. Similarly, physical order in the city is a matter of the governor's attention. The ornamentation of the university building's façade, the laying out of the English-style garden by the Institute of the Blind, the beautification of the hill next to the *Ossolineum*, and the closing down of the Jewish Cemetery in the cholera year of 1855 were made following his suggestions. The expanded Łyczaków Cemetery is also presently being transformed into a [beautiful] garden, while the Former Jesuit Garden is being transformed into a beautiful and large public park....The kiosks (*budki i kramiki*) scattered around our streets and squares marred and spoiled the city, compli-

cated traffic, and even caused a fire hazard. The large square in front of the theater...until recently dirty and filled with garbage, is now already cleaned and planted with trees, and looks beautiful.[80]

This obvious continuation of the Vormärz official appreciation for city cleanliness and green spaces is cited as one of Governor Gołuchowski's major achievements. The 1850s were a time of neoabsolutist reaction, when public freedoms were once again severely restricted and special legitimization of the new governor's activities was needed. Yet the newspaper *Przyjaciel domowy* was no official periodical, and the appearance of this type of argument there signifies how deeply the Vormärz notions on the beauty of greenery, cleanliness, and order, together with its rhetoric on a healthy urban environment, had rooted themselves in public beliefs. With these activities echoing Governor Lazansky's actions in the early 1840s, Gołuchowski erected a "monument" to himself in the 1850s.[81]

Gołuchowski's rejection of one particular proposal for a statue to the Russian tsar suggests that in 1853, as in the previous Vormärz period, the Gubernium would neither allow any architectural symbolism other than imperial, nor would it take much interest in erecting the latter. In 1853, a certain Szalowski, village mayor of Jasielki, suggested building a monument to Russian Tsar Nicolas I in the town of Zmigrod, where the tsar had temporarily resided in June 1849 during the Russian campaign against the Hungarian revolutionary uprising. The issue had, therefore, political connotations: the erection of a monument to a Russian tsar implied support of the Habsburg rule. Gołuchowski rejected the idea:

> Every supporter of Austria must remember with grief and humiliation those sad events, when a disgraceful betrayal and an unfortunate civil war brought the monarchy to the edge of a precipice and necessitated foreign military help. These events do not therefore deserve to be called back into the people's memory and preserved for a longer time in their recollections by the erection of monuments. As a witness to this unfortunate period, you [*WPan*] must know that during the Russian supportive action, certain casualties took place that…even today have not been forgotten. Thus an erection of a monument in memory of these events cannot but cause certain bitterness.[82]

Gołuchowski's argument suggests one reason why the Neoabsolutist Gubernium's interest in the physical restructuring of the city did not include the erection of monuments. Every such monument, even those dedicated to "approved" persons, such as Tsar Nicolas I, in this case, had the potential to cause dissatisfaction in one of the many ethnic and civic groups. In a multiethnic and multireligious context such as Lemberg, an undertaking of this kind would be even more troublesome than elsewhere.

Edmund Mochnacki and Tadeusz Rutowski

During the Vormärz and neoabsolutism, the Crown Land administration's Building Department memorialized city spaces by changing the names of its streets and squares in memory of particular great statesmen, such as Reitzenheim and Gołuchowski. By the final decades of the nineteenth century, and especially at the fin de siècle, the concomitant lack of interest in memorial architecture would change, as mere sanitary improvement was no longer sufficient to demonstrate authorities' commitment to city beautification. Even Gołuchowski, who previously avoided all possibly troublesome architectural projects, accepted on his deathbed the idea of being memorialized in stone.[83]

By the late 1880s, architecture was used as an argument in political agendas where the idea of "curative" greenery was combined with new elements throughout the Habsburg Monarchy. In Vienna, Budapest, and other larger cities of the monarchy, ideas from contemporary urban planning were combined with newly emerging information about the new health and penitentiary institutions, and at times even with such issues as the restoration of churches, the erection of new banks, and the building of aristocratic palaces, all to demonstrate general Municipal achievement. An implicit suggestion in Municipal reports of the time was that by putting effort into such purely architectural matters, the state could actually solve many urban social problems, such as crime, poverty, and prostitution.[84]

As the political organization of the Habsburg Monarchy gradually transformed itself from a neoabsolutist into a constitutional organization, provincial politics acquired strength and independence they had not previously experienced. After 1870, Municipal governments too could make independent decisions on Municipal affairs, as long as they concerned social and physical changes within the offices' respective cities. As the city mayor's term became a three-year position through election by members of the Municipal Council,[85] individual mayors gave reports on their Municipal achievements to the City Council at the end of their term. In these reports, architecture was seen not only as a symbol of good and legitimate administrative rule, but also as propaganda for national projects.

By education a lawyer, Edmund Mochnacki had a long bureaucratic career in the Crown Land administration prior to his election as Lemberg vice mayor in 1885 and as Mayor in 1887. In the late 1890s, Mochnacki was Lemberg's longest-ruling mayor to date, and his major achievement in this position was proclaimed "an astonishing (*zadziewiający*) development of the city in every direction."[86] Whatever his successes, he demonstrated the potential use of architectural improvements in electoral campaigns. An illustrative case is his *Sprawozdanie Prezydenta k. st. miasta Lwowa z trzechletniej czynności Reprezentacyi miasta i Magistratu (1886, 1887, i 1888)* [Report on the Activity of the Municipal

Council and Administration during 1886-88] to the Municipal Council, 1889.[87] As becomes evident from the text of the report, he viewed his position as a cultural mission. In principle, "the most important and the most urgent"[88] actions were "the improvement of the city's health conditions, support of the poor, and the systematic organization of efforts against the beggars...thus caring about the well-being...and development of this city."[89] The insertion of new green areas, however, occupied a leading place in the "Pavement" section of his report:

> Walking/recreation institutions (*zaklady spacerowe*) noticeably increased in number, even though the greatest portion of municipal funds was used for the conservation of the existing parks and gardens. I will mention here only that in addition to the existing plantings in Municipal Park, Castle Hill, Stryjski Park, Governor- and Hetmanwälle,... many new parks were established and...trees were planted....In the time span of the last three years, about sixty thousand trees were planted in city parks, squares, [and] streets.[90]

The composition of the Municipality might have changed profoundly over the century, yet the belief in the beauty and curative quality of green spaces remained as a Vormärz legacy.[91] To illustrate "progress," Mochnacki mentioned architecture: the erection of several cultural institutions (such as the Museum of Industry and the School of Industry - *Muzeum przemyslowy, Szkola przemyslowa*); health and penitentiary institutions (including the House of Forced Labor - *Dom przymusowej pracy*); the restoration of churches (such as St. Ann Church and St. Mary of Snow Church); and the renovation and adaptation of cultural institutions.[92] Further, he forged a link between Lemberg's new buildings – more often than not erected from private, rather than public, funds – and the activities of the Municipality:

> Speaking of the city's development, it would not be out of place to mention which buildings – both public and private ones – have been or are being erected in past years in our city and how important they are [for its general development]. It is perhaps not our exclusive achievement, but rather a fortunate coincidence. Nevertheless, I believe that the Municipality contributed greatly to this development and blossoming of our city. First of all, I shall mention the following projects: the channeling of the Pełtew River underground is to be without exaggeration considered as a monumental work..., building for the Greek Catholic Seminary, Post and Telegraph Office, Municipal Map Archive..., Alfred Potocki palace, Galician Savings Bank, Museum of Industry, School of Industry..., and the Opera Theater building.[93]

Although the importance of the erection of the monument to Gołuchowski was great for Mochnacki, as we shall see in the following chapter, his report on Municipal activities did not speak of memorial architecture. There he remained a follower of the deceased Governor Gołuchowski in paying great attention to architectural projects as part of the city's "healing," rather than dedicating concern to "memorializing" of any kind.

◆

Quite a different approach can be found in the text of an appeal made by the Municipal Presidium on 15 June 1907 to the general public regarding an artificial mound previously erected to commemorate the Union of Lublin. The nature of this appeal was largely due to another Lemberg vice mayor, Tadeusz Rutowski, who took upon himself responsibility for issues related to culture and art:

> The last rains caused severe deterioration to the Union of Lublin Mound. Serious cracks and ruts indicate that the whole structure [was] built on poor foundations [and] is gravely endangered. The [future] catastrophe concerns not only Lwów: the anniversary mount erected to the memory of the memorable (*wiekopomny*) act of the Union of Nations, a visible landmark of Lwów, the most beautiful decoration of its landscape, is endangered! The voice was born the bosom of the whole nation (*z piersi całej ludności rwie się jeden głos*): one should quickly save, strengthen, and preserve the Union Mound![94]

By then the Union Mound had a long history since Franciszek Smolka had proposed it in 1869. Although the Municipality gradually understood the issue of the mound's erection as its own responsibility, the memorial became the site of several Polish national celebrations, as in 1869 and 1871.[95] In light of Rutowski's understanding of architecture as a national affair, such an appeal to Lemberg professionals and the wider public on the condition of the Union of Lublin Mound is not surprising.

His view on the role of architecture in cultural politics became most pronounced during an impassioned debate in the local press on the issue of the national art gallery and its envisioned depository, the Palace of Art. The major point in the debate was whether the fine arts gallery was "worthy" of the Galician capital and whether, consequently, such an undertaking would improve the city's image. The discussion was invigorated by Rutowski and directed against the idea's greatest opponent, university professor and architectural conservation curator Jan Bołoz Antoniewicz.[96] For Rutowski, the issue was not only a matter of establishing yet another institution of culture, but also of creating a national collection and of addressing city planning from the aesthetic point of view, with the future Palace of Art as a beautifying factor.

Tadeusz Rutowski, who was Lemberg's vice mayor from 1905 on, though not a native Lemberger, was a man of two careers: one cultural and one political.[97] During his studies in Vienna in 1873, he had outlined his own political program based on cultural and linguistic nationalism, coupled with the economic well-being of cities and the general education of society.[98] As a "journalist in the sphere of politics and economics," he outlined this agenda even more precisely in 1883.[99] Although a parliamentarian at the Provincial Diet and the Austrian *Reichsrat* from 1889 on, he actively worked in the cultural field, serving, for example, as a president of the Artistic and Literary Circle (*Koło artystyczne i literackie*).[100] A professional journalist,[101] he assisted in the intensification of local press activity and in the change of its style to a more emotional and polemical one, as evident in the transformation of the newspaper *Słowo polskie* [Polish word], which he edited.[102]

Acting as vice mayor responsible for cultural and art affairs from 1905 on, well traveled and educated, Rutowski was, in fact, an expert in artistic matters rather than in politics. Because of his personal involvement, the establishment of national institutions became a political agenda in early twentieth-century Lemberg. Although Mochnacki's major pride in the late 1880s was the rechanneling of Lemberg's Pełtew River and the founding of health institutes, Rutowski's primary goals were the art gallery, Palace of Art, and the Museum of King Jan III (Sobieski). In 1907-8, the conflict between Rutowski and Antoniewicz over the issue of the art gallery developed in local newspapers and separate publications.[103]

In these, Rutowski argued that a national gallery, compiling a collection of modern *Polish* art and of historic paintings from the region, was a necessary facility for a modern capital. He employed foreign commentary for his argument, especially writings by Viennese musicologist Theodor Frimmel (1853-1928), whose report on the Lemberg art collection in his *Blätter für Gemälde-kunde* Rutowski reprinted in his *Galerya miejska w swietle polskiej i obcej krytyki* [City Gallery in the light of Polish and foreign criticism].[104] Aleksander Czołowski, director of the Municipal archive and a respected historian, joined the discussion.[105] The art gallery became for Rutowski the principal point of his cultural program and a major argument for his political success:

> Having understood the great mission of artistic collections, such as the gallery of old and new masters, [generally] for the national cause and [especially] for national culture in the capital of the Crown Land that is almost the far borderland of a national dominion (*niedaleko ostatnej rubieży narodowego posiadania*), we should be happy about any acquisition into the national treasure [rather than be critical about it].[106]

Further, Rutowski argued for the need of a "scientific" link between all of Lemberg's national cultural institutions and the academic world, and for the specific need to house such an institution in an adequate, separate building:

> One needs a scientific (*naukowy*) connection between the emerging cultural and national institutions, such as the art gallery and the museum in the name of King Jan III, with the university and [in general] with academic science....Changes in Lwów will...come through the existence of an art collection, the gallery, which will develop...into the best classroom for the development of artistic taste, love of art [and] national culture....Lwów's new art collection has already started its educational and cultural mission. Every civilized city of the world is familiar with such a mission when it creates rows of museums from public funds, and it has already become a slogan in America: the educational work of the museum. [Here in Lwów] there is a [pressing] need for a Palace of Art, supported by the Crown Land (*kraj*) and state [funds]."[107]

Possessing a "palace of art" was seen at the time by renowned art critics such as Frimmel as necessary for any self-respecting city.[108] For Rutowski, however, the issue was more than just a "worthy" collection; it was to be a national issue.

In comparing views on architecture during neoabsolutism (1848-67) and dualism (1867-1918), a shift from seeing architecture as a sign of technical and cultural advancement to its use as an argument in political programs becomes evident. This change, however, found expression only after 1905, when Rutowski's political program was solely responsible for successfully politicizing the question of a national art gallery and the Palace of Art. Yet in the Municipal view of the role of architecture prior to Rutowski, as seen in Edmund Mochnacki, architecture became a symbol of cultural and technical progress; in this, it was similar to the Vormärz views espoused by Kratter, Rohrer, Gołuchowski, and their contemporaries: the appreciation of parks, promenades, and greenery. Both Gołuchowski and Mochnacki remained faithfully loyal to the Habsburg throne and – in the context of the rise of nationalism – felt the increasing need to propagate this loyalty through monuments.

Poles: Historicism, Historians, and "Technicians"

As late as the 1860s, there existed within Polish intellectual discourse no consensus on local history, and various competing interpretations abounded. Franciszek Jaworski (1873-1914), the city's long-term archivist and a devoted collector, who will be treated at greater length later in this chapter, compiled a file of newspaper clippings on Lemberg and Galician history.[109] In this collection, Ivan Vahylevyč's article "Początki Lwowa" [Lwów's Beginnings, 1860] stressed the Ruthenian origins of the city, as well as Ruthenian medieval sources (*Ipatijevśkyj litopys*),[110] while a popular historical novel made an account of the Lemberg siege of 1648 by hetman Bohdan Chmel'nyćkyj's (Polish spelling Chmielnicki) troops from the Polish national perspective.[111]

At about the same time the introduction of Galician autonomy and Lemberg self-government in the late 1860s pressed Polish Municipal politicians to reconsider their views on Lemberg's architecture, a serious historical interest in local architecture emerged. This resulted in several books, written mostly in Polish, illustrative of local views on architecture near the turn of the century and similar to what the memoirs of Kratter and Rohrer had been for the Vormärz.[112] As Polish fin-de-siècle literature by Stanisław Schnür-Pepłowski, Franciszek Jaworski, and Michał Lityński based itself on earlier *Polish* histories,[113] these writings introduced a vision of Lemberg architecture that radically differed from the German Vormärz accounts.

At a time when the notion of style had crystallized into a term symbolizing a particular artistic period, "baroque" was no longer synonymous with "bad taste," but rather become a signifier for the art of the seventeenth century. In contrast to the Vormärz German writing, Polish late nineteenth-century authors chose the local, official school of neoclassicism as a major point for their criticism. Vormärz became synonymous with stylistic and architectural vulgarity, with planning practices that were heavy-handed and lacked respect for historic monuments, and with a pitiful poetization of Nature that because of its imperial overtones deserved ironic treatment at best. Thus in the late nineteenth century, the architecture of the Vormärz became viewed as "in bad taste" because of its "German" character, similar to the way that "baroque" had become a poor "Polish" style for Kratter and Rohrer. The curious belief that Lemberg "lacked" worthy architectural buildings was derived from standard comparisons with Cracow.

Conversely, the Polish prepartition periods were glorified as "national" years, and the existence of the medieval Ruthenian period, together with the strong Ruthenian presence in the city, was downplayed. As we shall see in the following chapters of this book, during the development of concepts on architectural restoration, the association of medieval styles with Polishness became even clearer. However, the familiar Vormärz biases – such as Lemberg's "ugliness," the city's perceived lack of monuments, normative comparisons with Western capitals, and the attribution of characteristic "ethnic" architectural styles – retained a presence also.

In fact, the attribution of national characteristics to styles and artistic periods fell within the stream of the prevailing historicist thought of the time. Thinkers as early as Gottfried Semper saw styles as carrying specific historical connotations for the artifact, and ancient buildings were thus the "fossilized receptacles of extinct social organizations," i.e., records of a "nation's" time-specific worldview.[114] Consequently, "German" architecture was built by a German architect in "German" times on "German" soil. Such views determined the nineteenth century's tendency to understand architectural history as a sequence of changing styles, but these beliefs also insisted on viewing stylistic change as a function of society's – and thus the "nation's" – worldview. However, the [local] application of this basic historicist concept ran into fundamental problems in Galicia.

In attempting to construct a Polish past for Lemberg's monuments, historians struggled with "Polish times" having been preceded by medieval *Ruś*, meaning that the national "soil" had for centuries been shared with others, and the architects of the time might have been altogether foreign. Several written accounts testify to this problem. Antoni Schneyder's unfinished *Encyklopedia do krajoznawstwa Galicji* [Encyclopaedia to the Sightseeing of Galicia],[115] for example, sees archaeological discoveries as "the greatest guides to Polish history" and artifacts "from the Polish land that now constitutes Galicia as well as ancient Ruthenian monuments in this Crown Land (*kraj*)."[116] In this view, medieval Ruthenian monuments are interpreted as a part of local Polish heritage.

A second account belongs to Franciszek Kowaliszyn (1860-1914), Lemberg's long-term archivist and another influential figure in the city's architectural history and restoration practices.[117] In his handbook on Galician political and architectural history, written for his personal use and never published,[118] Kowaliszyn represents a fusion of Polish romantic nationalism[119] and local patriotism. For him, Lemberg was poor in architecture as compared to "other Polish towns," especially Cracow. Once again, the nature of state rule was seen to be mirrored in architecture. While Cracow was, according to Kowaliszyn, a "capital city, the ancient capital of Poland, [and] the site of monuments, arts, and crafts," Lemberg's architecture did not deserve commentary, and the city's historical significance dated from 1340, the year it fell to the Polish crown.[120] In this view, Lemberg's medieval heritage simply had no place of significance in historical events.

Late nineteenth-century Polish writers associated the positive features of Lemberg with its similarity to Western capitals, such as Vienna, Paris, and London, while they subjected what they did not like to ironic commentary, blamed its presence on others, or ignored it. The first of these strategies was particularly evident in their treatment of the wider public's ignorance and what some called "exaggerations." An anonymous ironical account of Lemberg and its public, published in 1852 in the Cracow conservative periodical *Czas* [Time], is illustrative:

> There is no doubt that just as Lwów differs in its physiognomy from other cities, so do Lwów inhabitants have their own peculiar character....Old Slavic hospitality is often intertwined with everyday life.... One may also notice that...many exhibit peculiar exaggerations that generally seem a novelty for foreigners who come from the West. For us who know those things better, this is easy to explain, since Lwów is a heart of the old *Ruś*, and *Ruś* has for centuries been a famous seat of sorcerers and charms![121]

In the Vormärz, the authors writing in German accused the local "Poles" of "baroque" exaggerations of state rule, of everyday life practices, of religious matters, and, finally, of poorly styled architecture. By insisting on Lemberg's peculiarity, the anonymous writer also ascribed the origins of this troublesome strangeness to another group, the Ruthenians, and to the heritage of that historical period that was troublesome – in his mind – medieval *Ruś*.

Yet "Germans" were to be blamed for most of the modern wrongs, according to this "national" Polish view. Michał Lityński noted in his *Gmach skarbkowski na tle architektury lwowskiej w pierwszej połowie XIX wieku* (1912) [The Skarbek Building as seen in the light of Lwów architecture in the first half of the nineteenth century]:

> In no other period of its history has Lwów witnessed such a profound reshaping as in the beginning of the nineteenth century when the Austrian government felt strong and safe in the newly occupied part of Poland (*w nowo zagarniętej dzielnicy Polski*). [After a period of uncertainty,] characteristic of every unrightfully acquired property [until 1815], the entire city's appearance was fundamentally changed. During the Polish times this was a fortified city,...now it [has] turned into a large Crown Land's capital. Out of a knight...watching the wild steppe (*ku dzikom polu*) attentively and Tartar roads in the southeastern direction, it turned into a gentleman and a bureaucrat, disrespectful of his subordinates and bowing toward Vienna.[122]

For Lityński, a writer active in the last decades of the Habsburg Monarchy and in interwar Poland, the culture of the Vormärz bureaucracy, disrespectful of local traditions, was also immoral: for example, the "Germans" "literally danced on corpses" during carnival balls at the German Theater, formerly a Franciscan monastery.[123]

Lityński also blamed the "German" population for the emergence of a particular type of neoclassical building with a colonnade on the main façade that was "lacking any individual expression and character."[124] He did not escape a contradiction in his own views: the Skarbek Theater, which he glorified as "a work of art of unusual cultural and artistic achievement, and a work that united aristocratic charitable activity with a guarantee of the Polish drama's survival... and therefore ensured Lwów's Polish character,"[125] was accidentally another example of exactly this building type.

Since "bureaucracy" then equaled "German" and "ugly," Austrian architecture was all three. The Viennese Court building adviser (*k. k. Hofbaurat*), Paul Sprenger, was represented as "the main representative of bureaucratic Austrian architecture of neoclassicism that had nothing in common with a true art of antiquity." The Austrian building tradition was until 1848 "in a hopeless state.... Architecture was at that time a mere building craft limited by a whole system of bureaucratic prescriptions and regulations. Nothing remained for art as such. There appeared in Vienna...a particular local version of the empire style next to the academic style of Nobile."[126] Thus national art (*sztuka rodzima*) – the "Polish" Renaissance and baroque – had completely deteriorated and had been replaced by this Viennese brand of – in Lityński's terms – "pseudoclassicism."[127] Elsewhere, as in Congress Kingdom, Polish historians applied similar criticism to Polish neoclassicism, but in Lemberg the "foreign" (i.e., Austrian) target remained too strong for them to attack their own. For Lityński, as a consequence of the "German" architectural bureaucracy's backward views – in comparison with France and England, with which Poland (and Galicia) allegedly had closer contact prior to the partition – the new architecture was bound to be provincial and ugly:

> While in France and England this new trend [classicism] could and did base itself [on] the local [building tradition] and therefore acquired a national character; in Germany this [tradition] did not exist, and one had thus to rely on secondary sources....German architects could not, however, learn from these [secondary] sources the full connection of architectural thought with antique building practices. Rather than [grasping] a sense of the inner fundamental principles of antique architecture, [they could only learn about] pleasant ornaments and motifs from the ruins of the antiquity, which inspired fantasy with their [mere] picturesque qualities[128]

According to Lityński, it is clearly this alleged "more direct" connection of Polish architecture with Paris and London that had caused the particular beauty of Polish Vormärz institutions in Lemberg. Indeed, he introduced a specific stylistic differentiation between Lemberg's neoclassical buildings of power and those of Polish cultural institutions. This theory, developed further in the twentieth century by such writers as Józef Piotrowski[129] and Tadeusz Mańkowski, the latter of whom viewed "Polish" classicism, which he termed "Renaissancism," in all the Polish lands as having "feminine," "decorated," and "elevated" characteristics. The official architecture of Pietro Nobile's school was, conversely, "masculine," "lacking decorum," and "heavy."[130]

This curious architectural view was a local adaptation of the theory of classical orders and building types by Marcus Pollio Vitruvius, expressed in his *Ten Books of Architecture,* arguably the first theoretical work on the art of building,[131] modified to fit the purposes of a local fin-de-siècle, pronational interpretation. Already in Vitruvius's work and consequently in that of Leon Battista Alberti's (1404-72), the famous Renaissance architect and a leading interpreter of Vitruvius, whose writings were the touchstone in architectural education until the eighteenth century,[132] there existed theoretical discussion as to which of the classical orders – Doric or Ionic – should receive priority.[133] This surviving normative Vitruvian differentiation was further reinforced by the special attention to Doric temples in the late eighteenth and nineteenth centuries, especially the temples of Paestum.[134] Doric became an appropriate style for buildings aimed at embodying "bare" ("male") and "unadorned strength," and the Ionic adequately personified "smooth" and resolute ("female") elegance.

In practice, this resulted in the choice of Doric for the buildings of power and military, while the Ionic was reserved for more buildings perceived as "feminine," such as institutions of culture. In ascribing these additional aesthetic qualities to the Vitruvian division of orders and building functions – that is, claiming that the Ionic was beautiful and the Doric ugly - early Polish twentieth-century architectural history found a way out of a conceptual deadlock. It was now possible to dismiss "Austrian" Vormärz neoclassicism and also to appreciate the buildings of "Polish" cultural institutions from the same period. For Piotrowski there was, alas, only one escape from the stylistic "clumsiness" of the Vormärz buildings, such as the Town Hall: to reinvent their historic Polishness through a new design for their façades, one that would refer to a glorious historic period.

> Other buildings such as…the Town Hall were built in a typically Austrian barrack style (*Kasernstil*) [and] should soon be renewed and rebuilt (*neu-, bezw. umgebaut werden*)....After the fall of the old tower, the current, unelaborated, and barrack-like (*plumpe, kasernenhafte*) Town Hall was erected at the expense of a half-million Austrian Gulden....The façade of the building should be refashioned in the style of a particular Polish Renaissance in the very near future.[135]

Yet writers such as Piotrowski judged Vormärz architecture by the quality of its façade ornamentation, rather than by the principles of functionality, simplicity, and symmetry that were valued by the Vormärz architects who had erected the Town Hall and Lemberg's other "barrack" structures. Piotrowski therefore neglected the fundamental principle underlying neoclassicism's understanding of beauty, which lay in the totality of a building, in its simple and symmetrical proportions – rather than in the beauty of specific parts, such as façade ornamentation – and in its being adequate for its function. Instead, what mattered for Piotrowski and his contemporaries was rather that clearly "Polish" structures such as the Skarbek Theater (1837-42) could be appreciated architecturally, but the Town Hall (1828-37) could and should not be.

Some, like Franciszek Jaworski, also blamed "Germans" for the general destruction of architectural heritage. Apart from Jaworski's commitment to Municipal archives, he was also one of the major writers of popular history in fin-de-siècle Lemberg and a founder of *Towarzystwo miłośników przeszłości Lwowa* [Society of the Admirers of Lemberg's Past]. In 1906, the society started its printing activity with Jaworski's book *Ratusz lwowski* [Town Hall] that was intended to provide information on "the historical significance of Lwów for Poland, for its eastern borders, trade, and industry."[136] Jaworski's major contribution was *Lwów stary i wczorajszy (szkice i opowiadania)* [Lwów of old and yesteryear. Sketches and short stories], in which he accused the Vormärz administration of destroying architectural heritage:

> Out of considerations for public health, the Austrian government acquired church graveyards that were full of skeletons and threw all remains out of the city and into new cemeteries in an unordered manner and without recording the names of the deceased. At the same time, [the Austrian government] damaged, crushed, and destroyed tombs and monuments and erased all inscriptions.[137]

On the other hand, Jaworski was ironic about the unexpected difficulties the Vormärz government had faced with the newly planned green belt around the city, caused by the urban criminal element. It is as if this element represented the "true spirit" of the Vormärz city, which refused to accept "German" innovations out of some higher, supposedly national concern:

> The Austrian Municipal *Bauamt* regularly met with such surprises at the end of the eighteenth century[...as] the traditional anger of the Lwów paupers. [They] instantly damaged and pulled out the trees...planted on the boulevards, smashed stone benches in the night, destroyed the lawns, and desecrated the *Haupt-promenade*, the only *rendez-vous* of stylish Lwów.[138]

Reluctant to acknowledge honestly the value of both Austrian architectural planning and its reflection in German-language accounts of the Vormärz,[139] Jaworski maintained that the city's "national" – that is, Polish – past had been damaged.[140] A few years after the appearance of Jaworki's book on Lemberg, Piotrowski developed Jaworski's idea of the Austrian "destruction of heritage" in his travel guide *Lemberg und Umgebung* and presented this supposed destruction in the light of the early twentieth-century concepts on restoration and architectural monuments:

> From 1777 on, the old fortification walls were gradually pulled down, unfortunately without understanding or any concern for the preservation of monuments, and in their place plantings, streets, and allées appeared....The Emperor Joseph II closed 18 churches, 3 Armenian Catholic churches, and 7 Greek Catholic churches, with some of them demolished, in the great loss to Lemberg architecture and the ancient appearance of the city.[141]

To expect an early twentieth-century understanding of architectural conservation and restoration from the Vormärz-era architects and planners was anachronistic. Yet to claim that the closing of churches and ecclesiastic orders caused the destruction of architectural heritage reflected wretched logic, unless this heritage held value only for its being imbued with the memories of "old" and "better" Polish times.[142]

The idea of preserving historic monuments is not necessarily associated with nationalism.[143] The Vormärz conception of a monument – as a memory, often of a royal person, rather than of an architectural piece – underwent a transformation in the late nineteenth century. Not only did the notion come to be linked with specific architectural structures, old and new, but also the importance of monuments was increasingly judged by their value to the nation. Although in the early 1840s monuments were appreciated for their age rather than for their national memory, as early as 1847 Antoni Schneyder suggested the new, national meaning in the passage on the restoration of Castle Hill, quoted at the beginning of this chapter in connection to the Polish context of Kratter's and Rohrer's writings.[144]

To lament the abandonment of a national monument in the middle of the steppe, as an anonymous writer to *Przyjaciel domowy* did in connection with the monument to hetman Stanisław Żółkiewski at Cecora,[145] was not the same as justifying the renovation of existing national monuments in the middle of the Galician capital. Late nineteenth-century thinkers needed to selectively pick from national history the figures that would be approved by the Habsburg court as loyal yet remembered by the locals as nationally relevant. King Jan Sobieski, who commanded the joint army in defense of Vienna in 1683, was a prime example of such selection. Although there existed no monument to Sobieski until the early twentieth century, Lemberg possessed a monument to his primary assistant, hetman Stanisław Jabłonowski (Fig. 16):

> This was a truly deserved monument that proved [our] hero's great popularity....One must acknowledge that it would be a great pity if this monument were abandoned, because it is doubly dear to us as a historic

Figure 16. Monument to Stanisław Jabłonowski. Photograph by Józef Eder, 1860-70. Ľviv Historical Museum.

artifact and as a memorial to the famous and recognized leader...He is a hero of our land who was born and died here, who so many times fought for his native *kraj* and so many times saved the Ruthenian land from a most terrible devastation. Let his memory, commemorated in stone, tell future generations about his deeds and about [our] national (*narodowa*) gratitude.[146]

As time went by, Polish intellectuals increasingly concerned themselves with explicitly Polish heritage. Any artifact or architectural structure linked to important political and cultural events in Poland's life became a "monument." In the early 1870s, Schneyder recalled the connection between the remaining Castle Hill fortifications and the personality of Casimir the Great, the key figure in early Polish presence in Lemberg,[147] and thus connected the preservation of architectural heritage to national history. His contemporaries began to treat architectural heritage in a deeply emotional manner and were personally hurt when it was vandalized.[148]

Although architects increasingly felt the need to be represented and acknowledged as a professional group, as late as 1877 no architectural society existed. With the foundation of the Lemberg Polytechnic Society in 1877,[149] which soon became an activist social organization, architects acquired a tool for channeling their claims and demands to the authorities, as well as for presenting themselves to the wider public.[150] The society lamented the condition of the nearby castle in Żółkiew in 1878 with "reminiscences of the former greatness of *Rzeczpospolita*" and "so many good memories of our national life."[151] This illustrated just how important national values were for architect "technicians" in the late 1870s: a "monument" became any artifact carrying a nationally charged valence to the Polish inhabitants of Galicia. National memory, associated with particular historic monuments, became the primary value for judging the worth of such artifacts.[152]

Yet another important concept in late nineteenth-century discourse on restoration was Eugène Viollet-le-Duc's notion of "stylistic purity," which was introduced locally by *Dźwignia* (1877-82), the Polytechnic Society's monthly, in the 1880s and translated variously as *czystość, jedność stylu* and *stylowość*.[153] Restoration meant the destruction of subsequent – most often meaning baroque – additions for the sake of stylistic purity and the reinvention of medieval and/or Renaissance designs, as interpreted in terms of "local motifs" (*motywy swojskie*). In so doing, a restorer hoped to recover the "damaged" monument's past and to demonstrate that valuable – i.e., Polish – monuments existed in Galicia.[154] Such an approach theoretically, and practically, neglected that the medieval and Renaissance periods were clearly not only Polish, but also Italian, German, Jewish, Armenian, and Ruthenian in affiliation.[155] Yet the baroque remained, as it had in the Vormärz, the embodiment of poor taste.

In writing historical architectural guidebooks, however, Polish fin-de-siècle authors aimed at creating a national manual to Lemberg architecture in which the Ruthenian period was downplayed, official neoclassicism interpreted as "ugly," and Vormärz planning as "damaging"; "beautiful" was reserved for Polish monuments.[156] One such example can be found in Bohdan Janusz's *Lwów dawny i dzisiejszy* [Lwów of yesterday and today], which contains Lityński's article outlining the city's history and providing a list of architecturally valuable buildings:[157]

> Beautiful Polish life starts to blossom again in Lwów, as it did once in the Renaissance era....Modern Lwów has also begun to throw light toward all of the Polish East as a disseminator of culture. This is illustrated by Lwów's magnificent public and private collections, its museums,...monuments, palaces, public buildings, beautiful parks, wide streets, and promenades that emerged in the place of its ancient walls and fortifications.[158]

For Lityński, even the neoclassical Town Hall, whose architecture he could not bring himself to deign with commentary, acquired national symbolism. Its interior was "decorated with 'Polonia,' a large painting by Jan Styka, which symbolizes Polish life in the time of subjugation (*niewolia*) and the nation's belief in rebirth, which so miraculously came true."[159] Such guidebooks were bound to include contradictions because Lemberg architectural heritage was too heterogeneous to fit into the straightjacket of national interpretation.[160] For example, many of the city's "museums, monuments, palaces, public buildings, and beautiful parks and promenades" were projects accomplished under the Habsburg rule. The conceptual problem was left unresolved: Lemberg architectural heritage defied interpretation as solely Polish.

Ruthenians: Russophiles, Ukrainians, and "Germanized Individuals"

Although the appearance of scholarly historical studies on Lemberg in Ukrainian, such as that of Ivan Krypjakevyč,[161] dates to the interwar period, the Ruthenian press enjoyed a variety of authors who dealt with Lemberg's history and its architecture in the 1880s to 1890s. Just as in the Polish case, however, there was no clear consensus among these writers on how to interpret Lemberg's Polish and Vormärz history, nor on what position to take on Josephinian planning and architectural politics, state neoclassical architecture, and the Ruthenian presence in the city.

The cultural and literary periodical *Zoria* (1880-97) discussed these issues intensively in the 1880s-90s[162] without, however, much consistency. In 1882, for example, *Zoria*'s commentator, when writing on Włodzimierz Łoziński, a respected local Polish historian, the editor of the official newspaper *Gazeta lwowska* and author of the new book *Galicja w prierwszym roku po rozbiorze Polscy* [Galicia in the first year after the Partition of Poland], expressed irony toward the Vormärz Austrian bureaucracy, as was typical for Polish accounts.[163] Just a few issues later, it republished Vormärz Police Director Leopold Sacher-Masoch's memoirs from the Leipzig journal *Auf der Höhe*, which was edited by Leopold Sacher-Masoch (son of the police director), who was sympathetic to the Ruthenian cause. The later editorial commentary in *Zoria* mocked Polish aristocratic virtues and joined Sacher-Masoch (father) in his judgment of the aristocracy's morals and affiliations.[164]

Ruthenian views on matters outside the political sphere were the traditional reserve of the Greek Catholic clergy whose training in artistic and architectural realms was far from thorough. F. Bilous's *Drevnija zdaniia v sravnienii z nynish-nimi* [Ancient buildings in comparison with contemporary ones], a monograph published in 1856 by the *Stauropigija* Institute, the oldest Ruthenian (clerical) institution in Lemberg, served as an illustration of such church dominance. It was notably one of the first Ruthenian publications to raise the issue of the value of architectural monuments.[165] Following an amateur historical outline of ancient civilizations and their architectural achievement, the author stated that by comparison there were no valuable historic Ruthenian buildings in Galicia. He made no mention of any buildings in Lemberg.[166]

Ironic as it may sound, Bilous's urging that vernacular structures be replaced with new, "better" buildings and his espousing the belief that vernacular architecture had no value fit within the general context of historicism. In historicism, vernacular architecture was seen as unchanged since ancient times – in a sense, it was seen as architecture "without history" – and leading architectural historians had thus profound problems fitting the vernacular into their historicist interpretations.[167] At least in Lemberg, this view helped to delay the application of vernacular motifs to new architecture until the twentieth century, when this occurred within the Art Nouveau movement. Conversely, in building renovation, which was literally understood as making the old new, the replacement of aging, vernacular structures with "modern" ones figured as completely natural.

Bilous's account also stressed the familiar features of earlier historiography: a "lack of" valuable historic buildings and a normative, comparative dimension, yet in his case, these comparisons were made with *earlier,* rather than Western, civilizations. His complete omission of Lemberg also reflects the difficulty that the older generation of Greek Catholic clergy had in seeing Lemberg as a Ruthenian town because of their understanding of Ruthenian identity as both "peasant" and "Eastern." Because the major historical periods of the Romanesque, Gothic, and Renaissance had already been appropriated by Polish national historiography, because there were no explicit relics of an "Eastern" (meaning, Byzantine) tradition in Lemberg, and because the vernacular as yet possessed no value, the Ruthenian view of Lemberg was left without historic and geographical coordinates with which to define itself.

One certain point of Ruthenian identity was imperial loyalty. Similar to many of their Polish contemporaries and to the Vormärz authors writing in German, Ruthenians saw the Habsburg throne as their prime protector and supporter. Just as the emperor had been praised previously for "giving" the Poles their cultural institutions, he was now admired by the Ruthenians for having "presented" them with their National Institute:

Our emperor gave Austrian nations their constitution and pronounced the crucial word of national equality. Beyond that, he presented us, the Galician Ruthenians, with a National Institute (*Narodnyj Dom*), supported our church and...education and, when visiting our institution [the National Institute] and *gymnasium* two years ago, expressed his foremost joy [at our existence].[168]

Many attempted to establish points of reference with Western cities, yet such comparisons did not provide for a positive interpretation of Lemberg's and Galicia's Ruthenian architectural heritage. *Zoria*, for example, published the following opinion in 1881, written under the pseudonym Danylo Lepkyj:

One may find many wooden and stone crosses and many statues of saints in *Ruś*....All these are poorly made, not as abroad, for example, where those German [monuments] decorate the streets of beautiful large cities; [and] not like the Italian [ones] that acquired worldwide fame for their aesthetic value. Our statues [and] our crosses stand far from those beautiful works by German and Italian artists. [They stand] as far away from them, as our poor, thatched huts stand from those monumental, beautiful, and great palaces, which seem to reach...the blue sky with their majestic towers.[169]

While for the Russophile Bilous in 1856, Ruthenian wooden churches were miserable in comparison with ancient civilizations; for Lepkyj, writing in 1881, peasant wood huts paled in comparison with Western palaces. At the times of historicism in Galicia, men of letters rather admired buildings of national institutions that other "more fortunate" nations had erected.

Yet others in Ruthenian circles blamed the lack of valuable Ruthenian architecture on historical misfortunes. Since the art of building was inherently linked to a "nation's" social structure – and while the latter was "underdeveloped and very poor...[and was] led to this condition by five hundred years of Polish rule" – the Ruthenian architect (*budownyčyj*) could only be expected to master the construction of a "simple hut."[170] A hut that, in the historicist's vision, had no value.

Although initially only aesthetic, such comparisons gradually acquired national dimension. *Zoria*'s editor, Omelian Partyćkyj, used architecture to illustrate the progress of Western Slavs as nations; his report on the fire at the Prague National Theater is full of admiration and sympathy for the "deeply patriotic" Czech nation. "Matured in numerous [historic] misfortunes," the Czechs would "no doubt build out of the present ashes (*zharyšče*) a new, even greater beauty."[171] Because Ruthenians clearly lacked a Western national center equivalent to Polish Cracow that could serve for comparisons with Lemberg, they cast Prague in this role as the center of the Czech national movement and a symbol of pan-Slavic rebirth. A metaphor of building as a symbol of national revival was born in the case of the Prague National Theater and was then extensively used in Ruthenian writing.

Compelled by Polish fin-de-siècle historiography to introduce their own centers of reference, and being prone to Ukrainian nationalism, Ruthenians looked for Eastern equivalents. While "Eastern manner" meant "Greek Russian" for Bilous, it signified Kiev in an anonymous *Zoria* article in 1880:

> The only thing that…[the] enemies could not deprive [the Ruthenians] of was their Eastern Ruthenian faith (*vira v vostočnom ruskom obriadi*). This faith required an adequate, majestic, and beautiful temple….Kiev became the center of Christian faith….Ruthenian architects emerged and developed a distinctive Ruthenian building style for their churches… with one and more (three, five, and seven) cupolas, with an iron cupola (*z bliašanoju baneju*) and gilded crosses. … Does this not demonstrate that Ruthenians possess a great natural gift that, if developed harmoniously, could at one point create miracles in the architectural realm?[172]

It is through this Byzantine heritage, rather than the vernacular one, that Galician "Ukrainians" attempted to prove that they were not "barbarians" whose medieval history was notorious for mere witchcraft and "exaggerations."[173]

The issue of the vernacular changed radically in the first decade of the twentieth century, as part of the general European trend of architectural folklorisms within the Art Nouveau movement. Here again, as in the early 1850s, a church leader took the initiative. Andrej Šeptyćkyj (in Polish spelling, Andrzej Szeptycki), the metropolitan of the Greek Catholic church, as well as a convinced Ukrainian from a Polish aristocratic family, captured the importance of vernacular sacral architecture of the Eastern rite in a 1914 lecture on art and architectural monuments at the opening of the Ruthenian National Museum in Lemberg:

> Valuable…monuments of culture should be analyzed and preserved only when all of the society, caught up in one spirit, sees in them sacred qualities delivered by its ancestors that need to be preserved for future generations. They are, then, monuments of archaeology and consequently of national (*nacional'noi*) culture. As long as they are in their original location…,they constitute…a true sign of a living national soul, of a living culture….One does not know what to admire more in those churches, either the spirit of style or the individual, often so aesthetic, style of the architect, or the tenderness of a line, or finally that Christian simplicity and humility….The need for larger churches and the age of [these] old wooden churches have resulted in those [wooden] monuments being more and more difficult to preserve. We consider our old

wooden churches as invaluable monuments of past culture and art, and their preservation as a service to our culture no matter how great the sacrifices it may require.[174]

Thus within the Greek Catholic church, by the 1910s a recognition existed of both the need to appeal to national sentiment through architectural heritage, and the need to incorporate the local vernacular into a positive national identity. Yet as Lemberg was obviously no center of Byzantine heritage, given its European architecture, even the nationalist Šeptyćkyj failed to see it as a Ruthenian town.

One of *Zoria*'s regular writers, Mychajlo Podolynśkyj (1844-94), was representative of the new secular generation that greatly influenced late nineteenth-century Ruthenian national discourse. Having received a secular education and being widely read, this generation had also seen "the West" firsthand. Podolynśkyj's written legacy is exceptional only in his incorporation of scholarship of the day — on topics such as art history and comparative linguistics - and his own memories from numerous travels into a coherent vision of architectural history.

The son of Vasyľ Podolynśkyj, the Galician Ruthenian cultural leader of 1848,[175] Podolynśkyj was a journalist, literary critic, translator, and teacher.[176] In Podolynśkyj, who studied authors as diverse as Jakob Burkhardt and Émile Zola,[177] we find an architectural and cultural historian who rivals Chambrez in Vormärz Lemberg. This Burkhardtian, who ironically described himself as "a completely Germanized character,"[178] also reminds us of such Vormärz writers as Rohrer and Kratter in his admiration of neoclassical architecture and its closeness to Nature, in his negative attitude toward the baroque, and in his normative comparisons with Western capitals. Curiously, though these features, coupled with his blaming of the aristocracy for Galicia's historical misfortunes, reveal his Ruthenian origins, they also render him quite similar to the Polish positivists located across the Russian border.[179]

In 1883, *Zoria* published Podolynśkyj's foundational art history work "Pro realizm v štuci" [On Realism in Art],[180] in which he outlined his views on architectural development, the semantics of style, and Galician architecture's place within this.[181] Podolynśkyj proposed his view of the history of architectural styles from a late nineteenth-century perspective, and yet it was profoundly influenced by the Vormärz writers in its view of the baroque. In his conception, a period of lethargic dreaming had occurred between antiquity and the Renaissance, and then a second serious gap took place between the Renaissance and late eighteenth-century neoclassicism.

For Podolynśkyj, the baroque and rococo were deviations from the Renaissance-inspired pattern of viewing only classical antiquity as possessing worthy artistic achievements; moreover, he viewed these two periods as gradual departures from Nature into a self-referential world of aesthetics and professional jargon. In short, the period between the Renaissance and the late eighteenth century was a time of "reaction,"[182] and only by the end of that century did artists finally remember a return to Nature.[183] According to Podolynśkyj, this did not occur because the Romantic medieval revival replaced the neoclassical ideal, with its call for a return to Nature. Although he appreciated the value of the medieval revival for its uplifting of national spirit, he viewed it as an outdated trend. Podolynśkyj was no romantic nationalist; his personal motto was, "Let us be realistic."[184]

Noting the negative stereotypes of "Germans, our Austrian compatriots,"[185] Podolynśkyj depicted the Austrian German-speaking lands – and especially their cities – as clean, orderly, and beautiful. For example, Salzburg and most notably Innsbruck, "as all German cities," were admirable in his eyes because they were "beautiful...and the houses, streets, and squares [were] good, well-ordered (*choroši*)."[186] Yet he went to the opposite extreme: "German" became for him a synonym of "beautiful," while Austrian Germany was a land where there could be no unpleasant surprises.[187] Moreover, as we shall see further in this chapter, his description of Jews and of Jewish quarters as urban vices demonstrated an anti-Jewish bias, one that had also been present in the earlier local Vormärz accounts.

In his views on classical heritage, Podolynśkyj was strongly Burkhardtian: Renaissance Italy was, for him, the "motherland of architecture," and contemporary Italy served as the "model and inventor of [good] taste in Europe."[188] Yet just as in his architectural theory, Podolynśkyj also revealed himself to be a neoclassicist. Besides the cleanliness he appreciated in the German lands of Austria, he especially admired the monumentality and picturesque quality of the landscape in Italy, as well as the beautiful integration of cities with their surroundings.[189] However, his perception of Western cities and their architecture was most closely linked with reminiscences of his homeland, comparisons that he made in a normative manner:

> One immediately notices a great number of good houses [in Milan]. Churches and palaces, private and public institutions, and statues and monuments...remind us that we have arrived in the motherland of architecture, in the land of "cities and palaces."...Our land stands out as a sad exception in this respect. So little has been done for the [flourishing of] art that [these efforts] would be shameful to mention. Only in the past years has the conservation of ancient monuments been finally considered....The Cracow Academy of Arts only recently started to move [in this direction] (*počynaje sia rušatyś*), though in Lvov no such institution exists. One could count our beautiful churches and buildings on

a single hand. In most towns, and even in larger ones, one cannot meet with a single good building, with the exception of some churches of very questionable aesthetic quality, though the works of sculpture and plastic arts are represented almost exclusively by St. Nepomuks and other monsters of this sort, which can only frighten sparrows.[190]

Podolynśkyj never used the word "baroque" to describe the "questionable aesthetic quality" of Galician churches; by the 1880s, the baroque already referred to an architectural style, rather than to a poor building mode. Yet as evident in the quote above, he still viewed baroque churches and monuments as good only for "frightening sparrows." He was ironic in his tone when writing about public monuments in Lemberg:

Even Lvov...can offer no valuable work of plastic arts to its visitor! Since one cannot call statues to Jabłonowski and St. Michael on Marian Square monuments of art....The former, proud and self-important, counts the rats in the Poltva River, while the latter looks at the dragon below it in such a manner as if he wanted not [to kill the creature], but rather to take some bone out of its mouth so that it does not suffocate....[191]

In the writings of Kratter and Rohrer, the "nation" of Polish "baroque" aristocracy was blamed for the poverty of Galician architecture. In Podolynśkyj, such blame was laid on the local aristocracy, regardless of its origin. He extended his general perception of Galicia as ugly to Lemberg, which he called Lvov, and especially to its "national" cultural elite:

It is true that the Tartar and other [Polish, M.P.] invasions have destroyed our dwellings, villages, and towns throughout centuries, and along with these misfortunes they eliminated all embryonic formations of culture (zarodky kul'tury). But it is also true that the leading strata of our nation, which are so proud of their historic mission, have never exhibited a particular commitment to cultural [development]. The aristocracy (vel'moži) in other countries, such as Italy, France, Germany, and England, possesses palaces as ancient and magnificent as their dynasties..., which are embodiments of their native lands' art history. Beyond that, numerous cultural institutions,...such as hospitals, roads, bridges, canals, aqueducts, and temples, remind us of their cultural mission almost every minute. We have nothing of this nature. We can count only a few true family houses of aesthetic and historical significance, all of which date, at the earliest, from the previous [eighteenth] century, though one does not even ask about valuable monuments from ancient times! Most of our "nobles" (jasne-urodženni) do not even know where their "native hut" (rodna chata) is. Their ancestors cared only for the accumulation of gold and silver, like those Asian khans.[192]

The definition of "nation" remained blurred in the quotation above, and was likely to have class overtones rather than ethnic ones. Yet in this view, Podolyńskyj remained well within the legacy of earlier German and Ruthenian writing. As a Ruthenian, he believed that his own folk had been deprived of its aristocracy. The gentry ("*veľmoži*"), whom he blamed in his writings, are described as Kratter and Rohrer depicted the "baroque" Polish gentry. In his views on Lemberg, just as in his architectural theories and in his perceptions of Austria and Italy, Podolyńskyj remained a faithful follower of the Vormärz memoir literature. A convinced neo-classicist, he disapproved of the baroque. Moreover, a convinced "German" who associated himself with the Crown Land as a whole, he despised Lemberg because it did not stand comparison with Western examples. At the same time, his dislike of Romanticism, his acute sense that his Galicia was backward, and his emphasis on what he called "realism" in culture and politics link him with Warsaw positivism, a parallel that merits further exploration elsewhere. Podolyńskyj's views reveal the extent to which the Galician "nations" remained discursively entangled in their thinking within several conceptual frameworks, notably that of German-speaking Europe and that of the formerly "Polish" lands.

Gentiles and Places of Filth and Stench

Lemberg's nineteenth-century historiography and much of its twentieth-century historiographical writings are characterized by an ascribing of blame for historical misfortunes on yet another group. As the Austrian bureaucracy blamed the Polish "baroque" aristocracy, as Polish intellectuals blamed the "German" Vormärz bureaucracy and Ruthenian "exaggerations," and as Ruthenians blamed the Polish "yoke," throughout the entire nineteenth century there existed a much more easily targeted group. This population had been vehemently pointed at, described, and imaginatively construed by nearly all authors: the Jews. Lemberg's Jewish quarter was subject to blame for social ills throughout history, but became the embodiment of physical and moral filth as well as degradation during Vormärz, if not earlier. (See Fig. 17. This area was not touched by "beautification" efforts throughout the nineteenth century.)

As early as in the first years of the nineteenth century, authors such as Kratter and Rohrer noted the extreme dilapidation and overcrowded conditions in the Jewish quarters in Galicia. While typically blaming the quarters' inhabitants for their own misfortunes, such accounts were part and parcel of a greater disregard for the inner city, for which German Vormärz writing was characteristic:

> The most miserable of all streets is the Jewish street, which is dirty in any weather....The houses are badly built and maintained; of some only the walls remain. The squares [in the Jewish quarter] are completely

Figure 17. "Golden Rose" Synagogue. Photograph by Józef Kościesza Jaworski, ca. 1912. Private collection of Ihor Kotlobulatov.

empty. This dirty, shabby, smelly...little people (*Völkschen*) thinks of all of nice, clean Christendom as unclean.[193]

For Kratter, the author of the passage cited above, the differentiation between value and vice, between good and bad, and between clean and dirty followed a broader differentiation between Christian and Jewish Lemberg.[194] Similarly, the dilapidated, dirty, and stench-ridden state of Jewish houses was linked in his eyes to the qualities of the Jewish ethnicity, just as were "Jewish" professions, such as the leasing of flats. Stanisław Pepłowski replicated this view on Vormärz Jews in his *Teatr polski we Lwowie 1780-1881* [Polish Theater in Lwów, 1780-1881] as late as 1889.[195] Acknowledging that Christian flats were rented at a higher price and that the luxurious Höcht hotel was simply unaffordable during the yearly fairs, Schnür-Pepłowski nevertheless accused the cheaper Jewish flats of filthiness:

[The Christian house-owners] preferred to keep flats unoccupied rather than to rent them at lower prices. [Thus one had to rent] the Jewish houses between contemporary Jagiellonian and Grodecka Streets.

Figure 18. St. Ann's Street. Photograph by Józef Eder, 1860-70. Ľviv Historical Museum.

> However, the *Kontrakty* [fair] participants ended up in a dirty room, in which there was no furniture apart from a hard bed [and] a shaky table, where...the housemaid was replaced by a dirty Jewish servant (*zamorusany myszures*).[196]

Such association curiously outlived the physical existence of Lemberg's historic ghetto. While Kratter and Rohrer wrote about the Jewish quarter during the period when Jewish residence was severely restricted to the limits of the historic city center,[197] late nineteenth-century Polish authors such as Schnür-Pepłowski attributed the same qualities to the new entrepreneurial Jewish quarter that appeared on the left bank of the Poltva River after the final abolition of the residential restriction in 1867.[198] Antoni Schneyder, for example, wrote the following about St. Ann's Street (later *Grodecka*, see Fig. 18) in 1869:

> For the reason that St. Ann's Street is almost totally inhabited by the Jews, it belongs among the most crowded streets in the city. There reigns the continuous lament of Jewish tradesmen, lasting until late in night, the noise of carriages and, consequently, a common Jewish dirtiness.[199]

In 1896, Schnür-Pepłowski echoed that the limits of the new Jewish quarter were "distinguishable not only by eye, but also by nose" (*nie tylko dla oka ale i dla powonienia*) and advised avoiding the district.[200]

In such late nineteenth-century Polish writers' views, not only the poor condition of Jewish houses, but also that of Christian ones, as well as the general economic and cultural backwardness of Galicia, was due to the Jewish population's entrepreneurial spirit. To Kratter, this spirit resulted in the dilapidated condition of city houses, in parallel with the negative qualities of the "Polish" character and of peasant poverty. In his eyes, the city recovered from this economic and physical ruin only under Austrian rule:

> [Lemberg], as other cities, fell into an indescribable ruin because of general Polish carelessness, the exclusive ownership of industry by the gentry, the poverty of the peasants...and, finally, to intense swindling by the Jews. At the moment of Austria's acquisition of Lemberg, one mainly saw empty, collapsing huts and houses....Prior to this, nobody had thought of cleaning the city.[201]

The Jewish preference for "dirty entrepreneurship" was continuously invoked against them in German and later Polish descriptions of Jewish houses. At times, such accusations often merged with simple human jealousy, as in Rohrer's following remarks:

> When one goes from the *Gouverneurwälle* in the direction of Janow and Cracow Streets, one comes upon a whole row of new two- and three-story houses. With the exception of one, and only one, house..., they belong purely (*bloss*) to the Jews....I cannot but regret, however, that precisely the Jews and so seldomly the Christians are in the position to demolish a wooden house and erect a new one of stone, and that only a Jew possesses so much wealth [and can] use the hands of Christian laborers to his own advantage.[202]

Just as Kratter and Rohrer connected filth with entrepreneurial activity, later Polish writers blamed the Jews for the extreme overcrowdedness of the Jewish quarter. Walerian Kalinka exhibited a remarkable continuity with the Vormärz German authors, whom it also profoundly criticized:

> Where is his [the Jew's] dwelling? On the street under the open sky. There he spends all day, from dawn till dusk; there is his world, his life and his forum. At home he hardly sleeps, since how could he out of necessity spend more than a single minute there? Three, four, and more families dwell in [his] narrow and dark house. Dirt, uncleanliness, bad air [prevail there].[203]

Figure 19. Market on Cracow Square. Photograph by Józef Eder, 1860-70. L'viv Stefanyk Scientific Library.

Figure 20. Bałłaban Building prior to demolition. Unknown photographer, ca. 1909. L'viv Historical Museum.

In reality, as has been outlined in the previous chapter, it was the Austrian housing policy, rather than a Jewish entrepreneurial spirit, that caused the extraordinary inflation of flat rents in the city center and the resulting overcrowdedness of the Jewish quarter. In parallel it was the lack of sanitary improvements that led to the district's unattended, dilapidated, and dirty character.[204]

Accusations of economic ruin become more explicit in writers' descriptions of their travels westward: the more a person moved toward the West and away from Galicia and the presence of Jews, the more noticeable economic prosperity and cleanliness became, and the more a person was inclined to link the decay of Galicia's cities with the Jewish presence. For Rohrer, dirty entrepreneurial activities stemmed from a dirty house, as well as the dirty Jew:

> The Jews have appropriated all matters entrepreneurial....The appearance of the nearby Jewish dwellings and the devastation that one could see [even] from the outside were for me overwhelming (*vergällt*)..... Unfortunately, the capital of the dominion, so rich with crops, fruits, and vines, belongs almost completely to this dirty folk [sic.].[205]

Kalinka echoed Rohrer's views in 1853, in his description of Galician towns:

> Sad is the appearance of the towns in Galicia. Overcrowded by swarms of Jews (*przepełnione rojami żydów*), dirty, [streets] seldom paved, with eternal mud on their marketplaces and on streets that only after several weeks of drying can be cleaned away; with their wooden houses of distinct architecture, they also have a distinctive system of streets and squares. Nearly every such town possesses an enormous marketplace that has seemingly been paved sometime in the past, yet the stones have almost disappeared and are now covered with grass. [During town celebrations (*odpust*)] the houses at the square are filled with mobile shops (*ruchomemi sklepami*), and Jews and Jewesses sit down [in these squares] and sell everything that a Polish peasant may need....[Polish] domestic savings (*przychowek domowy*) remained in the hands of a Jew.[206]

In Kalinka, as in the Vormärz German writings, the Western Austrian lands were more prosperous primarily because there were no Jewish inhabitants. Kalinka radicalized Rohrer's vision further: Jews, the cause of "decay and disorder" in Galicia, also controlled "movement and trade" and caused "demoralization" in border towns.[207] The connection between trade, Jewishness, and physical and moral filth becomes even more pronounced in late nineteenth-century Polish authors' writings on the adaptation of architectural monuments, such as the Dominican Cloister's catacombs, for secular use by the Austrian government.

For Schnür-Pepłowski, who disregarded the considerable improvement to public hygiene through the Austrian adaptation of old churches, Jewish immoral entrepreneurial activities only benefited from the Austrian Vormärz religious reforms and so led to the destruction of Polish architectural heritage.[208] Similarly, the economic failure of Polish cultural institutions, such as the Skarbek Theater, was also due to their proximity to – or, in fact, in his view, within – the Jewish quarter (Figure 19 shows the Skarbek Theater bordering the Cracow district with its noisy market on Cracow Square):

> The building of the theater, [its] monumental inside, caused wonders among the wide strata of society. The press called it *"Palais Royal"* [and] envisioned shops, a hotel, a restaurant, and a confectionery in it....However, because the theater was located in the quarter inhabited mostly by Jews, [it] was not favorable for such an enterprise [as the institution of culture]....Later attempts to keep a first-class restaurant and confectionery on the ground floor of the building did not improve the situation.[209]

In reality, the matter was clearly one of prestige, rather than economic advantage: the local Christian population did not wish to have an institution of high culture – let alone one of national culture – in proximity to the city's filth.[210] The economic well-being of the Skarbek Theater in the 1850s could in no way be influenced because that area was partly inhabited by those Jews who could afford to leave the ghetto, rent flats, and live according to the strict lifestyle requirements of the Gentile society. Equally, in the Vormärz the proximity of Höcht's Casino and Hotel to the area on the left bank of the river, which in the late nineteenth century became a large Jewish quarter,[211] could cause no economic misfortunes to the former institution.

Although unable to discern the true cause of the Jewish quarter's density and unsanitary conditions, writers such as Kratter and Rohrer attributed these conditions to the qualities of Jewish ethnicity and especially the entrepreneurial profession, thus cementing the conceptual link between poverty, Jewishness, and entrepreneurship. Appropriated, developed, and radicalized by later Polish writings, this interpretation was applied in the late nineteenth century to the new entrepreneurial quarters, though by that time very little was "Jewish" about these districts (Figure 20 shows the Bałłaban Building before its demolition in 1909. Nothing on this photo shows the proximity of the former inner city Jewish ghetto).[212] Second to the dilapidation of the Jewish quarter and the city center, Jewish entrepreneurial activity came to be seen as a cause of economic misfortune, the loss of architectural heritage, and the economic failure of Polish cultural institutions. Yet besides these continuities between Vormärz authors writing in

German and later writers, several characteristics attributed to the Jewish quarter remained exclusive to either the Vormärz or to later national writings.

The earliest accounts of Habsburg Lemberg, such as that of Kratter, frequently complained of the rise of prostitution and bordellos, known as *Kaffezimmer*, in the city center and associated it at this early date with Jewish activity. This view was especially evident in writings by Franz Kratter, who despised bordellos largely because they abused useful city space, blocked the development of commerce and culture, and raised the rent of flats.[213] Kratter connected the wealth of the bordellos with the moral "filth" of what were called "Jewish agents" (*Judenfaktoren*), who involved themselves in "all types of dirty businesses with various clientele" and forced women of all Lemberg ethnicities into prostitution.[214]

The rise of prostitution largely resulted from the government's ignoring the issue.[215] Although the city's first serious attempts to combat prostitution in the city center of the 1870s did not immediately produce the desired results,[216] the Municipality did succeed in gradually moving prostitution out of the city center. Thus the issue of location, so often lamented later by the Polish writers concerning the proximity of Polish cultural institutions to "Jewish" quarters, could no longer be linked to the issue of prostitution. Because the presence of Jews in the city center remained visible, contemporary non-Jews were left with the option to connect their own economic misfortunes with "Jewish" entrepreneurial activities, rather than "Jewish" bordellos.

The most common accusation in the second half of the nineteenth century directed toward the Jewish quarters was of frequently causing great fires that had consequently destroyed *most* of the city's houses throughout history. Typical examples of such accusation can be found in popular historical fiction of the time, such as the 1857 novel "Krzysztof Arciszewski" published in the popular journal *Przyjaciel domowy*:

> Zarwańska Street was peculiar among old Lwów's streets for the same quality as today, namely, for the unusual dirtiness of its houses and their inhabitants. Added to that, the houses were then [in the mid-seventeenth century] mostly built of wood and inhabited by the uncountable swarms of various mobs ruled by the Jewry (*roje niezliczone rozmaitego tałatajstwa, w którym prym niepospolity wodziło zawsze żydowstwo*). No wonder that no other part of the city was so often subject to fires. Fires in the Zarwańska area were an everyday occurrence.[217]

Schnür-Pepłowski expressed the same idea, adding to it the familiar notion of Lemberg's center as "lacking" historic architecture, allegedly a result of "Jewish negligence."[218] As regards the belief that the Jewish quarter was the major cause of the city's main fires, that it was perpetually dilapidated, and that it was built of wooden huts, this thought had been anachronistic in nature since the early seventeenth century forward.[219] From the middle of that century onward, the Jewish quarter could not have been the prime cause of the great fires[220] because the quarter's urban fabric was no longer made of wood. Furthermore, late nineteenth-century Polish historians overlooked the fact that negligence relating to buildings did not figure as the sole factor causing fires, especially in the case of the Jewish quarter. Instead of associating the city's main fires with Jewish negligence and poverty, they should have linked them to the numerous pogroms throughout Lemberg's history.

Other Polish historians of the late nineteenth century introduced yet another crucial element in the perception of the Jewish population in Lemberg, its "foreign" character, versus the "local" Polish and Ruthenian populations. In these historians' eyes, the Germans and Jews were grouped together as "foreigners," as opposed to the true, local inhabitants. "Foreigners," who supported themselves with "dirty" entrepreneurial activities, were seen as being indifferent to the misfortunes of the land, rather than as the main target of Cossack violence. For example, the popular Polish press's interpretation of this issue on the eve of Chmel'nyćkyj's 1648 siege makes this clear.

> The German and Jewish occupation was primarily one of trade, with the help of which they gained great wealth here and were primarily afraid of being robbed. For them, Chmielnicki held no particular importance....For them, the motherland extended as far as their goods (*kram*) and full carriages could contain. Local inhabitants (*krajowcy*) understood the matter differently....Evil voices whispered to some: You are a Pole, you are a master! And to the others: You are a Ruthenian, you are a serf![221]

Ruthenian writing, as we have seen, experienced profound difficulties in integrating Lemberg into its own national vision, and thus writings on the Jewish quarter occupied a very marginal place in their publications. In the recollections of their travels westward, on the other hand, Ruthenian authors echoed earlier German and Polish accounts in their comments on Jewish quarters and Jewish towns in Galicia. Podolynśkyj, for example, admired the Austrian cities of Salzburg and Innsbruck that were beautiful because there were "no Jews there"; thus the streets were clean and the houses orderly.[222] *Zoria*'s anonymous article "Obrazky z svita Al'pejśkoho" echoed this in 1887:

> Even poor [Alpine] villages have their own community houses and their own schools...The local nation (*narod*) favors cleanliness and is religious....Neither does one hear about theft or any other violence

there. It is safe to walk in the woods [and] the mountains: nobody was ever attacked there....Although one must mention [the reason for this]: there are no Jews there![223]

Thus although one finds little commentary on the Lemberg Jewish quarter in late nineteenth-century Ruthenian writing, statements like the one quoted above illustrate striking similarities with literature in other languages on the description of Jewish quarters. Just as for the Vormärz German authors and Polish fin-de-siècle historians, the presence of the Jewish quarter was for Ruthenian intellectuals a sign of filth, immorality, and criminality.

In one aspect, however, Ruthenian writers radicalized earlier accounts and introduced perhaps the most curious accusation found in the late nineteenth-century popular writings. This notion was introduced in the writings on Halicz (in Ruthenian, Halyč), a town that Ruthenian intellectuals viewed as central to Ruthenian history and identity, indeed, even more central than Lemberg. Ruthenian writers of the period attributed Halicz's economic slump and decline in a minor regional town in the second half of the nineteenth century to its growing Jewish population, and viewed this as a misfortune of historical proportions, rather than a mere economic shift:

[The city] used to be glorious [in the Middle Ages], but how miserable [it is] now! It once threw wealth into the air,...today it has fallen low... under its former royal castle, now a ruin and an ironic monument to centuries-long subjugation (*dovhovikovoji nevoli*)....It has fallen into the unsatisfiable pockets of the Jewry and lost its ancient, truly Ruthenian character....Once the sound of trumpets and horns thundered within its fortified walls, spreading the glory of its nation, but today only the Jewish drum can be heard there, which spreads the glory and pride of a "chosen" nation....[224]

This quotation from *Zoria*'s commentary on 1882 excavations in the vicinity of Halicz is highly reminiscent of Rohrer's earlier account: "This city [of Halyč] was once the seat of the king, but now it is so miserable that it can be much better described as a Jewish nest."[225] Yet it introduces a new, national dimension to the view of the urban Jewish population: a Jewish presence in a Ruthenian town signaled national decline.

Notwithstanding the 1860's abolition of residential restrictions and the subsequent geographical intermingling of the emancipated Jewish population with the Gentile ones, Christian writers ascribed to the new quarters preferred by Jews the "traditional" qualities of Jewish districts – filth and stench. These, in turn, were linked to Jewish ethnicity and other city vices, such as swindling and prostitution. This connection, already present in German Vormärz accounts, was appropriated for a variety of purposes by late nineteenth-century Polish and Ruthenian writers. In its presentation of Lemberg Jewish quarters, nineteenth-century Polish and Ruthenian historiography revealed one of its fundamental misconceptions: the assumption of a direct link between the nature of state rule, ethnicity, and architecture. In so doing, it also contradicted one of its own fundamental principles, that of a great qualitative change in architecture and building practices in the Autonomy era: had there been such a qualitative change, the issue of physical and moral filth would have ceased to exist, just as the restrictive measures against prostitution had removed the connection between the inner city and the bordellos.

Fin de Siècle, Architects: Julian Zachariewicz and Artistic Civilizations

"The days when Vignola's scheme of architectural orders served as a complete arsenal for architectural inspiration have passed. [This] arsenal…is today so… rich that a single person can hardly comprehend it mentally." This quotation from the technical periodical *Czasopismo techniczne* in 1883 summarized the new conditions under which architecture was being created.[226] *Czasopismo techniczne* (published 1883-1918), a journal of the Lemberg Polytechnic Society and a descendant of its earlier *Dźwignia*, (published 1877-82), served as a mouthpiece for the opinions of local "technicians," opinions to which architects also adhered. By the 1880s, an entire system of culturally specific symbols existed that determined which style corresponded with building functions, as was demonstrated by Carl Schorske for the Viennese *Ringstrasse*. Yet until the 1900s and the arrival of the Viennese Art Nouveau in Lemberg, the arsenal of styles and epochs from which architects could draw was limited to European medieval styles, the Renaissance and the baroque.[227]

Two concepts within architectural historicism further prevented the search for architectural stylistic expression: the notion of imitation and the survival of a belief in the universal principles of beauty, as exemplified by simple, ancient Greek architecture. The concept of imitation did not carry the specific negative connotations ascribed to it later in the twentieth century. In imitating older historic styles, especially those of the medieval period, artists hoped to spark a deep emotional response of those historic periods: "If one cannot pioneer something, one should not view imitation only as the last resort!"[228]

The belief in the universal principles of architectural beauty, which survived as late as the 1880s, also figured as a general trend in European architectural

Figure 21. Polytechnic University building by Julian Zachariewicz. Photograph by Franciszek Rychnowski, 1894. Private collection of Ihor Kotlobulatov.

history of the day[229] and was deeply espoused by Lemberg's leading historicist architect, Julian Oktawian Zachariewicz (1837-98). For Zachariewicz, this belief not only resulted in his early buildings bearing similarity to earlier *Biedermeier* projects in Vienna, where he had studied, but it also led to the introduction of a theory of architectural "civilizations." This theory radicalized earlier local beliefs into a unified architectural program, one that Zachariewicz extensively used himself in his restoration practice.

Julian Zachariewicz was a Pole, a Protestant, and a true Lemberger, and therefore he was an individual who did not fit into the straightjacket of national history.[230] His complexity can best be illustrated by the name he chose on the occasion of his ennoblement, Julian Oktawian Lwigrod (*z Lwigrodu*) Zachariewicz. "*Z Lwigrodu*" literally meant "from the city of Leo" and was a poetic, medievalized term for Lemberg. After having studied in Vienna under Joseph Stummer, an architect of the Polytechnic Institute, and Friedrich Schmidt, the architect of the Viennese Rathaus,[231] Zachariewicz made a career as a railway engineer.[232] From 1871 on he was in Lemberg as one of the most outstanding professors of the Technical Academy, later renamed the Polytechnic University, and was honored and ennobled for the completion of the Polytechnic University building (1874-77, Fig. 21).[233] "A man who represented an entire institution,"[234] a practic-

Figure 22. Franciscan Church and cloister. Photograph by Edward Trzemeski, ca. 1890. Private collection of Ihor Kotlobulatov.

ing architect, and a theorist of architecture, he was also an active member of the Polytechnic Society.

Several publications by Julian Zachariewicz in *Dźwignia* in the 1870s-80s are valuable sources of his views and the views of his contemporaries on the validity of universal architectural principles. His first such article, "O poglądach J. Świecianowskiego na harmonię w architekturze" [On J. Świecianowski's views on harmony in architecture],[235] characteristically advocates the classical ancient Greek canon. Informed by the writings by Vitruvius, Vignola, and Alberti, as well as by ancient philosophy, Zachariewicz presents an argument of continuity in architectural history and the supremacy of the classical canon. Greek art was for him "a materialization of the rules of Nature, and this is the clue to its eternal beauty."[236]

Like the neoclassicist architects of the Vormärz, Zachariewicz believed that the universal principles of architectural proportion and beauty could be derived from mathematical calculations. For him, beauty lay in a building as a whole, rather than being derived from its individual parts, let alone from ornamentation only.[237] His and many of his historicist contemporaries' interest in the vernacular architecture, together with their active support for the vernacular crafts,[238] did not signal a serious questioning of accepted stylistic conventions.[239] The success and recognition brought to him by the completion of the neoclassical Polytechnic University building in 1877 did not prevent Zachariewicz from gradually shifting toward a Romantic rediscovery of medieval styles. From that time forward, he remained an ardent advocate of the neo-Gothic and neo-Romanesque, especially in sacral architecture. His *Odczyt o architekturze* [Report on architecture, 1877] admires medieval sacral architecture:

> The building of a church is topped (*pietrzy się*) by small and large towers of wonderful and proportionate forms. Upon entering its interior through the gate, we are struck by its magnifying and earnest charm. From the bright sunlight we enter, foggily and mysteriously, into illuminated aisles. Majestic pillars and ceilings...At a distance...the presbytery in a foggy light.[240]

It is this type of aesthetic appearance that Zachariewicz aspired to in his own neo-Romanesque and neo-Gothic churches. Yet at the same time he remained a cold rationalist: as evident in his explanatory note on his Franciscan Church and cloister (Fig. 22), his own adherence to the supposedly universal principles of architecture could complement the emotional appeal of neo-Gothic structures.[241] The historicist canon dictated the use of the "medieval" style for a modern cloister – which, in reality, became a mixture of simplified Romanesque and northern European Renaissance elements. Yet despite this, and despite his belief that medieval architectural proportions were a matter of intuition (*poczucie*), he thought it appropriate to apply geometrical formulas, as developed in neoclassical architecture, to this project.[242]

Together with the rediscovery of the medieval styles, the 1880s saw a profound rise in the prestige associated with restoration work, a shift that left no serious architect untouched, let alone Zachariewicz.[243] In Galicia, a major archaeological discovery complicated the architect-restorer's job even further; it was Izydor Šaranevyč's (in Polish spelling, Szaranewicz) 1881 discovery of medieval foundations near Halicz, the early capital of the medieval Ruthenian kingdom that gave Galicia its name.[244] This discovery, equally crucial for Ruthenian and Polish scholars, signaled the need for a reconceptualization of all of medieval Galician history in terms other than those of Polish "civilization."[245] Besides classical, medieval, Renaissance, and at times baroque styles, architects were additionally confronted with the need to conceptualize and integrate "Eastern," or Byzantine, stylistic elements into local architecture, an influence that in fact historically predated the glorified Polish period of Casimir the Great.

The Ruthenians immediately claimed the find to be "theirs." The discovery of the medieval churches was made by a Ruthenian scholar, who predicted their location with impressive precision and exclusive reliance on Ruthenian sources, such as medieval chronicles and oral tradition. The Ruthenian National Institute's board acquired the relics in short order and exhibited them in the building's museum.[246] Having taken an active part in the Halicz excavations,[247] Zacharie-wicz soon delivered his own interpretation, in which he drew a major differentiation between "Eastern" Byzantine civilization and the "Western" Romanesque one.[248]

The latter had, according to Zachariewicz, exerted its dominant influence on Galician architecture from the thirteenth century onward, but the former was part and parcel of the great Byzantine architecture that spread as far as the Caucasus, the Adriatic, and Central Russia between the ninth and twelfth centuries. The late twelfth and early thirteenth centuries, the time to which the excavated foundations in Halicz were dated, signified a threshold between the civilizations and the point at which the Western (Catholic) influence superseded the Byzantine in sacral architecture. The significance of the unearthed foundations lay for Zachariewicz precisely in the fact that they belonged to this period and consequently reflected the stylistic *synthesis* of both civilizations.

Here lies the important issue of stylistic consensus, as understood by the leading Lemberg historicist architect: in his own way, he attempted to reconcile Galicia's various histories and to reflect on them in a harmonious manner. Yet in the age of rising nationalism, this aspect of his approach was doomed: as the Poles saw themselves as Western and Westernizing, and as the Romanesque and Gothic became their preferred styles (as architect Teodor Talowski stressed in Cracow), the Ruthenians appropriated the Byzantine, especially in their sacral architecture (as architect Vasyl' Nahirnyj emphasized in his church projects throughout Galicia). Zachariewicz's theory soon found its most controversial application in his own restoration practices on Lemberg's medieval churches, as we shall see in the last chapter of this book. The reconciliatory character of the theory of civilizations notwithstanding, his restoration practices radically transformed the style of Lemberg's oldest architectural monuments into "the Western" neo-Romanesque.

The 1880s also witnessed different reactions to Zachariewicz's theory. Count Włodzimierz Dzieduszycki, Galicia's leading patron of the arts and conservation-curator, became a proponent of Zachariewicz's theory, yet stressed the importance of the Western elements in Galician architecture.[249] The Ruthenian *Zoria* periodical also attempted to integrate the theory into its own divergent beliefs. On one occasion, it reprinted Zachariewicz's article with an excessively positive commentary,[250] but on another it inverted the argument and claimed that "civilization" came to Galicia, and particularly to medieval Cracow, from the East via the Ruthenians, rather than vice versa. The article went so far as to claim that the

Polish kings prayed to "Ruthenian gods," that King Jagiello decorated his chapel in Cracow with "Eastern ornaments," and that his wife, Jadwiga, "had written her first letters in the Ruthenian alphabet."[251]

In 1887, *Zoria* published Volodymyr Kocovśkyj's article, "Ohliad nacionaľnoï praci halyćkych rusynov" [A review of national work by Galician Ruthenians], in which he concluded that Ruthenian culture lay on the threshold (*siny*) between civilizations and claimed that such conditions could not but hurt its "national" culture:

> No matter from which direction one looks at the fate of our Galicia, one cannot avoid seeing signs of incompleteness and unclarity....Galician Ruś had always been a threshold (*siny*) between Western Europe and the East....This is stamped on its history, literature, culture, and [especially] on the national development of the Ruthenians....Tartar attacks and bloody wars with the Poles and the Hungarians destroyed the embryos of our indigenous culture, which originated during the times of [Ruthenian medieval] princedom. Later, under Polish rule, foreigners (*čužyna*) squeezed in here from all directions, unobstructed: German colonists settled in our towns...and Polish magnates built their country houses and palaces thanks to royal "privileges"....German soldiers resided in Galician castles....As a result [one gets] a mixture of Eastern and Western, foreign and native, new and old [elements], and the foreign influence cannot but harm the Ruthenians.[252]

This telling quotation summarized the development of Ruthenian historical thought and illustrated its profound dependence on earlier German and Polish accounts and Zachariewicz's architectural theory. In Kosovśkyj's view, the lack of valuable cultural heritage was due to the years of statelessness and foreign domination, which destroyed the "indigenous" culture of the Ruthenians. In inverted negative terms, the latter belief is a replication of Zachariewicz's view of "Western" culture's victory at the time Galicia fell to the Polish crown.

At the turn of the century, historic styles acquired "national" connotations, and new styles were forged into "ethnic" categories, with the neo-Gothic and neo-Romanesque as Polish, and the neo-Byzantine as Ruthenian. Partly a consequence of late nineteenth-century thought on architectural development along national lines, this curious phenomenon also resulted from Zachariewicz's theory of architectural civilizations. In architecture, stylistic and generational changes within the Lemberg school illustrated how, moved by heated local debate, architects gradually recognized the possibility – and the need – to explore historic styles and local vernacular architecture inasmuch as the Art Nouveau and, later, modernist canons allowed. As a result, a synthesis of folkloric elements and historic styles, to which national connotations were already ascribed, became "true" architecture, just as neoclassicism and imperial historicism had been before.

◆

Polish historiography of the fin de siècle chose the architecture of Austrian neoclassicism as the major point of its criticism, yet it borrowed and inverted the Vormärz understanding of architecture as being inherently linked to the "baroque" nature of state rule. Notwithstanding such a profound continuity, this Polish writing introduced an approach into architectural history that required the complex architecture of Lemberg to be seen in national terms. Trapped between a view of Vormärz architecture as "ugly" on the one hand, and the clear planning achievements of the Austrian administration and the contemporaneous foundation of several Polish cultural institutions during the Vormärz on the other, Polish authors needed to rethink their conceptual approach to architecture. Because no consensus existed on the issue of Ruthenian identity, Ruthenian writing experienced even greater difficulties in interpreting Lemberg as a Ruthenian town, and hence followed either Vormärz German accounts or later Polish ones in its thinking. Yet these views all echoed one another when describing the Jewish quarter as an embodiment of urban vice, even following the abolition of Jewish residential restrictions in the late 1860s.

Architects' writings closely echoed the thinking of earlier professionals in the late nineteenth century, but the architects were less inclined to frame their work within the straightjacket of nationalism. This link is evident from the continuity in professional terminology on the belief in universal architectural beauty, which was present both in writings by the leading Vormärz architect, Ignac Chambrez, and in those by the late nineteenth-century historicist architect, Julian Zachariewicz. The basic historicist principle – that of seeing style as representative of a particular epoch and of using style to evoke the emotions associated with this epoch – merged with the need to incorporate recent archaeological discoveries into existing architectural systems. In late nineteenth-century Lemberg, such a rethinking led to the advent of a theory of architectural "civilizations," with the consequence that historic architecture was rethought, and new "national" styles were created to fit this theory.

Although it is clear at this point that the major assumptions found in the writings of the "long nineteenth century" on architecture require careful revision, it also emerges that this very literature demonstrated diverse and, at times, entangled identities and loyalties. Although Habsburg loyalty can be understood as the primary, overarching identity for the high-ranking bureaucrats, historians, and architects of Lemberg, the change of political climate in the 1860s did cause a shift in thinking about architecture. For the Vormärz writers, architecture had only imperial representational properties, but for the mayors of the Galician capital, in the federalized monarchy, it also became a visual material that could both demonstrate technical achievements and serve as a propaganda tool for political campaigns. Yet it was only in the 1900s and largely through Tadeusz Rutowski's personal efforts that buildings of culture came to be seen as contributing to national progress. It was largely due to such a view that Julian Zachariewicz's theory of architectural civilizations was appropriated by both Polish and Ruthenian thinkers for their own purposes.

Notes

1   See Mańkowski, *Początki Lwowa*, 591.

2   The key figure on the late eighteenth- and early nineteenth-century Viennese architectural scene, the Swiss-born and Rome-educated architect is remembered for his work in Trieste (the San Antonio Church), and Vienna (the *Theseion* and the *Burgtor*). The recent study in Italian by Gino Pavan is the first monograph on Nobile, and it largely concentrates on his architectural contribution to Trieste (Gino Pavan, *Pietro Nobile. Architetto (1776-1854)* [Trieste: Istituto Giuliano Di Storia, Cultura E Documentazione, 1998]).

3   Nobile's involvement in Lemberg was largely due to his high position at the court, notably because this concerned his work on the governor's palace and other buildings of political power, and also the *Ossolineum* Institute. See Franz Tschischka, *Kunst und Alterthum in den oesterreichischen Kaiserstaate. Georgaphisch dargestellt von* (Vienna, 1836), 268, and Stanisław Łoza, *Architekci i budowniczowie w Polsce* (Warsaw: Budownictwo i Architektura, 1954), 217.

4   Prokopovych, "Lemberg (Lwów, Ľviv) Architecture."

5   As in Jacek Purchla, ed., *Architektura Lwowa XIX wieku* [Lwów Architecture in the 19th c.] (Cracow: International Cultural Centre, 1997).

6   Maria Kłańska, *Daleko od Wiednia*; idem, *Problemfeld Galizien in deutschsprachiger Prosa 1846-1914* (Vienna: Böhlau, 1992). Also see Wolff, "Inventing Galicia."

7   Research conducted for this book did not allow for a comprehensive coverage of Jewish opinions. On the history of the Jewish quarter, see Melamed, *Yevrei vo Lvove;* Bałaban, *Dzielnica żydowska*; idem, *Historya lwowskiej synagogi postępowej*. On the history of Jews in Lemberg and Habsburg Galicia, see Wierzbieniec, "The Processes of Jewish Emancipation"; Mahler, *Hasidism and the Jewish Enlightenment;* Mendelsohn, "Jewish Assimilation in Ľviv"; Magocsi, *Galicia: a historical survey*, 228-31.

8   These included Winckelmann's *Geschichte der Kunst des Alterthums* (Dresden, 1764), Piranesi's *Vedute di Roma* (Rome, 1850), and Vignola's *Regole delle cinque ordini d'architettura* (Rome, 1562). See Mańkowski, *Początki Lwowa,* 7. On a summary of classicist thought, see Caroll William Westfall, "Excursus: A Short History of Typological Thought in Architecture," in Robert Jan van Pelt and Caroll William Westfall, *Architectural principles in the age of historicism* (New Haven: Yale University Press, 1991), 140-51. The antique temples were a major source of architectural inspiration and what we may call stylistic imitation, since the final goal of architects of the time was to come as close to the classical ideal as possible.

9   See Mańkowski, *Początki*, 7.

10 Sebastian Sierakowski, *Architektura obejmująca wszelki gatunek budowania i murowania* [Architecture as overarching all kinds of building and mural works] (Cracow,

1812); Stanisław Potocki, *O sztuce u dawnych czyli Winckelmann polski* [On the art of the ancients or Polish Winckelmann] (Warsaw, 1815).

11 Some of them, such as the traveler Baltasar Haquet, did not concern themselves with architecture, though others, such as Police Director Sacher-Masoch, recalled Lemberg as a place of turbulent military and political events. See Baltasar Haquet, *Haquets neueste physikalisch- politische Reisen in den Jahren 1788 und 1789 durch die Dacischen und Sarmatischen oder Nördischen Karpaten* (Nürnberg: Verlag der Raspischen Buchhaltund, 1790-91).

12 Typical of their generation, they were in principle advocates of full religious tolerance, anti-Jewish bias notwithstanding, and deeply criticized their contemporaries, such as the Roman-Catholic Bishop Gensakowski, for their religious and social conservatism. *Kratter, Briefe,* vol. 1, 9; 48.

13 During his studies in Vienna, Kratter became one of Joseph II's sincere admirers and kept his Josephinian views until his death in Lemberg in 1837.

14 Rohrer was appointed Galician police director in 1800 and headed the faculty of political sciences and statistics at Lemberg Lyceum, which later became the university, from 1806 on. Apart from his *Bemerkungen*, Rohrer was also the author of several statistical surveys on Western lands under the Habsburg rule. He retired in 1827 (Constantin Ritter von Wurzbach-Tannenberg, *Biographisches Lexikon*, vol. 26, (Vienna, 1874).

15 Rohrer, *Bemerkungen*, 162; 166-67.

16 "[Even] between the youngest generation (*Klasse*) of officials, it is noticeable how little they care about the respect of the public, as they behave in a manner in which one cannot receive any respect. In public they usually talk about whores. I was astonished how people who should have a better education could use the most elaborate expressions of the worst slang. A stable servant might hesitate to use such expressions, even when among his peers." (Kratter, *Briefe*, vol. 2, 226-227). On Kratter's bitter criticism of the new Austrian bureaucracy in Lemberg, see ibid., 177-81; 198-244.

17 Kratter, *Briefe*, vol. 2, 164-66.

18 Kratter, *Briefe*, vol. 2, 140-41.

19 The biased nature of such comparisons have already been noted by Tadeusz Mańkowski, who correctly pointed out that postrevolutionary eighteenth-century Paris was likewise dirty and poorly paved (Mańkowski, *Początki Lwowa*, 9).

20 Dora Wiebenson and József Sisa, eds., *Architecture of historic Hungary* (Cambridge, Massachusetts: MIT Press, 1998), 148-49; Waissenberger, *Vienna in the Biedermeier Era*, 62.

21 Rohrer noticed the unusually relaxed manner in which the Polish gentry walked along the *Gouverneurwälle* (Rohrer, *Bemerkungen*, 171).

22 Moreover, the air on the tops of hills was believed to have curative properties, as compared to the dirty and unhealthy city center (Kratter, *Briefe*, vol. 2, 182-83).

23 "The outer districts are very large…but mostly [consist of] poor, bad-looking (*schlechten, unansehnlichen*) buildings…There are beautiful, large, shady gardens, mostly laid out by nature, outside the city center, among which Jabłonowski Park stands out with its large, long, majestic shadiness and the Lonchamp Park with its diversity of hills, shrubberies, vivid allées, and wonderful sightseeing spots" (Kratter, *Briefe*, vol. 2, 176).

24 Kratter, *Briefe*, vol. 2, 184.

25 Rohrer, *Bemerkungen*, 297.

26 The park founder's name has three alternative spellings: French "Lonchamp," Germanized "Lonschamp" (as in *Lonschamplische Garten*), and Polish "Lonszan" (as in

Lonszanówka). For example, Kratter (*Briefe*, vol. 2, 176) writes of "Lonschampische Garten" and then quotes a Latin inscription on the memorial in the garden "Pofitum a Franc. Lonchamps, Leopol. Magistratus Confiliario VIII Maji A. D. MDCCLXXXI" (ibid., 177). Here and further in the text I have used "Lonchamp Park" and "Lonszanówka" interchangeably.

27   Lemberg had 42,000 inhabitants in 1800 and 68,000 in 1850 (Bairoch, Batou, and Chevre, *La population des villes*, 62). The growth accelerated in the second half of the nineteenth century and, in 1910, Lemberg's population reached over two hundred thousand (Steed, *A Short History of Austria-Hungary*). The occasional destruction of gardens met with critics' disapproval (Rohrer, *Bemerkungen*, 170-71).

28   "Jabłonowski Park possesses an excellent grand allée (*eine vorzüglich prächtige Allee*), and if it would be extended to the foot of the hill, it could become a fine (*herrlich*) English park. In this case, however, the palace in front of it would need to have a different appearance....The disorder that rules [over the palace's façade] today would undoubtedly displease an eye hungry for aesthetically pleasing buildings" (Rohrer, *Bemerkungen*, 170).

29   Antoni Schneyder (?-1880) was one of the first local Polish "heritage collectors" of historical artifacts who compiled an unfinished encyclopedia to Lemberg. See Der Verfasser [Antoni Schneyder], "Auflösung der im Nr. 8 gegebenen Total-Charade," [Cancellation of the complete charade printed in no. 8], *Mnemosyne* 10 (1846), 36. For a biographical study, see Oleksandr Šyška, "Tragična dolia Antonija Šnajdera" [The tragic fate of Antoni Schneyder], *HB* 5-6 (1995).

30   Anonymous (Dr. B.), "Wzorki Lwowskie" [Lwów Ornaments], *Czas* 282 (1852) (See CDIAU F. 52, Op. 1, Sp. 950, L. 11).

31   In his recent book, Christopher W. Thompson explores a thread of francophone "pedestrianism," a genuine enthusiasm for walking that translated into literary themes and formal practices. For Charles Didier as for other, more well-known French Romantics, walking provided a vehicle for a genuine encounter with the others – peasants, laborers, tourists, foreigners – outside the social constraints of class, gender, and profession. See Christopher W. Thompson, *Walking and the French Romantics. Rousseau to Sand and Hugo* (New York: Peter Lang, 2003).

32   Rohrer, *Bemerkungen*, 168-69. On Kratter's admiration of Joseph II's visit to Lonschamp Garden, see Kratter, *Briefe*, vol. 2, 176.

33   *"Ein kleines Monument dem Andenken des grossen Monarchen"* (Rohrer, *Bemerkungen*, 169).

34   *"Stolz trage ich des edlen Grafen Namen,/ Der sich in mir ein Denkmal hingestellt / Ein Denkmal seine Güte, seiner Würde / Der Auges [sic] Luft und – Lembergs schönste Zierde!"* (Moritz Siegerist, "Total-Charade," *Mnemosyne* 8 (1846), 31-32 (Also see CDIAU F. 52, Op. 1, Sp. 950, L. 13).

35   CDIAU F. 52, Op. 1, Sp. 950, L. 5.

36   In practice, the irrelevance of the concept of style as an ultimate tool for differentiating between "good" and "bad" architecture is demonstrated by the fact that the leading Lemberg architects of the Vormärz engaged in new planning techniques and erected new buildings of power (in line with Francesco Milizia's planning theory), while they also assisted the remaining ecclesiastical orders with renovations of their baroque and rococo churches. For an excellent summary of classicist and historicist concepts of style and building types, see Caroll William Westfall, "Building Types," in Robert Jan van Pelt and Caroll William Westfall, eds., *Architectural Principles in the Age of Historicism* (New Haven and London: Yale University Press, 1991), 138-67. On the neoclas-

120   ◆   CHAPTER TWO

sical concept of style in the Polish context, see Tadeusz Makowski, *O poglądach na sztukę w czasach Stanisława Augusta* [About the Views on Art in the times of Stanisław August] (Lwów: Nakł. Towarzystwa Naukowego, Drukarnia Uniwersytetu Jagielloskiego, 1929).

37   Emphasis mine. Franz Tschischka, *Kunst und Alterthum*, 267-68.
38   Kratter, *Briefe*, vol. 2, 167.
39   Mańkowski, *Początki Lwowa*, 9.
40   Francesco Milizia, *Principii di architettura civile di Francesco Milizia* (1781). On the application of Milizia's theory to Lemberg city planning, see Bevz, 51-69.
41   Mańkowski, *Początki Lwowa*, 44.
42   Kratter, *Briefe*, vol. 2, 159-60.
43   Leon Battista Alberti, *On the art of building in ten books,* trans. by Joseph Rykwert, Neil Leach, and Robert Tavernor (Cambridge, MA.: MIT Press, 1988).
44   Mark-Antoine Laugier, *An Essay on Architecture*, trans. Anni Herrmann with an introduction by Wolfgang Herrmann (Los Angeles, 1977), 90. Laugier's most important contribution to classicist architectural theory was the idea of the primary rustic (Greek) hut's universal beauty. Anyone who understood the beauty of the hut could therefore judge architecture without reliance on extensive knowledge.
45   "*Geschmackvoll, einfach, und majestätisch in ihrer Pracht*" (Kratter, *Briefe*, vol. 2, 160).
46   "*Lemberg ist ziemlich regelmässig angelegt, die Gassen laufen in geraden Linien fort, und einige davon haben eine bequeme Breite*" (Kratter, Briefe, vol. 2, 156).
47   Kratter, *Briefe*, vol. 2, 158.
48   The anatomy hall, on the contrary, was large and light, and its entrance reminded Kratter of Bavarian equivalents. (Kratter, *Briefe*, vol. 2, 5-7).
49   Kratter, *Briefe*, vol. 2, 156.
50   Kratter, *Briefe*, vol. 2, 154.
51   Kratter, *Briefe*, vol. 2, 153.
52   Rohrer, *Bemerkungen*, 172.
53   This quote is from the novel *Krzysztof Arciszewski*, written on the events of 1655 Chmeľnyćkyj's siege from the Polish national perspective. See anonymous, "Krzysztof Arciszewski. Obrazek historyczny z dawnej przeszłosci Lwowa" [Krzysztof Arciszewski. A historical image from old Lwów's past], *Przyjaciel domowy* 1-16 (1857), 26.
54   Mańkowski, *Początki Lwowa*, 27.
55   Chambrez was born in Holleschau (Holešov) in Moravia in 1758 to a family of Czech-Moravian descent. He retired and died in Lemberg in 1842. Thanks to Petr Kroupa's publication of Chambrez's original text *Nachlass eines mährischen Künstlers zur Belehrung seiner Söhne*, together with his concise commentary, we know much more about Chambrez than any of the other Lemberg local architects of the Vormärz. See Petr Kroupa, "Odkaz moravského umělce k poučení svých synů (umělecký cestopis z konce 18. stoleti), [Moravian artist's testament to his son, artistic manuscript from the late 18th century]. "Nachlass eines mährischen Künstlers zur Belehrung seiner Söhne, Zweites Heft Worinnen die in Prag Gesehenen Arbeiten der alten Mahler, Bildhauer, und anderer Künstler Böhmens beschrieben stehn," *Studie Muzea kroměřižska* 83, 123-31).
56   His works *Versuch eines architektonischen Katechismus*, believed to have been printed by Piller in Lemberg, 1821, and *Bertachtung über der Charakter der Gebäude und über die darauf anzubringenden architektonischen Verziehungen* (Vienna, 1807), remain unavailable to us. See Mańkowski, *Początki Lwowa*, 27.

57   His diary is written in the simple German of a fluent, nonnative speaker, with minor stylistic mistakes. (Kroupa, "Odkaz," 123).

58   Kroupa, "Odkaz," 124, footnote 6. Chambrez returned to Holleschau, via Vienna, in 1783.

59   Kroupa, "Odkaz," 124.

60   From 1793 on in Teschen, from 1803 on in Cracow, and from 1815 on in Lemberg (Kroupa, "Odkaz," 124). According to Mańkowski, Chambrez taught at the Lemberg lyceum from 1812 until retirement in 1834 (Mańkowski, *Początki Lwowa*, 26).

61   From his architectural practice, we know only that he managed the adaptation of the former monastery building as the headquarters of Lemberg University in 1826-28 (Mańkowski, *Początki Lwowa*, 27), and he designed the first neoclassical Alfred Potocki palace (1822).

62   Although at one point in his *Nachlass* he writes of the surroundings of Prague as "one of the most beautiful (*einer der angenehmsten*) in Austria," in the next paragraph, he mentions his trip from Prague "to Austria." German-speaking territories *outside* the Habsburg borders (Prussia) were unquestionably "*Ausland.*" (Chambrez, *Nachlass*, 130).

63   Chambrez, *Nachlass*, 127.

64   He retained his admiration of its church altars, statues erected "by native (*vaterländischer*) sculptors," and Kilian Diezehhofer's gardens and cloisters (ibid.).

65   Ludwik Finkel and Stanisaw Starzyski. *Historya uniwersytetu lwowskiego* [History of Lwów University], 2 vols. (Lemberg: Senat Akademicki c.k. Uniwersytetu lwowskiego, 1894), 240.

66   "*Alles Antique reizt die Einbildungskraft*" (Mańkowski *Początki Lwowa*, 28).

67   Full citation in Chambrez, *Nachlass*, 130.

68   van Pelt and Westfall, 140. See *Vitruvius on architecture/edited from the Harleian manuscript 276,* ed. and trans., Frank Granger (London: W. Heinemann, Cambridge, Massachusetts: Harvard University Press, 1931).

69   Chambrez, *Nachlass*, 130.

70   Similarly, the only Prague sculpture he commented on negatively in his diary was baroque St. Jan Nepomuk's statue on the Charles Bridge (ibid.).

71   He acknowledged, however, the subjective character of the notion of beauty when he wrote "The characteristic signs of beauty are [only our] attraction and inspiration. [Its] quality has not yet been explained by anyone, and would lose all its value when it would be explained. Where it exists it touches every heart, but to bring it is the highest art." (Mańkowski, *Początki Lwowa*, 28).

72   Chambrez, *Nachlass*, 131.

73   Chambrez, *Nachlass*, 127.

74   These were, curiously, churches in "*gotischen Maurischen Style*"; yet, Chambrez argued, talented local architects built them differently than elsewhere in Europe, and according to the principles of universal architectural beauty (Chambrez, *Nachlass*, 128).

75   He also stressed the importance of nuanced light effects in successful architectural work (quoted in Mańkowski, *Początki Lwowa*, 27).

76   Kroupa, "Odkaz," 124.

77   For example, see Walerian Kalinka, *Galicya i Kraków pod panowaniem austryackiem* [Galicia and Cracow under Austrian domination] (Paris: W komisie Księgarni polskiej, 1853), 37-38; Bohdan Janusz, *Lwów stary i dzisiejszy. Praca zbiorowa pod redakcyą* [Old and today's Lwów] (Lwów: Nakl. Wyd. "M.A.R." (Malop. Ajencja Reklamowa),

1928), 27, 48; Volodymyr Ovsijčuk, *Klasycyzm i romantyzm v ukraïnkomu mystectvi* [Classicism and romanticism in Ukrainian art] (Kyiv: Dnipro, 2001), 65; 87-91; Purchla, *Architektura Lwowa XIX wieku,* 32, 34; Olaksandr Šyška, *Naše misto – Ľviv* [Our city Ľviv] (Ľviv: Centr Jevropy, 2002), 142-49.

78   See Unowsky, *The Pomp and Politics,* 145-74; Richard S. Geehr, *Karl Lueger: Mayor of Fin-de-Siècle Vienna* (Detroit: Wayne State University Press, 1990); Karin Brinkmann Brown, *Karl Lueger, the Liberal Years: Democracy, Municipal Reform, and the Struggle for Power in the Vienna City Council, 1875-1882* (New York: Garland Publishing, 1987); John W. Boyer, *Political Radicalism in Late Imperial Vienna: Origins of the Christian Social Movement, 1848-1897* (Chicago: University of Chicago Press, 1981); Susan Zimmermann, *Prächtige Armut: Fürsorge, Kinderschutz und Sozialreform in Budapest: Das "sozialpolitische Laboratorium" der Doppelmonarchie im Vergleich zu Wien, 1873-1914* (Sigmaringen: J. Thorbecke, 1997); Gerhard Melinz and idem, *Über die Grenzen der Armenhilfe: kommunale und staatliche Sozialpolitik in Wien und Budapest in der Doppelmonarchie* (Vienna: Europaverlag, 1991). Also see Schorske, *Fin-de-siècle Vienna,* 116-80.

79   Born in Galicia in 1812, Gołuchowski became one of Austria's leading conservative politicians during neoabsolutism: he served as the Minister of the Interior from 1859-60 (*Minister des Inneren*) and as Minister of State (*Staatsminister* in 1860). He died in Lemberg in 1875. See Bronislaw Łoziński (Dr.), *Agenor Hrabia Gołuchowski w pierwszym okresie rządów swoich (1848 - 1859)* [Count Agenor Gołuchowski in the first period of his governorship, 1848-1859] (Lemberg: Nakl. Księgarni H. Altenberga, 1901).

80   Anonymous, "Agenor hrabia Goluchowski," *Przyjaciel domowy* 10 (7 March 1857), 76-78.

81   In line with the Vormärz notion of a monument, the city council decided to name the square in front of Skarbek Theater after the governor and planned to erect a fountain there in his name.

82   Łoziński, 116.

83   A rather unreliable source tells us that he wished to have a monument that would depict the two major scenes of his political life, the proclamation of the October Diploma (1860) and his return to Lemberg (CDIAU F. 165, Op. 5, Sp. 230, vol. III, L. 7).

84   See Geehr, *Karl Lueger,* 143-69; Zimmermann, *Prächtige Armut,* 244-99; Gerhard Melinz and idem, *Über die Grenzen der Armenhilfe,* 92-102; 136-41.

85   *Szematyzm król. Galicyi i Lodomeryi z Wielkim Księżstwem Krakowskim na rok 1872* [Schematismus of the Crown Land of Galicia and Lodomeria together with the Great Principality of Cracow, 1872], Lemberg: Winiarz, 1872, 86.

86   See Leon Gustaw Dziubiński, *Poczet prezydentów, wizeprezydentów i obywateli honorowych miasta Lwowa. Odbitka z "Księgi pamiątkowej," wydanej w 25-letni jubileusz autonomii krolewskiego stolecznego miasta Lwowa* [Account of Mayors, Vice-Mayors, and Lwów's honorable citizens. Reprint from the "Memorial Book" issued on the occasion of the 25th anniversary of the capital city of Lwów's autonomy] (Lemberg: Nakl. Gminy m. Lwowa, 1896).

87   Edmund Mochnacki, *Sprawozdanie Prezydenta k. st. miasta Lwowa z trzechletniej czynności Reprezentacyi miasta i Magistratu (1886, 1887 i 1888) wygloszone na posiedzeniu pełnej Rady dnia 19. Stycznia 1889* [Report by Lwów's Mayor on the occasion of the three years (1886, 1887, and 1888) of the Municipal Council's and Municipality's operation, presented at the full Council's meeting on 19 January 1889] (Lemberg:

Nakl. Gminy m. Lwowa, 1889). Also see *Miasto Lwów w okresie samorządu, 1870-1895* [The City of Lwów in the Times of Municipal Self-Government, 1879-1895], intoduction by Mochnacki (Lemberg: Nakl. Gminy m. Lwowa, 1896).

88 Mochnacki, *Sprawozdanie*, 1.

89 As a proof of improvement in health conditions, Mochnacki mentioned the additional actions of the rechanneling of the Petłew River underground, the introduction of the sewer mains, and the planning of the new section of the Janów Cemetery (Mochnacki, *Sprawozdanie*, 1-2).

90 Ibid., 9.

91 See "XVI. Corso i arena wyścigowa" [Bulevard and the sports arena] (ibid., 11).

92 Just how important the appearance of the city was for the mayor's program is evident in the discussion over the new city guide. See "XII. Sprawa nowego skorowidza i przewodnika," [The issue of a new guidebook] ibid., 11).

93 Ibid., 12-13.

94 CDIAU F. 165, Op. 5, Sp. 110, L. 150.

95 Despite the initial enthusiasm, the issue of the mound's erection was never central in municipal affairs. It was only because of Smolka's personal involvement that the construction was completed by the end of the nineteenth century – badly and unprofessionally, as evidenced by its serious deterioration by 1907 (For further discussion, see chap. 4 of this book.).

96 The idea of an art gallery was first introduced in 1861 by the artist Kornel Szlegl; yet it was realized only through Rutowski's personal involvement in the late 1900s. For Antoniewicz, the idea of having a public art collection was unthinkable because of what he viewed as the low quality of the collected works.

97 Born in Tarnów, Rutowski held degrees from both the Viennese Polytechnic University and the Viennese University's faculty of philosophy, where his thesis topic was Herder's philosophy of history. Employed from 1884 on at the Statistical Bureau of the Crown Land Department in Lemberg, he became Lemberg's vice mayor in 1905.

98 See Henryka Kramarz, *Tadeusz Rutowski. Portret pozytywisty i demokraty galicyjskiego* [Portrait of Galicia's positivist and democrat] (Cracow: Wydawnictwo Naukowe AP, 2001).

99 In provincial matters, Rutowski saw economic reform as the most necessary issue, and administrative reform of the municipal administration and its further independence from the superior imperial bodies were his goals at the municipal level. See *Mowa Dr. Tadeusza Rutowskiego na zgromadzeniu wyborców m. Tarnowa dnia 19. Maja 1883* [Dr. T.R's Speech at the meeting of the electorate in the city of Tarnów, 19 May 1883] (Cracow: Drukarnia Związkowa, 1883).

100 In 1884, he organized the first exhibition of the Polish painter, Artur Grottger.

101 In 1881, he founded the journal *Muzeum* in Cracow, which discussed political and cultural matters in a liberal, democratic tone. After the failure of the *Muzeum*, together with Adam Asnyk and Tadeusz Romanowicz, he organized the journal *Reforma* (known from 1883 on as *Nowa Reforma*), intended as a counterpart to the successful *Czas* of the conservatives (Stańczyki). He was also author of *W sprawie przemysłu krajowego* [On the issue of Crown Land industry] (Cracow, 1883).

102 Founded in 1896, *Słowo polskie* was edited by Romanowicz. After Rutowski replaced Romanowicz as editor, the newspaper doubled its number of daily issues and soon started to come out twice a day. In parallel, its style changed to a much more polemical one. In Lemberg, Rutowski also edited the stylish and informative art journal *Sztuka*

until 1913, which while presenting modern Polish culture also provided information on local Ruthenian, Armenian, Jewish, and Hucul traditions.

103 See Jan Bołoz Antoniewicz, "Nasz Rafael," [Our Rafael] *Słowo polskie* (19 August 1907); idem, Nasz Rafael, (Lemberg, 1908); Tadeusz Rutowski (Dr.) "W sprawie Galeryi miejskiej," [To the issue of City Gallery] *Słowo polskie* (5 June – 24 August 1907); idem, *W sprawie Galeryi miejskiej z planem "Pałacu Sztuki"* [On the issue of a City Gallery with a plan of the "Palace of Art"] (Lemberg: Księgarnia H. Altenberga, Drukarnia i litografja Pillera, Neumanna i sp., 1907).

104 Tadeusz Rutowski (Dr.) *Galerya miejska w swietle polskiej i obcej krytyki* [City Gallery in the light of Polish and foreign criticism] (Lemberg: Nakl. Gminy Miasta z drukarni W. A. Szyjkowskiego, 1908).

105 Aleksander Czołowski (Dr.) *W sprawie Galeryi miejskiej. Odpowiedź prof. Dr. Janowi Bołoz Antoniewiczowi* [To the issue of the City Gallery. An answer to Dr. Jan Bołoz Antoniewicz] (Lemberg, 1907). An anonymous author, Dr. M. Sz., connected the idea of the palace with the commemoration of the Grunwald battle in 1910 (CDIAU F. 165, Op. 5, Sp. 1163, L. 30-35).

106 Rutowski, *Galerya,* 11. Rutowski's principle was to collect "first of all, modern Polish works, while not forgetting, at the same time, to collect old masters, where one would not introduce a national criterion." Thus the city of Lemberg bought a large number of Renaissance and baroque pieces of art from the Ruthenian collector Jakowicz, thus constituting the core of the future collection of old masters. Similarly, local professionals thought to fill the "German" section with the graphics of a Czech artist, Antoni Lange (ibid., 85).

107 Ibid., 60-61.

108 Ibid., 66.

109 Thanks to Jaworski, the city's archivist and a devoted collector, we can reconstruct the interpretation of Lemberg's history in the mainstream Polish print media of the second half of the nineteenth century, such as *Kółko rodzinnne* [Family circle] and *Przyjaciel domowy* (Home Companion). (see CDIAU Fond 101, Op. 1, Sp. 5, 22, and 23).

110 Jan Wagilewicz, "Początki Lwowa" [Beginnings of Lwów], *Kółko rodzinne* 7 (1860), 114 (CDIAU F. 101, Op. 1, Sp. 5, L. 1). Together with Markian Šaškevyc and Jakiv Holovaćkyj, Ivan Vahylevyč (Jan Wagilewicz) was one of the major players in the Galician Ruthenian-Ukrainian national awakening and an editor of the first collection of poetry written in the Ruthenian vernacular, *Rusalka Dnistrovaja* (Buda, 1837).

111 Anonymous, "Krzysztof Arciszewski."

112 There were, however, earlier Polish histories of Lemberg that dealt with its architecture, such as Ignacy Chodyniecki, *Historja stółecznego Królewstw Galicyi i Lodomeryi Miasta Lwowa od założenia jego aż do czasów terazniejszych w r. 1829 wydana. Wydanie wznowione tanie* [History of the Crown Land of Galicia and Lodomeria and the City of Lwów from Its Foundation to the Present, published in 1829] (Lemberg: Karol Wild, 1865).

113 Michał Lityński, for example, called J. Chodyniecki, Fryderyk Papée, Walerian Kalinka, Stanisław Schnür-Pepłowski, and Władysław Łoziński "the first Galicians" and admired them for their pioneering works in the history of Lemberg and its Crown Land under early Habsburg rule. See Michal Lityński, *Gmach skarbkowski na tle architektury lwowskiej w pierwszej połowie XIX wieku* [The Skarbek Building on the background of Lwów architecture in the first half of the 19th century] (Lemberg: Makl. Fundacyi Skarbkowskiej, 1912).

114 The personality of an architect, his *stylus* (the Latin word used by Romans to describe a writing and drawing instrument from which Semper derived the German word "*Styl*") is for Semper determined by the spirit of his age, rather than by his creative genius. See Harry Fracis Mallgrave and Wolfgang Herrmann, eds., "On Architectural Styles: A Lecture Delivered at the Rathaus in Zürich," *Gottfried Semper: The Four Elements of Architecture and Other Writings* (Cambridge: Cambridge University Press, 1989), 268.

115 Antoni Schneyder, *Encyklopedia do krajoznawstwa Galicji pod względem historycznym, statystycznym, topograficznym, orograficznym, hidrograficznym, geograficznym, etnograficznym, handlowym, promyslowym etc.* [Encyclopedia to the Sightseeing of Galicia from the historical, statistical, topographical, orographical, hydrographical, geographical, ethnographical, and industrial perspectives, and the perspective of trade, etc.] (Lemberg, 1869), vols. 1-2.

116 Schneyder, vol. 2, 140. For example, we learn about the deep appreciation for the busts of Krzysztof Arciszewski and Grodzicki, Lwów's defenders against Chmel'nyćkyj's siege, on the walls of municipal armory buildings in the Jewish quarter (Schneyder, vol. 2, 325-29).

117 From his writing we know about historic building conditions in the second half of the nineteenth century, while his drawings present us with the invaluable visual material. "Franc Kowalyšyn – grafik i archivist" [Franc Kowalyšyn, the graphic and the archivist] *HB* 5 (February, March, April 1995) "Krajeznavstvo Halyčyny," 24-25.

118 CDIAU F. 137, Op. 1, Sp. 1.

119 His personal file of letters from 1900-1911 contains postcards with the texts of major national songs such as "*Pieśń do serca Jezusowego (Z dymem pozarów)*" [Song to the heart of Jesus - With the smoke of fires], the mourning prayer for the commemoration of the deceased of Warsaw in 1861, and others. (CDIAU F. 137, Op. 1, Sp. 1, L. 14, 15).

120 "In 1340, King Casimir the Great gave it the Magdeburg law, assumed power over it from governors, castellans, and honorables (*wojewod, kasztelanów and starostów)*, and abolished the Ruthenian law and all Ruthenian traditions. From the [1340] issue of [his royal Magdeburg law] document, the significance of the city is counted." (CDIAU F. 137, Op. 1, Sp. 1, L. 102).

121 Anonymous, "Wzorki Lwowskie" [Lwów Ornaments], *Czas* 282 (1852).

122 Lityński, *Gmach,* 5-6.

123 Ibid., 11. Since "Germans" were to blame, it was obviously insignificant that Polish aristocracy took equal parts in regular performances, the balls, and the masquerades during the *Redoute* at the German Theater.

124 Lityński, *Gmach,* 34.

125 Lityński, *Gmach,* 13.

126 Lityński, *Gmach,* 27.

127 Lityński, *Gmach,* 30.

128 Lityński, *Gmach,* 19.

129 Józef Piotrowski, a Polish fin-de-siècle art historian, wrote an architectural guide to Lemberg that was characteristic of Polish national interpretation and that is analyzed later in this chapter. See Piotrowski, *Lemberg und Umgebung,* 70.

130 Mańkowski, *Początki Lwowa,* 9-16. No self-respecting fin-de-siècle architectural historian would describe Nobile's own design in such negative terms.

131 Vitruvius was active in the first century BC. See, for example, Pollio Vitruvius, *Vitruvius on architecture* (London: W. Heinemann, 1931-34).

132 See Leon Battista Alberti, *On the art of building in ten books* (Cambridge, Massachusetts: MIT Press, 1988). According to Mańkowski (*Początki Lwowa*, 7), Alberti's writing was fashionable in Polish architectural circles.

133 This discussion had its roots in antiquity, especially in the surviving works of the Roman architect Vitruvius, who attributed qualities of "virile strength" and male solidity ("male, bare, and unadorned") to the Doric, and feminine delicacy ("delicate, adorned and feminine") to the Ionic. For further discussion, see Martin Goalen, "Greece seen from Rome (and Paris)," in Iain Borden and David Dunster, eds., *Architecture and the Sites of History: Interpretations of Buildings and Cities*, (New York: Whitney Library of Design, 1995), 23-37.

134 Goalen, "Greece," 34-36.

135 Piotrowski, *Lemberg und Umgebung*, 70, 130-31.

136 Franciszek Jaworski, *Ratusz lwowski z 21 rycinami w tekście* [Lwów Townhall with 21 illustrations in text] (Lemberg: Towarzystwo miłośników przeszłości Lwowa, 1907), 4.

137 Jaworski, *Lwów stary*, 46.

138 Jaworski, *Lwów stary*, 242.

139 Jaworski, *Lwów stary*, 350.

140 "Around 1776, the city started to plan promenades in the place of the old fortifications...and therefore destroyed the [architectural] landscape that filled the Lwów inhabitant's heart with pride" (Jaworski, *Lwów stary,* 242).

141 Piotrowski, *Lemberg und Umgebung,* 33.

142 Rather than demolishing these structures, the new Austrian government actually located military, archive, and government offices in the emptied cloisters and churches, thus taking as much care of them as any government would of its own buildings.

143 See Françoise Choay, *The invention of the historic monument* (Cambridge: Cambridge University Press, 2001).

144 In 1846, the official periodical of the Crown Land administration, *Gazeta lwowska,* expressed the need for the renovation of the Jesuit Garden for its historical (memorial) significance, without specifying which historical moments were to be remembered (CDIAU F. 52, Op. 1, Sp. 950, L. 5; 14).

145 "Pomnik Żółkiewskiego pod Cecorą," [Żółkiewski monument near Cecora] *Przyjaciel domowy* 4 (25 January 1857), 28.

146 "Stanisław Jabłonowski, hetman wielki koronny" [Stanisław Jabłonowski, great royal hetman], *Przyjaciel domowy* 9 (28 February 1857), 68-69.

147 CDIAU F. 52, Op. 1, Sp. 950, L. 5.

148 Ibid.

149 *Towarzystwo Politechniczne we Lwowie,* established in 1877 as the Society of Graduated Technicians of Lemberg/*Towarzystwo ukończonych techników Lwowa/Verein ehemaliger Politechniker.*

150 Largely consisting of the professors of the Polytechnic University, the Lemberg Polytechnic Society was not a union of architects *per se*. With Julian Zahariewicz's efforts, at the request of the society's board an architects' section was later created within the society, (*Dźwignia* 12 (1878), 89-90; 1 (1879), 2).

151 *Dźwignia* 9 (1878), 72; 10 (1878), 80.

152 This became even more evident when particular buildings were judged positively, such as the German Theater in Lemberg, where Polish troops performed during the Vormärz because of the absence of a separate stage, (Schnür-Pepłowski, *Obrazy z przeszłości*, 35-36).

153 Polytechnic Society members and a Cracow University professor, Władysław Luszcz-kiewicz, made this explicit in his 1883 article on Włocławek cathedral in Western Galicia (Władysław Łuszczkiewicz, "Katedra Włocławska i projekt p. Stryjeńskiego jej restauracyi" [Włocławek Cathedral and the project of its restoration], *CzT* 5 [1883], 57).

154 Luszczkeiwicz, "Katedra," 69.

155 Medieval and Renaissance buildings were often designed by Italian architects, and built by German, local Polish, and Ruthenian craftsmen. Moreover, Jewish and Armenian architecture maintained their own distinctive traditions. See Vujcyk and Lypka, 10-62.

156 See, for example, *Kronika Lwowa*.

157 Lityński listed the following significant buildings: St. Elizabeth Church (the "wonderful modern temple"), the Polytechnic University, St. Mary Magdalene Church, the *Ossolineum*, the University (former Galician Diet), the monument to King Jan III (Sobieski), the Opera Theater, the Skarbek Theater, the Museum of Industry ("which hosts the National Gallery that above all represents Polish art"), the monument to Adam Mickiewicz, the city Casino, the monuments to Kornel Ujejski and Alexander Fredro, the Bernarnide Monastery, the City Armory, the Royal Armory, and the Dominican Church. He mentioned Ruthenian institutions, such as St. George Cathedral and Woloska Church, as well as the Armenian Cathedral, only in passing while totally omitting the precious Golden Rose synagogue in the city center (Michal Lityński, "Oblicze dzisiejszego Lwowa" [The face of contemporary Lwów], in Janusz, *Lwów stary i dzisiejszy*, 81-89).

158 Ibid., 84.

159 Ibid., 89.

160 On an alternative and much more coherent interpretation approved by the Habsburg military, as expressed by the military's Colonel Mathes [identity unknown], see Anonymous [von Mathes], "*Geschichtliches über Lemberg*" (1901, CDIAU F. 52, Op.1, Sp. 953). For educational purposes, Mathes also drew up a list of selected buildings and sites he considered of historical or artistic value that diverges from the Polish fin de siècle accounts discussed above.

161 Ivan P. Krypjiakevyč, *Istoryčni prókhody*.

162 Initially "a literary-scientific publication for Ruthenian families" (*pyśmo lit.-nauk. dlia ruśkych rodyn*), *Zoria* was edited by Omelian Patryćkyj (1880-84) and became the official publication of the Scientific Society in the Name of Taras Ševčenko (NTŠ) in 1895, which resulted in the expansion of its readership to the Russian Ukraine. In the early 1890s, *Zoria* lost its polemic character and stopped reporting on general cultural issues, while transforming itself into a strictly literary journal.

163 "Halyčyna v peršom roci po rozbori Poľšči" [Galicia in the first year after the Partitioning of Poland], *Zoria* 15 (1882), 237-38.

164 *Zoria* 20 (1882), 320.

165 F. Bilous, *Drevniia zdaniia v sravnienii z nynishnimi* [Ancient buildings in comparison with contemporary ones] (Lemberg: Stauropigija, 1856).

166 Naming a few examples of vernacular wooden churches that were accidentally set on fire, he lamented the population's wish to erect similar wooden churches on the places of the old ones. According to Russophile Bilous, these new churches were not built after the "Greek-Russian taste" (*po obrazu i vkusu grechesko-russkomu*) and thus had no artistic value (Bilous, 9).

167 For a critique of this perspective, see van Pelt and Westfall, 29.

168   "Promova otcia Vasylia Iľnyćkoho," [Vasyľ Iľnyćkyj's speech], *Zoria* 24 (1882), 387.
169   Danylo Lepkyj, "Zamitky artystyčni" [Artistic notes], *Zoria* 2 (1881), 23.
170   Anonymous [V. D. Sm.], "Lysty artystyčni", *Zoria* 6 (1880), 87.
171   Omelian Partyckij, ed., "Čeśkij narodnyj teatr" [Czech national theater], *Zoria* 15 (1881), 188. On a similarly sympathetic account of the fire in the Viennese theater, see "Požeža v Ringtheatru" [The fire in the Ringtheater], *Zoria* 1 (1882), 15-16; 10 (1882), 160.
172   Anonymous [V. D. Sm.], "Lysty," 87.
173   Concerning the Congress of Galician archaeologists (Lemberg, July 1883): "It would be useful to organize an exhibition of ancient printed and written books...[that would] represent the cultural life of medieval Ruś...[from the times of] Byzantine and until the times when we were touched by the cultural spring from the West. [It would] bring proof that we were less barbarian than we were thought in Europe to be." *Zoria* 1 (1885), 12.
174   CDIAU F. 358, Op. 2, Sp. 22, L. 1-12.
175   Vasyľ Podolynśkyj (1815-76), a Ruthenian from the Lemko region, had written the famous "Word of warning" (*Głos przestrogi,* 1848) to Ruthenian intellecturals, in which he had pointed out the segregation of Ruthenians into four different political "camps" (*Encyklopedija ukraïnoznavstva* [Ľviv, 1996, vol. 6]).
176   During his studies in Vienna, Podolynśkyj became one of the founders and the head (1868-69) of the Viennese Ruthenian society "Sič." Later he taught in the Lemberg and Brody *gymnasiums.* He wrote for the Ruthenian periodicals *Pravda, Dilo,* and *Zoria* and translated extensively from Russian, French, and Italian (ibid.).
177   Judging from his "Pro realizm v štuci" [On realism in art] *Zoria* 1-8 (1883), Podolynśkyj was particularly influenced by Burkhardt's *Civilization of the Renaissance in Italy* (1860) and *History of the Renaissance in Italy* (1867).
178   "M*oja na-skroź zgermanizovana natura, jak mene vpevnialy bulo znakomi ukraïnci v Vidni.*" Podolynśkyj, "Z podorožej po Italiï" [From the trips to Italy], *Zoria* 1 (1885) 9.
179   There is no evidence of Podolynśkyj's being in contact with anyone from the school of Warsaw. The only possible link in Lemberg is Kazimierz (Jerzy Skrzypna) Twardowski (1866-1938), a student of Brentano, a Lemberg University professor and the founder of the Lwów-Warsaw School of logic. However, there is no evidence of contact between Podolynśkyj and Twardowski.
180   Podolynśkyj, "Pro realizm," *Zoria* 1 (1883), 7.
181   Realism as a philosophical principle meant for Podolynśkyj being "true to the matter of things," "material," and "taken from nature" (*rečevyj, predmetnyj, zniatyj z pryrody, virnyj pryrodi*): while in nature "beauty is what one likes; the artistic world is completely different from the world of nature." (Podolynśkyj, "Pro realizm," *Zoria* no. 1 [1883], 7-8; 2 [1883], 22-23; 7 [1883] 110-11; 126-28).
182   Podolynśkyj, "Pro realizm" Zoria 7 (1883), 127-28.
183   "By the end of the previous [eighteenth] century, voices finally rose throughout Europe demanding a correction and return to nature, to natural life" (ibid.).
184   "This rediscovery of the medieval times was also beneficial for the revival of most European nations' spirit because the beginnings of modern nations' history lie in that... time....Only recently, after Romanticism had sufficiently blossomed, was it generally noticed that the return to Nature and to real life, expressed in the previous [eighteenth] century, has not yet been accomplished....We have had enough of those imitations

(*perežyvannia*) of Ševčenko, Kvitka, and Marko Vovčok. Enough of those cries, tears, complaints, stereotypic and unnatural idylls, and stories! Let us be realistic" (ibid.).

185 Podolynśkyj, "Z podorožej" *Zoria* 1 (1885), 9.

186 Podolynśkyj, "Z podorožej," *Zoria* 2 (1885), 20.

187 With a touch of irony, Podolynśkyj describes his shock at heavy frost in southern Austria: "This news shocked us so much, as if I had not been born in the land of bears (*im Bärenlande*) and my friend was not raised in Orel and Vladimir, where winter frost is no surprise" (Podolynśkyj, "Z podorožej," *Zoria* 6 [1885], 71).

188 Podolynśkyj, "Z podorožej," *Zoria* 9 (1885), 104.

189 Podolynśkyj, "Z podorožej," *Zoria* 10 (1881), 124.

190 Podolynśkyj, "Z podorožej," *Zoria* 9 (1885), 105.

191 Ibid.

192 Ibid.

193 Kratter, *Briefe*, vol. 2, 157.

194 Concerning the Jewish leasing of flats, Kratter, for example, wrote that it "spread to everything that could be leased: Christian and non-Christian, Jewish and non-Jewish, holy and unholy" (ibid., 2, 27-29).

195 Karl Feyerabend, *Kosmopolitische Reisen durch Preussen, Wolhynien, Podolien, Galizien in d. Jahren 1795-1798*, I. B.4 (quoted in Stanisław Pepłowski, *Teatr polski we Lwowie 1780-1881* [Lemberg: Gubrynowicz & Schmidt, 1889], 29).

196 Schnür-Pepłowski, *Obrazy z przeszłości*, 40-41.

197 *Evreiskaia entsiklopediia*, 405-12.

198 Melamed, *Evrei vo Lvovie*, 107-9.

199 Schneyder, *Encyklopedya*, 108-9.

200 Schnür-Pepłowski, *Obrazy z przeszłości*, 169.

201 Kratter, *Briefe*, vol. 2, 153-54.

202 Rohrer, *Bemerkungen*, vol. 2, 172. A similar vision is expressed in Lemberg's popular Polish press in connection to Jewish taverns: "Mr. Icko's tavern stood out from other depositories of alcohol by its even greater sloppiness (*niechlujstwo*) and the totality of Jewish vileness (*obrzydliwość*), yet despite that, it enjoyed good fortune because it was widely frequented by various guests who drank there all day long" (Anonymous, "Krzysztof Arciszewski," 106).

203 Kalinka, *Galicya i Kraków*, 64.

204 *Evreiskaia entsiklopediia*, 410; Melamed, *Evrei vo Lvovie*, 105.

205 Rohrer, *Bemerkungen*, 278-80.

206 Kalinka, *Galicya i Kraków*, 36-38.

207 Ibid.

208 Schnür-Pepłowski, *Obrazy z przeszłości*, 67.

209 Schnür-Pepłowski, *Obrazy z przeszłości*, 47.

210 Because the core of a new Jewish settlement outside the walls of the ghetto lay elsewhere, on the left bank of the Pełtew River, such a location within the "predominantly Jewish" quarter – notably outside the restricted limits of the ghetto – did not cause particular misfortunes for other cultural institutions in the same neighborhood, such as the Ruthenian National Institute.

211 When the Polish landed gentry and aristocracy came to Lemberg to attend the *Kontrakty* fair, the "Jewish houses between today's Jagiellonian and Grodecka Streets" were available for rent at lower prices. Thus there must have been a considerable amount of such houses as early as the 1830s to 1840s, the peak of the *Kontrakty*'s significance.

212 As correctly noted by Melamed (108-9), even the first out-of-ghetto Lemberg inhabit-
     ants were not religious Jews, since, first, they escaped the ghetto at the time of various
     restricting regulations, suggesting that these individuals were secularized Jews who had
     accepted the norms of the mainstream society, and second, the Orthodox Jews retained
     a preference for residing within the ghetto, close to the oldest synagogue.
213 Kratter, *Briefe*, vol. 2, 187.
214 Ibid., 193-97. As reported by Majer Bałaban, there was only one bordello in the inner
     city ghetto, maintained by an Italian, in the sixteenth century (See Bałaban, *Dzielnica
     żydowska*, chap. 3, "Walka o rozszerzenie ulicy."
215 Worth noting are several complaints by Jewish inhabitants on various state officials'
     sexual abuse of their daughters. Such was the case, for example, with the district com-
     missar, Baron Rzykowski, a lawsuit against whom was made by a Jakob Menkel, who
     accused the former of sexually attacking at least three Jewish women in 1824 (CDIAU
     F. 146, Op. 6, Sp. 323, L. 1920-23, 1962).
216 One such attempt was made in 1872, when the police headquarters forbade bordellos in
     the city center, allowing them to reside only in the outer districts. Yet while city gossip
     held that Police Director Grossmann allowed bordellos in the center and received ille-
     gal payment from their owners did not reflect the truth, the reporter commented, it was
     true (and lamentable) that the Jews Zizyk Szapira and Herz Ulmer did maintain public
     houses in the Jewish quarter (CDIAU F. 146, Op. 7, Sp. 3989, L. 11-12).
217 Anonymous, "Krzysztof Arciszewski," 106.
218 Schnür-Pepłowski, *Obrazy z przeszłości*, 1-2.
219 Already Bohdan Janusz argued that not only was the loss of stone-masonry buildings
     greatly overestimated in city fires, such as in the one of 1527, but that also the Jews
     were not the prime cause of these fires (Janusz, *Lwów stary i dzisiejszy*, 26-39). After
     the devastating fires of 1571 and 1616 destroyed the Jewish quarter, it was entirely re-
     planned, and instead of wooden huts was filled with multistory brick houses (*Evreiskaia
     entsiklopediia*, 410).
220 Lemberg witnessed 27 main fires throughout its history. The fire of 1623 almost en-
     tirely destroyed the Jewish Cracow district, and in 1703 the Jewish quarter was again
     put to fire.
221 Anonymous, "Krzystof Arciszewski," 2.
222 *"Jak vsi nimećki mista, tak i Innsbruck misto harne (nema żydov), domy, ulyci i ploščadi
     choroši"* (Podolynśkyj, "Z podorožej," *Zoria* 2 [1885], 20).
223 Anonymous [Denys], "Obrazky z svita Al'pejśkoho," *Zoria* 9 (1887), 152. Similarly,
     "The town of Gozav [?] is orderly and clean because there are no Jews there" (*Zoria* 17
     [1887], 282).
224 Konst. Bobykevyč, "Na rozkopkach pod Halyčem," [At the excavations in the vicinity
     of Halyč] *Zoria* 10 (1882), 190-91.
225 Rohrer, *Bemerkungen*, 108.
226 W. Luszczkiewicz, "Katedra," *CzT* 5 (1883), 56.
227 See Alofsin, *When Buildings Speak*, 55-79, 127-59. On Vienna, see Christian Brand-
     stätter, ed., *Vienna 1900 and the Heroes of Modernism* (London: Thames and Hudson,
     2006), 49-64, 239-91; Waissenberger, *Vienna, 1890-1920*, 171-208; Kirk Varnedoe,
     Vienna 1900: Art, Architecture and Design (Boston, 1986), 25-75; Peter Vergo, *Art
     in Vienna 1898-1918: Klimt, Kokoschka, Schiele and Their Contemporaries* (Ithaca:
     Cornell University Press, 1975); 87-147. On Budapest, see János Gerle, Attila Kovács,
     Imre Makovecz, *A századfordulo magyar építészete* [Fin-de-siècle Hungarian architec-

ture] (Budapest: Szépirodalmi Könyvkiadó, 1990). On Prague, see Marie Vitochova, Jindrich Kejr, and Jiri Vsetecka, *Prague and Art Nouveau* (Prague: Vraji, 1995); Petr Wittlich, *Prague: fin de siecle* (Paris: Flammarion, 1992); Wiebennson and Sisa, 223-42. On Lemberg, see Jurij Biruliov, *L'vivka secesija. Katalog vystavky* [Lviv Secession. Exhibition catalog] (Lviv, 1986); idem, *Secesja we Lwowie* [Secession in Lviv] (Warsaw: Krupski i S-ka, 1995).

228 "*Kto w czym nie może przodkować, nie poślednia i wtorkować!*" was Karol Knaus' motto, which he inscribed on the interior of his Cracow Savings Bank building. Anonymous, [H. L....t, Henryk Lindquist?], "Kasa Oszczędności w Krakowie" [Savings Bank in Cracow], *CzT* 11 (1883), 151.

229 See Caroll William Westfall, 140. In the local context, *Dźwignia*, for example, lamented a "total lack of knowledge of the principles of beautiful architecture, but also a negligence of the need for adequate interior arrangements and the prescriptions of hygiene" (see *Dźwignia* 2 [1877], 14).

230 Born in Lemberg on 17 July 1837 to a Polish family, he dedicated most of his creative life to the city and was to die there in 1898. Marrying Anna Josefa Dawid, a woman of Danish descent, he converted to the Evangelical church and remained a devoted Protestant thereafter. Recently, Zachariewicz has received disproportionate praise in Ukrainian scholarship: Oleś Noha, for example, has called him "one of the most famous architects of Europe" (Noha, 9-10).

231 Martin Kubelik, "Das k.k. Polythechnische Insitut in Wien zur Zeit des Studenten Julian Zachariewicz," in Tscherkes, Kubelik, and Hofer, 89-98; Luszczkiewicz, 70.

232 In Vienna in 1858, in Temesvar from 1860 to 1865, and in Tschernowitz from 1865 to1870. Zachariewicz designed his first significant public project for the railway: the railway station in Jassi (1869-70), thought to be a prototype for his later Lemberg Politechnic University. Wladyslaw Zajaczkowski, *C. k. Szkola Politechniczna we Lwowie. Rys historyczny jej zalozenia i rozwoju, tudziez stan jej obecny* [The Polytechnic School in Lwów. A historical sketch of its foundation and development, together with its current condition] (Lemberg, 1894), 141; Ihor Żuk, ed., *Julian Zachariewicz, 7.*

233 Żuk, *Julian Zachariewicz,* 7.

234 A devoted traveler and recorder of historic monuments in drawings, Zachariewicz was also a collector of Carpathian (Hucul) ceramics (Żuk, *Julian Zachariewicz,* 11).

235 Julian Zachariewicz, "O poglądach J. Świecianowskiego na harmonię w architekturze przez Juliana Zachariewicza" [On J. Swiecianowski's views on architectural harmony, by J.Z.], *Dźwignia* 3 (1879), 17-19. Zachariewicz's most valuable lecture at the Polytechnic Society's meetings, "On Lemberg buildings," was never published (see *Dźwignia* 3 [1879], 34).

236 Although Zachariewicz did not consider Świecianowski's idea on the correspondence of architectural proportions with musical tones persuasive, he nevertheless thought it appropriate to praise the "new attempt to compare these principles" (Zachariewicz, "O poglądach," 18-19).

237 Zachariewicz, "O poglądach," 18.

238 For example, he conceived the idea of a vernacular ceramic school in Lemberg with very relaxed admission procedures: only basic reading and writing skills, combined with experience in vernacular ceramic technology, were to be required (*Dźwignia* 5 [1880]).

239 For Zachariewicz in the 1880s, vernacular architecture could be appreciated for a short time and geographically *outside* of his native Galicia. This was a belief that related to

the leading classicist theoretician Laugier's appreciation of the ancient Greek rustic hut.

240 Julian Zachariewicz, *Odczyt,* 19.

241 Julian Zachariewicz, "Budowa kosciola i klasztoru PP. S. Św. Franciszka i Przenajśw. Sakramentu we Lwowie" [The building of the church and the cloister of the order of St. Francis and the Holy Sacrament in Lwów], *Dźwignia* 12 (1879), 92.

242 "In my point of view, this [intuition] is a very valuable means of using for the senses of the eye (*dla poczucia oka*), which is especially useful in the erection of a building" (ibid.).

243 Julian Zachariewicz, "Wykopaliska w Zalukwi nad Dniestrem" [Excavations in Zalukwa and near Driestr], *Dźwignia* 9 (1882), 139-141; 10 (1882), 152-154. On a reflection of this shift in the importance of restoration, see, for example, Luszczkiewicz, 56.

244 For coverage of the excavation process and subsequent events, such as the 1855 Archaeological congress in Lemberg, see, for example, *Zoria* 12 (1883), 203; 15 (1883) 203, 251-52; 19 (1885), 223-24; 20 (1885), 249-50.

245 "It is sad that our Galician school [of history] connects *kraj* history to such absurdities (*nebylyć-durnyć*) as Krakus and Wanda, rather than to local monuments. Now both the [historic] school and the city inhabitants can only feel ashamed at not knowing their own history. The Cracow [periodical] *Czas* greatly criticized Halyč's inhabitants for their indifference and ignorance." (*Zoria* 15 [1883], 252).

246 The Ruthenian National Institute actually bought the land where the excavations were dug in order "not to give away valuable artifacts of antiquity to unnknown hands, and thus valuable items among the excavated artifacts will become the property of the Ruthenian National Institute." ("Sprava rozkopov starokniažoho Halyča" [The issue of old-princely Halyč's excavations] *Zoria* 12 [1883], 203).

247 In June 1883, Zachariewicz was one of the members of the Crown Land Department's committee that ventured a trip to Halicz for further excavations. Other members of the commission included Professor Izydor Šaranevyč and the conservation curator for eastern Galicia, Wojceh Dzieduszycki (*Zoria* 12 [1883], 203).

248 Julian Zachariewicz, "Wycieczka do Zalukwi, Halicza i na Krylos" [A trip to Zalukwa, Halicz, and Krylos], *Dźwignia* 11 (1882), 164-65; 12 (1882), 175-95.

249 CDIAU F. 55, Op. 1, Sp. 217.

250 "Rozkopy pod Halyčem," [Excavations in the vicinity of Halyč], *Zoria* 24 (1882), 388.

251 This statement was made on the occasion of the discovery of Byzantine frescos during the restoration of Cracow's Wawel Castle (1885), which soon became a political issue (*Zoria* 21 [1885], 249-50).

252 Volodymyr Kocovśkyj, "Ohliad nacional'noï praci halyćkych rusynov" [A review of the national work by Galician Ruthenians], *Zoria* 21 and 22 (1887), 361-62.

CHAPTER THREE

Making the City:
Institutions, Parks, Monuments

As early as the Vormärz, provincial and Municipal Building authorities in Lemberg were not the only actors in the rebuilding of the city, even if at times their role was decisive in a project's fulfillment. For a project to succeed, even the most zealous commitment by some state administrators was not enough, and even commitments of this kind were often in short supply. For success, a project required a coherent construction plan, regular monitoring of the building process, sufficient funds and, in the absence of funds, committed volunteers. Although an increasing number of cultural societies claimed the right of decision on architectural issues after the 1867 establishment of Galician Autonomy and the 1870 introduction of Municipal self-government, such claims were often limited to intellectual speculation. Together with purely intellectual works on Lemberg's foundation, its university,[1] and a democratically elected Municipal and Crown Land government,[2] they belong to the broader discourse of inventing a "national" historic and modern Lemberg.

This chapter offers an interpretation of Lemberg's nineteenth- and early twentieth-century *de facto* building practices, viewing them as complex interactions between several actors: the Gubernium and the Municipality, as well as various societies and individuals. Symbolic and practical issues additionally figured as a part of the construction processes. The chapter presents several cases of historic continuity in building practices, as well as examples of the gradual transformation of Vormärz institutions during the later era of provincial autonomy and nationalism. I argue that throughout the entire Habsburg period, the role of public officials, and especially that of publicly employed architects and building engineers, was decisive in the success of building projects. Along with their participatory influence, their attitudes and preconceptions shaped building practices.

The city's constant concern with maintaining existing greenery and with establishing new green areas was ongoing throughout Habsburg Lemberg's architectural history. Yet, closer to the fin de siècle, as the notion of public space gradually expanded from city streets to include areas of greenery, Lemberg gradually recognized the need to "memorialize" green areas and turn them into public statements that largely reflected a conglomerate of imperial and local values. However, even in the Autonomy era, this space was more often than not free of explicit, national statements made in architecture. As the fin de siècle Municipality engaged in the construction of several monuments to selected Polish historical figures, it never came to fulfill its greatest aspiration, that of reconstructing the Town Hall into a romantic, Polish, neo-Renaissance structure.

Institutions: *Vaterland*, Nation, and the Arts

Just as historical buildings symbolic for national history justified interpretations of Lemberg's character as Polish or Ruthenian, as discussed in the previous chapter, the presence of new landmarks such as the *Ossolineum* Institute (1821-40s) and the Skarbek Theater (1837-43) for the Poles, and the National Institute (1851-54) for the Ruthenians, would justify their recently asserted national presence. Thus in the second half of the nineteenth century, the cultural and political activities of diverse social organizations and individual enthusiasts, which received varying degrees of support from the authorities, centered on the creation of architectural landmarks – such as monuments – and building enclaves in the otherwise architecturally uniform Lemberg.

Narratives of national histories have assumed the existence of a great national agenda on the part of the founders of these cultural institutions, while architectural historians have assumed the same for their project designers, architects, and construction supervisors. Thus historians have attempted to discern specific stylistic characteristics that would, in the absence of agendas explicitly expressed by the actors, implicitly signify nationalistic beliefs. This was done even if the style provided minimal or no grounds for such an interpretation. In contrast, I argue here that the institutions' founders did not see themselves exclusively as great national missionaries, nor did the buildings' styles represent any "national" agenda at the times of construction. Rather, the Vormärz founders aimed to establish cultural institutions within the framework of the Enlightenment's recognition of the multiplicity of high cultures and maintained simultaneous deep loyalty to the Habsburg Court, to local patriotic beliefs, and to an array of ethnic-specific sentiments. Stylistically the appearances of these buildings reflected the predominant understanding of ornamentation as needing to be appropriate to its purpose, a major neoclassicist dogma.

Ossolineum, vaterländisch-literarische Institut

Kazimierz Tyszkowski, a Polish scholar of the interwar period, described the creation of the National Institute and Library, the *Ossolineum*, by Count Józef Maksymilian Ossoliński (1748-1826) as a great national endeavor, realized in times of foreign violence against the nation.[3] In those times, he claimed, the best sons of Poland either took up arms, as Kościuszko did, an obvious reference that he did not invoke, or "retreated to domestic privacy (*zacisze domowe*) and collected cultural artifacts, as Czaski, Czartoryski, and Ossoliński did."[4]

Tyszkowski cited a significant event from the *Ossolineum*'s history as an example of the institution's symbolic power. In 1848, when the commander of the Austrian army, General Hammerstein, bombarded revolutionary Lemberg, he allegedly regretted that the *Ossolineum*'s outlying position did not allow him to target and destroy it.[5] If true, this would illustrate what strong feelings a cultural institution such as the *Ossolineum* could evoke in the Habsburg military elite, and indeed how dangerous and explosive cultural politics could become in the years of turbulent revolution and subsequent reaction. Thus scholars such as Tyszkowski portrayed the *Ossolineum* as a national revolutionary institution when treating the history of its establishment. In so doing, they assumed that as the *Ossolineum* became a secret publishing house as early as 1840 and as it united the most free-thinking Polish intellectuals, it possessed such a revolutionary spirit from its very foundation.

Yet Tyszkowski accurately described the *Ossolineum* as initially a *private*, exclusive, and aristocratic institution. Furthermore, the institution's founder, Count Ossoliński, a resident of Vienna from 1793 on, was anything but a revolutionary. Hailing from the Galician Polish gentry and educated at the Warsaw Jesuit College, Ossoliński was one of the authors of the Galician letter of grievance to Emperor Joseph II, known as the *Magna Charta,* sent in 1789 and published in 1795.[6] Hugo Lane has argued that despite this document's harsh criticism of Austrian policy, its signatories were incapable of conceiving a serious alternative to Austrian rule; thus their conception of a Galician "nation" was distant from our modern understanding of the word.[7] It was in Vienna that Ossoliński, in line with the fashion of the day, started to collect old books, lithographs, and manuscripts; it was from Vienna that he financially supported the creation of the first Polish dictionary and the creation of the Department of Polish Language and Literature at Lemberg University. Further, he left a large literary legacy in the spirit of the Enlightenment: he authored dialogues, philosophical treatises, didactic romances, and largely unfinished studies of the history of Poland and Polish literature.[8] By collecting books, prints, maps, manuscripts, and lithographs, Ossoliński aimed to "make a donation to the nation and the sciences."[9] The Vormärz *Ossolineum* fits well within the cultural activities of the late Enlightenment in which all historic languages and high cultures deserved promotion and support, and in which libraries and museums would serve as "encyclopedias" for such cultures. The noble founder of the *Ossolineum* thus may have had sound reasons to hope for the success of his "patriotic-literary institute" (*vaterländisch-literarische Institut*).[10]

The earliest precedent of requesting imperial approval for the establishment of a public library in the Galician capital dates to as early as 1811, and it was not made by Ossoliński. Rather, in that year the bookkeeper Karl Wild submitted such a request and waited twenty-three years for imperial approval. According to existing imperial legislation, the Police Department reasoned, only *one* public library was allowed in Lemberg.[11] Ossoliński's aristocratic title and his connections in Vienna and the Galician Diet, albeit a symbolic Vormärz institution, made him privileged.[12] Although he officially established his institution in 1817,[13] a decade was needed for the *Ossolineum* founder to purchase an adequate building to house his Viennese collection.[14] Ossoliński's money was short, yet his aspirations grand: the future institution was to replace the renowned first aristocratic library open to the public, the Warsaw Zaluski collection, which the Russian government had moved to St. Petersburg. Yet only after the founder's death in 1826 was his Viennese collection moved to Lemberg, and only from 1832 on was it open to the public.

The institution was housed in a former Carmelite cloister, which Emperor Joseph II had given to the Roman Catholic seminary during his visit to Lemberg in 1783 and which later fell into military possession.[15] Ossoliński showed great loyalty to the Habsburg Court when he requested that the letter granting him imperial approval for the establishment of the library in its new premises be signed personally by the emperor. This met enthusiastic bureaucratic support in the Gubernium and the Court Chancellery. A Gubernium official maintained that Ossoliński's request was "modest (*billig*)," "adequate and deserved (*gerecht*)," and recognized "the purest love and deepest dependency for the monarch."[16]

The building of the *Ossolineum* would have never been finished without personal financial support from the governor, Count August Lobkowitz,[17] in 1827 and from the Galician Diet in 1828. Ossoliński, whose finances severely lagged behind his aspirations, lacked the resources needed to realize his "literary offering to the public."[18] The *Ossolineum*'s function during the Vormärz period is best described in a phrase used during the institution's reorganization after Ossoliński's death in 1826 and in connection with Lobkowitz's mercenary activities. By supporting the *Ossolineum*, Lobkowitz – and Ossoliński[19] – demonstrated their "love for science and learning that expressed itself fully through the support for the national institute (*vaterländischer Institut*)."[20] In its design, as in its function, the *Ossolineum* continued to serve as an Enlightenment institution of high culture throughout the Vormärz.[21] The institution's loyalty to the Habsburg Court would be exemplified by a request made by Henryk Lubomirski, the *Ossolineum*'s curator, for the "highest grace" (*allerhöchste Gnade*) to honor the library with a portrait of its *alledurchläuffigste Protektor*, Emperor Franz I, in 1831.[22]

Several related projects remained unrealized either from a lack of finances or because of Count Ossoliński's unrestrained ambitions. In 1820 a detailed plan existed for renovations to the old cloister building.[23] Yet Ossoliński's wish was to commission the work to Pietro Nobile, the leading architect of the Habsburg Court (*Hofbaurat*) and a personal acquaintance. He called Nobile "one of the most outstanding architects, known in Europe for his wonderful architectural works," and requested in his will that "the building be executed in strict correspondence with...Nobile's plans, thoroughly and forever (*trwale*)."[24] Ossoliński ordered that the former church building to host his mineral, numismatic, and manuscript collection be "stripped of its church façade...and decorated with a flat façade in the Italian spirit (*w guście włoskim*) in accordance with [Nobile's] design."[25] Although Nobile's work in Lemberg, such as the governor's palace,[26] was largely due to his high position at the court, in the case of the *Ossolineum* his involvement stemmed from personal connections. His project for the *Ossolineum* Institute of 1823 is illustrative of his vision of Doric as the appropriate style for public buildings[27] and the use of mathematically calculated proportions.[28] Had the Ossolineum building been erected according to Nobile's plan, it would have become an outstanding monument of Doric neoclassicism of the time.[29]

Nobile's plan for the building's adaptation envisioned a fundamental rebuilding

Figure 23. Nobile's façade design for the Ossolineum.
Mańkowski, *Początki nowożytnego Lwowa w architekturze*.

of the structure, a plan in correspondence with its founder's wish, but not in accordance with his means. Because of these financial limitations, the renovations fell short of Nobile's grand design. The later choice of a different architect, Józef (Zachariasz) Bem (1794-1850), was dictated by very similar financial considerations: Bem agreed to make designs and lead the construction *pro bono*. Subsequently famous as a revolutionary general in the events of 1848 in Hungary and later in Turkey, Bem was not an architect by training, but a former civil engineer employed by the military. Yet the extent to which he was told to modify the initial plan by Nobile revealed local attempts to deal with financial problems by criticizing the original as inadequate. The institution's Polish board, finding itself unable to realize the grand design as envisioned by the institution's founder and designer, came to blame Nobile for inadequate planning and lack of familiarity with "local circumstances." Thereafter it attempted to redress the situation by insisting on different ornamentation for the façade. The *Ossolineum*'s board interpreted Nobile's stylistic preferences as "heavy, fortress-like," and "German" as early as the late 1820s and into the 1830s. Short of rational arguments, Count Stanisław Dunin-Borkowski, the *Ossolineum*'s curator, argued in 1827 that Nobile "had never been to Lwów and had seen neither the site nor the building itself" and thus "made his design from the plan that had been sent to him from Lwów, an imperfect one."[30] The institution's board went in search of "outstanding architects" who could "improve" Nobile's plans.

Figure 24. Ossolineum in 1846-48. Lithograph by Karol Auer. Mańkowski, *Lwów przez laty osiemdziesięciu.*

Figure 25. Ossolineum. Photograph by Edward Trzemeski, 1874-77. Private collection of Ihor Kotlobulatov.

Ironically, its first choice was that a civil engineer, rather than an architect, Józef Bem, the future revolutionary general who otherwise was a typical, albeit not outstanding, neoclassicist[31] and who explained his *pro bono* commitment of willing service to the Austrian Crown Land.[32] The resulting plan drawn up by Bem, with the assistance of Lemberg's leading building engineer, Franz Trescher, largely followed Nobile's design for the façade (Fig. 24). It received praise from the Crown Land commission that met on 4-11 June 1828 for its "simplicity," "appropriate ornamentation for an institution of this type," its adherence to the Corinthian order, a lack of "details or unnecessary architectural elements," and the practical use of the interior.[33] Bem's incompetence to implement it, however, had been a matter of his contemporaries' complaints and led to the appointment of a new supervising architect in 1837.

Like Bem, Jan Salzmann (1807-69), Lemberg's leading architect of the Vormärz period, agreed to manage the building process free of charge because of the institution's "noble purpose" and its benefit to the Crown Land. Salzmann, however, was no Polish patriot. He was a Vienna native, trained at the Viennese Polytechnic Institute and later at the Academy of Fine Arts, who moved to Lemberg to assume the position of professor of architecture at Lemberg University and that of Building Inspector with the Municipal government.[34] He argued that although Nobile's plan was most adequate to the building's purpose, it was impossible to realize; Bem and Trescher had already managed much of the building process according to subsequent plans. It was under Salzmann and Wilhelm

Figure 26. Ossolineum after the fights of 1918. Unknown photographer, 1918.
Ľviv Historical Museum.

Schmid's stewardship that the former cloister and church building acquired its pediment roof – a feature Nobile had not envisaged, yet one that was neoclassical in nature (Fig. 24).[35]

It took decades before the *Ossolineum* could be transformed from a collection of Enlightenment-era knowledge, tucked away in a wing of a run-down building, into a monumental Polish collection. This brings the Lemberg institute in line with similar developments in other parts of the Habsburg Empire, notably Prague and Budapest. In both Bohemia and Hungary, the role of the nobility as patrons of what was later termed national institutions was crucial.[36] The beginning of the Prague National Museum, for example, was in 1796, when the private Society of Patriotic Friends of the Arts was founded by Count Kaspar Maria Sternberg (modern Czech spelling Kašpar Maria Šternberk) and a group of other prominent nobles. The avowed purpose of the endeavour was "the renewed promotion of art and taste," and in 1800 the group founded the Academy of Fine Arts to train students in art and history.[37] In Budapest, similarly, Count Ferenc Széchenyi played a key role in the foundation of the National Museum and the National Library in 1802 along very similar lines, and only with the events of 1848 – especially Sándor Petőfi's famous twelve-point speech – was the building fully connected to the Hungarian national struggles.[38] His son István (Stephen), the greatest Hungarian reformer of the Vormärz, founded the Hungarian National Academy in 1825 and a National Casino (Nemzeti Kaszinó) in 1827. The latter especially became a forum for the Hungarian nobility active in the reform movement.[39] Both Sternberg and the Széchenyis were convinced supporters of Austria, whose actions were only later reinterpreted along nationalist lines.

Founded by the enlightened aristocrat, the *Ossolineum* became a seat of secret revolutionary activity in the 1840s, yet many of the adjacent buildings that belonged to the same complex – and indeed, even the rooms in the main building – were routinely rented out to other institutions for profit. This was a matter that caused the *Ossolineum* board regular frustration;[40] in fact, however, this situation mirrored the general approach to buildings of this sort in Lemberg. Rather than become "national houses," they were routinely complex structures in terms of legal ownership, residence, and activity. For example, a matter of special concern from 1822 on was the maintenance of the building known as the "Greek Chapel" (*Griech. N. unirtes Bethaus*) in *Ossolineum's* courtyard. It proved difficult to get the "Greeks" (i.e., mostly Orthodox Ruthenians) out of the building because they were granted legal protection on the grounds that the chapel served the military.[41]

Not until the 1850s did the local Polish press, which had for long been critical of the extensive and seemingly never-ending building process, link the *Ossolineum*'s architecture exclusively with issues of ethnicity. Only was it then noticed that both Salzmann and Schmid were ethnic Germans, while their involvement in the *Ossolineum*'s construction became associated with what was known as the Germanization epoch.[42] It was largely due to the *Ossolineum*'s role as an illegal Polish printing office in the early 1840s, and to its exclusive right to publish schoolbooks during the Autonomy era, that the institution became one of the Polish landmarks in the city during and after the 1848 events. In 1918, the *Ossolineum* was vandalized by Ukrainian troops during the street fighting as one of the key Polish enclave strongholds and the most obvious symbol of Polishness (Fig. 26).[43] Yet a closer examination of its history reveals a much more complex interplay of actors and loyalties than nationalists prefer to see. Its architecture corresponded to the basic principles of neoclassicism, which were shared by its Polish curatorial board: modest in ornamentation, appropriate to the building's purpose, and beautiful in totality. As Nobile's heavy horizontal architrave was replaced with a pediment roof in 1854, an inscription was placed in the pediment, memorializing the institution's founder and declaring a faithful neoclassical message: "Deliberately brought from Vienna in golden euphonies."[44]

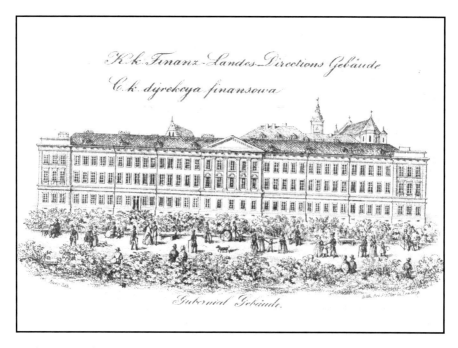

Figure 27. Finanzlandesdirektion Building. Lithograph by Peter Piller, 1800s. Mańkowski, *Lwów przez laty osiemdziesięciu*. The roof of the former Franciscan Church, accommodating the German Theater and the Jesuit Cloister, is visible behind the building.

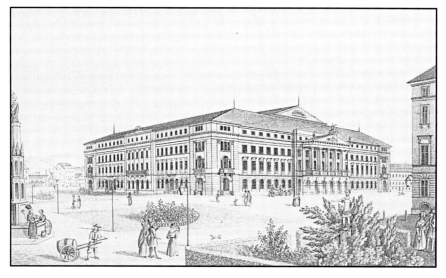

Figure 28. Skarbek Theater. Lithograph by Peter Piller, 1840s. Mańkowski, *Lwów przez laty osiemdziesięciu*.

Skarbek Theater, *"Der allgemein genüssende Wunsch"*

The Austrian arrival in Lemberg in 1772 was marked by several enterprises in support of the high imperial culture, of which German theatrical performances were an integral part. Because there previously had been no public theater in Lemberg, certainly no German dramatic performances, the new government adapted the former Franciscan Church for this purpose shortly after it firmly established its rule in Galicia.[45] The choice of this church was not accidental. Standing next to the former Jesuit Cloister, which the Gubernium had taken possession of for its own use, and to which the *Dicasterialgebäude* office building had been added in the early 1800s to host the Crown Land Finance Department (*Finanzlandesdirektion*), this complex created a powerful enclave of official power and German culture in the historic city center (Fig. 27 shows the *Finanzlandesdirektion* Building and the roof of the Franciscan Church with the Jesuit Cloister behind it).[46] A monumental entrance gate to the theater was added,[47] and the renovated building soon became an important place of entertainment and socialization for the local elite, both German and Polish, who hosted carnivals, balls, and *Redoutes* (Fig. 14).[48] In 1798, the German traveler Karl Feyerabend described the theater as "decent, quite small, and oval in plan," and its decoration as "appropriate," and he further noted that Polish and German plays were performed in turn, with the public widely in attendance.[49]

Because Polish culture seemed high enough – at least to local Polish aristocracy – to merit its own stage, several attempts were undertaken to establish a Polish public theater in Lemberg[50] before the great initiative by Count Stanisław Skarbek (1780-1848) in 1834. While the directors of the German theater were frequently changing, Wojciech Bogusławski, who brought his Warsaw troupe to perform Polish plays at the Lemberg stage in 1794, brought the German theater to success in just a few years.[51] Bogusławski's opera *"Krakowacy i górale"* [Cracovians and Mountaineers] became the stage hit for the rest of the century and later served as the inspiration for a decorative motif for the fin-de-siècle Opera House.[52] Bogusławski also restored the former Franciscan Church's building, involving Viennese building specialists in this work. In 1795, a separate *Redoute* hall was attached to the main building of the former church.[53] Supported financially by local Polish aristocracy, he initiated the construction of a Polish summer theater in the fashionable Jabłonowski Park,[54] a counterpart to Franz Kratter's earlier German theater in the *Żelazna Woda* forest.[55]

That the former Franciscan Church was not ideally suited for theater performances was an acknowledged fact by the early 1800s,[56] though performances were held there until the late 1830s when this became no longer workable. In March 1834, the Gubernium's report to the *Oberste Kanzler* – possibly written by the governor Ferdinand d'Este[57] – asked for the official approval of Count Stanisław Skarbek's initiative and described the present theater as "too small,... in winter too cold and a fire hazard." He noted the wish, "generally relished" (*der allgemein genüssende Wunsch*) by the local public, to have a better theater in Lemberg and Count Skarbek's "useful proposal to build a regular theater in Lemberg exclusively at his own cost."[58]

The empty *Castrum* Square in the vicinity of the German governmental-cultural cluster became the site of the future building that was to host a permanent theater, a *Redoute,* and a hotel.[59] It took years until the building process could start in 1839, fully approved by Crown Land and Municipal representatives,[60] and be finished in 1842[61] (Fig. 28). The building was received enthusiastically by Lemberg's diverse local public,[62] and the role of its founder in the accomplishment of the project, as well as its later management, was evident and acknowledged.

The only time an ethnic issue explicitly entered the discussion of the plans and building of the new theater occurred in 1842 when the question was raised about whether to let Jewish tenants into the building. Possibly following Skarbek's wish, Salzmann made several new arrangements that angered the authorities, who saw them as threatening "security considerations": Jews, as we have seen, were believed to be the sources of physical and moral decay. As the Court Chancellery reasoned in 1836:

> If the flats in both aisles would be let to the enterprise of a pub orga-nized by the Jews, the basis for a permanent residence of two Jewish families in the new hotel, with which the entrances are also connected, would be secured. This would undoubtedly result in the tendency of a gradual spread of police surveillance and repressive practices (*Mass-regeln*), which usually take place there....[With] such familiar experi-ences in mind, there would remain the worry that this large building, in which one with such great aspirations hoped to have organized a new hotel, modeled after the hotels in larger cities, would gradually transform itself into a Jewish inn....In connection to this, the right to maintain the pub in the theater building, practiced on behalf of the city until now, is to be eradicated.[63]

Further in the text of the document, the authorities also restricted Skarbek in his wish to rent the back *mezzanine* flats of the building – which stood across the street of the Jewish Cracow outer district – to Jewish tenants. It allowed such an undertaking only on the condition that as provided by Pichl's original plan, there would be no access whatsoever between the back flats and the building's courtyard.[64]

In 1842, the building authorities were already concerning themselves with greater planning matters related to the theater building: the rechanneling of the

Pełtew River underground and the placement of pedestrian paths around it because of greater public traffic in the area. Expecting "a great concentration of people" because of the new theater building, and hoping to house a hotel (*ein Gast- und ein Kuhrhaus*), a café, and other "public functions (*öffentliche Zwecke*)," the Gubernium envisioned what would later become "one of the most favorite public pedestrian areas (*eine der belebtesten Verkehre des Publikums*)."[65]

The theater, later admired in national scholarship as a deeply Polish institution, was intended to satisfy the general public's desires, rather than Polish national sentiment. There was little explicitly "Polish" in the building's appearance, theatrical direction, or repertoire. One of the few philanthropists and private patrons of art, Skarbek was an educated aristocrat and himself a Romantic writer.[66] He not only supervised the building process, but also concerned himself with the theater's administration and influenced its repertoire. He was, first and foremost, a loyal Habsburg subject, though not without aristocratic dignity and conviction of his enterprise's usefulness. He maintained that "the state, the provincial capital, and the public all benefited from my building work." The first received a "purposively constructed" (*zweckmässig eingerichtetes*) theater in Lemberg, while the city was released from years of repairs to the run-down building and the public "obtained a much better locale for its entertainment." He stressed his desire to dedicate a public (*öffentliche*) building to the capital of Galicia and asked for due imperial support.[67]

The architecture of the building would exude *Biedermeier* simplicity and grandeur, marked by Jan Salzmann's personal style.[68] The Gubernium's report of March 1834 described the future building's architecture simply as "built in the Italian manner" (*nach italienischer Art*).[69] Typical of theater architecture of the time, the completed structure took the form of a late neoclassical building with an Ionic portico topped with a wooden statue of Apollo.[70] The repertoire included both European drama and Polish comedy. As reported by *Lemberger Zeitung*, the theater opened its doors with a production of Grillparzer's drama, "*Das Leben ein Traum,*" followed the next day by Aleksander Fredro's comedy, "Husband and Wife" (*Mąż i żona*).[71] Skarbek directed both the German and the Polish stages, and his choices in repertoire revealed his preference for local writers of less serious productions, such as Aleksander Fredro and Józef Korzeniowski.

The issue of whether to issue the Royal Privilege[72] to the Polish troupe at the Skarbek Theater led to a later conviction in Polish national historiography that the Polish stage had been severely discriminated against. It is true that in accordance with the imperial decree, Polish performances were not to interfere with plays in German, thus assuring the survival and dominance of a German culture.[73] Yet as is evident from the imperial decree giving performance privileges to the

Skarbek Theater, the issue was to secure *coexistence* between the German and Polish stage*s* while ensuring the priority of the German stage.[74]

The Skarbek Theater was arguably too big for mid-nineteenth century Lemberg's modest theater-going population.[75] Its size undoubtedly played an important role in weakening the German theater's position after 1848 in addition to the impact of political events. A large house cost more to run, and there was a need to ensure that more people would attend a show. Yet, as in the second half of the nineteenth century, the existence of a separate national stage came to be seen as an integral part of a larger national project, and the Skarbek Theater, by then exclusively Polish, was no longer seen as adequate to meet the variety of national aspirations that had emerged. When by the late nineteenth century the desire for new opera and operetta buildings had already been expressed,[76] the creation of separate national stages took place outside the Skarbek Theater. Several attempts to create a uniquely Polish summer stage were made in the 1870s,[77] and in 1889 a group of actors from the Skarbek Theater applied to the viceroy for permission to open a summer people's (*ludowy*) theater.[78] The organizers needed to ensure the authorities that their initiatives would not conflict with the established stage, this being the Skarbek Theater, by then exclusively Polish, or with future Municipal projects, notably the Opera House.[79] Although permission was granted to these Polish initiatives, the Ruthenian "*Ruśka besida*" theater remained without a permanent home. Yet all these late nineteenth-century national initiatives had a much more radical program than Skarbek's initial agenda. While Skarbek aimed at satisfying the "general wishes" of a heterogeneous public with light theatrical productions and European drama, these initiatives concentrated exclusively on introducing emotionally charged national drama.

The Ruthenian National Institute, One's Own Truth in One's Own House

When in 1882, the Habsburg dynasty's 600th anniversary, the local Ruthenian paper *Zoria* commented on what was called the emperor's "generous visit" to Lemberg, his act of granting the Galician Ruthenians their national institute, the Ruthenian National Institute (*Narodnyj Dom,* in later Ukrainian orthography, *Narodnyj Dim*), in 1851 was described as a "gift" for Ruthenian loyalty during the events of 1848.[80] Ruthenian initiatives to establish cultural institutions in the second half of the nineteenth century were shaped by a deep imperial loyalty following the political support provided to them by Governor Franz Stadion in the turbulent year of the "spring of nations," but their efforts to realize their cultural aspirations were also marked by a certain lack of engagement. In the Autonomy era, Ruthenians grew distrustful of the Municipal and provincial governments;

Figure 29. Ruthenian National Institute. Photograph by Józef Eder, 1860-70. Ĺviv
Stefanyk Scientific Library.

Figure 30. The ruins of the Lemberg University building after bombardment in
1848. Ĺviv Stefanyk Scientific Library.

the latter had become increasingly Polish, and the Ruthenians themselves were deeply divided in their orientation and tactics.[81]

The university building, granted to the Ruthenian institution by imperial decree in 1851, had initially been a Trinitary monastery, but it was later adapted in 1783 to house the university and had been severely damaged during Hammerstein's bombardment of Lemberg in 1848.[82] The offer of a plot of land in the historic center to a Ruthenian institution was one of the strategies of the Crown Land administration to counter the growing Polish influence in Galicia, and it only marginally figured as a sign of gratitude for the Ruthenians' traditional conservatism and loyalty. In fact, the emperor's "gift" was virtually a burned ruin (Fig. 30). Yet the location in the very center of the city would prove highly advantageous and, at times, troublesome in the future.[83] Its proximity to the Town Hall, as we shall see in the next chapter, would become a matter of police concern in the early twentieth century, and the Preobraženska Church, a part of the same Ruthenian enclave, would be seen as dominating the area (Figure 31 depicts this church; the building of the Ruthenian National Institute is visible in the background). Although few realized the importance of the site of the Ruthenian institution at the time – with perhaps neither the Ruthenian elite nor the emperor fully cognizant of it – the location proved much more advantageous than it initially seemed in 1851.

As Lemberg was preparing for Franz Joseph's visit in October 1880, *Zoria* recalled the institution's founding twenty-nine years earlier, emphasizing its vitality: "The emperor's words, spoken in the memorable year of 1851, have finally come true: 'When I return, you will greet me in your own house.'"[84] These words, as it happens, were invented: the only phrase that Emperor Franz Joseph ever uttered during the 1851 ceremony in Lemberg was "*Da bin ich unter meinen Ruthenen*" (Here am I among my Ruthenians). Naturally, the Ruthenians were not his primary interest. Rather, the emperor's reasoning instead lay in a concern for public peace and rewarding his loyal subjects.[85] During his visit in 1851, when he was met with full imperial pomp, Ruthenians had to submit to their presence in the city being expressed materially in only one temporary triumphal arch, through which the imperial procession had passed.[86] After important matters were settled, on the third day of his visit the emperor laid the founding stone of the future Ruthenian university and church.[87] At the end of the ceremony, he was presented with a printed verse from the Ruthenian community that included the words *Zoria* had attributed in 1880 as being the emperor's own:

> You are my children! You are a bright jewel (*krasne svitylo*)
> In my Crown!...
> I will meet your children in this house,

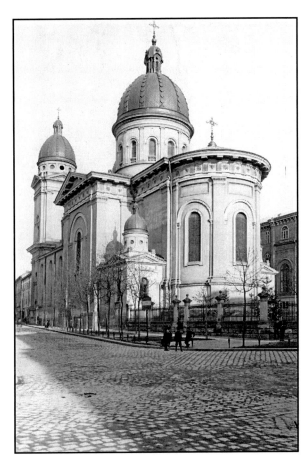

As a father meets his offspring. And when I return, you will Greet me in your own house.[88]

Thus the Ruthenians expressed their aspirations for their presence in Lemberg by placing words anachronistically in the emperor's mouth. The construction of the Ruthenian National Institute, completed in 1864 (Fig. 29), established the first Ruthenian enclave in the historic center and was conceptualized as an embodiment of Ruthenian presence. Other Ruthenian institutions of populist, Ukrainophile, Russophile, and academic orientation, such as Kačkovśkyj Society, *Prosvita,* and the Taras

Figure 31. Preobraženska Church. Photograph by Teodozy Bahrynowicz, 1900s. Private collection of Ihor Kotlobulatov.

Ševčenko Academic Society *(Naukove Tovarystvo imeny Tarasa Ševčenka,* NTŠ), did not become national enclaves to the extent that the Ruthenian National Institute did.[89] It was only at the great public meetings there, despite the institution's deeply conservative administration – evident in its preference for Old Church Slavonic rather than the vernacular – that Ruthenians, who themselves were bitterly divided, could enjoy a sense of being a nation:

> *Prosvita* Society and the NTŠ organized a musical evening in the great hall of the Ruthenian National Institute to commemorate the 20th anniversary of Taras Ševčenko's death. The Ruthenian *(ruśkyj)* House... is our symbol and prerequisite *(porukoju)* [to nationhood], captured by

our great Taras with the words "Our own truth, strength, and will lie in our own house" (*v svojij chati svoja pravda, i syla, i volia*). The flower (*cvit*) of Ruthenian intelligentsia assembled in the brightly illuminated hall of the building....This was another proof that Ruthenians, until recently divided, now feel themselves to be as one large family, as one nation (*narod*), and that they are now attempting to proceed with their national renaissance. The hall was completely full.[90]

Thus *Zoria* commented overoptimistically in 1881 on the unifying role of the Ruthenian institution. The paper significantly conceptualized such a large meeting's intimate character through a reference to the words by a Ukrainian national poet, Taras Ševčenko. For Ruthenians as late as in the 1880s, their "own truth" could be practiced only *within* their "own house," even if that house – formally a public institution – was somewhat inadequate to hold most of of the progressive parties. In this sense, the Ruthenian National Institute was an accurate representation of the Ruthenian vision of themselves as late as the 1880s: self-restrained in the limits of their oldest, most conservative and inert institution, yet not adept enough to move out into the street and claim their right to the public sphere[91] to the extent that Polish societies had through commemorating activities.

The emperor's presence legitimized the very existence of a secular Ruthenian institution and the increased Ruthenian presence in the historic center. This great imperial honor was invoked whenever the institution was attacked for its conservatism, either by Polish liberal nationalists or by the new generation of Ruthenians from the Radical Party. During the imperial visit of 1880, for example, the building of the Ruthenian National Institute was decorated with a large banner depicting the events of 1851: the contemporary Ruthenian National Institute, and the future Preobraženska Church that would be built next to it.[92] The building's architecture expressed an adherence to the predominant style known as *Rundbogenstyl*.[93] The interior of the Ruthenians' "own house" exuded loyalty and conservatism both in its aesthetics and its political orientation. As commented on by the *Dilo* newspaper, the organ of the Ruthenian National Democratic Party, "All the evil voices of the enemies of Ruś (*vsi neprychyľni holosy protyvnykov Rusy*) fell silent: the Austrian emperor stood among the representatives of the Ruthenian nation (*narod*) in the Ruthenian National Institute....Walls, draped in gold, beautifully decorated ceilings, delicate ornamentation on galleries and windows: everything reflected true aesthetic taste."[94]

Yet despite the Ruthenian National Institute board's conservative orientation, something that displeased the emerging populist generation of Ruthenian intellectuals, the building served as the site of national meetings and regular imperial visits, as well as a Ruthenian stronghold with a growing number of functions. Housing an academy, it was also soon to rent its hall to the Ruthenian theater "*Ruśka besida.*" Yet some great aspirations remained unrealized: Neither a separate university[95] nor a worthy museum collection was created; in parallel, the debate on whether to allow "*Ruśka besida*" use the Ruthenian National Institute's spaces was still ongoing[96] in the 1880s, and the Preobraženska Church remained unfinished.

Ultimately, the church was erected despite inaction by the Ruthenian National Institute's board and largely thanks to Municipal pressure. The first official plans for the church were designed in 1850,[97] yet by the late 1860s, the board, which was responsible for the erection of the church, tended to view the task as an unnecessary burden. Only in 1872 was the issue again raised seriously at a general meeting of the foundation, largely resulting from the demands of delegates from the countryside.[98] As the Ruthenian National Institute dallied with the construction work, the Municipality threatened to impose financial sanctions several times throughout the 1870s and 1880s, and the scaffolding was removed only in 1892.[99] If not for pressure from the Municipality, the building would never have come into being.

Throughout the late nineteenth and early twentieth centuries, many radical Poles blamed high-level Austrian officials, beginning in particular with Governor Franz Stadion in 1848, for having, as they put it, invented the Ruthenians. The history of the first Ruthenian cluster of cultural institutions in the historic center, however, reveals that the Polish-dominated Municipality played an equally important role in this cluster's appearance. The conflicting Ruthenian identities in circulation at the time were too contradictory to form a significant independent political force or to lobby for representation, political or architectural.[100] Thus the Municipality's repeated letters urging construction and threatening to impose fines for building delays actually galvanized the process of the Ruthenians' establishing a presence in Lemberg.

In an atmosphere of architectural conservatism,[101] of distrust of the authorities and of a general shortage of funds for architectural projects, other Ruthenian cultural institutions failed to create additional ethnic strongholds in the fin-de-siècle city. One proposal put forth the idea of erecting a monument to Taras Ševčenko[102] in front of the NTŠ building.[103] Simultaneously, it was suggested that the nearby medieval Powder Tower (*Pulverturm – Baszta prochowa - Porochova veža*)[104] be rented to the chronically stageless "*Ruśka besida*" theater.[105] In the neighborhood of the *Stavropigia* Institute, Ruthenian Street, and the Ruthenian Church, this would have created a powerful ethnic institutional cluster. Because of the Municipal rejection of the proposal on the grounds that the square was unsuited to the construction of the monument, such a cluster never came into existence.[106] Yet the board of the NTŠ demonstrated equal caution, concern for regulations, and indecision in dealing with the Municipality in even mundane construction matters.[107] In comparison, radical Polish architectural initiatives that were modeled on Smolka's Union Mound, actively put forward by skillful politicians and supported by Municipal backing, clearly enjoyed much better odds of being realized. As the debate over a Ruthenian University increasingly dissolved into an abstract political slogan that lay beyond Municipal jurisdiction and that irritated Polish activists, the project never came to fruition.[108]

Town Hall, "*Edelstein im schönen Ringe*"

Like many buildings in Lemberg's historic core, the Town Hall was in a sorry state at the time of the Austrian arrival in Galicia in 1772.[109] Several architects made designs for the new Town Hall building, all of which envisioned retaining the tower and stylistically "upgrading" to the new architecture.[110] The tower had unexpectedly collapsed on 14 July 1826, causing panic among the bureaucrats and attracting large crowds of a curious public (Fig. 32).[111] Several artifacts saved from the tower's remains – among them statues of lions, known from Lemberg's coat-of-arms – would figure as objects for architectural preservation, appropriation, and contestation over national heritage later in the century.[112]

The new building, designed by Lemberg's leading architects Joseph Markl and Franz Trescher and approved by the Viennese *Hofbauamt*, was completed in 1835 and inspired wonderment among the city's public (Fig. 33). Some contemplated its huge size and radically modest ornamentation, while others admired the rich neoclassical decoration of the main hall, made of marble and gilded stucco.[113] This was perhaps the most radical neoclassical addition to the city center since the arrival of the new rule in 1772, with ornamentation added only to the south side in the form of a relief by a renowned local sculptor, Jan Schimser, in 1847.[114]

The ceremony opening the building took place on 2 October 1835[115] and was accompanied by the installation of a gilded sphere (*der Thurmknopf*) on the top of the spire, the lion as Lemberg's coat-of-arms, and the eagle, the Austrian imperial symbol. The 1835 inauguration ceremony was appropriated for local political purposes: the exclusive public was presented with the copies of Galician *Schematismus,* which, together with the newly renovated Town Hall, were intended to demonstrate recent successes at urbanization as well as the benevolence of Austrian rule.[116]

The crucial element of this ceremony, however, was not this symbolic arrangement, but rather the speech of the mayor detailing the story of the building's construction and the great advancement that Lemberg had experienced under Austrian rule, as demonstrated by statistical data.[117] In contrast to late nineteenth-century historiography's understanding of the building as ugly "barrack classicism" and as also evident from the odes written in both Polish and German for its

Figure 32. The collapse of the old Town Hall in 1826. Lithograph by Karol Auer. Lviv Stefanyk Scientific Library.

Figure 33. Town Hall before 1848. Lithograph by Karol Auer. Lviv Stefanyk Scientific Library.

opening, the new Town Hall's austere architecture was perceived as beautiful. As one of the German-language texts called it, the new tower was "a precious stone in a beautiful ring" (*Edelstein im schönen Ringe*). German texts emphasized the new building's usefulness and viewed it as a sign of the Austrian state's reliability, while stressing the imperial role in its construction. Polish texts, such as those by Jan Nepomucen Kamiński, and German writings both commented with admiration on the Austrian imperial and Municipal symbols incorporated into the new structure.[118]

The Town Hall was one of the sites of the Polish revolutionary brigades during the events of 1848, and it was heavily bombarded by triumphant Austrian troops led by General Hammerstein (Fig. 34). Because of Jan Salzmann's personal efforts that earned him a place in both Polish and Lemberg history, a greater fire was avoided. Yet the university – the future site of the Ruthenian National Institute – and the Town Hall were both seriously damaged (Fig. 35). A year later, the question of the Town Hall's restoration was brought up at a meeting of the Municipal Building Department on 11 July 1849, especially in a discussion on "repairs

Figure 34. The Fire in the Town Hall in 1848. Lithograph by Ridl. Ľviv Stefanyk Scientific Library.

Figure 35. Town Hall after the Bombardment in 1848. Drawing by J. Dzewoński. L'viv Stefanyk Scientific Library

to [and] the eventual beautification of the Town Hall's building and tower."[119] The purpose of the meeting was to approve Salzmann's drawings for the Town Hall's reconstruction – which had been submitted two years earlier on 11 June 1847. While preserving most of the existing building's design, Salzmann envisioned restoring the sculptures of lions located on the previous Renaissance tower and installing them on the new one.[120] His particular attention to the historic symbols of the Renaissance Town Hall building, topped with the eagle, the symbol of the Austrian state, was evident. The building commission approved Salzmann's design, but because the Town Hall "dominated all private buildings on the square," it expressed hope that the main risalit be "decorated with some ornament to create a nice impression to the eye."[121]

Salzmann, who understood the idea of "beautification" as "to decorate the roof of the southern risalit to be as dominating as possible," submitted three sketches a week later. Two of the sketches ("A" and "C") envisioned "5 intruding, empty fields, on which the main 5 moments in the history of Lemberg would be presented as pictures; the selection of these presentations would be a matter of further discussion," to be located above the arched windows on the first floor. The Building Department chose the final, most expensive, and least practical option (Sketch C).[122] As it had often happened in the past, however, though Municipal aspirations were great, finances were severely limited. On 25 July 1849, the Building Department decided to abandon the grand beautification project;[123] therefore we do not know what five "major events in the history of Lemberg" the Municipality would have chosen in 1849. The renovation, finished that same year under the supervision of Wilhelm Schmid, was completed on a much lesser scale and included only pressing, practical interventions.[124] Nevertheless, we do know that the notion of decorating the Town Hall building with symbols of medieval Lemberg's strength and independence – coupled with more general aspirations of imparting to the building a more "medieval" appearance – was a desirable idea even in that difficult year.

The attempt to reshape the neoclassical Town Hall as a "Polish fortress" – as it was seen following the introduction of Municipal self-government in 1870 – took place much later. By the early 1900s, future changes to its façade that would transform it into a neo-Renaissance structure reminiscent of Cracow's Cloth Hall (*Sukiennice*) were anticipated.[125] In 1907, the Municipal Council announced an architectural competition for the Lemberg Town Hall reconstruction. *Czasopismo techniczne* published the winning projects, along with the committee's reasoning and its own commentary, which later came out as a separate publication.[126] The entire undertaking, however, portrayed as a "restoration," had a symbolic rather than a practical purpose. That was because the Municipality had no intention of realizing any of the winning projects.[127]

From period writings, it appears that in the early 1900s everyone considered the neoclassical Town Hall, an embodiment of Vormärz "Germanization," no longer beautiful. The competition committee's idea was thus to recall referentially the previous medieval building in the building's new façade. Although the discussions over the projects remain unknown to us, it is quite likely that Tadeusz Rutowski's zeal, supported by Cracow architects on the committee, exerted a decisive influence on the outcome.[128] Five of the projects submitted had clearly nationalistic titles: "Hard nut" (*Twardy orzech*), "On our land" (*Na naszej ziemi*), "In the year 1340" (*Roku pańskiego 1340*), "A. D. 1700" and "In the spirit of our fathers" (*W duchu ojców*).[129] Two submissions were chosen for recognition: "Hard nut," by a Cracow architect Roman Bandurski, won first prize (Fig. 36), and "On our land," by a Polish architect from Friedenau, Sylwestr Pajzdzierski, won third place. Although the committee seems to have taken seriously the competition's narrow architectural considerations, the winning project was selected based on whether it reflected the "local spirit" (*duch swojski*).[130] Ironically enough, third prize was won by a project that received sharp architectural critique and whose only positive feature could be found in references to national themes, though the decision committee judged them unsuccessful.[131]

Intellectuals' discussions of the projects' representation of local and national motifs and historic references speculated on the implications of their falling short of expectations. None of the restoration projects was built. The aspirations of some Municipal employees and most Polish intellectuals notwithstanding, no symbolic references to prepartitioned Poland or medieval Polish Lwów were placed in the Municipal Building, with the exception of an interior decoration, Jan Styka's painting "Polonia." The Town Hall remained as it had been since Salzmann's and Schmid's adaptation in 1849, a grand *Biedermeier*

Figure 36. Roman Bandurski. The winning "Twardy orzech" project for the Town Hall reconstruction, 1908. *CzT* (1908).

complex physically dominating the Renaissance square, modest in symbolic ornamentation, and deeply disliked by intellectuals for what they termed its "barrack style." Thus the Municipal Building remained a stylistic hybrid of imperial loyalties and Polish aspirations.

Parks: From Places of Solitude into Memorialized Spaces

The design of green spaces was one of the few aspects of urban planning in which the building authorities enjoyed a lack of restrictions throughout the entire nineteenth century, and in which they could also make a crucial imprint on the city's built environment. The city's largest, ecclesiastic baroque parks came into public ownership with the establishment of the new power in the early 1770s. By then their condition was seriously deteriorated; they, too, had fallen prey to the eighteenth-century's "ruin." As the new Austrian administration demolished the city walls, it introduced a new system of parks and green boulevards in their place. The planting of trees became a regular practice along the emerging ring road and in the outer districts. The beautification plans of the 1770s and 1780s viewed the regulation of the Pełtew and the subsequent greening of the surrounding area as a crucial and urgent issue.[132]

Practical considerations aside, public green promenades figured as spaces of symbolic representation, ones in which the Crown Land authorities could demonstrate their achievements to honorable visitors and ones in which the "respectable public" could show itself. But the planning process yielded no immediate results. Until a visit to Lemberg in 1817 by Emperor Franz I, there were still few places for such public expressions of state efficiency.[133] By 1816 this had changed. In front of the governor's palace, a promenade was laid out that very soon became the city's favorite; named after Gubernium Councilor Joseph Reitzenheim, it was known as *Reitzenheimówka* (Fig. 4). The emperor's visit seemed to have catalyzed a larger process.

The Gubernium decreed the demolition of the north fortification walls toward the (Jewish) Cracow outer district, and in 1821-25 the replanning of the area near Castle Hill was undertaken. A row of villagelike houses, streets, and plantings emerged. In 1826, the city started planting trees on the western side of the historic core. This was to become the most prestigious part of the ring project at the fin de siècle. Exclusive hotels, the opera house, government buildings, and expensive private houses were to set its distinctive urban look. In 1837, Castle Hill again came up on the Municipal agenda. Because the city walls were demolished, the area on which they had stood became public property and was planted over with trees. The German-language periodical *Mnemosyne,* remarked in 1846 on the decisive role of the governor, Count Leopold Lazansky,[134] in the reconstruction of this area, through which it was transformed from the city's "burden rather than decoration" (*mehr eine Last als eine Zierde*) into "the most beautiful splendid park (*Prachtanlagen*) of this *genre.*"[135]

The Municipality also attempted to gain legitimacy from the Crown Land's project by advertising it in the official press (*Lemberger Zeitung / Gazeta lwowska*) and even promoted its greening initiatives abroad.[136] The reaction of the well-off citizens was appreciation.[137] Not only did they admire the new ruler's "greening" of Lemberg's public areas, but many also followed this example and surrounded their own cottages in the new outer districts with previously unseen rich greenery,[138] in line with the *Biedermeier* ideal of the private house. Very few, however, followed Kratter and Rohrer's orderly attitude toward greenery that required walks into the "wilderness," an ideal into which Caste Hill was designed to fit. While the Gubernium concerned itself with a further creation of neoclassical park architecture – promenades, paths, fountains, vistas, and grottoes – the liveliness of the area was fundamentally transformed only by the establishment of a café in the late 1840s.[139] The neoclassical public park was appreciated most when people could socialize there in an informal environment.

Perhaps the most illustrative example of how greenery and park architecture could be manipulated for different purposes, and with varying success, is the story of the Vormärz Municipal Park (*Ogród miejski*), formerly in the ownership of the Jesuits. The story of its transformation has already been told in great detail.[140] In brief, the park was planned in the baroque fashion (or "Italian manner"): straight-line alleys, geometrically pruned trees, and labyrinths full of dark shadows. When it entered the public realm, it was not in the best condition and was sold in a sorry state in 1799 to Höcht, a wealthy entrepreneur and owner of the City Casino and Hotel on the site, with the obligation to maintain it.[141] Höcht rebuilt it in a neoclassical style by adding public baths, arbors, and a carousel. At first, the curious public visited it eagerly. The Casino Building, designed by the architect Mörz, soon became a center of upper-class socialization and was honored several times by imperial visits (Fig. 37).

Figure 37. Höcht's Casino Building. Photograph by Józef Eder, 1860-70. Ĺviv Historical Museum.

Figure 38. Municipal Park. Unknown photographer, 1900. Ľviv Historical Museum.

Yet time revealed that although the private entrepreneur cared for the public buildings in the park, he neglected the greenery of the park itself. In 1813 the park's decline became apparent.[142] The disappointed public soon turned its attention to outlying private gardens: *Kortumówka (Friederikenhof)*, *Pohulanka*, *Woda Żelazna*, and *Lonszanówka* (Lonchamp Park). After half a century of private ownership, in 1855 the park was taken back by the city in a state of deterioration.[143] On 12 April 1855, the Council of the City Administration accepted a plan for a new park design by the city's famous gardener landscape architect, Bauer, who subsequently transformed it into its now familiar late nineteenth-century appearance.

Care for plantings – the basic principle of *Biedermeier* planning – figured as one of the Municipal Building authorities' priorities for the rest of the century.[144] Thanks to Governor Gołuchowski's personal initiative, the university's botanical garden was created in 1853, the northern side of the *Wronowskiberg (Kalecza góra)* above the *Ossolineum* was planned, and Stryjski Park was also planted;[145] it was later turned into the site of the 1887 provincial exhibition. A key concern with greenery is evident from Mayor Mochnacki's report of 1889, discussed in the previous chapter. However, in the age of historicism and nationalism, the vision of green spaces as merely "beautifying" and curative was no longer sufficient.

Closer to the fin de siècle, the city authorities attempted to turn green spaces into public space in the full sense of the term by erecting monuments in them. We shall see how the statue of Galicia's neoabsolutist governor, Agenor Gołuchowski, came to be in the Municipal Park as the result of such an initiative. Thus from a curious hybrid of privacy and publicity enjoyed by the Vormärz public, the public parks were turned into truly public spaces where monuments were erected, celebrations organized, and beside which meetings and demonstrations were held. Until this became a reality, however, a strong stimulus was needed to force the Municipal authorities to reconsider their understanding of green spaces and of public space in general.

Monuments represented landmarks associated with nationality and were illustrative of the interplay between the city authorities, professional architects, and society. Diverse social organizations and individuals used "politically correct" historical personalities of the time to legitimize their activity. One way to assure the longevity of such self-legitimizing activities was to carve them in stone. Thus in late nineteenth-century Habsburg Lemberg, several locally important Polish historical personalities were used and abused, approved and appropriated, for diverse purposes.

However, selective as the Municipality was in choosing historic names to commemorate, its role in the "nationalization" of Lemberg's most significant memory, its cemeteries, was secondary at the fin de siècle. For Lemberg's most prestigious cemetery, Łyczaków, the Municipality decided which graves to restore and to which new graves it would allocate prestigious plots close to the cemetery entrance. In the Municipal vision, though, the cemetery remained a place of intimacy, recollection, and solitude, even if its heroes were chosen somewhat selectively. The most illustrative example of this Municipal vision is the small Wiśniowski Park, created in 1895 in the location of the (former) execution grounds of 1848.[146] Wiśniowski and Kapuściński's execution site was to become an intimate graveyard, a place where one pondered great philosophical questions and was absorbed in lofty emotions, in the solitude of green spaces and away from everyday city noise. Independent societies thus would focus their attention on "nationalizing" those Lemberg gardens and cemeteries that they viewed as contested sites, and in which the Polish-dominated Municipality saw its own engagement as crucial. Other gardens of symbolic national significance but not contested space, such as Wiśniowski Park, remained within the realms of Municipal responsibility and maintained their intimate settings.

Kiliński Park and the Resistance of Political Power

In the 1870s and 1880s, several memorializing initiatives were taking place in Lemberg's green areas, provoked by Smolka's idea of the Union of Lublin Mound.[147] In parallel with debates about the mound, several smaller yet no less telling projects took place in the city. Several Polish intellectuals decided in 1888 to erect a monument to Jan Kiliński in Lemberg's Stryjski Park. The future exhibition grounds, the Stryjski Hills, had been developed a few years prior to 1894, the year of the greatest provincial exhibition in Lemberg, and probably had developed already with the idea of a provincial exhibition in mind. Even during the Vormärz, the hills featured a park, restaurant, and villa complex.[148] The provincial authorities became seriously concerned. This memorializing initiative could lead to yet another "Polish demonstration," and the police director requested that the viceroy administration's presidium inform the members of the executive committee that the erection of the monument would under no circumstances be permitted.[149] Jan Kiliński (1760-1819) had been a historical personality to be treated cautiously. Initially a cobbler by profession, he was elected to the position of Warsaw city council deputy in 1791; from 1793 on he took part in the preparation of the Kościuszko insurrection, and in 1794 fought against Russia and was promoted to the rank of colonel. After the suppression of the uprising, Kiliński was arrested in Poznań and imprisoned in the Pertopavlov fortress in St. Petersburg. He was subsequently released in 1796. This "colonel of the people" from the Kościuszko insurrection had begun to enjoy popularity in Lemberg in the early 1810s. At the fin de siècle, his personality not only demonstrated a Polish patriotic commitment to resurrect greater Poland as the descendant of the Polish-Lithuanian Commonwealth (*Rzeczpospolita*), but it also delivered a message supporting democratic change from the quarters of Polish nationalism.

Moreover, the site suggested for the monument, Stryjski Park, was a green area that symbolized Municipal involvement in urban planning. Before becoming the site of the Galician provincial exhibitions in the 1870s, the park had been replanted through the efforts of the Stryj outer district authorities. By the fin de siècle, it would become a famous site of both temporary and permanent pavilions that were distinctive in their mixture of imperial and national symbolism, as were those erected for the exhibition of 1894. Yet until this great initiative of the Crown Land administration of the 1870s, Stryjski Park remained a place of solitude and informal socialization for the affluent residents of the city.

Of the three individuals who served as the executive committee for the Kiliński monument project – these being Austrian parliament deputy Stanisław Niemczynowski, Julian Zachariewicz, and Piotr Gross – Niemczynowski was the central figure of the group.[150] As noted in a police report to the viceroy administration's presidium, he was both the initiator of the idea and the driving force behind it.[151] Notwithstanding the sharp opposition to the idea of the monument from the provincial political authorities, the committee had purchased a stone block for the memorial by August 1888.[152] The carved likeness of Kiliński, which would rise four meters high on a six-meter pedestal, was to stand with a sword in one hand and a Polish national flag (*Nationalfahne*) in the other. Further, the figure would sport a *kontusz* (historic outer garment worn by Polish noblemen in the times of the Polish Lithuanian Commonwealth) and hat typical of the failed 1768-72 Bar Confederation, known as the *konfederatka*.[153] Both became Polish national symbols in the course of the nineteenth century. Julian Markowski, a sculptor already involved in other Polish national monuments in Lemberg such as that to King Jan Sobieski, had already been commissioned for the memorial. As the report of the viceroy's administration from 13 August 1888 stressed once again,

> In circles loyal to Austria (*in österreichisch gessinten Kreisen*), there is serious concern over such demonstrations of national sentiment, which has sparked separatist powers and opposition to Russia....After such developments (*nach einem solchen Vorgange*), it is incomprehensible that also in Austrian Galicia, as we have learned from Italy, where their national hero Garibaldi *e tutti guardi* is now commemorated in his own land (*im eigenen Lande*) with monuments and celebrations, personalities who conspired [against Austria] in Poland and fought against Russia...would be honored in a declarative way with public monuments (*öffentliche Standsäulen*).[154]

The interdiction by the viceroy's administration was definitive. In September 1888, the next report of the viceroy's administration to the Ministry of the Interior stressed that per its previous resolutions, any further steps toward the monument's completion were to be stopped.[155] Because the funds collected for the construction of the monuments were minimal, Niemczynowski still hoped to organize an official opening of the park in September 1888 when the Diet had its regular meeting, but the celebration was postponed until 1892.[156] When on 11 June 1892 the committee was finally allowed to organize an informal event for the purposes of collecting funds, its program was modest; the police authorities had grown somewhat more tolerant to national celebrations. As reported by the police director to the viceroy administration's presidium on 11 June 1892, there were "no legal grounds to oppose" the event, and the police limited its actions to explicitly prohibiting the use of a military orchestra.

In the same year, 1892, when the artist Julian Markowski had finished his work on the figure, he made an important conceptual modification to it. He decided to enhance the design of the pedestal with a white Polish eagle.[157] This caused a final outrage at the police department. On 21 August 1892, the police

Figure 39. Kiliński monument. Unknown photographer, 1900s. L'viv Historical Museum.

director made an appeal to the governor to prevent the statue's completion, and this time enjoyed success.[158] The governor took the necessary measures at the director's request, and the monument indeed remained in Markowski's workshop until 1895. As reported by an informer to the secret police, its transportation to its future location in the park was planned for the spring of 1895,[159] but the actual transportation would not have taken place without two crucial changes in 1894: the provincial exhibition being held in the grounds of the park, and a change made in the executive body championing the Kiliński monument. The latter move was a deliberate tactic designed to allow the Municipal Council, dominated by Polish deputies, to take over the project. Indeed, at a meeting it held on 17 April 1894, the Council members decided to place the project under Municipal ownership, to erect the monument with Municipal funds, and to do so under the supervision of the Municipal Building Department and of a special Municipal Council commission.[160]

The day of the monument's unveiling was set for 3 May 1895. The Municipality's role in the successful completion of the project was crucial. The scenario, used repeatedly in the fin-de-siècle Lemberg, of a group of enthusiasts initiating a memorial architectural project and then, after being restricted by provincial authorities in its fulfillment, delegating the task to the Lemberg Municipality proved successful also for the Kiliński monument. In the late 1890s, the Municipality was even more inclined than before to embark enthusiastically on a project that could be viewed as part of city "beautification" work, and yet at the same time put national symbolism on display. Lemberg's mayor at the time, Edmund Mochnacki, may or may not have been a nationalist, but he certainly declined to assist with police efforts to block the opening ceremony in a direct refusal of the police director's request of 23 June 1895. Having become a matter for the Municipal government, and therefore by definition a *public* affair, the celebration of the Kiliński monument's unveiling thus not only received all the official pomp, but it also became a means of legitimization for the Municipal Council and the mayor personally.[161]

Yet as nationalist as some council deputies were, the Municipality would have never initiated by itself a project such as the monument to Kiliński. A great external stimulus was needed to demonstrate to the Municipality the extent of popular interest in a project of this kind. Only under these conditions could the Municipality play the role of a public body that could execute projects initiated by others.[162] In the case of the Kiliński monument – as in others, notably that of the monument to Agenor Gołuchowski – the existence of a professional cohort of intellectuals who were interested in and capable of working with Municipal Building authorities was central to project success. Throughout the late nineteenth century this type of cooperation succeeded in "nationalizing" Lemberg's contested public greenery[163] and in transforming it from a Vormärz-era garden of solitude into public space for meetings, celebrations, and architecturally embedded political beliefs; the Stryjski Park was renamed as Kiliński Park after the erection of the monument to a legendary Polish "colonel of the people" there.

Memorializing Agenor Gołuchowski

Financial difficulties accompanied the Building Department's memorial projects throughout the nineteenth century. Yet a comparison of the projects having clear imperial connotations with those not initiated by the authorities and rather possessing national symbolism reveals a clear difference. When in 1889 the provincial budget commission issued its report on the previous year's expenditures,[164] the difference between the fund for the erection of the monument to Kościuszko in Cracow and the one financing the Agenor Gołuchowski monument in Lemberg was striking. Although the former had by 1887 an independent executive committee, the fund of the latter was almost twice as large.[165]

Hardly any figure in nineteenth-century Polish history would have met with less resistance from any level of the Austrian state than Count Agenor Gołuchowski, a long-term Galician governor and one of the most prominent figures in Galician and Austrian politics of his day. Lemberg's efforts to erect a monument to such an unproblematic figure – at least in eyes of Vienna – enjoyed great success, standing in sharp contrast to a later initiative to memorialize the great Polish national hero Tadeusz Kościuszko. They are thus instructive of the existence in Lemberg of a larger commemorative project that gave preference to memorializing Polish dynastic and aristocratic commitment and loyalty to Vienna.

In 1875, when the Crown Land Department (*Wydział krajowy*) decided to collect funds for a monument to Gołuchowski,[166] the deceased governor's achievements for the Polish nation were not self-evident to the general public. Thus a major promotional campaign was needed to collect funds for the memorial: the city and the Crown Land were, as always, short of funds for expensive symbolic projects. On 14 September, an appeal to the Galician population appeared in print, signed by the Diet's Vice Speaker Oktaw Pietruski and four members of the Executive Department of the Crown Land Department, including Franciszek Smolka.[167] The text was significantly similar to an earlier 1873 appeal for private donations to the Memorial Foundation for Youth in the name of Franz Joseph,[168] quoted in the introduction to this book. The 1875 request regarded the governor as "a loyal adviser to our Monarch and, at the same time, a citizen deeply attached to his homeland" and also as a "citizen and statesman *(obywatel i mąż stanu)*," and it appealed "to the hearts of our citizens in the name of...our nation."[169]

The appeal was to no avail: a lack of funding prevented the monument from being built until 1890. The issue of a memorial to Gołuchowski came up again on the Municipal agenda, thanks to Lemberg Mayor Edmund Mochnacki's personal inquiries into the matter.[170] Mochnacki's involvement in the construction of the monument to Agenor Gołuchowski was a decisive force, and it revealed both his understanding of the importance of monuments as public statements and his own identities and loyalties, which merged local patriotism with imperial loyalty and nationalism. Had Mochnacki not personally provided impetus for the project, hopes for this monument might have died unfulfilled, just as several other projects had throughout the nineteenth century because of a lack of "practical" purpose, enthusiasm, and finances.[171]

Mochnacki not only revived the idea in 1890 of a monument to Gołuchowski, but he also became an active member of its executive committee.[172] At a regular meeting of the committee on 25 July 1891, he offered several building site options to the group on behalf of the Municipality, free of charge.[173] Such sites were relatively rare. In 1891, they included only the remaining open plots on the ring road (*Gouverneurwälle, Hetmanwälle,* the Marian, and Gołuchowski Squares) and the Municipal Park (the former Jesuit Garden).[174] Opinions on the committee were split, and the disagreement well illustrated the disparate symbolic implications for the city of a monument's location. The Municipal Park would offer a Vormärz-like solitude in greenery, and the ring road location would create a strong landmark in the new modern city. Julian Zachariewicz argued for the garden option, but Mochnacki supported the downtown site.[175] The final vote was in the favor of the latter.

When the decision to place the monument on the Municipal Park site was finalized in 1900 (Fig. 40), the Crown Land Department established an executive committee to manage the project. Contrary to the previous decision committee, the new one was a larger body whose mandate focused on the artistic aspects of the future monument, yet both bodies were exclusively Polish in constitution. Besides the previously involved individuals,[176] new members were invited to take part on the committee: historians Dr. Jan Bołoz Antoniewicz and Władysław Łoziński; architects Zygmunt Gorgolewski and Juliusz Hochberger; and artists Antoni Popiel and Jan Styka.[177] The choice of these particular individuals demonstrated first that the monument's aesthetic appearance had begun to assume greater importance than its national references, and second that by 1900 a cohort of Polish intellectuals and artists existed that was ready to work on architectural projects in collaboration with the authorities.[178] The importance of having such a group of intellectuals would become evident soon thereafter when Ruthenians, operating without such a group, would fail to get official approval for similar projects. In terms of national sentiment, the cohort of Polish intellectuals and artists supporting the Gołuchowski monument was heterogeneous; rather than being united by a single national belief, they were rather linked through personal friendships and the desire to collaborate with the authorities to achieve their goal.

It was this committee that invited the Paris-based Polish sculptor Cyprian Godebski to prepare a design for the monument.[179] This choice would subsequently cause the committee many headaches because the artist proved to be careless, stubborn, and convinced of his own artistic authority.[180] Since the site had already been chosen, a discussion of the aesthetic aspects of the monument centered on two issues: the material to be used and the symbolic reliefs to appear on the base. Curiously, the representation of the deceased governor did not figure as a crucial point in discussions about the monument – the only requirement was that the statue represent Gołuchowski as realistically as possible.[181]

These heated issues were not purely aesthetic ones. The debates over them illustrated that firmly established symbolic associations existed for materials and motifs, turning choices about them into statements defining values as "old" – meaning imperial, or "new" – signifying modern, and often also national. While marble and neoclassical ornaments indicated the old *Biedermeier* values of the Habsburg Empire, bronze and realistic depictions stemmed from late nineteenth-century historicism and, enhanced by architects' practical knowledge of the material's adequacy for local climate, were imbued with national pathos. When

Jan Bołoz Antoniewicz, by training a historian and by coincidence a conservation specialist, spoke in favor of marble and allegoric side reliefs, he implicitly thought of the Viennese monument to Mozart on the Ringstrasse, as Popiel quickly pointed out.[182] Neoclassicism, marble, and greenery were inseparable, while for some in this camp – like Antoniewicz – bronze was also not as fine as marble in its aesthetic appearance. He thus voted for marble, which, "with proper conservation, can be preserved well."[183]

Most, however, recognized the aesthetic and practical qualities of bronze, often bringing up Polish examples rather than Viennese ones, such as the monuments to Mickiewicz in Warsaw and to Copernicus in Cracow.[184] Also stressed was the adequacy of bronze for the monument to the great statesman: climatic considerations aside, for this camp neoclassical symbolism was also no longer appropriate for modern architectural statements.[185] While arguing in favour of bronze for the monument to statesmen, curiously, the participants did not seem to notice that the aforementioned bronze monuments in Warsaw and Cracow – to Mickiewicz and Copernicus, respectively – actually represented *literary* and *scientific* figures rather than political ones.[186]

In accordance with the Gołuchowski family's wishes, and allegedly with those of the late count, the side reliefs on the monument – debated so heatedly by the executive committee – were to represent two major events in his life: the October Diploma of 1860 and his return to Lemberg as Galician governor. Although Godebski insisted on a realistic representation, the committee stood behind an allegorical one.[187] Some of the new committee members made radical suggestions. The librarian of the Baworowski Library, Józef Korzeniowski, even suggested removing these scenes completely and replacing them with "something else, such as wreaths and garlands, for example, concise inscriptions, and the city and Crown Land's coats-of-arms."[188]

The final decision, made on 11 February 1900, was a compromise: the monument, to be of bronze, was to stand on a pedestal made of gray stone. Godebski stubbornly refused to include allegories in his design, having modified his initial proposal to feature a heavily polychromatic pedestal decorated with realistic historical reliefs; this caused the committee to specify on 29 March a precise outline of why his proposal was unacceptable:

1. Neither of the historical scenes from Count Gołuchowski's life is readable, in general, and both today cannot do without a commentary; to future generations they will be absolutely *unclear*.[189]
2. Neither of the reliefs represents what it aims to. The October Diploma scene *is not* a historical scene because *no such scene ever occurred*. This is...only...an allegory of an act, a *realistic* allegory, and

Figure 40. Monument to Agenor Gołuchowski. Unknown photographer, 1900s. Private collection of Ihor Kotlobulatov.

thus a false one....
The scene [representing] the late Mr. Gołuchowski in Lwów does not create the impression of the impressive applause.[190]

While thus describing the flaws of Godebski's second design, the committee outlined its preferences for the monument: "A female figure (*postać niewieścia*) representing the monarchy or history and writing in a book the words 'The October Diploma' and the date 'MDCCCLX,'" and "A female figure personifying the Crown Land at the base of a column or beside a memorial plaque bearing the dates of the late Mr. Gołuchowski's political activity and deeds for the Crown Land, 1849-75."[191] Such allegories stemmed from the repertoire of familiar neoclassical motifs. Pressed to comply with the committee's requirements – and yet reluctant to incorporate the required changes – Godebski first used his personal acquaintance with the late Count Gołuchowski as a reason not to make changes, later pretending not to have understood,[192] and finally complied only after the deceased's son, Count Adam Gołuchowski, penned a letter on 15 April 1900 expressing his family's agreement with the demands of the committee.[193]

Cast in France, the monument was transported to Lemberg and unveiled in an official ceremony on 27 June 1901, thus memorializing in stone the great Pole's contribution to Habsburg Austria and its loyal Galician Crown Land.[194] The heated debates over the style of the monument and the legibility of the historical events revealed the great importance that the provincial and Municipal authorities placed on memorializing imperial values. At the same time, they also laid bare the complexity of the memorializing process and of the intellectual and political elite's artistic worldview – one in which national and historicist values merged with neoclassical allegorical representations, building materials held particular symbolism, and the actual appearance of a memorial statue was almost trivial.

Monuments on the Street: Imperial Symbolism and Aspirations Unfulfilled

Introducing national symbols into gardens was much easier than doing so in explicitly public areas, namely Lemberg's crowded streets and squares. This more difficult and problematic work often met with Municipal and Crown Land administration resistance and, as we shall see, fell short of success.

Because of the prevailing Vormärz understanding of a monument as a memory site, versus a physical object, the city concerned itself little with the construction of memorials in prominent public spaces until the late 1880s.[195] Although the Crown Land administration corresponded with regional offices in 1838-48 about collecting funds for the Lemberg construction of monuments to the Emperor Franz I and to the Archduke Franz Karl, neither of the projects was realized.[196] Although "the first and foremost duty (*Pflicht*) of each country's inhabitant" remained "to prove love, obedience, and faithful attachment to their God-given Monarch" and out of such love regularly propose the construction of memorials,[197] no monument to an Austrian emperor was ever erected in Lemberg. Over the course of the second half of the nineteenth century, the decisive events of 1848 directed the government's attention to more pressing issues.

In the second half of that century, the Municipality grew increasingly sympathetic to the inclusion of Polish national symbolism in architecture. Yet most of the monuments erected in Lemberg at the fin de siècle were not explicitly nationalist in meaning. Usually a kind of compromise between imperial values and old social hierarchies was sought, even if the figure to be "memorialized" was drawn from Polish national history. This was so with the monument to King Jan III Sobieski, a major hero in Polish national history, who was also renowned for his defense of Vienna against the Turkish army in 1683.[198]

Various city groups participated in the memorializing process of King Jan III.[199] The city first commemorated Sobieski with a memorial stone on Castle Hill in 1883, and subsequently erected a monument to him on the ring road in 1898. The idea of capping the western end of the ring road with the Opera House, together with the suggestion of erecting the monument to Sobieski (Fig. 41) and of

Figure 41. Monument to Jan Sobieski. Unknown photographer, 1898. L'viv Stefanyk Scientific Library.

building several city covered passages – all later to become landmarks in modern Lemberg – were made in the early 1880s (Fig. 42). Julian Zachariewicz played the leading role in the design of this plan.[200] The proposal by the newly created Society for the City of Lemberg's Development and Beautification (*Towarzystwo rozwoju i upiększenia Lwowa*) to place along the ring road busts of Lemberg's great historical figures, such as Leon Sapieha and Stanisław Skarbek, was yet another imitation of the *Ringstrasse* idea imported from Vienna.[201]

The existence of a Polish intellectual lobby for the erection of a monument to Adam Mickiewicz was clear in Lemberg in 1904, but even in this case the sculptor, Antoni Popiel, modeled his work on Mozart's monument in Vienna rather than on the existing monuments to Mickiewicz in Warsaw and Cracow.[202] Ruthenians, however, lacked an independent set of intellectuals who were willing to work with the authorities on matters of architectural symbolism and had a relationship with the Municipality that could be described as suspicious and later hostile in the early twentieth century. As such, this group could contemplate only in private the possible site of a monument to a great Ukrainian poet, Taras Ševčenko. The decisive role the Municipality played in urban planning affairs at the fin de siècle led to a marking of the city with statues of great Austrian officials who were aristocratic Poles, such as Agenor Gołuchowski. Great figures of other

Figure 42. Mikolasz passage. Unknown photographer, 1900s. Private collection of
Ihor Kotlobulatov.

Lemberg "nations," such as the Ukrainian poet Ševčenko and the Polish revolutionary leader Tadeusz Kościuszko, who was deeply valued by democratically
oriented Poles, were marginalized from official representation.

Failing with Tadeusz Kościuszko

When a monument to Tadeusz Kościuszko was proposed a second time by the
Cracow Municipality in 1893, the reasoning behind the idea seemed to make
sense. The monument was to be erected in the place where the legendary Polish
general had taken his oath of allegiance to the *Rzeczpospolita* a hundred years earlier, in the *Rynek* Square in Cracow.[203] Yet in 1897, when the Cracow Municipal
Council informed its Lemberg counterpart of this and of the viceroy administration's approval and financial support, received in 1896,[204] its proposal met with a
chilly response from Lemberg. The mayor of Lemberg, Godzimir Małachowski,
was outraged at the thought that Cracow might appropriate the greatest hero of
recent Polish history for itself, while, he claimed, it could not even manage the
task of constructing a monument to Mickiewicz:

The thought of erecting a monument to the Polish nation's leader (*naczelnik*) is a beautiful one and deserves unconditional support. The fact that until today there is no such monument can be explained only by matters of a political nature and by the age-old discrimination against the divided Polish nation. Kościuszko is as dear to Cracovians as he is to Lwówians, and for years there has existed the idea to erect a proper and beautiful monument to him in Lwów, which has not been realized only because of a lack of finances. The city of Cracow would like to decorate itself with a new ornament using funds from the entire Crown Land....Yet until today it has not accomplished the task of erecting its monument to Mickiewicz....On the other hand, the Municipality of Lwów has proven its...patriotism by erecting a monument to King Jan III [Sobieski] and would undoubtedly be able to meet the task of a monument to Kościuszko's too.[205]

The curious competition between the two Galician cities for the title of Poland's national capital is a related subject that awaits further exploration by scholars. In the context of nineteenth-century memorializing, the presence in the Galician Crown Land of the ethnically Polish, historic city of Cracow – its large Jewish population notwithstanding – made Lemberg Poles particularly sensitive to issues of national commemoration, and these sociocultural differences clearly led to more outspoken nationalist arguments over memorial spaces in Lemberg's multiethnic urban context. For Lemberg's Mayor Małachowski, Jan Sobieski, the Polish king who defended Vienna against the Ottomans, was obviously as much a great Polish military hero as Tadeusz Kościuszko, who took an oath to Poland in Cracow and fought for Polish independence.

Financial constraints were only one of several reasons that caused lengthy delays in the construction of a monument to Kościuszko in Lemberg. The involvement of the Municipal Building Department director, Juliusz Hochberger (1840-1905), introduced yet another argument against the construction of explicitly national monuments in fin-de-siècle Lemberg's public spaces. Hochberger maintained that Lemberg's historic architecture was inadequate, that is, not grand enough to serve as a background for great monuments; yet he simultaneously dismissed the idea of radically reshaping this historic fabric to accommodate new monuments, as had been attempted in the Vormärz period. Hochberger, trained in his native Poznań and in Berlin[206] in the solid neoclassical tradition,[207] moved to Lemberg in 1872 and by 1896 had designed numerous public buildings, such as the Diet Building (1877-81), several schools and *gymnasiums*,[208] pavilions at the Provincial Exhibition (1894), and churches, and he also directed several restoration projects in Lemberg.[209] A decisive figure in issues related to the city's new and old architecture, heavily involved in building and restoration practices, and disliked by many,[210] Hochberger reasoned this way:

The most appropriate place for the Kościuszko monument...would be...Market Square. However, one must bury this wish...for the last time, since there is no adequate space for Kościuszko there....[My] opinion is that the only two suitable locations are Halicki Square and the Municipal Park. The former is better because it is closer to the life of the people (*bliższy życia ludu*), yet as a square it is of no particular worth [...especially because] the tramway rails go through it and would desecrate [the monument...]. Placing [the monument] in the Municipal Park also has its vices. It would lose its monumentality and would degenerate into a mere park decoration...Moreover, the neighborhood of the Provincial Parliament (*Sejm*) leads to the thought of a connection between the two, which does not exist. Nevertheless, the location is beautiful...and it improves one's mood to such an extent that, although not all, but at least certain [crucial] preconditions speak in favor of it.[211]

For Hochberger, professional ethics clearly took priority over concerns stemming from national sentiment. Prone to neoclassicist views on green spaces, he also recognized the inappropriateness of architectural statements of nationalism, such as a monument to Kościuszko, to the private character of the Municipal Park:

Expansive and remarkable thoughts are connected with the monument to Kościuszko. He was a hero of the people and a representative of the idea of national awakening (*bohater ludu i przedstawiciel ... narodowego odrodzenia*) with the help of that [Polish] nation. Therefore his monument should first and foremost stand where the nation gathers (*dzie lud się gromadzi*), and where Kościuszko's figure will always be before the nation's eyes and will record itself in its memory and heart.[212]

National symbolism required a grandeur of scale that the city's architecture was unable to provide. Thus professional adherence to the neoclassical architectural canon contradicted national aspirations and assumed priority over them. Hochberger's further reasoning demonstrated that the very same conceptual problem arose in other cases of public monuments:

As early as during the search for an adequate place for the monuments to Sobieski, Gołuchowski, and Mickiewicz, one encountered the damned (*dosadne*) difficulties that arise [every time] that one attempts to select a location for a monument in Lwów. The reason is that there is no single adequate (*porządnego*) square..., one that would, through its size, symmetry, beautiful architectural surroundings, and appropriately formal location (*położeniem reprezentacyjnym*), be adequate for the placement of monumental sculpture and that would inspire uplifted

Figure 43. Haliciki Square. Photograph by Antoni Wodziński, 1890s. L'viv Historical Museum.

emotion (*uroczysty nastroj duchowy*)[.] One should [however] experience such emotion in places where great works of art and dear national monuments (*drogie pamiątki narodowe*) appeal to us....There are only little squares...in respectable districts...while the main Marian Square is too asymmetrical and, because of the presence of a miniature statue of the Virgin Mary, inadequate for any other use as a result of the most basic of aesthetic considerations.[213]

Curious as it may seem, at the fin de siècle, Marian Square – today the site of one of the most prominent city landmarks, the monument to Adam Mickiewicz – was not seen as architecturally suitable for memorials (Fig. 44). For Hochberger, just as for the older generation of Lemberg's Vormärz-era architects and planners, beauty was to be found in strict geometrical shapes, broad streets, and monumental proportions, which Lemberg's fabric "lacked." Thus Hochberger refused to acknowledge any aesthetic value in the square that shortly after his death would become the site of the first high-rise building in Lemberg, of the monument to Adam Mickiewicz and of dense commercial and leisure activity in the covered passages.

Once discussions of the monument's location resumed in 1903, financing for the project required attention too. The Polish Gymnastic Society "Sokól" volunteered in 1904 to support the monument with its own funds and to establish a committee for its construction to "our national leader and a patron of Polish

Figure 44. Marian Square. Photograph by Edward Trzemeski, 1890s. L'viv Historical Museum.

'Sokols'" (*naczelnika narodu i patrona sokolstwa polskiego*), yet these monies were insufficient.[214] Thus another decade was needed before the issue could be resolved. In 1917, the honorary committee for the construction of the Kościuszko monument – which included the Diet speaker Stanisław Niezabitowski and Lemberg's Mayor Tadeusz Rutowski – printed a public appeal that exuded Polish political nationalism and, for the first time, refused to consider the legitimacy of the Habsburg state:

> This only name – Kościuszko – speaks so much to every Pole that all other words beside it would be superfluous. It has become a signpost, a kind of palladium, a sanctity (*drogowskazem, jakby palladium, świętością*). We failed to remember the hundredth anniversary of Kościuszko's death in the terrific whirlwind of the World War. The 15th of October is approaching. Every Pole's duty should be to turn this day into a national holiday (*święto narodowe*) until the triumphal *Zygmunt*[215] in honor of our leader (*Naczelnik*) will thunder in our new, free motherland.[216]

Yet despite all such appeals, construction of the monument did not move forward, and the issue was indeed brought up again in a "new, free motherland," that is, in interwar Poland, but only in 1928. That, however, was a different story; by that time, nearly all members of the former committee had joined the Polish legions during the war and were no longer living, and the collected funds had been lost to inflation.[217]

◆

The Vormärz building authorities who created city parks and promenades presented their initiatives in terms of "public security considerations" and the improvement of health conditions, all portrayed as efforts at "beautification." Yet the realization of such public projects by other groups revealed that green spaces and park architecture could serve a variety of purposes. The Crown Land and Municipal authorities concerned themselves with the architectural expression of imperial symbolism, and the city's well-off public frequently engaged in local promenading and thus appreciated such public spaces. Private entrepreneurs assumed the maintenance of city parks, yet often neglected to maintain the plantings themselves. Although only the Municipal Building authorities could perform the latter task over the long run, by the 1860s such city initiatives had proven greatly insufficient. As the century drew to a close, the national memorializing project as initiated either by independent bodies or a rival Municipality had gradually been taken over by the city administration. In fin-de-siècle Lemberg, however, the construction of a monument that was simultaneously national and anti-imperial in character, such as that to Tadeusz Kościuszko, remained a problematic affair. Although financial difficulties played a role, the failure of the Kościuszko monument project was derived primarily from the allocation of Municipal attention, funds, and efforts elsewhere. Royal or aristocratic figures such as Gołuchowski, Sobieski, and Jabłonowski were chosen for memorialization, rather than military leaders who fought for Polish independence. Kościuszko belonged to the latter group, and a monument to him was placed in a Lemberg public square only after the fall of the Habsburg Monarchy.

The activity and professional dominance of state-employed architects ensured that until the early twentieth-century invention of "national styles," Lemberg's overall architectural appearance remained free of locally defined characteristics and was implicitly Habsburg in style. Just as the local involvement of Nobile and Salzmann guaranteed this appearance for the Vormärz period, the work of Juliusz Hochberger, the architect of the Provincial Parliament building, and Zygmunt Gorgolewski, the designer of the opera house, allowed for the predominance of *Ringstrassenstyl* in the second half of the nineteenth century. With architects routinely following stylistic fashions, there is nothing stylistically "national" in the architecture of Lemberg's leading cultural institutions of the period of Vormärz and neoabsolutism, such as the *Ossolineum*, the Skarbek Theater, and the Ruthenian National Institute. These buildings are among the most outstanding edifices of their period, together with major structures associated with political power, such as the Town Hall and the governor's palace. Similarly, historicist architecture, as represented by Julian Zachariewicz's Polytechnic University (1874-77, Fig. 21) and Hochberger's Diet (*Sejm*, 1877-81, Fig. 45), also fits well into the predominant architectural trend of the period. The evolution of Lemberg's architecture can thus be seen as a sequence of traditionally recognized styles – neoclassicism, *Biedermeier, Rundbogenstyl,* and *Ringstrasse* historicism, again – until the arrival of Art Nouveau.

Yet in both Zachariewicz's Polytechnic University and Hochberger's *Sejm,*

Figure 45. Galician Sejm Building by Juliusz Hochberger. Photograph by Edward Trzemeski, 1894. Private collection of Ihor Kotlobulatov.

the architects invited academy-trained painters to work on the interior. In the local context, these painters were the first to add to historicist architecture what was understood locally as an ethnic element. By 1900, the universal aesthetic canon – however sincerely it was shared by local architects and matched their professional affiliations – needed to be appropriated to the local context of contested identities and claims for representation.

It is in this light that the search for a national style in Lemberg Art Nouveau can best be understood. Yet the notion of national styles expressed within local schools makes too immediate and direct a link between folkloristic symbols and the national identity of the individual architect: this interpretation fails to account for the multiplicity of the inventor's identities. Ivan Levynśkyj, by now an icon in Ukrainian architectural history, for example, the creator of "Hucul Sezession," which is elsewhere termed a "Ukrainian style" (Fig. 46), also executed purely "Viennese" projects in the Galician capital in tandem with Polish architects while

Figure 46. "Dnister" Building by Ivan Levynśkyj. Photograph by Mojżesz Fruchtmann, 1900s. Ľviv Historical Museum.

maintaining a deep Habsburg loyalty.[218] Zbigniew Lewiński, a local Polish architect, merged criticism of "foreign," meaning Viennese, influence with aspirations for local (*swojski*) style and ethnic sentiment.[219] In 1913, the Polish architect Czeslaw Thullie envisioned the original roof of the Korniakta tower – the Renaissance structure over the Ruthenian (Ruśka, Uspenśka) Church – to assume a pyramidal shape,[220] which would later be seen as an attribute of the "Ruthenian Sezession" as understood by Levynśkyj. Generally, Polish architects participated in the invention of the "Ruthenian style," and Levynśkyj concluded a few projects in the "Polish" Zakopane style; in parallel, nearly every local Art Nouveau architect designed a building in the Viennese cliché of Sezession. The stylistic and generational changes within the Lemberg Art Nouveau school illustrated how, moved by the ethnically colored local debate, architects gradually recognized the possibility, and the need, to explore folklore, inasmuch as the Art Nouveau and, later, modernist canons allowed.

By the late 1910s, however, the age of Art Nouveau and the search for a "national style" along with it had passed as a result of political and cultural influences on the art world. The younger generation of architects was more inclined to separate their professional affiliation from their personal sense of ethnicity and loyalty. Designs inspired by folklore had achieved the status of "true" architecture, but only temporarily. Irrespective of local scholars' grand narratives on national architecture, late nineteenth-century architecture failed to create a single national form through the use of fragments and motifs derived from historic or vernacular architecture. Instead, by the early twentieth century the profession's practitioners were turning their hopes toward international modernism.

Architectural history is not just a narrative of stylistic change, limited to architects' visions and built projects. Alhough interventions into green spaces were just as central to the Crown Land and Municipal building departments during the Vormärz period as in the Autonomy era, enthusiasts who did not support official Austrian cultural policy in Galicia, and sometimes opposed it, initiated projects of a different nature. Polish intellectuals, convinced of their "citizen's right" to demand representation in the form of monuments to Polish national heroes and historical events, constituted an important urban lobby for such architectural initiatives. The resulting radicalization of the city's public space – more often than not, its green space – caused worries in the Crown Land administration despite simultaneous Polonization.

With a shortage of Municipal finances and human resources, intellectuals within and outside of the state administration engaged in heated debates over theoretical issues about the new architecture, focusing on such topics as the style of a building of symbolic significance and the location of future monuments, but they often neglected the real issues related to construction. Only the Municipality could afford to provide regular supervision of the building process and (often badly) of the workers. In such a situation, only those projects that enjoyed full support by the Municipality reached realization. As great as the nationalistic aspirations of some Municipal employees were, these projects most frequently embodied imperial, rather than nationalistic, values.

The Municipality, while increasingly Polish in composition, was first forced to spy and then to report on pro-Polish civic architectural initiatives, and it gradually assumed control over them. The city's prestigious Łyczaków cemetery, both conceptually and practically a private realm, was transformed into a national pantheon, with this occurring through Municipal effort. This change was possible because public cemeteries and, for that matter, public parks, did not, strictly speaking, figure as part of the city's public space. Such spaces, as we have seen, were dominated by symbols of imperial loyalty, such as monuments to Gołuchowski and Sobieski, even if some individuals simultaneously understood these memorials to be Polish landmarks. Successful as some of the Polish initiatives were, the history of Lemberg's nineteenth-century architecture is primarily a history of unfulfilled aspirations, of coexistence, and, even if reluctant, of tolerance. Deep loyalty to the Habsburg Court proved to be a strong and tenacious feeling, even if at times such loyalty appeared as a misfortune rather than an advantage, as with Ruthenian institutional centers and in the life of Ivan Levynśkyj. Like the wording of the Municipal collections appeal to Galicia's population for the Gołuchowski monument, many nineteenth-century documents employed terms such as "citizen," "nation," and "homeland" in their complex, multivalent texts. Loyalty and patriotism to the existing Habsburg state was combined with an inclusive, egalitarian concept of nationalism or, alternatively, with place-specific, ethnic sentiments. Manipulative as this use of terms might have been, it was precisely this polyvalence that appealed most strongly to most of Galicia's inhabitants. The context of the Dual Monarchy allowed for multiple loyalties and mosaic identities, taking them as both acceptable and comfortable, even if the composite elements seemed too incongruent to form a whole.

Notes

1   This discussion among Polish intellectuals came as a reaction to the official Austrian founding of a modern university in Lemberg by Joseph II, and claimed a historic continuity between Lemberg University and the earlier Jesuit College.

2   This was interpreted as a continuation of the earlier Magdeburg law, abolished by the Austrians shortly after 1772.

3   "The national institution in the name of Ossoliński was created in a difficult moment for the Polish nation when foreign violence (*przemoc*) conquered [our] political independence and when an orgy of Germanization and Russification spread unrestrained throughout Polish lands" (Tyszkowski, 51).

4   Dr. Kazimierz Tyszkowski, "W stulecie Ossolineum," in Janusz, *Lwów stary i dzisiejszy*, 50.

5   Tyszkowski, 51. Wilhelm Karl Konrad Freiherr von Hammerstein was governor-general of Galicia in June and July 1848.

6   Ernest Traugott Kortum, *Magna Charta von Galizien oder Untersuchung der Beschwerden des Galizischen Adels polnischer Nation über die österreichische Regierung* (Iaşy, 1790). See Wolff, 828-33. According to Lane ("Szlachta Outside the Commonwealth," 526-42), it was published in Heinrich Moritz Gottlieb Grellmann, *Statistische Aufklärung über wichtige Theile und Gegenstände der österreichischen Monarchie*, vol. 1, Göttingen 1795.

7   Lane, "Szlachta Outside the Commonwealth," 530-42; Wolff, 828-33.

8   See Eva-Maria Hüttl-Hupert, "Die edle Leidenschaft. Das 'Ossolineum' und sein Schöpfer," in Bisanz, 26-32.

9   As expressed by Joseph Maus, a German university professor with Enlightenment leanings and sympathies to Polish culture (Mańkowski, *Dzieje gmachu*, 29).

10   A government official warmly commented (in German) in 1826 on the quality of the *Ossolineum*'s natural collection, seeing it as equal to other European collections (CDIAU F. 146, Op. 7, Sp. 1615, L. 24).

11   Inherited by his son Ludwig Wild in 1836 and by the latter's brother-in-law Eduard Winiarz, Wild's library was finally closed in favor of Franz Galiński, who in 1839 asked for permission to open his own public library in his bookstore (CDIAU F. 146, Op. 7, Sp. 2293, 11-21, 29-30).

12   The Diet supported his project, as became evident again in his request, albeit unsuccessful, for a tax-free land lease in the 1820s (Mańkowski, *Dzieje gmachu*, 36).

13   On the Galician Gubernium's correspondence with the Austrian Ministry of the Interior about its establishment of the *Ossolineum* (1817-18) see CDIAU F. 146, Op. 7, Sp. 860.

14   Apparently during Ossoliński's visit to Lemberg in 1817, he was already in search of an appropriate building (Mańkowski, *Dzieje gmachu*, 29).

15   Negligence caused a great fire in 1804, and the building stood in ruins thereafter, which allowed Ossoliński to buy it with his modest means (ibid., 24).

16   CDIAU F. 147, Op. 7, Sp. 860, L. 5.

17   August Longin Fürst von Lobkowitz served as governor-general of Galicia between 1826 and 1832.

18   Mańkowski, *Dzieje gmachu,* 35.

19   His own intentions, merging imperial loyalty and noble pride in making such donations, were articulated in his letter to the Galician governor in 1819 (ibid.).

20   CDIAU F. 146, Op. 7, Sp. 1615, L. 1. In this letter to the court chancellery, the governor's administration recognized Ossoliński's "citizens' eagerness...and work on the [establishment] of the *Ossolineum* Library (ibid., L. 43).

21   In 1836, for example, Franz Tschischka laconically commented on it: "Many items related to art can be found in the public library, founded by Count...Ossoliński, which is particularly rich in Polish literature, [and] has antique and coin collections" (Tschischka, 268).

22   CDIAU F. 146, Op. 7, Sp. 860, L. 12.

23   Mańkowksi, *Dzieje gmachu,* 38.

24   Ibid., 39.

25   Ibid., 54.

26   See Tschischka, 268, and Łoza, 217.

27   Yet neither were Ionic and Corinthian stylistic taboos; in some of the sketches for the *Ossolineum,* Nobile envisioned Corinthian columns. His final choice of the Doric for the building of culture was rather a matter of his personal stylistic preference and financial considerations. Nobile's governor's palace (1821), together with the *Redoute* of the German theater (arch. Mörz, 1784-1795), reveals that the elegant, resolute, and elevated style reminiscent of the French style of the Second Empire could also at times be appropriate.

28   Mańkowski, *Dzieje gmachu*, 42.

29   Ibid., 45.

30   Nobile designed *Ossolineum* in Vienna, having been provided with the parameters by Municipal Building Department employees and heavily relying on his earlier model projects (ibid., 43).

31   In the situation of chronic lack of finances, the search for an "outstanding architect" expectedly ended with the cheapest one. Józef Bem, who had not previously been commissioned for any serious architectural work of his own, agreed to make new plans and curate the building process free of charge. Bem admired Vignola, routinely made mathematical calculations of proportions of the building's parts, and was informed by Sebastian Sierakowski's theoretical work (ibid., 58-64, 70).

32   "The Prov. Dpt appreciates Captain Józef Bem's citizen's readiness to serve the public good, whose work puts a duty of gratitude on both the Prov. Dpt. and the whole publicity" (ibid., 63).

33   The commission's members included Józef Dzierkowski, Tadeusz Wasilewski, and Wincenty Zietkiewicz (ibid., 77-78).

34   Salzmann was born in Vienna and later died there. In 1840, he became Municipal Building Department director in Lemberg. His involvement with the construction of the Skarbek Theater, the *Ossolineum*, the archbishop's palace (1844), and the reconstruction of the Town Hall (1848-49) established his professional presence in Lemberg (See Jaworski, *Ratusz lwowski*, 83, 90; Piotrowski, *Lemberg und Umgebung*, 141, 145, 206; Mańkowski, *Początki Lwowa*, 370-71; Łoza, 268).

35   Mańkowski, *Dzieje gmachu,* 91-94, 115-17.

36   On Bohemia, see especially Eagle Glassheim, *Noble Nationalists: The Transformation of the Bohemian Aristocracy* (Cambridge, Massachusetts: Harvard University Press, 2005) 10-49; also see John F.N. Bradley, *Czech Nationalism in the Nineteenth Century* (Boulder: East European Monographs, 1984), 8-11, 15-16. On Hungary, see Janos Varga, *A Hungarian Quo Vadis: Political Trends and Theories of the Early 1840s* (Budapest: Akademiai Kiado, 1993), 22-42, 160-213. Also see Alice Freifeld, *Nationalism and the Crowd in Liberal Hungary, 1848-1914* (Washington, D.C.: Woodrow Wilson Center Press, 2000); András Gerő, ed., *Hungarian Liberals* (Budapest: Uj Mandatum Konyvkiado, 1999). On István Széchenyi, see Bettina Gneisse, *Istvan Szechenyis Kasinobewegung im ungarischen Reformzeitalter (1825-1848): ein Beitrag zur Erforschung der Anfange der nationalliberalen Organisation im vormarzlichen Ungarn* (Frankfurt am Main: Peter Lang, 1990); Andreas Oplatka, *Graf Stephan Szechenyi: Der Mann, der Ungarn schuf* (Vienna: Paul Zsolnay Verlag, 2004); also see George Barany, *Stephen Szechenyi and the Awakening of Hungarian Nationalism, 1791-1841* (Princeton: Princeton University Press, 1968).

37   The museum did not collect historical artifacts until the 1830s and 1840s, and its first association with Czech nationalism dates to the 1820s and is connected to the activity of František Palacky. In fact it was solely due to the Sternbergs that Palacky became involved. See Joseph Frederick Zacek, *Palacky: The Historian as Scholar and Nationalist* (The Hague: Mouton, 1970), 18-19; Derek Sayer, *The Coasts of Bohemia: A Czech History* (Princeton: Princeton University Press, 1998), 53-69, 98-102, 120, 142; Peter Demetz, *Prague in Black and Gold: Scenes from the Life of a European City* (New York: Hill and Wang, 1997), 278-79; Katerina Beckova, *Wenceslas Square in the Course of Bygone Centuries* (Prague: Schola Ludus Pragensia, 1993).

38   Freifeld, 45-58.

39   Gneisse, *Istvan Szechenyis Kasinobewegung*; Freifeld, 32; Oplatka, 217-43, 337-72; Barany, 36, 118, 138, 220, 222, 245, 273-77, 301, 308, 355-56.

40   The former Carmelite Cloister housed the *Ossolineum*, and it rented residences and offices to other insitutions. The demolition of the adjacent buildings was completed in 1837-39, during the reconstruction of Szeroka Street, though the buildings in the back courtyard were retained.

41   Such efforts were made in 1832, 1839, and 1844. It is believed that for this reason the chapel was associated with a Bukowina religious fund, from which its rent was paid. Lemberg's renowned playwright, Aleksander Fredro, who rented the backyard building as his private residence, did not see the urgency of removing the chapel from the building complex (ibid., 100-102).

42   The debates in the press were started in 1850 by an anonymous article in the Poznań-based newspaper *Gazeta polska*, which was soon echoed by Karol Szajnocha in *Ty-*

godnik lwowski (no. 22, 1850), and followed by publications by the Ossolineum's vice curator, Jan Szlachtowski, in the same periodical (ibid., 126).

43 The Ossolineum acquired this printing monopoly in 1878. It is believed that during the turbulent Polish-Ukrainian street fighting of 1918, the Ukrainian regiment that seized the building used books from the library as shields in the windows (ibid., 134).

44 *"W głoskach złocistych z Wiednia umyślnie sprowadzonych."* See Mańkowski, *Dzieje gmachu.*

45 Prior to the former Franciscan Church's adaptation of the building, the German theater was located in a primitive wooden construction across from the Jesuit Gate. Because its condition became critical in 1783, it was soon reassembled (Piotrowski, *Lemberg und Umgebung,* 28). For a concise summary of the history of the Lemberg theater during the Vormärz, see Victor Proskuriakov, Jurij Jamaš, "Skromni škicy pro dijanisť poľśkoho teatru u Lvovi," [Modest Sketches of the history of Polish theater in Ľviv] *HB* no. 11, January 1996, pp. 14-15; *HB* no. 8 "Teatr," November 1995. For a general discussion of the history of Lemberg theater, see Jerzy Got, *Das österreichische Theater in Lemberg im 18. und 19. Jahrhundert. Aus dem Theaterleben der Vielvölkermonarchie* (Wien 1997); Zbigniew Raszewski, *Krótka historia teatru polskiego* (Warszawa 1977).

46 For plans of this bureaucratic quarter, together with the theater site, see, for example, CDIAU F. 146, Op. 7, Sp. 3365, L. 1-7. For the correspondence between the Building Department and the Municipality concerning the construction of the Skarbek Theater, see CDIAU F. 146, Op. 78, Sp. 23 (1833-44), Sp. 24-27 (1834-48). For an overview of Lemberg's theater history, see *HB* 8 (November 1995) "Teatr."

47 While acquiring a plot from the former Minoriten Cloister for Henrich Bulla's theater enterprise in 1792, the authorities ensured that the parcel outside the church wall, on the side of Fowls Square (*Hühnerplatz,* destroyed in 1848), would remain unbuilt and would be used as a public pathway as well as an access route to the theater building (CDIAU F. 146, Op. 7, Sp. 3365, L. 11-12).

48 *Redoute* referred both to the building in which the elite's balls and masquerades took place and – especially in the absence of a dedicated building – to the event itself.

49 Feyerabend, *Kosmopolitische Reisen,* 4; quoted in Pepłowski, 30.

50 Polish plays were traditionally performed in the residences of the aristocracy, as at the Wronowski palace.

51 Wojciech Bogusławski (1757-1829) was the leading neoclassical playwright, a theater director, revolutionary, and Freemason. He first resided in Lemberg in 1781, and he moved to Poznan in 1783 because of a financial concession to a Polish stage there. Until his longer stay in Lemberg of 1795-99, he directed plays in Grodno, Wilno, Dubno, and Warsaw. In Lemberg, he cooperated with his student and future leading local playwright, Jan Nepomucen Kamiński. See Zbigniew Raszewski, *Bogusławski* (Warszawa 1982).

52 Bogusławski also staged Shakespeare's "Hamlet" in Polish, in his own translation based on the text of a German adaptation.

53 Plans by a local architect, Mörz, 1795.

54 1820s, local Italian arch. Maraino.

55 Pepłowski, 27.

56 The theater's deteriorating condition and occasional accidents were reported as early as 1807. The court adviser (*Hofrat*) Mitscha, for example, reported in 1807 the critical condition of the theater building that could "collapse at any time." Police Director Joseph Rohrer also reported on the same issue (CDIAU F. 146, Op. 6, Sp. 46).

57   Ferdinand Karl Joseph d'Este, Erzherzog von Österreich served as governor general of Galicia between 1832 and 1846.

58   CDIAU F. 146, Op. 1, Sv.76, Sp. 1426, L. 2. In consequence, Alois Ludwik Pichl (1782-1856), Viennese architect and a member of St. Lucas Academy in Rome, traveled to Lemberg in 1833 to examine the site for the future theater (Łoza, 233).

59   On 30 July 1783, Emperor Joseph II presented the square to the city on the condition that it would be developed as a site for a permanent theater, a *Redoute,* and a hotel. When the building was erected, it also housed rental units and a café.

60   Lityński, 46; 62.

61   As a consequence, Skarbek was awarded the medal of St. Stephen, (CDIAU F. 146, Op. 1, Sv. 76, Sp. 1429, L. 6, 8, 14). On the interwar-period plans of the building, see DALO F. 2, Op. 4, Sp. 1092.

62   CDIAU, F. 146, Op. 1, Sp. 1426.

63   Ibid., L. 42-45.

64   Ibid., L. 45-48.

65   CDIAU F. 146, Op. 1, Sp. 1428, L. 17-18. For further detailed issues concerning the river rechanneling and the pedestrian paths around the theater building, see ibid., L. 18-19. In the intervening time, the old theater building was adapted for archival use in 1838 (CDIAU F. 726, Op. 1, Sp. 385, L. 1-6).

66   In the humanist tradition, Skarbek established the Institute of the Poor in Drohowyż, his country estate. His novels *Tarło* and *Damian Ruszczyc* follow a literary trend in mid-nineteenth century Romantic literature known as Walter-Scottism.

67   "In the opposite case," he reasoned, he would have to "resign from this enterprise, patronized by Your Majestic Dignity, with great regret" (CDIAU F. 146, Op. 1, Sv. 76, Sp. 1426, L. 8-10). Further see ibid., L. 5-29; 38-60.

68   According to the imperial decree, the future building was to correspond as closely as possible to the original plan and design by Alois Pichl. Skarbek's wish, motivated by greater expenses to be caused by a close following of Pichl's plans, was to keep the original design for the main (theater) building, but the remaining parts, which together occupied the whole quarter, were to be erected after Salzmann's cheaper plan. (Pepłowski, 174).

69   CDIAU F. 146, Op. 1, Sv. 76, Sp. 1426, L. 4.

70   The statue soon became the topic of local urban folklore: it was blown away and destroyed by a strong wind shortly after the official opening of the theater.

71   Lityński, 62. According to Pepłowski (183), the Polish play was titled "*Śluby panieńskie,*" also a comedy by Alexander Fredro.

72   The Royal Privilege freed the Skarbek Theater from state tax for thirty years.

73   Lityński, 74.

74   "Count Skarbek also (*allein*) asks to allow him to maintain (*freylassen*) a Polish stage and…to perform plays in Italian and French. One could mention this in its proper place in the [text of the] Privilege, though according to its general formulation, the [German theater's] exclusive right to hold plays, *redoute*s, and masquerade balls, no second Polish stage could be opened [separately]" (CDIAU F. 146, Op. 1, Sv. 76, Sp. 1426, L. 55.

75   Lane, *State Culture and National Identity.*

76   Although for a variety of reasons Polish operetta has always been more successful on the Lemberg stage than German drama, this popularity stemmed from the termination of Skarbek's privilege, which also caused the final decline of the German stage in the

late nineteenth century. On national symbolism being superseded by an imperial one as regards symbolism of ornamentation in the Opera House, see Lane, *State Culture and National Identity*. For the building process of the Opera House, see Pavlo Grankin, "Ľvivśkyj opernyj teatr: istorija budovy i restavraciï." *Budujemo inakše* 6 (2000), 1 (2001).

77   In 1872, the Municipality refused to support a proposal for a summer theater in the Municipal Park. In 1874, a Wolenski erected a temporary wooden theater in the Riflemen's Shooting Range, which, however, failed (Pepłowski, 341; 357).

78   The idea was conceived of by an actor, Lucian Kwieciński, who aimed at incorporating the nation's "legends, history, [...and] vast musical material" into national (*swojskie*) operettas for the future theater. Kwieciński suggested *Rundbogenstyl* (*styl altanowy*) as the theater's architectural style, using the Warsaw theater as a model (CDIAU F. 146, Op. 7, Sp. 4471, L. 11-13).

79   Ibid.

80   "Ročnycia 600-litnioho panovania Habsburskoï Dynastiï," *Zoria* 24, (1882), 386-87.

81   See Wendland, *Russophilen*; Mick, "Nationalisierung in einer multiethnischen Stadt."

82   The Ruthenian National Institute's designer was the aforementioned construction manager of the Ossolineum, German architect Wilhelm Schmid. On the collection of funds for the establishment of the Ruthenian National Institute and the church by the Ruthenian National Council (*Nacionaľne Sobranije*) in 1851, see CDIAU F. 146, Op. 7, Sp. 3117. For the plans of the building, see DALO F. 2, Op. 4, Sp. 1080.

83   The *Ruthenian National Institute* was a place for Ruthenian socialization in the 1880s: Ruthenians held meetings on its premises rather than on the street because "important for their nation" issues were to be discussed in "their own house," rather than in public ("Zamitky i visty," *Zoria* 21(1880), 283-84).

84   "Zakladyny Narodnoho Domu (Zhadka z roku 1851)," *Zoria* 17 (1880), 235-36.

85   As the emperor commented at the end of his visit to Galicia in 1851, after a similar ceremony in the district town of Sambor: "It pleased me to lay the foundation stone for Ruthenians for their future development (*zu ihrer künftigen Ausbildung*). I am grateful. Ruthenians always showed order and loyalty. I will take care to support the Ruthenian nation" (ibid.).

86   This arch was constructed by a "Ruthenian M." on Grodecka Road, and was decorated with blue-and-yellow strips and an inscription in Ruthenian reading "Hail to Franz Joseph" (ibid.).

87   An initial proposal had been put forth as early as 1849 to build a Ruthenian university and church on this plot of land, for which purpose the National Institute Foundation was established and donations were collected for the project throughout Galicia (Žuk, 5).

88   "Zakladyny," 235.

89   The *Prosvita* (est. 1868) society was established by a younger, educated, and nonclerical generation of Galician Ruthenians who sought to secure ties with what they believed to be their conationals in Ukraine across the Russian imperial border. NTŠ (founded in 1873) was similarly established by Galician Ruthenians, but it became a serious institution only of academic excellence with Mychajlo Hruševśkyj (in Polish spelling, Michał Hruszewski), a leading historian from the Russian Ukraine, assuming the position of its head in 1897. In consequence, the older institution of the National Institute (*Narodnyj Dom*) became a stronghold of the older, Russophile, clerical Ruthenian elite. See Wendland, *Russophilen*, Mick, "Nationalisierung in einer multiethnischen Stadt."

90 "Muzykaľno-deklamacijnyj večir v XX-ij rokovyny smerty Tarasa Ševčenka," *Zoria* 5, (1881), 66.

91 In the 1880s, for example, a much greater demand existed for indoor busts of Ukrainian national leaders, such as Ševčenko and Chmeľnyćkyj (*Zoria* 5, [1881], 67-68; 11[1881], 132; 139), although the explicit demands for national monuments had been given only voice by very few individuals, mostly in connection with the Chmeľnyćkyj monument in Kyiv. "Has it really been decided to abandon the idea of allegorical figures, so beautiful and so touching to every Ruthenian-Ukrainian's heart: the freeing of the Ukrainian nation (*narodu*) from the Polish yoke with the inscription, 'It could not be better than in our own country, in Ukraine, where there would be no Poles, there would be no Jews'" ("Z svita artystyčnoho" *Zoria* 11 [1881], 167).

92 Brightly illuminated at night, the banner is reported to have attracted crowds of curious passers-by. The Ruthenian press emphasized that during his evening tour around Lemberg, the emperor asked to stop in front of the building where he gazed upon the banner "as if recalling the solemn ceremony of the laying of the foundation stone" ("Jeho Velyčestvo Cisař meži rusynamy," *Zoria* 18 [1880], 247-48).

93 This first application of the historicist style, which enjoyed wide application to structures as varied as the military citadel (1852-54), the *Invalidenhaus* (1855-63), the first railway station (1860s), and the triumphal arch (1851), illustrated the readiness with which neoclassical architects such as Jan Salzmann adopted new architectural trends. On the emergence of the *Rundbogenstyl* in connection with the medieval revival and Romanticism in Germany, see Wolfgang Herrmann, "Introduction," in Harry F. Mallgrave, *In What Style Should We Build? The German Debate on Architectural Style. Essays by Heinrich Hübsch, Rudolf Wiegmann, Carl Albert Rosenthal, Johann Heinrich Wolff, and Carl Gottlieb Wilhem Bötticher* (National Gallery of Art, 1992).

94 The banner of the Ruthenian volunteer garrison that had kept "order in our *kraj* against the troublemakers (*suproty vorochobnykov*) [i.e., Polish revolutionary legions]" in 1848 was prominently displayed. (Quoted from "Jeho Velyčestvo," 248).

95 The idea of the original building's adaptation into a Ruthenian university was never realized largely because of a chronic shortage of professionally trained teachers and professors hailing from the Ruthenian population. In 1880, the emperor was invited to visit the academic secondary school, located on the premises of the Ruthenian National Institute. On a detailed account of the emperor's visit to the Ruthenian National Institute in 1880, see "Jeho Velyčestvo," *Zoria*, 247-48.

96 *Zoria* 19 (1882), 304.

97 The plans were designed by Crown Land Building Department employee Anton Frech and were typical of Vormärz Lemberg bureaucratic architecture: simple, minimal in decoration, and adequate in planning. The interior was stripped of much of its baroque decoration, the Corinthian was replaced with the Doric, and the building's plan envisioned the construction of three cupolas, characteristic for vernacular Galician Ruthenian sacral architecture. See Ihor Žuk (ed.), *Preobraženska Cerkva*, Istoryko-architekturnyj atlas Lvova, Series II: "Vyznačni budivli," Bind 2 (Lviv: Taki Spravy 1997).

98 The approved project of 1874, also designed by a bureaucratic architect from the Crown Land administration's Building Department, Sylvestr Havryškevyc – a man of Ruthenian origin – did not make great changes to Frech's initial design (Žuk, *Preobraženska Cerkva,* 7).

99   Because of a conflict between the board of the Ruthenian National Institute and the metropolitan of the Greek Catholic Church, Andrej Šeptyckyj, the official blessing of the church, which had been initially set for 1898, did not take place until 1906 (ibid.).

100 Most notably in the case of the Ruthenian National Institute's board, its Russophile orientation hindered the full realization of the project rather than supported it. Moreover, as in many cases when an ethnic cultural foundation collected funds for a certain project, its administration tended to use the funds for its own purposes: the donated money allowed the foundation to enjoy a significant yearly profit (ibid.).

101 Both the old and new generations of Ruthenian intellectuals adhered to the official style (notably, *Rundbogenstyl*) and supported state-employed architects (such as Wilhelm Schmid and Sylvestr Havryškevyč), as well as those who were deeply loyal to the Habsburg Empire (such as Ivan Levynśkyj). At the architectural competition for the Ruthenian "Academic House" in 1905, for example, the jury consisted of Sylvestr Havryškevyč, Ivan Levynśkyj, and Julian Mudrak. None of the six applications received "suited the required program," and the building was later commissioned directly to Ivan Levynśkyj (CDIAU F. 309, Op. 1, Sp. 50).

102 Ivan Krypjakevyč, 81-82.

103 Ivan Krypjakevyč, 78. On building adaptations, see DALO F. 2, Op. 2, Sp. 3455, L. 56-58, 67. For the neighboring building (no. 26) from 1898 on in NTŠ possession, see DALO F. 2, Op. 2, Sp. 3456, L. 173-174.

104 In the state's possession from 1772 on, the building was bought by the Municipality for use as a museum or library (*Kronika Lwowa, Jego zabytki, osobliwoci z przewodnikiem oraz planem Lwowa, Lemberg: Nakl. Lwowskiego Biura Adresowego*, 1909, 22-23).

105 Ivan Krypjakevyč, 78.

106 Ibid., 81-82.

107 Such caution in mundane construction matters is evident, for example, from a request in 1900 for a municipal concession for courtyard adaptations to building no. 26 (DALO F. 2, Op. 2, Sp. 3456, L. 173-74).

108 On Polish 1914 demonstrations concerning the imperial decree for the creation of the Ukrainian University in Lemberg, see CDIAU F. 146, Op. 8, Sp. 1583.

109 Built in the fifteenth century, the Town Hall was in ruins by the late eighteenth century, at which time it was also being used as a prison. By the 1820s, the only remaining element of the building was its tower, surrounded by a wealth of small private houses in the center of the square. Although the new government initiated the process of purchasing these small houses as early as the 1790s, a few remaining hovels were still standing in 1830. In 1832, the last such building in the center of the square was demolished (Franciszek Jaworski, *Ratusz lwowski*, 70).

110 The author of one such project was a Jarosch and Christian Marischer, and Antoni Steinkeller designed another one (ibid.).

111 This event had become a topic in urban folklore, and figured later as the subject of verse and plays. Jan Nepomucen Kamiński penned the comedy, "The falling of the Town Hall tower, or a chimney–sweeper and a miller," (*Zawalenie się wieży ratuszowej czyli kominiarz i młynarz*); Alexander Fredro authored the play, "The troubles of a young husband" (*Kłopoty młodego męża*), ibid., 74.

112 Ibid. The Municipality called in local heritage experts to evaluate the quality of the excavated artifacts. Through the attendance of *Ossolineum*'s director, Konstanty Slotwiński, historic coins retrieved from the ruins became part of the *Ossolineum* museum collection.

113 In 1827, the basement of the new building was begun. See Jaworski, *Ratusz lwowski*, 76-77, for a full description of the ceremony and Jan Nepomucen Kamiński's verse written for that particular occasion.

114 This relief was lost the following year during street fights and the bombardment of Lemberg.

115 For the official report on the celebration, see CDIAU F. 146, Op. 1, Sv. 76, Sp. 1427, L. 15-17.

116 Along with the administrative handbooks (*Schematisma*) issued by the imperial government in Vienna beginning in 1778, which covered the administrative structure of the entire Habsburg Empire, another series, published locally, was devoted solely to Galicia. See *Schematismus der Königreiche Galizien und Lodomerien* (Lemberg: Piller, 1789-1843); *Provinzial-Handbuch der Königreiche Galizien und Lodomerien* (Lemberg: Piller, 1844-84); *Handbuch der Lemberger Statthalterei-Gebietes in Galizien* (Lemberg: Piller, 1855-69); *Szematyzm Królewstwa Galicyi i Lodomeryi z Wielkim Ks. Krakowskim* (Lemberg: Piller, 1870-1914).

117 After the speech, the document including these data, as well as the basic statistics on Lemberg's population and housing, were left inside the *Turmknopf* for future generations, together with an issue of Galician Schematism (ibid., L. 16-17).

118 For the texts glorifying the event in German, written by Schiesser, Karlmann, and Tange, and in Polish, by Jan Nepomucen Kamiński, see ibid., L. 19-28.

119 Dr. Michal Gnoiński, the first Lemberg mayor elected by the municipal council (1848), took part in the meeting. See CDIAU F. 52, Op. 1, Sp. 30, L. 2-5.

120 "This is especially important because they are an antiquity that stems from the times of the [former] tower's erection in 1481, and it is therefore purposive that they survive and be exhibited on the aforementioned place" (ibid., 3-4).

121 Ibid., L. 5-6.

122 Ibid., L. 7-8.

123 "In light of the limited funds, and in the name of the whole city, whose interests [the Municipality] exclusively represents, it can under no circumstances allow for such extensive spending and, at the same time, maintain its public responsibility" (ibid., L. 11).

124 On 22 November 1849, the Municipal Council had already met in the Town Hall, though previously that year its sessions were held in the hall of the Riflemen's Range (Jaworski, *Ratusz lwowski*, 91).

125 See *Kronika Lwowa*.

126 The editorial board of the journal limited itself to mentioning that it did not agree fully with the outcome of the competition; though it recognized the competition as useful. See *Konkurs na projekt rekonstrukcyi gmachu ratuszowego we Lwowie (z 10-ma tablicami), Odbitka z Czasopisma technicznego* (Lemberg 1908).

127 Even the organization of the competition was for the Municipality a very difficult undertaking, both financially and in terms of architects' attendance (ibid., 1).

128 The decision committee included state-employed architects, as expected – such as Emil Förster, ministerial adviser and an architect from Vienna; Lemberg municipal construction inspectors Wincenty Górecki, Jakob Kroch, Hippolit Śliwiński, Artur Schleyer, and Wincenty Rawski; as well as Cracow building instructors Slawomir Odrzychowski and Jan Zawiejski. Also members were the city's mayor, Stanislaw Ciuchciński, and vice mayor Tadeusz Rutowski.

129   The project title, "Impenetrable nut," referred to the medieval and Renaissance (pre-Austrian) strength of the city, which was in the possession of the Polish Crown from 1340 to 1772. Second prize was awarded to a project mysteriously called "Three Red Circles" by a Polish architect working in Darmstadt, Germany, Józef Handzielewicz. Other projects had more neutral titles, such as: "New raiment" (*Nowa szata*), "*Senatoribus*," "*Ideal*," "*Pro publico bono*," and "S. P. Q. R.").

130   First prize: "The entire project is outstanding from the architectural point of view; it exhibits unusual freshness and an extraordinarily pleasing aesthetical appearance and is completely conceived in a national spirit." The "Three Red Circles" project gave priority to the national issue too, but unsuccessfully: "The project exhibits good architectural proportions, a characteristic and harmonious appearance of the building as a whole, yet the national character is not clearly signified" (ibid., 2).

131   "The idea behind the basic layout is in general good, though the asymmetrical arrangement, inadequate dealing with the stairs, and the lack of [other elements required by the competition program] were seen as unpractical....Although the author incorporated many national motifs (*motywów swojskich*), he did not succeed in achieving a general, artistic national character in the building (*rodzimej cechy*)" (ibid., 3).

132   CDIAU, F. 52, Op. 1, Sp. 17, L. 2-6. On the other hand, the river's water had been a matter of dispute between various city groups: in 1787, the amount of water was insufficient for the needs of all citizens, and the water itself had a truly foul smell, as reported in 1785 (ibid., L. 3).

133   On the western and northern sides, where the fortification walls still stood, a walking alley existed, yet the walking paths were narrow and interrupted at every turn with mud and swamps. On the eastern side, the fortifications had been demolished, yet the site of the future *Reitzenheimówka* promenade was full of garbage and dangerous holes, and the streams and sandy winds from the Sand Hill (*Sandberg*) made it accessible only to cattle (ibid).

134   Leopold Graf Lazansky von Bukowa, later Governor of Moravia. On Lazansky's concern with the Jewish issue during his Moravian governorship, see Michael L. Miller, "Samson Raphael Hirsch and the Revolution of 1848," *CEU Jewish Studies Yearbook*, II yearbook (1999-2001).

135   "With the return of Count Lazansky..., the plantings [of Castle Hill] received a new impetus" (CDIAU F. 52, Op. 1, Sp. 950, L. 36).

136   T. W. Kochański, the editor of the weekly magazine of farming and industry (*Tygodnik rolniczo-przemysłowy*) traveled in the late 1840s to Bern to participate in the congress of German agricultural societies and to present "the method in which the local Municipality managed to bind the sand on our hill within just a few years" (CDIAU F. 52, Op. 1, Sp. 950, L. 12).

137   A commentator wrote in 1813: "Considering the major need of the...population, the caring government has taken responsibility for the city's management and engaged in taking care of places adequate for walks, for attractions for the people, and by so doing wishes to improve sanitary conditions." Quoted in Zygmunt Stankiewicz (Inż.), "Ogrody i plantacje miejskie," in Janusz, *Lwów stary i dzisiejszy*, 63.

138   Ibid., 63.

139   CDIAU F. 52, Op. 1, Sp. 950, L. 6. On municipal measures concerning the beautification of Castle Hill in 1840-58, also see CDIAU F. 146, Op. 109, Sp. 101.

140   See, for example, Stankiewicz, 63. The park's name obviously troubled the new rulers. The first renaming of the garden took place in 1824, when it came to be called

Hechtschen Garten, derived from the owner of the casino and hotel on its premises (CDIAU F. 146, Op. 6, Sp. 322, L. 727). From the early 1840s on, it started to be officially called Municipal Park, although the new Polish administration often used the old name in the late nineteenth century (*Ogród jezuicki*). For the plans of the Jesuit Garden (1786-1844), see CDIAU F. 720, Op. 1, Sp. 623.

141 Stańkiewicz, 63-64.

142 Ironically, it also turned out that extensive plantings, designed to resemble fashionable Italian gardens and fitting the *Biedermeier* ideal, were not suitable to Lemberg's notoriously wet climate. The change of ownership in 1847 did not produce a positive change. In the nineteenth century, private entrepreneurs repeatedly attempted to free themselves from the obligation to maintain the park (Stańkiewicz, 64-65).

143 For a complete history of the changing ownership of the former Jesuit Garden (1840-59), see CDIAU F. 146, Op. 78, Sp. 377; F. 146, Op. 6, Sp. 212, L. 1727-28. For the plan of the park from 1876, see CDIAU F. 165, Op.5, Sp. 103.

144 One example is the resolution against the *Militär Stadtcommando*, signed by a Building Department employee, Alfred Bojarski, in 1858 (CDIAU F. 146, Op. 109, Sp. 101, L. 8).

145 *Wronowskiberg* was previously notorious for its neglect and criminality. In 1853, the city employed Bauer to plant trees in the Łyczaków cemetery; Stryjski Park was planned and arranged by another leading Lemberg landscape architect, Arnold Röhring (Stańkiewicz, 65).

146 In July 1895, a memorial obelisk was erected on the place where the Polish revolutionaries of 1848, Teofil Wiśniowski and Józef Kapuściński, were executed, and rich greenery was planted around it (Stankiewicz, 70).

147 For the erection of the mound and the transformation of the Union of Lublin celebration, see chap. 4.

148 Jaworski, *Lwów stary*, 346.

149 CDIAU F. 146, Op. 7, Sp. 4437, L. 1.

150 CDIAU F. 146, Op. 7, Sp. 4437, L. 3, 5.

151 Ibid., L.14-16.

152 Zachariewicz headed the building preparations and, probably using his own connections at the Galician Railway, deposited the purchased stone block on its premises. Apparently, the organization committee appealed to the board of the Galician Railway to redeem itself from paying the prices connected with transporting the stone block from the nearby Mikołajów (Mykolaïv) and received approval.

153 Ibid., L. 3.

154 Ibid., L. 4.

155 Ibid., L. 11.

156 Ibid., L. 17-19. In 1888, the sum collected amounted to 630 crowns. Niemczynowski also intended to lay the foundation stone for the future monument at that time and to appeal to the "dignity" of parliamentarians and other officials to procure donations for his project (ibid., L.14-15). For more on this, see Markian Prokopovych, "The Lemberg Garden: Political Representation in Public Greenery under the Habsburg Rule," *East Central Europe/l'Europe du Centre-Est: Eine wissenschaftliche Zeitschrift* 33 (2006) 1–2, special issue "Urban History in East Central Europe."

157 Ibid., L. 23-24.

158 Ibid.

159 Ibid., L. 25-26.

160 The municipal fund for the monument's construction was 3000 crowns (ibid., L. 27-29).

161 "Do wysokiego Prevydium c. k. Namiestnictwa we Lwowie – Sprawozdanie Prezydenta Miasta w sprawie pomnika Jana Kilińskiego (18 June 1895)," (ibid., L. 42-43).

162 On a similar process through which the Municipality gradually assumed maintenance of Artur Grottger's tomb in the prestigious Łyczaków cemetery, a process initiated by the Mlodnicki family in 1894-1905, see CDIAU F. 55, Op. 1, Sp. 191. In 1905, the Municipality did not care to restore several artistically valuable tombs of leading Lemberg personalities of the Vormärz period, such as Franz Kratter and Jan Sacher, father of Police Director Leopold Sacher-Masoch. Instead, the Municipality freed itself of this responsibility by assigning it to the deceased individuals' nonexistent descendants ("Ogloszenie magistratu od 18 Maja 1904" CDIAU F. 55, Op. 1, Sp. 190, L. 24).

163 On the "nationalization" of Łyczaków Park with the erection of a statue to Bartosz Głowacki (ca. 1758-94), a peasant from the vicinity of Cracow and a hero of the Kościuszko uprising, and renaming the park after him, see CDIAU F. 55, Op. 1, Sp. 191, L. 50.

164 On the public donation collection for the erection of the monument to Gołuchowski (1875-98), see CDIAU F. 165, Op. 5, Sp. 230, L. 37-45. For several preserved plans and architectural drawings of the Monument to Jan Sobieski, see DALO F. 2, Op. 4, Sp. 1261.

165 33.874 zlr for the Gołuchowski monument, and 15.207 zlr for the Kościuszko monument. As a consequence, it took long years for Kościuszko's monument to stand on its place in Cracow, and by then it was stylistically outdated and sharply criticized (CDIAU F. 165, Op. 5, Sp. 230, L. 37-45).

166 CDIAU F. 165, Op. 5, Sp. 230, L. 6-7.

167 Other members of the Crown Land Department included Dr. Joseph Wereszczyński, Maciej Zenon Serwatowski, and Dr. Jan Czajkowski (ibid., 17).

168 The 1873 appeal for private support for the Memorial Foundation for Youth in the name of Franz Joseph was written by the same officials who had composed the 1875 appeal, including Smolka (ibid., L. 12).

169 Ibid., L. 17.

170 Ibid., L. 33-35.

171 The first proposal for the monument came from the Crown Land Department in 1875, following Gołuchowski's death, but no action was then taken for fifteen years. In 1890, Edmund Mochnacki wrote to the Diet Speaker to inquire about the status of the project. Although the latter took seven months to answer, his reply suggested the organization of a committee that would determine the location and terms of the monument's construction (CDIAU F. 165, Op. 5, Sp. 230, vol. II).

172 The committee was established in March 1891 by the Crown Land Department and included Vice Speaker of the Diet Antoni Jaxa Chaniec, Crown Land Department member Edward Jedrzejewicz, Edmund Mochnacki, Count Adam Gołuchowski (the descendant of Agenor Gołuchowski), and Julian Zachariewicz (ibid., L. 46-47).

173 Ibid., vol. II, L 49.

174 In 1893, the square in front of the Crown Land Department was suggested as a location for the monument to Gołuchowski, even though the location had already been earmarked for the Kościuszko monument (ibid., vol. II, L. 59).

175 Zachariewicz was informed in 1891 that the plantings committee had already developed a site plan for the garden, though for different purposes, and that it had taken into consideration the neighboring Gołuchowski palace in its work (ibid.).

176 Previously involved on the committee were Antoni Jaxa Chaniec, Dr. Josef Wereszczyński, Mayor Małachowski, and Adam Gołuchowski.
177 ibid., vol. II, L. 1.
178 Jan Bołoz Antoniewicz enjoyed a reputation as a distinguished Lemberg University professor and historian. Zygmunt Gorgolewski was the government councilor and director of the Lemberg School of Industry, as well as the designer of the winning project for the Opera Theater. Juliusz Hochberger served as the Municipal Building Department's long-term director, and Professor Władysław Łoziński was a renowned historian. Antoni Popiel and Jan Styka figured among Lemberg's leading historicist artists; the former was recognized for his monument to Mickiewicz, and the latter had painted "Polonia" that decorated the Town Hall and the *Racławice panorama* featured at the 1894 Provincial Exhibition.
179 Ibid., vol. II, L. 6-7.
180 Ibid., vol. II, L. 9-10.
181 All the committee's members acknowledged the value of the statue: Łoziński and Gorgolewski thought it was "perfect" (*doskonały*) and made the best impression, while Antoniewicz felt that it was "splendid" (*wyborny*) (ibid.).
182 "Marble sculptures are absolutely impossible in our climate, for which the best evidence is the monument to Mozart in Vienna, which after merely a few years is so marred that it is no longer recognizable" (ibid., vol. II, L. 8).
183 Ibid., vol. 2, L. 7.
184 Gorgolewski acknowledged that Godebski's model was "more beautiful than the Mickiewicz monument in Warsaw." Godebski justified the choice of the Pietro Lippi firm, of Pestoa for the casting of the statue, stressing that the firm was "the leading [firm] in Europe and the one where...the figures for the Mickiewicz monument in Warsaw and the Copernicus monument in Cracow were cast." (ibid., vol. II, L. 7; 14-16).
185 Łoziński suggested that "the statue should be made of bronze not just out of climatic considerations, but also purely artistic ones: the latter material is in any case more adequate for the statesman's monument than marble." Gorgolewski also acknowledged that it "represents a man of the state ideally" and insisted that "out of climatic considerations a marble figure would need to be covered most of the year" (ibid., vol. II, L. 7).
186 Similarly, nobody seemed to have noticed that even in neoclassical planning, bronze statues of the great rulers were placed in major public squares rather than in the solitude of gardens.
187 Gorgolewski reasoned: "The reliefs are not well readable because the scenes that they represent are difficult in general to translate into sculpture." Even Antoniewicz was opposed to the side reliefs, but suggested that the back one, representing Gołuchowski's schooling, "should be kept because of the view from the side of the garden above" (Ibid., vol. II, L. 7).
188 Ibid., vol. II, L. 7.
189 Emphasis in the original.
190 Ibid., vol. III, L. 5.
191 Ibid., vol. III, L. 3
192 Ibid., vol. III, L. 7.
193 Ibid., vol. III, L. 10-11.
194 Ibid., vol. III, L. 15, 35, 39.
195 One of the very few exceptions can be found in the Crown Land administration's correspondence with the Court Chancellery and the Lemberg Mayor in the late 1820s about the construction (restoration) of a monument to Count Jan Gaisruck, Governor of

Galicia (1795–1801) (CDIAU F. 146, Op. 7, Sp. 1805). Excluding provisional work on the existing sacred monuments to St. Michael, St. Jan Nepomuk, and St. Jan of Dukla, only one received extensive work in the city center during this period: a statue of hetman Stanisław Jabłonowski, restored and reerected in the 1860s.

196 CDIAU F. 146, Op. 7, Sp. 2243.

197 "Die erste und heiligste Pflicht jedes Staats Bürgers ist dem ihm von Gott gegebenen Monarchen Liebe, Gehorsam und treue Anhänglichkeit zu beweisen," in connection to the construction of the monument to Franz I in Stanisław in 1844 (CDIAU, Fond 146, Op. 7, Sp. 2468).

198 The statue of Sobieski, largely a municipal initiative, was finished and unveiled with all the requisite imperial pomp in 1898. For the official unveiling of Sobieski's monument in 1897, see CDIAU F. 739, Op. 1, Sp. 130. The eighteenth-century statue of hetman Stanisław Jabłonowski, Sobieski's key adviser, was restored with Governor Gołuchowski's personal encouragement and returned to its pedestal in 1859, representing Polish heroism and faithfulness to the house of the Habsburgs.

199 On a summary of monument construction in Lemberg, see Ihor Siomočkin, "Pamjatnyky," 14-15.

200 The Municipality approved the project in 1887 and completed it after the river was channeled underground in that section of the ring road (Ihor Siomočkin, "U tradycijach ľvivśkych ambicij, abo u hlybyni navkolotvorčych konfliktiv kincia XIX st" [In the Traditions of L'viv Ambitions, or in the Debth of Art Conflicts at the End of the 19th c.] *HB* 11 (1996), 15).

201 Apparently this idea was not realized, and the busts were placed in front of the Diet building in the late 1890s (Siomočkin, 14). The last imperial symbol to be erected on the ring road was a curious wooden statue known as the "iron warrior," built 1916-18, on which everyone who wished to donate to the Austrian military could pin an iron nail.

202 See Ihor Siomočkin, "Pamjatnyk Mickevyču v Lvovi" [Monument to Mickiewicz in Ľviv] *HB* 2: 38 (1998), 14-15.

203 Tadeusz (Andrzej Bonawentura) Kościuszko (1746-1817) was the leader of the 1794 insurrection that started in Cracow and led to the defeat of the Russian army at the battle of Raclawice (4 April 1794). Imprisoned in the Petropavlov Fortress in 1794, he was released in 1796 and emigrated to the United States. In 1798, Kościuszko returned to Paris and formed the Polish legion battalions. He died in Switzerland and was buried in the Wawel Castle in Cracow.

204 On a full discussion over the issue of the Kościuszko monument in Lemberg / Lwów (1893-1928), see DALO F. 2, Op. 4, Sp. 829.

205 Ibid., L. 2-3.

206 Before starting his studies at the Royal Architectural Academy (*Bauakademie*) in Berlin, Hochberger completed a required year of professional practice in 1859 in the municipal office in Poznań (*Staatsrath* Koch). (see "Nekrologia," *CzT* (1905), 170-172).

207 In 1866, for example, he was awarded the silver Karl Friedrich Schinkel medal at an architectural competition held by the Architectural Society of Berlin. From the literature consulted, it appears that he was the first Pole to be awarded the prestigious Schinkel prize. See. Stanisław Łoza, *Architekci i budowniczowie w Polsce* (Warsaw: Budownictwo i Architektura, 1954).

208 Graduate *Realschule* (1876), St. Ann School (1883), Franz Joseph *Gymnasium* (1886). He also designed the fire station.

209 Hochberg's sacral projects include his design for the Powder Tower's reconstruction and plans for churches in Poznań and Pszczew (Łoza, ibid.).

210 See "Sprawozdanie Komisyi wybranej przez Towarzystwo politechniczne, o organiza- cyi urzędu budowniczego miejskiego we Lwowie," [Report of the Commission Elected by the Polytechnic Society about the Organization of Municipal Building Regulations in Lwów], *CzT* 3 (1910), 32-34.

211 DALO F. 2, Op. 4, Sp. 829, L. 21.

212 Ibid., L. 24.

213 Ibid., L. 24.

214 Ibid., L. 25-26. The idea was welcomed by the Municipality, which delegated its six representatives to the new committee.

215 The bell of Cracow's Wawel Cathedral.

216 With this reasoning in mind, the Municipality arranged a celebration, the aim of which was "not only to have the character of a national demonstration (*manifestacyi naro- dowej*) and an evening event in the Opera Theater, but also to serve as an occasion to collect funds for the support and development of Polish culture in Lithuania" (ibid., L. 36-37).

217 Ibid., L. 41, 53-54.

218 Levynśkyj was of a mixed ethnic descent: his mother came from a German col- ony in Galicia, and his father was Ruthenian. His wife, Maria Bronikowska, bore a Polish-sounding name and had relatives in Zakopane. See Ivan Oleksyn, "Žyttia i dijaľnisť Ivana Levynśkoho," in *Ivan Levynśkyj, Joho žyttia ta pracia* (Lwów: Nakl. Agronomično-technilčnoho tovarystva "Pracia" im. Ivana Levynśkoho, 1934), 9.

219 Zbigniew Lewiński, "Polski styl importowany z Wiednia," [The Polish Style imported from Vienna], *CzT* 31 (1913), 20-21.

220 Czeslaw Thullie (Dr.) *O kościolach lwowskich z czasów Odrodzenia* (Lemberg: Ksie- garnia W. Gubrynowicza i syna, 1913), 11.

CHAPTER FOUR

Using the City: Commemorations, Restorations, Exhibitions

The meaning of architecture speaks not only through the peculiarities of the building process and the art historian's commentary, but also through its uses: buildings can be adapted, restored, or preserved in a particular form and decorated with new symbols and inscriptions for particular occasions. Temporary architecture can be erected to commemorate a historic event, such as a royal person's visit or a provincial exhibition. Conversely, the reasons for the destruction or elimination of access to buildings can hardly be viewed as "practical."

In Lemberg, where rulers changed frequently throughout early modern and modern history, the symbolic uses of architecture were commonplace. This chapter deals with the three major symbolic uses of architecture where identities became most pronounced: the city celebration, historic preservation, and late nineteenth-century provincial exhibitions (*Landesausstellungen*). Commemorations, historic preservation practices, and temporary exhibition architecture figured importantly as statements of – and as supporting reasons for – specific loyalties, aspirations, and identities, all of which were expressed through the use of architecture. In its treatment of commemorations, this chapter follows the current of recent research on public celebrations in the Habsburg Monarchy with a particular focus on multiethnic Galicia.[1] Following this lead, this chapter argues that public participation in celebrations and later in provincial exhibitions revealed the population's multilayered identities and loyalties. It additionally highlighted the way in which various projects for Galicia were imagined; the uses of architecture demonstrated diverse agendas behind the celebrations' organization. The increasing use of national symbolism in celebrations, including "nationalized" provincial exhibitions, and in historic preservation practices became evident at the fin de siècle, thus further nationalizing public space. Broad societal participation in these events, however, limited neither to imperial celebrations nor to nationalistic projects, demonstrated a public need for such attractions and much more inclusive and overlapping identities than was previously believed by late nineteenth-century historians.

Dynastic Ceremony, Imperial Pomp, and National Celebration

The importance of public events, such as street celebrations, for the wider public during the early Austrian rule is best understood within the general political context. This atmosphere of early nineteenth-century Lemberg was captured, albeit in a way typical of national histories, by historian Bronisław Pawłowski: "This absolutist-bureaucratic oppression...was tolerated quietly, and one attempted to drown out the torments of life's colorlessness with various kinds of attractions and parties....Therefore one did not complain about contemporary life, but attempted to make it not only bearable, but also pleasant, in those circumstances."[2] Obviously in conditions where the only high culture recognized was German, where the aristocracy was restricted from enjoying its medieval honors, and where literature and the press were severely censored, it was the buildings of entertainment that became centers for upper-class social life, and public celebrations figured as the rare occasions to enjoy urban space.

Provincial and Municipal files are replete with records on the city's loyalty to the Habsburg throne. In 1828, the eight city council representatives, five of whom were Polish, noted that it was the common wish (*allgemeiner Wunsch*) of the city of Lemberg to mark the 60th anniversary of the emperor's coronation with celebrations.[3] The Crown Land administration's report of 13 November 1828, similarly noted that the celebrations allowed Galicia's inhabitants a much-desired occasion to demonstrate their love for and loyalty to (*Liebe und Anhänglichkeit*) the emperor.[4] One may of course doubt the veracity of these early Vormärz records: not only did the officials see the event from a rather biased perspective, since their contact with potential anti-Habsburg intellectuals was limited, but they were also bound to report positively on a commemoration event they themselves organized. Yet several facts illustrate that the population's sincere commitment to and enjoyment of imperial commemorations went beyond mere official rhetoric.

In honor of this celebration of 1828, the Polish Theatrical Society took action a day before the actual ceremonies to hang a banner (*Tableau*) before the theater wishing the emperor a long life on behalf of the Polish subjects. On the day of the celebration, the imperial anthem was sung in the local vernacular, (*in der Landessprache*) i.e., the Polish language, to a specially composed tune. Performed under the emperor's portrait inside the theater, the event was attended by a "sizable crowd" that exhibited "unmistakable joy." The ceremonial mass at the Metropolitan (Roman Catholic) Cathedral was also widely attended, not only by officials, but also by representatives of "all the classes."[5] Much of the historic center, as well as the outer districts – including not only the buildings associated with institutions of power, but also numerous private dwellings – was brightly illuminated in the evening. About 80 large slogans written in both German and Polish were hung from buildings, the *Ossolineum* among them, to commemorate the emperor's anniversary. An article in the official city newspaper *Lemberger Zeitung* described the celebration as brimming with a "general feeling of thankfulness" and with a "joy and enthusiasm for Austria."[6]

These descriptions indicated that the greater public truly enjoyed the numerous public ceremonies and celebrations organized by the new Austrian rulers in the early nineteenth century and the Vormärz period. Lemberg's long-time Police Director Joseph Rohrer could find little material for his "reports on the public mood" (*Stimmungsberiche*), nearly all of which concluded with a cliché: "The mood of the local public has until today remained largely unchanged."[7] This statement could well be extended to the second half of the nineteenth century, when a large crowd attended Governor Agenor Gołuchowski's funeral in 1875. As one Municipal official commented, "Accompanied by voluntary participation from all social strata, the funeral procession, true regret for the loss, and the prior acute attention to his illness were clear signs that our Crown Land (*kraj*) was able to see the value of the late governor's deeds."[8]

Yet did this public mood extend into the early years of the Austrian rule in Galicia, and especially into the events of 1809? If so, how can one reconcile the facts that both the Polish and Austrian troops arriving in Lemberg that year were met with grand mass celebrations, organized by the Municipal government? Similarly, if the local public had truly become so loyal to the Habsburgs by the Vormärz, what transformations, if any, did royal ceremony undergo to accommodate local sentiments? The following discussion will trace the appropriation of the rich tradition of medieval street celebrations that had survived in Lemberg into Habsburg imperial celebrations. The survival and transformation of this ancient urban tradition is a key to understanding the events of 1809 and the fate of Lemberg's Riflemen Confraternity. This examination of imperial ceremonies will also reveal how a national celebration was invented from these same celebrations, and how the insertion of national symbols into official celebrations gradually became commonplace by the fin de siècle. Although recent research has teased out the culture of politics surrounding the commemorations of 1851, 1868, 1880, 1891, 1894, 1898, 1910, and 1913,[9] the analysis of the 1809 events, the celebrations associated with the Union Mound, and the 1905 anniversary of the 1655 siege of Lemberg, offer new insights into the understanding of Galician ceremonies with a more complex coding than the purely imperial or purely national celebrations.

The Spectacles of 1809

Historians tend to stress the official, regulated, and therefore constructed character of early Austrian celebrations in Lemberg, versus the improvised and supposedly much more spontaneous Polish ones, thus assuming that this spontaneity was an expression of the population's sincere loyalty to the Polish cause. The historian Bronisław Pawłowski emphasizes that contrary to the welcome given to the Napoleonic troops in 1809, the subsequent return of the Austrian army was greeted "in a highly solemn way, following a printed program, established from above. [It] prescribed who, where, and in what order to stand for the greetings, and even prescribed when to exclaim '*Vivat*' and to fire salvos."[10] To prove what he views as the artificial character of the ethnic German inhabitants' joy at the Austrian troops' return and to demonstrate the event's essence, Pawłowski writes, "The evening was spoiled by someone breaking windows in the Jewish houses that were not illuminated."[11] Schnür-Pepłowski, similarly, reasoned as follows:

> They were greeted with the full royal ceremonial at *Grodecka* tollgate, with salvos and the ringing of church bells. The Municipality's deputies, together with the guilds and the militia, went to greet them, led by the orchestra. One could hear greetings here and there, and yet they sounded somewhat cautious, artificial....Such manifestations could not have been pleasant for the Polish society...since it not so long ago had enthusiastically sung, 'We shall follow the golden eagle to widen our lands' (*Za złotym orłem pójdziemy, Rozszerzyć nasze ziemice*). This was a beautiful dream....Better it would have been not to dream, than to wake up so painfully.[12]

In contrast, a full Municipality "accompanied by the music band, the guilds, and the Jewish kahal" attended the prior welcome celebration given to the Polish troops. "The general public joyfully observed the national (*ojczysty*) decorations."[13] Yet the written description of both 1809 ceremonies is very similar, and accounts on public attendance for both the imperial and the Polish national ceremonies provide similar testimony.

In comparison with earlier medieval and baroque ceremonies, both 1809 celebrations, as well as the generally Habsburg celebrations staged in Lemberg in the early nineteenth century, were simplified and rationalized.[14] A typical example of a larger street celebration of this period can be found in the 1814 celebration of the emperor's name day, connected with the First Peace Treaty of Paris signed on 30 May 1814.[15] The procession for this event included the guilds – with their coat-of-arms, schools, *Gymnasiums* and the *Lyceum*, both seminaries, the clergy of all the city churches, representatives from the Municipality, officials from other public institutions, and high-ranking military officers. Starting at the

Figure 47. Roman Catholic Cathedral. Lithograph by Karol Auer, 1837-38. L'viv Stefanyk Scientific Library. Most of the imperial celebrations started in the cathedral.

Dominican church early in the morning at 9 a.m., the procession passed market square by the Town Hall, entered the Roman Catholic Cathedral to attend the "*Te Deum*" mass at 10 a.m., and sang the anthem "*Gott erhalte*" (Figure 47). Strict order was to be maintained: in the morning, the Municipal police, which would also fire salvos during the mass, encircled both churches, the major streets, and the Ringplatz. For this occasion a triumphal arch – an almost indispensable element for imperial celebrations – was constructed, and the city boulevards along the ring road, by then laid out and planted, or sometimes just covered, with greenery, were decorated with lamps. All the church bells pealed for a quarter of an hour, beginning at the start of the mass. In the evening, public buildings were illuminated, along with private homes that had requested special permission from the Police Department to do so. A fitting production was staged at the theater, which was decorated with a portrait of the emperor; before the curtain was raised, and the anthem "*Gott erhalte*" was sung again.[16]

On selected occasions, the city militia and the military were stationed on the *Ringplatz* and the neighboring streets, creating living corridors through which processions would pass. More simple arrangements were made, for example, during Emperor Franz I's visit and the opening of the Diet in 1817,[17] for the celebration of Emperor Franz's 60th birthday in 1828, [18] for events marking the Austrian Constitution in 1849[19] and in honor of Franz Joseph's wife after the prince's birth in 1856 (Fig. 48).[20] The official celebration's format remained largely unchanged until the twilight of the monarchy,[21] and the Polish celebrations of 1809 followed exactly the same pattern.

Figure 48. Procession during Franz Joseph's visit to Lemberg in 1851. Collection of the Foundation for the Preservation of the Historical-Architectural Heritage of L'viv.

As discussed earlier, as significant as the events of 1809 may have seemed at the time, the most striking fact about them in the long run was how readily Habsburg authority was reestablished.[22] The most radical, extreme reactions of support and of opposition among local Poles to the political events of 1809 came from a winery owner Waigner and Archbishop Kajetan Kicki, respectively.[23] Waigner is reported to have removed Emperor Franz's portrait from the wall of his pub, having thrown it on the ground, having spat on it while stomping on it with his feet, and finally having offered a glass of wine to everyone who would volunteer to follow his example. On the other hand, Archbishop Kicki, known for his loyalty to the Habsburgs, allowed neither the performance of the *Te Deum* in the Cathedral nor the ringing of the bells in honor of the Polish troops. When his order was not obeyed, he "excommunicated" – that is, deconsecrated – the bells, so that they later needed to be consecrated a second time. These two episodes taken together suggest the range within which a variety of attitudes to the Austrian rule took shape. Most of the public remained somewhere in between these two extremes, as a passive observer of the street spectacle.

The reasons for these diverse actions, however, might not have been ideological. In early 1809, the political situation was still uncertain, and the population rather tended to think that Napoleon would never be defeated. Thus by showing their loyalty to Roźniecki and Kamieński, the inhabitants were making a long-term investment in what appeared to be a promising political outcome. Similarly, the population knew very well the irregularities that would come with the establishment of Polish rule in Lemberg. So it had reason to feel a greater fear of punishments handed out impulsively by Polish troops for disloyalty than of measures from the Habsburg state, since for the Polish military being a "non-Pole" corresponded to being a suspicious foreigner.[24] It is quite likely that public unrest of the time – the Jewish pogroms included – stemmed from political instability and change, unconnected to who was about to assume power in the city. It is also very likely that it was not only the German population that was "moved to tears" at the sight of Habsburg troops marching into the city. The devastating arrival of the Russian troops in Lemberg later that year definitely left even the most committed enthusiasts disabused of the notion of Poland's rebirth.

The illumination and decoration of private homes for special occasions had emerged as a custom during the Middle Ages, and the organization of a standard ceremony upon the arrival of every king, archbishop, *hetman*, *wojewoda*, governor, or other dignitary had become an established practice in Lemberg by the eighteenth century.[25] Precisely because public attendance of imperial ceremonies was impressive and difficult to disregard, serious historians with pro-Polish national agendas explained it as "imposed from the above" and "artificial." A well-known episode of vandalism of the Austrian coat-of-arms on Kicki's palace, perpetrated by an unknown Polish nun of noble descent, served precisely this purpose, and mention of it was reproduced throughout Polish national scholarship. According to this interpretation, the greater public's enjoyment of such events was "artificial" and the celebration itself was "imposed," though the public's "true" identity was exemplified in the anonymous nun's "noble" act of vandalism.[26] Yet while there certainly were individuals who caused public disruptions during official celebrations, the general assumption of prevailing popular disapproval of the Austrian return to power requires reexamination.

Król Kurkowy and the Transformation of the Riflemen Confraternity

The transformation of Lemberg's most unusual annual street celebration under Austrian rule illustrates the Vormärz state's ideas about its exclusive possession of public space, as well as its understanding of the relationship of fraternal societies, such as the Riflemen Confraternity (*Konfraternia strzelecka*), to the public sphere. Besides royal ceremony, Lemberg also had its own celebratory traditions and its own sites of reference within the city that have been treated only marginally in the historiography. These included traditional religious rituals and buildings of socialization, most especially pubs. As regards traditional popular rituals, one that is widely recorded is that of the Ruthenian *Haïvky*, attended by the urban lower classes, village inhabitants who came to Lemberg specifically for the event, along with craftsmen and low-ranking military personnel.[27] Many popular celebrations, including the *Haïvky*, took place in the vicinity of Kurkowa Street, the site of the Riflemen shooting range associated with Lemberg's oldest confraternity.[28]

Figure 49. Riflemen shooting range. Lithograph by Peter Piller, 1800s.
Mańkowski, *Lwów przez laty osiemdziesięciu.*

This celebration, known as the election of the "shooting king" (*król kurkowy/ König der goldenen Hahn*), was an annual shooting competition, derived from medieval roots, and its own ceremony was organized by the confraternity. This included a solemn mass and a procession starting from the old riflemen's range building (called the "*Celsztat*"). The route crossed through the city wall, continued through the city center in a peculiar, picturesque order, and finished at the shooting range, where the actual competition, and the election of the best marksman, *król kurkowy*, took place.[29] Franciszek Jaworski commented on the similarity of this procession – with the members of the confraternity dressed in colorful, traditional costumes walking along with the parade bearers of the competition's prizes – to the mythological ceremony of the arrival of Bacchus. The lowest-ranking prize, a sheep with painted horns, headed up the procession, and was followed by the two top prizes, one, a wool cloth, and the second, an ox with gilded horns crowned with a wreath. The final member of the procession was the previous year's "king" in a carriage.[30]

The confraternity was an old institution dating from prepartitioned Poland that was transformed under the Austrian rule into the Municipal militia and artillery. It had been traditionally honored with royal and Municipal privileges by the Polish kings.[31] A part of local street celebrations, the confraternity traditionally appeared with its members in their unmistakable costumes at various church holidays, such as Corpus Christi, the Resurrection, Easter, and Pentecost, and at members' burials.[32] Under Austria, it never lost imperial protection: as early as 1793, the state provided the confraternity with a new statute replacing its old privileges, and in 1795 it requested that members wear redesigned uniforms at imperial functions. Thus from a medieval confraternity, it was transformed into a part of the state's apparatus, that is, from the *Konfraternia strzelecka* into a *bürgerliches Scharfschützenkorps*. Its very survival was due to the chance fact that in Austria, notably in the Tyrol, there was a similar confraternity with which the Lemberg riflemen kept close connections.[33]

The Austrian state also made use of the riflemen on numerous occasions in the early nineteenth century. Their appearance both provided for local legitimization and imparted a quaint quality to state processions. After the reestablishment of the Diet in 1817, for example, the confraternity was asked to participate in the official opening ceremonies. The Riflemen's shooting range building was regularly visited by Austrian emperors on their trips to Lemberg in 1817, 1851, 1855, 1880, and 1894. The day following the celebration of the emperor's 60th birthday in 1828, for example, the shooting range was the site of the confraternity's hosting of a ball attended by the governor, the aristocracy, high-ranking clergy, military officers, representatives of the *Stände*, and a "previously unseen numerous" public.[34] Yet this period witnessed a gradual transformation of imperial ceremonies, and of the confraternity itself, to suit the worldview of the new rulers. Not only did the confraternity's public appearances change dramatically, but its right to physical representation in the city center was also severely curtailed.

The riflemen possessed a plot of land north of the city walls, and from the first discussions of a ring road in the late eighteenth century among city planners, this plot had been seen as an obstacle to the project. Thus the confraternity was soon forced to vacate that land for a new location outside the city center.[35] It was not the mere existence of the confraternity that bothered the new rulers, but rather the diverse symbolic associations it had acquired in its long history that disturbed the newly established rule. The Austrian bureaucrats favored the idea of a riflemen's community in their city, and even enjoyed participating in military-like activities themselves in their free time. It was the unusual medieval ceremony, coupled with the confraternity's autonomous legal status, that remained incomprehensible and problematic for them. They thus attempted both to restrict the confraternity's autonomy and to rationalize its ceremony to conform more closely to state regulations.

As soon as the new two-story confraternity's building (*strzelnica*) was completed in the late 1820s,[36] it began to attract new members and visitors. But the confraternity was soon changed into a casino and a private club for the officials, and its hall became an important venue for balls and carnivals of the period, both entirely foreign to the medieval nature of the riflemen's association. The transformed confraternity occasionally marched through the city in their "masquerade costumes,"[37] accompanied by an amateur band recruited from among Crown Land and Municipal officials. Later, it became joined with city militia public appearances. Another transformation took place in 1832 when a local townsman was killed during one of the Riflemen's public appearances. Thereafter the members were forbidden to carry their rifles and became a simple and somewhat ridiculous embellishment to official ceremonies.[38] Little remained of the medieval symbolism once held by an independent confraternity honored with royal and Municipal privileges in their public use of space and associated self-representation.

Through a series of gradual measures, the confraternity and its public activities were transformed from a medieval civic association honored by the Polish kings into an integral part of the Vormärz Austrian state's official culture. Its residence was relocated to the city periphery, where its building and shooting range became the site of officials' leisure activities and imperial visits. The organization was restricted from carrying out its annual shooting competition in the traditional form and from using its old costumes and weapons; in their place, the members were to wear Austrian-designed uniforms and to participate in state ceremonies. During the events of 1848, the confraternity became a part of the Polish National Guard and with it was dissolved shortly thereafter: the neoabsolutist state did not foresee the existence of a paramilitary society that had roots in prepartition Poland, even in a revised version. Only in the 1890s was the confraternity revived again as a "national society," yet another project of traditions invented from local

Figure 50. Riflemen Range Building during the Vormärz. Lithograph by Karol Auer, 1840s. Ľviv Stefanyk Scientific Library.

Figure 51. The Riflemen Shooting Range Building. Photograph by Edward Trzemeski, 1900. Ľviv Historical Museum. Jan Sobieski's bust was placed in front of the building in 1883.

customs. (Figure 51 shows the Riflemen Shooting Range Building after 1883, when the bust to Jan Sobieski was installed in front of it.) The Lemberg riflemen became part of an all-Polish network of riflemen that held congresses and carried their own, specially designed banner.[39] The confraternity's function as the bearer of a medieval legacy characterized by the grotesque, or as a promoter of "enlightened" leisure activity was never recovered, however. The development of official royal ceremonies and the emergence of new, purely national celebrations were longer, more powerful processes within which various groups came to express themselves through the use of public space.

The Lublin Union Mound in 1869, 1871, and 1874 and the Later Construction

Since the Compromise of 1867, several issues related to city celebrations came to be disputed in Lemberg, including the right to charge entry and collect donations; the right to use city illumination, music, costumes, flags, salvos, and fireworks; and the rights to use the Municipal guard, to close shops, to stage performances in theaters, and to hold holiday masses in church. The authorities were not willing to grant these rights easily. Thus those who organized popular celebrations were generally forced to limit their ambitions to modest commemorations. Those with greater hopes attempted to assure the authorities that theirs would be a quiet celebration in order to acquire Municipal permission. Others, such as Franciszek Smolka, chose a more radical method of suggesting an outrageously alternative celebration and then contesting the authorities on legal grounds (something that became possible only after the 1867 constitutional reform), thereby forcing them to compromise. Smolka, a liberal politician and professional lawyer, had previously been a revolutionary.[40] In 1869, he organized Lemberg's first celebration of a different symbolic nature, in which the use of streets and buildings became a political weapon for their cause.

That a public celebration could be turned into a political tool is well illustrated by the decision of the Cracow gentry in 1872, on the 100th anniversary of the First Partition of Poland, to not participate in the dancing during the traditional annual carnival. The governor's secret agent argued against their decision in this way:

> Experience teaches us that statements of political significance, which I would classify such as [an expression of]...mourning, often starts from seemingly innocent actions. A mourning of the Austrian rule's hundredth anniversary would touch the highest spheres [of the government].[41]

In Lemberg, this type of weapon was first used at a large public event on the 300th anniversary of the Union of Lublin. The man-made edifice on Lemberg's Castle Hill in commemoration of the Union of Lublin was the city's first public monument initiated by an independent society rather than by the authorities. For Smolka, who developed the idea of the monument to the Union of Lublin (*Kopiec Unii Lubelskiej*), the future mound being erected in Lemberg's green surroundings stemmed from several reasons. First, a model in Cracow, the Kościuszko Mound, had existed since 1823.[42] Second, as will be argued in the following pages, the official Vormärz notion of public parks as semipublic space was central to Smolka's position. The authorities concerned themselves little with any symbolic activities that took place in parks, and memorial plaques and obelisks were routinely placed in memory of an honorable visitor to the city. Smolka, by education a lawyer, could skillfully manipulate with this understanding of public space. And we must not forget that the site was marked by Habsburg imperial symbolism. Following Joseph II's visit in 1780, a memorial obelisk had been erected there, and after Franz Joseph's visit in 1851, the hill itself was named *Franz-Joseph-Berg*. The idea to erect a monument in the emperor's memory was greeted with enthusiasm by the Lemberg public. In 1852 an anonymous writer, who was quite likely Polish, mused about it in his writings:

> I am hoping that Castle Hill, that is, Franz Joseph's Hill, will soon be beautified with a new embellishment. Once having passed in a large company by the same spot where Our Majesty had wished to stop for the longest time, at the terrace overlooking Żolkiew Road, I revealed my thoughts of how wonderful it would be to erect some adequate monument at this spot in memory of Our Majesty's visit. Those words convinced the entire company, the thought was adopted unanimously, and soon someone had already made a sketch and worked out the costs, which...should not exceed 4000 Gulden. This total is a trifle, almost nothing.[43]

Given that Smolka's idea was first expressed only two years after the establishment of Galician Autonomy, it was bound to be seen by the Gubernium's authorities as radical. Smolka's pioneering initiative was furthermore significant because it was followed later by many other enthusiasts who conceived of ideas of monuments to national leaders and also because it resulted in the invention of a new type of yearly celebration in fin-de-siècle Lemberg.

The Union of Lublin of 1569 was one of the key treaties in Polish history: it symbolized Polish greatness and encouraged national pride. The Union resulted in the creation of the medieval Polish-Lithuanian Commonwealth, which united the Kingdom of Poland and the Grand Duchy of Lithuania, and lasted until its final partition in 1795. The state covered the territory of what is now Poland, Lithuania, Latvia, Belarus, and large parts of Ukraine and western Russia.[44] It also fit into the revolutionary idea of the union of free nations under the leadership of the most progressive one, Poland. Thus whatever the organizer's political intentions – which were, as previously mentioned, far from questioning the political legitimacy of the monarchy – to commemorate the Union of Lublin would seem to suggest a radical alternative to the Habsburg project and one in which Poland would play the leading role.

The ambitions of the organizational committee were grand. When Smolka submitted for approval the proposal for initial construction work on the Union Mound, along with the program of the accompanying public event on 10 August 1869, his proposal included outrageously bold suggestions. This was one of the first documents submitted to the authorities in the Polish language, in which Smolka suggested not only laying the foundation stone for the mound, but also an extensive celebration program. The event was to attract international attention, and therefore "celebrities from other Slavic nations" were to be invited; furthermore, "all European nations" were to be informed of the ceremonies. Smolka's idea was that the authorities need not interfere with the celebration at all. [45] He wanted a two-day celebration held on 10-11 August 1869, with 11 August as a national holiday. The organizing committee, led by Franciszek Smolka, envisioned a *theatre pavé* in the Skarbek Theater on 10 August, and a celebration ceremony of the greatest possible scale on 11 August. The second day would begin with 100 mortar shots at dawn, around 5 a.m., and a holiday mass held at all churches that would include appropriately themed sermons. After the mass, the procession participants would assemble at Market Square, brandishing national emblems and flags and dressed in national costumes. Accompanied by music – a chorus and an orchestra – and with further salvos, the procession would head to Castle Hill. Smolka even envisioned a citizen guard (*straż obywatelka*) to accompany the procession and help supervise the event.[46] The procession would then wind through Ruthenian (*Ruśka*) Street and pass by the Carmelite Cloister and the palace of Roman Catholic archbishops, which would be decorated with flags and banners.

All the ceremonial arrangements described above recall the structure of the official celebrations detailed earlier in this chapter. However, the purpose of this celebration was far from glorifying the Habsburg throne; rather, this event was to support a revisitation of the "Jagiellonian idea" – the Polish-Lithuanian Commonwealth interpreted as a voluntary, "brotherly" union of the Polish, Lithuanian, and Ruthenian nations.[47] After official greetings from the chairman, Smolka then envisioned that a speaker would "explain the importance, value, and significance of the Union, at which time he would point out the duties of the nation deriving from it. He would further solicit adequate contributions that would express the feelings and beliefs of the Polish nation regarding the duties described in the Union."[48] The practical measure of having a guard and a predetermined list of speakers was intended to ensure that no mishap would serve as a pretext for the police to intervene and thereby stop the ceremony.

However, by copying the organizational structures and methods of the state authorities, the committee also aimed to eliminate those same authorities from the event and to demonstrate that – at least for this event – Polish Democrats were in control of the city. To legitimize their right to use public space and buildings, notably the theater, for a national celebration, Smolka invoked a connection with Vienna: the anniversary of the Viennese Riflemen society, he claimed, was to "uplift the spirit of the German unity's revival."[49] As if forgetting that the Ruthenians demonstratively claimed their opposition to the commemoration, Smolka reasoned:

> Is in this case also a different interpretation given to the application
> of constitutional rights on the one hand to Germans and, on the other
> hand, to other, non-German nations?! – and this in opposition to [the
> principle of] equal rights for everyone?![50]

The reaction was predictable. The police director's report to the Crown Land and central administration of 14 June 1869 noted that an agreement between the Democrats (meaning Smolka and his followers) and the Ruthenians was not reached.[51] Therefore his report prohibited the celebration altogether on the grounds that it would cause "irritation to the majority of inhabitants of the city and the Crown Land" and thereby threaten public peace.[52] The 11th of August was to be a usual working day, and his proposal for a public procession and illumination of the city was rejected.[53] However, thanks to Smolka's legal skillfulness, the authorities could not prohibit the celebration altogether. He reasoned that since the organizing committee had changed the program to a celebration of a "private" nature, the state could not prohibit people from gathering in the morning for church services and then, in small groups and without "disturbing public peace," from proceeding through the city to Castle Hill. In the end, he succeeded in having the celebration in 1869 be as grand as possible, even if he had to submit to official restrictions that prevented it from being "public."

Police records provide a coherent picture of the actual celebration that was held on 11 August 1869 and that started with an expected mishap: brochures detailing the Ruthenian protest against the celebration were sold on every corner, causing several minor conflicts in the streets.[54] In general, disturbances continued throughout the day and were not limited to the opponents of the celebration:

There was no shortage of disturbances and excesses....The members of the Democratic Party took part in the celebration and naturally showed their dissatisfaction with the nature of the government's prohibition [of the commemoration].[55]

The city maintained its typical appearance: no holiday cleaning was done and public offices were open all day. A small crowd gathered for the church service in the Dominican Church (Fig. 52), and an even smaller group convened at the Bernardine Church. Few wore national costumes, and the aristocracy and peasantry did not attend.[56] The local priest referred to the union in his sermon as of an act of brotherly love and unity, and then he sug-

Figure 52. DominicanChurch. Lithograph by Karol Auer, 1837-38. Lviv Stefanyka Scientific Library. This is where the Union of Lublin celebration started on 11 August 1869.

gested that its principles be observed in the present, once a quiet political engagement would become appropriate, and concluded with praise for the Austrian throne. After the *Honorationi* and the guilds left the church, the remaining public sang "*Boże, coś Polskę*" [God, Thou protected Poland] and "*Z dymem pożarów*" [With the smoke of fires], Polish religious songs that were associated with the Polish insurrection of 1863. In small groups, the participants then made their way to Castle Hill. Altogether numbering about five hundred, the group included representatives of the district and city councils. When the foundation stone, bearing the Polish coat-of-arms and the inscription "Free among the free and equal among the equal – Poland, Lithuania, and Ruthenia unified by the Act of the Lublin Union on 11 August 1569," was in place, Smolka gave his speech:

> We cannot afford marble and bronze to erect an adequate monument to the most magnificent moment in our historic past. Thus let us erect a monument...from the soil taken from all Poland. Let it be a symbol of the indivisible union of the brotherly nations that inhabit this land.[57]

Figure 53. Smolka's speech on Castle Hill on the occasion of the Union of Lublin anniversary in 1869. Aleksander Czołowski, *Wysoki zamek z 19 rycinami w tekscie* (Lemberg: Towarzystwo Miłośników Przeszłości Lwowa, 1910).

Smolka expressed his gratitude to the city council for their efforts to date on the construction of the mound. He threw the first handful of soil, saying, "In the name of God, in the name of love for the motherland, and for the sake of equality and brotherhood, let us now, citizens, begin to mold this monument that will symbolize these principles and that will commemorate this great anniversary."[58] Smolka's words made a connection between God, the motherland, and democratic principles, a link that was a standard ideological feature in Polish nationalism.[59] City representatives and foreign guests followed Smolka in metaphorically initiating construction of the mound.[60] Soil had been brought from various symbolically significant places, such as from the battlefield of Grunwald. This military event, also known as the Battle of Tannenberg (15 July 1410), was the decisive engagement of the Polish-Lithuanian-Teutonic War (1409-11) and one of the greatest battles of medieval Europe. It was fought between the Kingdom of Poland, the Grand Duchy of Lithuania, and their allies on one side, and the Knights of the Teutonic Order on the other. Other symbolic places included the tombs of Kościuszko, Lelewel, Mickiewicz, Kniaziewicz, Słowacki, and Ostrowski,[61] the Tomb of the Five Victims in Powązki,[62] and the tomb to those deported to Siberia. Soil had also been brought from more bizarre and faraway places, Jerusalem and San Francisco.[63] Some deputies, such as Dworski, spoke in the name of Polish *Emigrationi*, and others, such as Ostrowski, whom the police report called "*ein obscures Individuum*," invoked the name of their late fathers who died in the "wars of liberation."

The fragment of Smolka's speech quoted above illustrates the most striking characteristic of national celebrations in Lemberg, this being a profound gap between aspirations and the achievable. Beyond official restrictions, which would ease with time as the Crown Land and Municipal administrations came to include members of the Democratic Party, national projects were chronically short of money and people. Thus the organizers of such endeavors were forced to compensate for this lack of commitment and funding by using more affordable designs for their symbolically charged projects.

On this occasion, the inclusive character of Polish nationalism, the "brotherly union of nations that inhabit this land," was clearly foregrounded. Later in the day, for example, at a concert at the restaurant on Castle Hill, a Ruthenian speaker was invited to attend, and a donation to the Ruthenian *Prosvita* Society was made.[64] The indoor, "private," per Smolka program continued in the same spirit in the Skarbek Theater in the evening, though the authorities had forbidden the full performance of Ostrowski's "Golden Mountains" (*Złote góry*), written specifically for the event. This historical piece to the three main events in the history of the Polish crown was intended as an educational guide to the main characteristics of Polish national identity: civilized, Catholic, and democratic.[65] At the end of the evening, the theater troupe performed Kamiński's "Krakowiaki," the opera "Ukrainka," the "Ruthenian Song" (*ruśka duma*),[66] and a fragment from "Zygmunt August on this throne." The last number, possibly taken from Ostrowski's monumental work, involved three female figures in folk costumes who symbolized the union of the Polish, Lithuanian, and Ruthenian "nations."[67]

Just as the Gubernium could not disallow the celebration altogether, it could not prohibit the spectacular lighting of private houses. If the accuracy of the police report of the time is to be believed, the city must have had a striking appearance that evening: "Simultaneous [with the theater performance], [the] illumination [of houses] got under way. Except for the dwellings of the Ruthenians, military officers, and some officials, and except for the buildings of the Crown Land administration and the Town Hall, all (*sämtliche*) private dwellings were illuminated."[68]

By the end of the day and with his ostensibly private format, Smolka appears to have created a truly national mass celebration. His idea for a Polish congress at the mound of the Union of Lublin[69] was realized two years later, in 1871. On 13 August of that year, a large gathering was held in Lemberg with participation by distinguished guests from greater Poland (*Wielkopolska*), Prussia, Silezia, and Cracow and involved a solemn procession to Castle Hill. Although Schnür-Pepłowski has left a detailed account of this event, primary source materials on it have not yet been discovered.[70] However, the information available allows us to trace an important change in the authorities' treatment of such events.

At the 1871 congress, the authorities did not attempt to restrict the commemoration ceremony that was planned in tandem, nor did they themselves pay lip service to the Ruthenians, as was done in 1869.[71] Despite the unusual summer heat, crowds assembled early in the morning at the train station to greet the visitors. The great procession started at the Municipal Park in the afternoon and headed through the city center toward Castle Hill, bypassing the ring road and Market Square. Gentry's hats (*kolpaki*) mingled with caps from the Bar Confederation (*konfederatki*) and the helmets of the fire brigade; some participants brandished flags depicting the Polish white eagle. At Castle Hill, Smolka spoke of the Union as "the most wonderful act in Polish history" that united "nations of different origin into one political entity for the defense of common interests so that they might march together on the road of civilization and progress."[72] The Riflemen Garden hosted the dinner and a "Cracovians and Mountaineers" performance in the evening; on 15 August a grand ball was held in a large tent in the Municipal Park.

A comparison of the two ceremonies on Castle Hill, 1869 and 1871, reveals an important difference between the two that speaks to a fundamental change in the way public space was used following the establishment of Galician autonomy and Lemberg's self-government. The gradual transition of Polish national celebrations from the "private" realm to the "public" realm can be observed. The celebrations of 1869 and 1871 were held on the site that had been renamed *Franz-Joseph-Berg* in 1851, physically the highest landmark in the city. Although both celebrations made use of public buildings such as the Roman Catholic churches, the Riflemen's shooting range building, and the theater, the outdoor expressions of national sentiment became much more explicit in 1871. Furthermore, in 1871 the celebration had been sacralized in the cathedral and legitimized by a grand public procession passing through the city center, past the Town Hall and the Dominican Church, actions ostensibly undertaken in a private mode in 1869. Other, modified and increasingly public, meaning outdoor, versions of Polish national celebrations can also be found in the late nineteenth and early twentieth centuries. As public buildings became increasingly available for such events, the speeches given at the Town Hall became integral parts of these celebrations, along with printed materials.

Castle Hill and the Union Mound came to witness yet another celebration in 1874, this one organized by a previously unknown Pole. Jan Pawulski, a war veteran, had been one of the guards responsible for supervising the construction of the Union of Lublin Mound[73] and was allegedly a member of the Democratic Party. Careful analysis of this celebration's complicated history leads to a further rethinking of the role of Lemberg's "*tromtadraci*" ("trumpeters," pejorative for the Polish Democratic Party)[74] in nationalizing Lemberg's public space and of the complex reality of the late nineteenth-century multiethnic city under the Habsburg rule. Furthermore, it provides an illustration of the constant reinvention of traditions, already constructed along the lines Hobsbawm has suggested, in continuous modifications to fit changing political realities. For Franciszek Jaworski, the celebration was a spontaneous but repulsive popular event, held without clear cause or purpose:

> Out of the blue (*ni z tego ni z owego*), the Lwów *tromtadracja* came up with the notion of solemnly transferring a lion from the old…Town Hall to Castle Hill. It was carried with great pomp, and the first day it arrived as far as Teatyńska [Street]. The police, out of a fear of possible demonstrations, however, made the subsequent procession impossible in such [a curious] way that the police itself moved the lion to Castle Hill during the next night. [The lion stood there and] in a peculiar Lwów dialect spoke: "For God's sake, may thunder strike me once I know why they have put me here and what all this is supposed to mean (*Dalibóg, niech mnie piorun trzaśnie, wenn ich weiss, na co oni mnie tu postawili, i co się ma znaczyć diese ganze Geschichte*)."[75]

Yet Pawulski was in fact driven by a clear idea derived from a mixture of loyalty, local patriotism, and nationalism. In August 1874, he wrote to the Municipality, suggesting a small party at Castle Hill five years after the commemoration of the union's 300th anniversary.[76] He fully realized that his request for approval to include elements of the traditional royal ceremonies in his celebration – even if it appeared to be in connection with the mound's anniversary and was made at the time the city administration was predominantly Polish – was not a promising strategy:

> There has been a gloomy silence at Castle Hill for five years [since 1869]. We plan a celebration on 11 August for the youths who remain

[in the city] during the holidays, children under their parents' eye, and the public of both sexes,...free of charge, without military orchestra or fireworks,...without the slightest resemblance to a political demonstration, and yet under the eye of the political authorities and the supervision of the Building Department in the person of Alfred Bojarski.[77]

After receiving preliminary approval, Pawulski's second letter to the Municipality revealed that he already had a much broader idea in his mind. He suggested that a medieval sculpture of a lion, one that prior to the construction of the neoclassical Town Hall had stood in Market Square and that remained in the ownership of the Municipality, could be presented to the celebration committee. The sculpture would then be ceremonially transported to Castle Hill where, Pawulski claimed, it would enjoy a more fitting location than it had previously:

> For many centuries the proud lion, the Ruthenian prince's and this city's founder's true coat-of-arms, stood...at the tribune of the Town Hall.... For decades now he stands redundant, presently near the stable and toilets, desecrated from the front and from the back [as if] condemned to shame and misery. Present him to us so that he may decorate the top of the city's future landmark, the mound. Already this Sunday (9 August) he could inhabit a place more appropriate to him: the residence of Casimir the Great, destroyed by the Swedes. Monument conservator Mr. Potocki will restore him and put him in new clothes, as [he did with] the statue to Hetman Jabłonowski....It would become a possession, a decoration, and a symbol (*wlasność, ozdoba i klejnot*) of yours, of the entire Crown Land (*Kraj*), of this city, and of us!"[78]

This quote reveals Pawulski, a regular member of Lemberg "*tromtadracja,*" as close to most public officials and monument conservators, two groups for whom historic monuments held significance by virtue of their age, rather than any national or other historic association. In this view, the Ruthenian prince coexisted with the Polish king, and the medieval monument with the new mound on Castle Hill, while local patriotism overlapped with imperial loyalty and ethnic affiliation.

On 15 August 1874, the city council approved of the commemoration on the grounds that the sculpture "was neither significant from an artistic point of view, nor through its age, and that there cannot be a better place for it than on the mound."[79] Moreover, the authorities allowed the incorporation of architectural landmarks traditionally significant in official ceremonies: the Town Hall would mark its starting point, and salvos were to be fired from Castle Hill when the procession would arrive at the triumphal arch at Kiselka Tollgate.[80] Thus Pawulski legitimized his ceremony with the use of elements from well-known official celebrations. By taking a more tolerant stance toward the authorities than Smolka's aggressive claiming of public space as a civil right, Pawulski allowed for the further institutionalization of an invented national celebration, and in so doing he set a precedent for later, innovative intrusions into official ceremonies.

While Smolka should certainly be granted the key role as Lemberg's first and foremost "master of ceremonies," the one to have successfully established a new tradition of street celebrations, the actual construction of the Union Mound seriously complicated his success story. Although brochures spoke emotionally of "constructing a new Poland with our own hands" on Castle Hill, the organization of the celebration was easier than the actual construction work on the mound. There neither the organizers nor the wider public was particularly enthusiastic about the actual outcome. A police report of 30 July 1869 mentioned the sorry sum that the committee had at its disposal and sarcastically concluded as follows: "It appears from this that the initial project has not been particularly well supported by the people."[81] The committee needed to seek approval from different organs of power and to use legal tricks to be able to continue the project. One such trick – invented by Smolka, yet the one we already met in the discussion of the Jan Kiliński monument – was that the initial committee for the commemoration of the 300th anniversary of the Union of Lublin ended its legal existence on 11 August. Instead, Smolka organized a new and larger standing (*nieustający*) committee for the Union Mound.[82] This committee needed to marginalize the Ruthenian opinion, which was explicitly negative, and to commit its own "nation" to the idea.

Smolka himself complained to the Municipality as early as 8 September 1869 that "because the public is not willing to be convinced and so to become involved in this pressing (*konieczna*) work," he had repeatedly asked the Municipal Building Department to provide workers, "or maybe prisoners," for the project.[83] There was the usual shortage of finances and public commitment. The former problem Smolka attempted to solve at the Crown Land Administration as early as August 1869, mentioning to the authorities the possible expenses, though still unaware that some quarters, especially historic preservation, would deal him more headaches than help in the future.[84] The viceroy administration was obviously not in a position to allow such an explicit public statement as Smolka proposed, nor did it have the intention of doing so.[85]

Yet as time went by, the Municipality seemed to have fallen into a familiar trap. Through the interplay of various forces, it was now compelled to view the construction of the Lublin Union Mound as a *public* affair, and thus as one that required its support. In Smolka's explanatory response to the Police Department of 11 August 1869, we read that by then he had already ensured Municipal permission for the building of the mound on Castle Hill.[86] Nothing could occur at the building site thereafter without the Municipality's knowledge and approval. As the road leading from the city to Castle Hill was being widened and renovated,[87] the viceroy administration's presidium ironically commented in an inquiry to the police director that "such an undertaking...would be difficult to explain...in the light of the prohibition of the entire celebration, and...the act of the assembly."[88] As the turn of the century approached, the latter became increasingly Polish, and indeed some of its members viewed the construction of the mound as a pressing national issue. The members of the Municipal Council attended the groundbreaking ceremony on 11 August 1869. By this time, an official from the Municipal Building Department, Alfred Bojarski, had become an active member of the executive committee for the construction of the mound.[89] Because of this, the Municipal authorities were left with two options: either refrain from any activity connected with the mound's construction, or support it openly and publicly as its own project. The first option, though attractive to the old neoabsolutist generation of Galician officials, would have left the Municipality to watch and wonder how, after permission to develop the land had been obtained, the Union Mound would rise as a monument to an alternative political agenda. Thus even if its construction would be long and difficult, as it indeed proved to be, choosing to support the mound's construction provided a way out of the deadlock. The political authorities could preserve their legitimacy and engage in an activity they traditionally favored, urban planning.

Even those public officials who would oppose the idea, such as the police director, acknowledged that the construction of the Union Mound was a *public* enterprise:

> Since the construction of the mound is taking place in full view of the government (*w obliczu rządu*), since [it] is connected with various large expenses, and since the committee has begun this activity without the government's permission – an activity that even if not viewed as a demonstration against Austria is nevertheless a political demonstration designed to have a different trajectory [than Austrian patriotism]. Consequently the government possesses the means to prohibit this illegal act.[90]

The Police Department and the Crown Land administration in general remained hostile to the proposal, and the Municipality grew more and more enthusiastic about it. In the early 1870s, yet another opponent entered the picture, one whose professional opinion it was difficult to ignore.

Beginning in March 1872, Juliusz Hochberger, the Municipal Building Department director, personally inspected the mound's construction and kept a close eye on any activity that might have compromised either good architectural taste or any existing historic monuments. The ruins of the medieval castle stood in close proximity to the building site. Few as the enthusiasts for the construction of

220 ◆ CHAPTER FOUR

the Union Mound were, they were deeply convinced of their professional authority. Opinions clashed in 1872, when it emerged that the committee had unilater-
ally decided to demolish the ruins in the center of the mound because it believed
it was in a position to decide which portion of the ruins was valuable and which
was not. Hochberger harshly replied to this decision:

> One is to oppose this proposed action as strongly as possible, since,
> first, such a dear national monument that, moreover, obstructs no one's
> way should not be demolished (*pamiatki takiej ojczystej, która nikomu
> nie zawadza...burzyć nie należy*). Second, those ruins add much to the
> picturesque quality of the area...I am convinced that quite a few of
> those who are today in support of the demolition of those ruins will
> feel their absence in the future.[91]

The committee seemed not to take notice, and the Municipality rather un-
willingly joined ranks with its Building Department director and on 4 December
1872 warned of its intent to limit the committee's rights to develop the site:

> The Municipality watches with great pain (*ubolewanie*) as the honor-
> able committee continues to demolish the historical monuments that
> are so rare here. [The Municipality] urges [you] decisively (*stanowczo*)
> to stop all demolition work as well as the planning of the site where the
> castle walls are situated. In the opposite case, the Municipality would
> feel urged (*widziałby się znaglonym*) to use adequate [legal] means to
> limit the scope of the committee's activity.[92]

Despite Hochberger's concern for the historic ruins, the Municipality remained passive out of political and administrative concerns. It was easier to let
Smolka's committee develop the ground for the scandalous project that had been
initially rejected at the provincial level than to protest its work at this late stage."
On the administrative side, it was unclear to what extent the Municipality could
indeed interfere.[93] Smolka himself was not willing to allow the work to stop
simply because one individual thought that the old castle ruins deserved greater
care.[94] It was only in September of 1875, when reports began to circulate that the
mound had started to deteriorate because of a poorly laid foundation,[95] that the
city finally decide to intervene.

A variety of other voices joined the discussion. Polish intellectuals of diverse backgrounds who had professional interests in historic preservation were,
by virtue of their profession, opposed to the mound's construction. Some, such
as Count Mieczysław Potocki, had strict professional affiliation with the Austrian
state and worked as regional curators of historic sites. Others, like Antoni Schneyder, were public activists committed to preserving local historic architecture.
Here the issue of defining national heritage began to play a leading role.

In the conservators' opinion, the abandoned remains of the medieval castle were at least as important, if not more so, as the construction of the Union Mound. Potocki and his deputy Stanisław Kunasiewicz followed conservative imperial values and maintained a deep belief in the Austrian state's good intentions and its ultimate authority on conservation issues.[96] As it happened, they had sound reasons to assume that the Polish Democrats committed to the mound's construction would not preserve the old medieval ruins in full, which could clearly serve as a better building material than sandy soil. A week after the ceremony of 1869, Kunasiewicz complained to the Municipality that "the hills are being dug out as [construction] material" and that "diverse artifacts of varying quality," found during the works, were either being shattered on the spot or reaching the hands of antique collectors."[97] A month after the celebration, Potocki appealed to the Municipality in connection to the organizers' continuing careless attitude toward the old walls and requested that efforts be made to preserve this "national monument (*narodowa pamiatka*)." The city should, he reasoned, "under no circumstances allow the erection of a new monument in the place of an old one, and a much more valuable one at that."[98]

With support from conservation enthusiasts and possessing clear evidence that Smolka's committee could accomplish its work neither qualitatively (technically) nor quantitatively (given the chronic lack of people and work delays),the Municipality finally took the initiative in 1876. The Union Mound was deteriorating, most notably on the side of the triumphal arch, through which all official ceremonies had to pass, and further building work was prohibited.[99] Because of the pressing situation, given its allocating a sum annually to fund the mound's construction and with *pro forma* recognition of Smolka's efforts,[100] in September of that year the Municipality finally made its position plain:

> So as not to unreasonably overburden the fund for the erection of the mound,...the Commission's opinion is that it would be natural that the expenses of the mound's construction and the technical control of it be undertaken by the Lemberg Municipality....Although Mr. Smolka's involvement in the building works deserves recognition, because of the lack of funding and, separately, his other time-consuming public duties, the progress of the works has often been delayed. [101]

Thus Smolka's initiative finally became the priority project of the Municipality. Yet it proved impossible, even for the professional city civil engineers, to save the Union Mound from deterioration. Municipal funds were insufficient to undertake an evaluation of the ground, or to employ an adequate number of experts, or, finally, to complete the memorial, for which there initially had been little official interest or public commitment.

The Municipality struggled with the project for nearly forty years and finally gave up in 1907 when strong summer rains caused new deformations to the mound. Lamenting the mound's "catastrophic condition" on 15 June 1907, the Municipal presidium, headed by Tadeusz Rutowski, appealed unsuccessfully to the public conscious once more, employing heavy national rhetoric.[102] Yet, as in previous years, the expected national commitment materialized only in written form, and the general public remained indifferent to issues other than popular attractions. The written commitment came from Teofil Merunowicz, a notorious deputy to the Provincial Diet and a chance participant in the ceremony of 11 August 1869,[103] in an open letter to the city's newly elected mayor, Stanisław Ciuchciński, on 18 June 1907.

This letter was apparently a polemical response to an article in the Ukrainophile newspaper, *Dilo,* which had simply paraphrased a popular proverb sarcastically and asserted that the Union Mound would soon be "blown away by the winds," just as the Polish-promoted idea of the "friendly union of nations" that it personified had been.[104] Merunowicz's letter asserted Municipal responsibility for the maintenance of the mound, appealed again to the "entire nation" for support for the project, and, ironically, blamed the "modern *hajdamaky*," i.e., the Ruthenians, for the mound's deterioration.[105] Ironically, the metaphor worked well: it was precisely the mound's foundation that had been badly constructed.[106] Having destroyed much of the medieval ruins, the initiators of the project had failed to construct a proper, lasting monument to the liberal values represented in the Act of the Union.

In the early 1900s the issue yet again became a matter of political dispute: from a question of the great unity of the three "Polish" nations, the deteriorating mound was transformed into a metaphor for the troublesome Polish-Ruthenian relations of the early twentieth century. The pathos of the press's polemics demonstrated how deeply emotional the issue of the Lublin Union Mound was for local intellectuals in the late 1900s, and also how reluctant they were to provide assistance for its actual completion. The Municipality remained reluctant to reconceptualize the notion of public space as a heterogeneous one, where many more actors could and should play. As a result, it was forced to consider the problematic project as its own and thereby to dedicate sums for the poorly begun, technically troubled, yet emotionally charged memorial at the top of *Franz-Joseph-Berg*. (Figure 54 captures the aerial view over Lwów during the interwar period, when the problems with the mound's maintenance continued.)

Instead of attesting to the victory of liberal values and to the greatness of the modern Polish national mission in the region of Central Europe, the mound became a run-of-the-mill Municipal worry throughout the remaining years of Habsburg rule.

Figure 54. View over Lwów. Photograph by Edmund Libański, 1928. Private collection of Ihor Kotlobulatov.

The City and the Ruthenians, 1905

Castle Hill found itself on the Municipal agenda once again in 1905, this time as a site of reference: this was the year of the 250th anniversary of the siege of Lemberg by the Cossack troops, led by Bohdan Chmelnyćkyj, during which the defense of Castle Hill had figured very significantly. The predominant Polish and Ruthenian historical interpretations of the siege, however, differed radically. Polish historiography viewed the attack as an act of violence, replete with notorious abuses of the Jewish inhabitants, and as a demonstration of Lemberg's spiritual strength and its unanimous loyalty to the Polish crown.[107] Ruthenian literature, conversely, understood the siege as an unsuccessful attempt to liberate Lemberg from the yoke of Polish rule and of Chmelnyćkyj's solidarity with the Galician Ruthenians, while they considered his demand that Lemberg give up its Jewish population in return for a cessation of the siege an act of long-awaited justice.[108] Thus the suggestion of a commemoration in 1905 was certain to stir up antagonisms within the local population and to make a clear political statement.

The idea of the celebration came from the city. On 5 October 1905, a meeting of the commemoration committee, led by Lemberg President Michał Michalski and including five members of the city council, took place in the president's office. The impressive program, which received immediate approval from the city council, concentrated on indoor activities: a solemn mass in all the churches and a service in the synagogue; a lecture by Aleksander Czołowski in the Town Hall; the printing of two publications, one scholarly by Czołowski and one popular by Jaworski; and lectures in all the Lemberg schools.[109] The Jewish community joined in with a terse brochure that simply quoted a Municipal archival source of 2 November 1655 in which Lemberg Mayor Marcin Grossmajer recorded his position on the Jewish issue and the Lemberg inhabitants' solidarity against Chmelnyćkyj's troops.[110]

Ruthenians felt seriously hurt. The celebration was initiated by the Polish-dominated Municipality and, despite its indoor character was to make use of a range of public buildings and printed material. Calling the proposed celebration "a chauvinist demonstration against the memory of [our] hetman and against the idea that led him to go to war against Poland," the Russophile newspaper *Galichanin* appealed that "the truth" be uncovered and that the "Russian" (*russkoje*, i. e., Ruthenian) clergy be exempted from the celebration:

> If the aforementioned members of the committee were familiar with history, and if they would have had at least a bit of political tact and common sense, they would have left the upcoming 250th [anniversary] unnoticed, as they left all its previous anniversaries without commemoration. Simple common sense should have led them to realize that such demonstrations could not be pleasant to Russian [i.e., Ruthenian] inhabitants and that it can neither support the peaceful relationship between the Russian [again] and the Polish population..., nor even moderate the existing national and political antagonisms.[111]

A document written in Polish by Semen Wityk, a Ruthenian Socialist and Austrian parliament deputy, illustrates that cold-minded and reasonable arguments against the celebration existed on the Ruthenian side.[112] The Ruthenian protest notwithstanding, the celebration went according to the program. Public officials, the guilds, a professional society (*Handwerksvereine*), and a few (*spärlich versammelten*) workers attended the sermon at the Roman Catholic Cathedral. Czołowski held his lecture in the Town Hall in the afternoon, where he described the Lemberg inhabitants' "decent conduct" (*wackere Haltung*) during the siege. Both Czołowski's and Jaworski's publications came out in print.[113] Seemingly a quiet celebration, the commemoration of November 1905 demonstrated that Municipal and education institutions, together with the official press, had become mouthpieces for the official Polish understanding of history and that Municipal celebrations could now be organized irrespective of the Ruthenian position.

The first attempt at a large Municipal scenario was in 1905, and its aspirations were realized in full in 1910, with the commemoration of the 500th anniversary of the Grunwald battle, organized as an exhibition of Polish art. The program included the insertion of a memorial plate onto Julian Zachariewicz's Galician Savings Bank, the building at the intersection of Jagiellońska Street and the ring road; the establishment of a foundation for the construction of a monument to King Jagiello, which was never realized; the official opening of the exhibition; the festive illumination of the entire city and the burning of tar barrels on Castle Hill; a gala performance in the city theater; smaller celebrations in each of the city districts, accompanied by lectures; and the printing of an appeal to the population of the Crown Land regarding the commemoration of the Grunwald anniversary.[114] The start of the procession was signaled early in the morning from the Town Hall tower. After a solemn mass at the Roman Catholic cathedral, at 9 a.m., the procession headed from *Rynek* Square toward Jagiełłońska Street. Then, after moving along 3 May, Słowacki, and Kopernik Streets and passing the Diet, the procession arrived at the monument to Mickiewicz, where speeches were presented. Thereafter it headed to the exhibition grounds.[115]

The situation was quite different with Ruthenian national celebrations that, until the early twentieth century and to a large extent until the monarchy's collapse, remained limited to religious and cultural organizations, notably the *Seminarium*, the Ruthenian National Institute, and the *Prosvita* society (the latter had acquired a prestigious Lubomirski palace building on the *Rynek* Square in the early 1900s).[116] The events of 1905 set light on why this was so. By this time, having "one's own truth in one's own house" was no longer seen as sufficient for Ruthenian political interests. The authorities had grounds to fear the unusual unity of the Ruthenians. According to a police report, the complete spectrum of Ruthenian national organizations (*sämtliche Ruthenen ohne Unterschied der Parteien...beiderlei Geschlechtes und verschiedener Stände*), numbering altogether over two thousand people, was present at a meeting on 13 November 1905 in the Ruthenian National Institute. Social Democrats and students of the *gymnasium* and the university made up most of those present. After the usual program was completed,[117] the Ruthenian newspaper *Dilo*'s editor, Jevhen Levyćkyj, called the Polish celebration "an act of chauvinist ingratitude (*Undankbarkeit*)" and invited the participants to "finish the siege that Chmelnyćkyj had begun two hundred fifty years earlier."

As a consequence, a column formed on the street and headed through Teatralna Street toward *Rynek* Square to demonstrate in front of the Town Hall. "According to a confidential source," continues the police report "they were determined to throw stones through the Town Hall windows."[118] Yet the police met them at Trybunalska Street, and prevented them from entering the main square. The crowd attacked with cobblestones; the police used force. After one gunshot from the crowd, the police scattered the demonstration before it could access

Rynek Square.[119] The Polish official indoor celebration of Lemberg's historic loyalty to the Polish crown and its inhabitants' heroism against the Cossack siege continued undisturbed. *Rynek* Square remained quiet and the Town Hall windows safe, thus confirming in practice the Polish version of Lemberg's past and the Ruthenian inability to change it.

The uses of architecture during street ceremonies figured as powerful vehicles for symbolic statements, and as one of the very few means of local self-expression in the Vormärz. Beginning with the celebration welcoming Polish Napoleonic troops in 1809, the uses of architecture in ceremonies represented the invention of traditions that grew ever more varied toward the end of the nineteenth century and the beginning of the twentieth. The success of these endeavors by the authorities and nationalist intellectuals was, however, questionable because the wider public attended all spectacular events, almost irrespective of what symbolic charge they carried. Although the Lemberg public became a powerful force on the street during these diverse celebrations, at times even requiring police force to safeguard key buildings incorporated into the transformed ceremonies, as in 1905 the working of mass nationalism was still years away.

Nationalizing Restoration and Westernizing the Past

Although diverse actors used Lemberg's urban space for their varying purposes during street celebrations and ceremonies, individuals who considered themselves experts in matters related to architecture were involved in much more narrow architectural practices that radically reshaped a large bulk of the city's historic architecture. The historic preservation of architecture represents a more specialized use of historic buildings and city space than the decorations of street celebrations, more than temporary architecture and the nighttime illumination of private homes; therefore the roles as well as the ambitions of architects and civic engineers were much greater in this arena than in those of their contemporaries. These ambitions notwithstanding, not only did architects' ideas on what and how to restore undergo profound transformations in the nineteenth century, but also their professional role was challenged by a range of institutions that also claimed the right to reshape historic buildings according to their own vision. The transformation of the idea of a historic monument, of style, and of the architect's role in the historic preservation process resulted in profound changes in preservation practices. In Lemberg's particular context of ethnic diversity, these practices acquired additional dimensions.

The belief that historic buildings possess inherent value and that they should be preserved in an "original" form is a late nineteenth-century concept. As late as the 1850s and 1860s, the idea of renovation implied renewal, that is, making new. An illustrative example of the related ignorance of local architectural matters can be clearly seen in a Bilous' brochure *Drevnija zdanija v sravnienii z nynishnimi* [Ancient buildings in comparison with contemporary ones], an early Ruthenian publication that dealt critically with the value of architectural monuments. There, as late as 1856, the author lamented the lack of Ruthenian historic buildings in Galicia, as well as the reluctance on the part of churches' governing bodies to build stylistically and technically up-to-date churches to replace old ones.[120] Largely a private matter, restoration entailed technical upgrading and the fashioning of facades and interiors according to current stylistic trends. Such was the case, for example, with Salzmann's historic preservation of the Town Hall after the bombardment of 1848.[121] The rediscovery of the value of medieval styles and the first attempts to save local Gothic buildings for their artistic and historic values arrived in the Crown Land in the 1820s; yet these efforts mainly concerned the Gothic structures in western Galicia.[122] Well into the 1850s, when the state attempted to take control of private historic preservation work on buildings that it saw as "national heritage," the practice of preservation had gone unchanged.

Vienna and the Honorary Curators

Beginning in the early 1850s, the state increasingly concerned itself with the preservation of architectural heritage, and owners and architects gradually lost their ultimate authority to fashion historic buildings to fit their own vision. Based on the previous emperor's decrees on the preservation of monuments, the Central Commission for Research and Maintenance of Architectural Monuments (*K.K. Central Commission für die Erforschung und Erhaltung der Baudenkmale*) was established in 1850 and appointed the first honorary national conservators (*Landeskonservatoren*) in 1853.[123] These positions were established "with the aim of recognizing, preventing from destruction, evaluating the scientific value of, and prolonging the life of historic buildings." This move represented an expansion of state control over monuments and their preservation: historic preservation practices became increasingly a public affair, funded by public resources.[124] These activities concerned any historic building – public or private – that "either through its artistic value or its historical significance" the state thought worthy of protecting as "national heritage": in practice, this included castle ruins, churches, cemeteries, fortifications, historic town halls, armories, towers, gates, and excavations.[125] In the view of the Central Commission, national heritage was in principle any piece of historic architecture built on the territory of the monarchy that had artistic and/or historic value.

The committee's beliefs were formulated at the beginning of the twentieth century, based on two concepts put forward by the Austrian art historian Alois

Riegl: that of the historic period, *Kunstwollen* – with every period having its own artistic value and thus requiring treatment outside a hierarchical system of superseding styles – and that of *Alterswert*, the concept of a historic artifact's age value. Riegl, who became conservator general at the turn of the twentieth century, is chiefly responsible for the legislation that safeguarded monuments (*Denkmalschutzgesetz*), issued in the year of his death, 1905. For the practice of historic preservation, Riegl's work led not only to the rediscovery of the value of classical, medieval, and Renaissance architecture, but also that of baroque. It was also implied that contemporary technology and stylistic concerns should not be applied to restore historic architecture, but rather that older structures should bear the signs of age. One should conserve, not restore, according to Riegl's writings.[126] This agenda was followed by Riegl's pupil and his successor to the position of conservator general from 1905 on, Max Dvořák. Dvořák assumed the control of preservation work in Lemberg on several occasions, notably in the re-building of the Armenian Cathedral, as we shall see in the following pages.[127] Yet in Lemberg itself, theory and practice differed profoundly: existing restoration methods prevailed toward the turn of the century, and, where they were applied, projects became increasingly national in orientation.

Despite the Riglean interpretation held by the Central Committee, its under-standing of heritage did not impart significance to the preservation of buildings of the recent past. It was commonplace throughout the entire Habsburg period to erect new buildings at central points in the city, in locations where significant architecture already stood. In Lemberg, perhaps the most illustrative example of this is the erection of the Diet building, the *Sejm*, designed by Juliusz Hochberger in 1870 (Fig. 45), on the site where the valuable neoclassical casino by Höcht stood (Fig. 37). The earlier building, significant not only for its richly decorated façade, but also as a meeting place for the gentry during the *Kontrakty* fairs, had hosted the emperor on several occasions. In contemporary discussions on the erection of a new Diet building, the potential value of Höcht's Casino never emerged;[128] neoclassicism was not yet understood as an artistic period to be val-ued and preserved.

The honorary national conservators were given responsibility for the com-prehensive supervision of historic preservation projects in their respected regions; for cataloguing buildings and artifacts; for supplying the Central Commission with those inventory lists; and, lastly, for informing the media about this state activity.[129] Galicia had two main offices: one in western Galicia and a second in eastern Galicia. Thus preservation practices were divided institutionally – and often disproportionately – between the Crown Land's "west" and "east."[130]

Following the establishment of Galician Autonomy in 1867 and the increase of provincial power after the *Ausgleich*, the Crown Land Department attempted to bring conservators' activity under its control. Their being placed under the Ministry of the Interior repeatedly figured as a matter of complaint from the Crown Land administration. In its 1872 report to the viceroy's presidium, the Crown Land Department argued that since the conservators were subordinated to the Ministry, and since they were working primarily on privately owned objects, it was very difficult to estimate their financial needs and expenditures and to monitor their activities.[131] However, the provincial budget for preservation work was limited, and Crown Land authorities therefore often advised those searching for funds to look elsewhere.[132] The 1872 report gives a rather detailed account of sites and objects that were the focus of the conservators' attention. Here western Galician heritage was given a greater value than that from the east: most of the buildings dealt with were in Cracow, and the only valuable historic objects noted in Lemberg were the Roman Catholic cathedral, the Ruthenian St. Piatnycia Church, and the sculpture of St. Michael.[133] In this light, it is revealing that a special fund was set up for the restoration of the Cracow Old Cloth Hall (*Sukiennice*) building in 1875.[134]

In the early twentieth century, the Central Commission attempted to sustain its exclusive authority over preservation practice. Because of its appeal to the Ministry of Religion and Education of 9 June 1909, the ministry on 3 March 1910 ordered that all preservation work undertaken with either state financial support or the help of the commission should note this with an adequate attribution.[135] This move illustrates a further decline in the Commission's authority, already limited to nonbinding decisions. Thus architectural heritage became a matter of contest in what Miroslav Hroch has termed the collection stage of nationalism. Crown Land conservators, appointed in Galicia and predominantly of the Polish gentry, were inclined to understand the concept of "national" in Zachariewicz's civilizational terms, which by definition favored the Gothic and Romanesque over the Byzantine. Consequently, monuments seen as Polish were given preference over those understood to be Ruthenian.

Laymen, "Technicians," and the Invention of Wawel's past

The broader city public was not indifferent to the issue of historic heritage, which by the era of Galician autonomy had already acquired specific symbolic connotations. However, besides suffering from a terminological and conceptual vagueness, early preservation work also struggled with a simple lack of organization and direction. Such was the situation with the ruins of the medieval fortifications on Castle Hill; since the undertaking of work on the Union of Lublin Mound, these ruins had become a curious obstacle to Smolka's volunteers. Antoni Schneyder commented on the continuous negligence of them during his archaeological excavations on Castle Hill:

> Last week a few handsome youngsters … destroyed the most beautiful part of those fortification walls by blocking with rubble the entrance to a place where previously the soil had been freely excavated. Such work, gentlemen, is by no means a contribution to the construction of the mound – it generally complicates progress. Thus now, because of this piled-up rubble…, there is a greater need to save it for which, as it turns out, it is not easy to find committed workers. Thus the respectable public is asked to listen to the advice and to the reminders by supervisors of the work and generally to older people who usually have in their possession an ordered plan of work.[136]

Elsewhere, Schneyder described a pitiful situation when the public, driven on by amateur archaeological fever, destroyed numerous excavated artifacts before he could obtain them. An enthusiastic attitude toward amateur archaeology did not mean volunteering for the preservation of works. On the contrary, the greater public was uninterested in the historic ruins: obviously those could not be taken home and exhibited in private collections, or sold in the antique market. It was therefore "citizens'…rights and the technicians'…duty"[137] to direct and guide public opinion, together with the actual preservation of newly discovered historic monuments, and this role was assumed by the Polytechnic Society. In the view of one of its members, who had obviously been inspired by the writings of Eugène Emmanuel Viollet-le-Duc (1814-79), a French architect, theorist on restoration, and central figure in the Gothic revival in France responsible for public discourse on "honesty" in architecture, the role of restorers was not to preserve the complex totality of the "original" design and numerous additions. Instead, the restorers needed to "return" a building to its "original" stylistic purity by demolishing "sad baroque productions" that marred it. This notion of restored architectural beauty was to lead not only to an "upgrading" of monuments' values, according to Viollet-le-Duc, but it would also serve as a means of turning laymen's attention to them.[138] Furthermore, it was to facilitate further study of local medieval traditions, and the restored historic monuments would thus become museums of medieval styles for further generations to study. The idea that some may in fact have favored the baroque and preferred it over medieval, was unthinkable in the second half of the nineteenth century, especially given the architects' sense of aesthetic hierarchy.

Although the Polytechnic Society had an aura of a professional, technical institution,[139] it took an active part in preservation affairs, which from the 1880s on were increasingly charged with symbolic meaning. Through the society's activities, a profound shift occurred in the prestige accorded to historic preservation by architects. A combination of an unprecedented increase in architectural knowledge and an awareness of the worth of local historic monuments resulted in both a need for and an appreciation of preservation work. In 1880, the Polytechnic Society proposed a resolution to the national conservator prohibiting the destruction of architectural monuments, which was "so common in Lemberg." The importance of the issue is illustrated by this resolution, which was to be delivered to the Municipal Building Department,[140] ultimately finding its way into the Lemberg Building Regulation Act (*ustawa budownicza*).[141] Yet it was not recent architecture that the Polytechnic Society, or anyone then concerned with the preservation of architectural heritage, had in mind. Rather, these were sites and buildings of historic, but Polish, national significance, and more often than not they were located west of the Galician capital.

Once again, Cracow emerged as an external factor that exerted political influence on affairs in Lemberg. The late nineteenth century included a process of the construction of Polish Cracow as the "treasure of national traditions" and as a "truly Polish" city.[142] Pressured by Cracow individuals working to make Cracow appear Polish, Lemberg preservation specialists were pressed to do the same, but their task proved more difficult. It was the Cracow Technical Society that put forward the idea of a systematic approach to significant historic monuments in Galicia.[143] The restoration of Cracow's Wawel Castle was an issue of such symbolic importance: Wawel was not just another historic castle, but the site of old Poland's past glory.[144] During Emperor Franz Joseph's first visit to Lemberg in 1880, the organizers of the official ceremony decided to entertain him with a specially organized performance at the Skarbek Theater of a fragment from Jan Nepomucen Kamiński's *Krakowiaki*, in which "ancient Wawel sparkled, revived."[145]

In 1881, upon the decision to restore the Wawel Castle, the "most magnificent national monument," the Cracow and Lemberg polytechnic societies issued a special joint statement:

> Just as the Polish language spreads wide and [with] as much honor as there will be accorded to the great tombs, so wide will the old Wawel be our dream, and thus our concern. Polish technicians and the Polish building profession cannot remain indifferent to what all the Polish folk love and to what was built with great effort and with splendid art.[146]

The role of the restorer was simultaneously that of a nation maker. In this light, the choice of a particular period to which the castle was to be restored was crucial. On the one hand, forms and styles were to be professionally considered, just as future uses might demand further technical considerations relating to construction. As an art historian, the restorer was to "examine the character of the past epoch in an unbiased manner." On the other hand, as an architect he was simultaneously "writing and making history." And although the requirements were demanding indeed, and despite the expertise and analysis to be applied to the aesthetic qualities of styles, the range of stylistic periods to which architects could restore the Wawel Castle was largely limited to one, the Renaissance, the era of King Zygmunt's glory. This choice was justified by the particular beauty of King Zygmunt's sixteenth-century castle and by the relatively damaging effect of the further modifications on the original structure.[147]

The concern of society at large that surrounded this issue was great: the First Congress of Polish Technicians had in the meantime issued a resolution demanding an architectural competition for the preservation, and the Crown Land Department in Lemberg had assigned an architect, Tomasz Pryliński, to make measurements and to prepare a plan of the castle as it had been in the sixteenth century. As Pryliński finished his work, his results were brought for evaluation to the Crown Land Department, which in turn sent them on to the Viennese court.[148] Although the plans for Wawel's restoration had been discussed since the early 1870s, much of Lemberg's other historic heritage, meaning its ostensibly non-Polish sites, had been abandoned. Thus as late as the interwar period, Bohdan Janusz lamented on the neglect of the Ruthenian St. Nicholas Church, arguably the oldest historic structure in the city. The building had kept its original shape until the mid-seventeenth century, the times of "the fire and the sword,"[149] and had been in ruins ever since. Attempts at renovation initiated under Austrian rule were in vain, a result of fires in 1785 and 1800, and thus the church stood forgotten until the end of Habsburg rule.

In this context, the restoration of Wawel Castle became a political issue. On the one hand, the congresses of Polish technicians that had been regularly held in Lemberg included it in their final resolutions as one of the most important topics of the day. This fact is even more illustrative given that there had been, as the congress reports repeatedly complained, little continuity between the congresses in their agendas. On the other hand, the Wawel restoration became the subject of Ruthenian political protest in the early twentieth century, in which context it was seen as an example of unnecessary public spending. On 30 December 1905, for example, the annual general meeting of the Ruthenian Ukrainophile *Narodna Rada*, held in the "*Ruśka besida,*" concluded with a secret conference. Apart from the usual points in the program, such as Julian Romančuk's lecture on the political conditions of the Ruthenians,[150] Kost' Levyćkyj's otherwise critical speech on the Ruthenian "opportunist" position at the Diet and the parliament cast the protest at the Diet over the restoration of Wawel.[151] In this case again, Ruthenians who held different political orientations demonstrated remarkable unity. The very same evening at the Russophile *Ruśka Rada's* meeting in the National Institute, the topics of general discussion were, in order of importance, the use of

Ruthenian taxes for the restoration of Wawel and the division of Galicia into two politically independent provinces.[152]

The City, the Municipal Archive, and the External Advisers

The Municipality assumed manifold roles in historic preservation. First, the Municipal Building Department monitored and supervised all building activities, regardless of whether they occurred at a historic building or on an empty plot of land.[153] Second, it financially supported the preservation of historic structures and monuments, and thus it provided for the realization of preservation projects making use of the advice of national conservators and external advisers. By the 1860s, it could proudly boast of the newly restored sculptures of St. Michael and hetman Jabłonowski, as well as the restored coat-of-arms on the city armory, for which Stanisław Kunasiewicz, the deputy conservator for eastern Galicia, generously praised the Municipality.[154] Until the early twentieth century, the Municipality's chosen historic monuments remained based on local patriotic criteria. A good example of this can be found in the discussions of 1888 on the installation of a memorial plaque on a new building on a Marian square. Following the national conservator's suggestion, given in 1877, the city council formally decided to install the memorial plaque on the spot where the Halicka Gate had once stood.[155]

In the 1860s, the city created the Municipal archive as a repository for historic written documents as well as other artifacts of historic significance. City archivists Wilhelm Rasp, Franz Kowaliszyn, and especially Alexander Czołowski figured importantly in Municipal historic preservation activities, especially for their opinions on architectural value.[156] Czołowski's peculiar handwriting is increasingly present in Municipal files on preservation at the end of the nineteenth century. For him, Lemberg's historic architecture was a "telling witness of Lwów's wonderful past," despite its "ruthless destruction" resulting from "the first years of the Austrian rule's extermination of all signs of Polishness."[157] In addition to the city archivist, the Municipality often solicited the expert views of external advisers on the value of a historic building. Such was the case, for example, when Czołowski addressed Izydor Šaranevyč on the destruction of old, aristocratic residences, located on Armenian Street and *Rynek*.[158] Šaranevyč's response is illustrative of late nineteenth-century concepts of stylistic purity, the value of older historic styles, and radical restoration practices.[159]

As long as there was an absence of overt symbolism, the Municipality was willing to grant concessions to historic building owners, and in such cases the role of external advisers, and especially of national conservators assigned to the Crown Land, became crucial.[160] Such was the situation when in 1903 the Ruthenian *Stavropigia* Institute decided to renovate its building.[161] On 26 May

1903, the Municipality issued a concession to the institute for the adaptation of several buildings on Blacharska Street according to the plans submitted.[162] The issue would have passed without note had Jan Bołoz Antoniewicz not learned of it. A university professor and the honorary national conservator, Antoniewicz was notorious for refusing to admit mistakes he had made on the location of the medieval Halicz, discovered by Šaranevyč, and for his fierce opposition in 1905-10 to the proposal by Lemberg President Tadeusz Rutowski for a national gallery. Offended by being bypassed, Antoniewicz requested a review of the issue. *Stauropigia* gave assurances that the adaptation of the building would be carried out exclusively according to the plans approved by Antoniewicz, but complained about a lack of funding. It therefore relied on the opinion of a master builder that a ledge had to be raised to fulfill the conservator's request and asked the Municipality for the permission to do so.[163] The Municipality, it seems, already disliked Antoniewicz, and so issued another building concession on 12 September 1903, as well as subsequent concessions on residency through 1906.[164]

Thus the only zealous proponents of historic preservation were the city archivists and conservators, such as Antoniewicz. The Municipality showed remarkable efficiency in granting concessions to the Ruthenian institute. These measures reveal how remarkably good relationships between Ruthenian institutions and the Municipality could be achieved when no symbolic charge complicated preservation issues. Later, in the 1910s, cases such as this one become increasingly rare.

Westernizing Medieval Churches: Julian Zachariewicz

Julian Zachariewicz's late nineteenth-century restoration practices have often been attacked for their brutal approach to extant historic buildings. Yet as we shall see, in Lemberg his work was neither pioneering nor exceptional in its radicalism. A telling example of heavy-handed restoration practices from the late nineteenth century, Zachariewicz's 1887 restoration of St. John the Baptist Church figured among a slew of restorations throughout the century that radically altered buildings' appearances. Contrary to previous preservation projects, which simply disregarded original structures and imposed new elements according to contemporary fashion, this one altered the church into what Zachariewicz understood as a "Western" medieval style, the Romanesque, although the original building may well have been constructed in the ostensibly "Eastern" Byzantine style.[165]

St. John the Baptist Church had undergone a series of renovations throughout the nineteenth century, with work done on it in 1836, 1855, 1861, 1868, and 1887, the last four interventions being a matter of intense interest for Lemberg's intellectuals (Fig. 55).[166] Zachariewicz undertook the final restoration in 1887,[167] following on the heels of the 1836 and 1868 projects that had begun to succumb

Figure 55. St. John the Baptist Church before Zachariewicz's restoration. Photograph by Teodor Szajnok, 1868. Private collection of Ihor Kotlobulatov.

to criticism in the late nineteenth and the first half of the twentieth centuries.[168] The renovation of 1836, for example, was viewed by Tadeusz Münnich as "the largest in scale [before Zachariewicz], yet the least diligent one,"[169] and Bohdan Janusz unconditionally declared it "fatal."[170] Their views grew out of the aforementioned preference of the day for medieval styles over the neoclassical.

The renovation of 1836 appears to have fallen very much within the tendency toward stylistic improvement common to late Vormärz work: the interior had been decorated with neoclassical pilasters and ceiling ornamentation, and an addition to the entrance hall (*predsionek*) had been built.[171] Because of the large-scale Vormärz renovation, even specialists failed to detect medieval remains in St. John the Baptist Church. National conservator Mieczysław Potocki, for example, stressed in 1869 that the present church was not remarkable for any particular historic or architectural value, but it did stand in the location of the first Christian church in Lemberg.[172] The church's importance was thus symbolic rather than architectural: it represented "the first church of Roman Catholic rite, and...therefore the first parish of this rite in the city. As such, it held crucial historic importance and therefore deserved attentive treatment."[173] The historic importance Potocki identified was an argument that even medieval Ruthenian Lemberg had had Roman Catholic – therefore, in his view, civilized – roots.

Despite these previous renovations, the church's deteriorating condition was regularly a source of Municipal worries. In 1868, the Municipal Building Department termed its condition critical and ordered that it be closed. In consequence, once Count Mieczysław Potocki, the national conservator assigned to the Crown Land, had been informed of this by his deputy Stanisław Kunasiewicz, he encouraged the Municipality to act immediately in support of a volunteer committee headed by the deputy. In Potocki's view, the church deserved attentive care, not only as "one of the oldest in Lwów," but especially as a "dear, national (*narodowa*) memorial, as well as a Municipal monument of bygone times."[174]

The Municipality, however, was restricted from action because St. John the Baptist was in the Roman Catholic church's possession. The Municipality could only appeal, as it already once had in 1854, to the church leader's patriotic feelings. In its letter of 17 February 1869, addressed to the church Cathedral Chapter (*Kapituła*),[175] the Municipality emphasized that it did not wish to involve itself in the restoration of the church's possession because it wanted to avoid unnecessary friction, but urged the church to take radical measures.[176] The head of the church hierarchy, however, did seem to have been easily moved by symbolic and cultural issues:

> The church's opinion is that this building is neither...a monument of art, nor does it contain any valuable parts. As regards its location, completely peripheral and distant, it cannot be considered as a municipal decoration, either. Its only value...lies in its historicity (*starożytność*). Yet it is precisely from this point of view that one needs to avoid everything that can deprive it of this quality. Therefore...to preserve it as it is, preventing it only from destruction, so that neither its interior nor its exterior is changed....If, however, Mr. Curator would like to lead the restoration himself, the church will not prevent it, but reserves the right [to see] that the restoration is accomplished in the aforementioned way.[177]

As early as 1869, the Church had been cautious of the radical stylistic changes initiated by professional architects and national conservators. And indeed, the costs of the proposed project reveal the radical nature of anticipated changes. The Vormärz-era hall addition was to be demolished and the organ removed, while the chief conservators, Rozsacziński and Kunasiewicz, also envisioned a mosaic decoration for the interior that had previously known no mosaic.[178]

In restoration, Julian Zachariewicz was a passionate advocate of the "medieval styles." His restoration work in Lemberg, in particular his rather radical adaptations of St. John the Baptist's Church and of St. Mary of Snow Church to the neo-Romanesque,[179] were typical of the restoration practice of his age and sparked controversy in later times.[180] While finally addressing the technical problems of construction that previous renovations had ignored, his 1887 restoration resulted in a reclothing of the building with a completely new appearance. For the sake of what he termed stylistic recovery, Zachariewicz invented numerous detail elements whose existence was neither documented nor possible in the original building: an oversized masonry cross topping the church; a three-meter-wide *rosette* window on the façade; a cross-shaped roof spire, (*Sygnatur*), characteristic of Zachariewicz; and decorative bricks on the corners of the façade and on the buttresses. The entrance hall was retained, but its style changed; the roof over the side transepts was lowered so that the building's silhouette was reminiscent of northern European Romanesque churches, with their dominating central naves and lower side aisles (Fig. 56). Thus the origins of the building, imagined – and constructed – as "Western," became visually expressed. However, because there was no clear evidence of the original building's façade, the inventive installation of a Byzantine appearance – with side aisles of equal height and the central nave and a cupola in the center – would have been equally feasible. Zachariewicz, however, did not consider such a possibility.

Although only one example of the heavy-handed restoration practices of the late nineteenth century, Zachariewicz's 1887 restoration of St. John the Baptist Church was radical in its symbolic reconfiguration of the church into an ostensibly "Western" medieval style, the Romanesque. Be-

Figure 56. Julian Zachariewicz. Restoration of St. John the Baptist Church, 1887. *CzT 6* (1888).

cause of Zachariewicz's appreciation of the Ruthenian churches in Halicz, such a radical approach is surprising and testifies to his deep belief in contemporary interpretations of the church's origins and to his own theory of stylistic civilizations. Since the church's origins were believed to lie in the thirteenth century and with a Catholic order,[181] he assumed that it had been built in stone and, consequently, in the Romanesque style, though he possessed no evidence for these preconceptions.[182] For him, the Western Christian rite was symbolized by a Western type of building, particularly by a three-nave basilica with characteristically lower side aisles; that St. Panteleimon Church in Halicz and St. John the Baptist in Lemberg both exhibited a characteristically Byzantine crosslike plan figured as an issue of minor significance. In the same fashion, St. Mary of Snow Church, founded by German colonists from the Rhine region, also acquired an invented neo-Romanesque appearance. The building's plan spoke of a typical provincial – simple – Gothic church, and the later additions most likely had been done in the Renaissance.[183] For Zachariewicz, however, the founding by German colonists was alone sufficient for his interpretation, and he disregarded that literally none of the material signified Romanesque origins.

Polonizing the Armenian Cathedral

In the early twentieth century, in the context of various groups' explicit contests to occupy public space in the city center both physically and symbolically, restoration practices took on an evermore pronounced and radicalized significance. As with the Armenian cathedral's restoration, such practices ostensibly nationalized the space around the renovated structures. Regarding the cathedral, this area had been previously dominated by two Ruthenian institutions – the Preobražeńska Church and the Ruthenian National Institute – and by Jewish stores.

Admiration of the Armenian Cathedral's architecture was common in the late nineteenth and the early twentieth centuries (Fig. 57). The anonymous author (known only as D. K.) of *Odnowienie i rekonstrukcya Katedry Ormiańskiej we Lwowie* [The renovation and the reconstruction of the Armenian Cathedral in Lwów], for example, expressed the prevailing views on the value of this historic building: "This is a true oasis of antiquity in our Lwów, a quiet and a self-indulgent one, and yet so attractive because of the general mood that it exudes. Those sensitive to beauty prefer to stop here for a while."[184] The Viennese Central Conservation Commission similarly viewed it as an "unusually worthy monument from the perspective of art history" (*ein kunsthistorisch ungemein wertvolles Denkmal*), emphasizing the building's older medieval core.[185]

Under Austrian rule, the Armenian Cathedral underwent major renovations in 1862, 1878, and 1908. Józef Piotrowski and the aforementioned anonymous

Figure 57. Armenian Cathedral. Postcard from around 1900.

author have left us lengthy accounts of the details of the Armenian Cathedral's restoration history.[186] We thus know that as late as 1925 there was little extant knowledge on what the "original" medieval church looked like: "We have no information about the original, Armenian-Gothic arrangement of the cathedral in the fifteenth century; no inventory catalogues have been preserved. We can only assume."[187] Despite this fact, earlier renovations of 1748 and 1878 were just as bitterly criticized as in the case of St. John the Baptist. Although first eighteenth-century intervention "finalized the complete change of the interior to the baroque, by so doing totally destroying the original polychromy and to a large extent the stonework decoration," the second of the late nineteenth century added a "clumsy, high portal...and a tower, made in a similar fashion" and "unnecessary and unrefined plastering that imitated stone," masking the sacristy between the presbytery and the portal, as well as the tower. Piotrowski believed that this nineteenth-century plastering "should be removed, and the ancient, refined (*szlachetna*) stonework [underneath] should be cleaned and repaired."[188] The restoration of 1908-25 removed the baroque furniture.[189] Just as mosaics had replaced the earlier frescoes, so now the new marble church furniture from the dismantled Russian Orthodox Cathedral in Warsaw replaced its well-made baroque predecessors.[190] Arguments legitimizing these radical changes ranged from familiar discussions on recovering the supposedly original appearance of the cathedral to statements that the baroque additions had been "severely damaged."[191]

Historic preservation experts would not fail to recognize the difficulty of the architect-restorer's work in such cases as this one. When outlining the consequences of archbishop Józef Teodorowicz's formal support of a comprehensive plan for the cathedral's "renewal," D. K. described the tasks of the architect in this way: "One needed to bring together a piety for the monument that does not allow for any change to the historic building, with the considerations of modern needs at every step."[192] A committee of experts was convened to legitimize the restoration.[193] Further, the archbishop is believed to have been in regular contact with the Viennese Central Conservation Commission, and in particular with Conservator General Max Dvořák, who came to Lemberg for these discussions. Legitimizing arguments were soon found: the committee simply repeated the assessment of the Viennese commission on the core building's architectural worth and, conversely, on the worthlessness of the recent additions.[194] When Józef Mehoffer's sketches for a fresco painting in the interior of the cathedral met with admiration in Vienna and approval had been secured, full legitimization existed for the restoration.[195]

The restoration, however, was motivated by deeper reasons than simple stylistic purification and the stripping from the façade of baroque and nineteenth-century additions. An additional detail reveals the multifaceted nature of restoration in this rather neglected district of the historic city core. The concern continuously had existed, it surfaced, that the cathedral had no entry to Krakowska Street. In 1908, Cracow architect Franciszek Mączyński attempted to solve this problem, much to the admiration of local architectural historians and art critics (Fig. 58). This resulted in a "completely new fact that one of our recognized conservators called simply epochal in the history of the cathedral."[196] Apart from pure artistic value, a particular feature of Mączyński's architectural solution was widely admired:

> This is a solution of a true master because...Krakowska Street [is now] joined through his artistic idea [with the Cathedral]. It is as if the Cathedral's enlargement and its opening from [this] street create a new Polish church on that noisy commercial street. This therefore takes on a truly contemporary (*aktualne*) and, I would [also] add, cultural meaning.[197]

One would think that the true meaning of Mączyński's new church entrance lay in its allowing an institution of cultural – and religious – significance to open its doors to people believed forgotten through their absorption in commerce. This argument in itself appears rather odd, since the old entrance to the Armenian Cathedral was just across the corner, and those hungry for spiritual matters could easily enter through it. The issue was, however, much more straightforward:

Figure 58. Project for the restoration of the Armenian Cathedral by Franciszek Mączyński, 1910. *CzT 23* (1910).

Among the many people who enter Lwów from Żolkiewska Street there are also Polish folk....Thus if it would be possible to have the entry to the Cathedral opposite the Ruthenian church, then the Polish folk that until now needed to go around... through the side streets will find support here for their spiritual needs.[198]

In this manner and with the Armenian archbishop's and the Central Conservation Commission's approval, the cathedral became the site of a cultural struggle: by challenging the Ruthenian Preobražeńska Church's (Fig. 31) dominance over the district; in a curious way it supported Polish claims to physical presence in the district. With this in mind, this restoration project, typical for the early twentieth century, acquired new meaning: it essentially "Polonized" the symbolically complex urban space in Lemberg's city center.

Preservation concepts allowed individuals within the Municipality and the restoration movement to treat this and other key historic buildings as sites of national reference; furthermore, they allowed them to make decisions on preservation matters depending on whether buildings corresponded to a certain historic vision. Conversely, in the case of the Armenian Cathedral, the rhetoric of current need was used not only to strip the building of its stylistically misguided nineteenth-century additions and to commission Mehoffer to embellish it, but also to legitimize a spatial contest with the Ruthenian church. As a result, the Armenian Cathedral was transformed into another ostensibly "Polish" church in the district.

Although Zachariewicz's intentions in his restoration projects were dictated by his own architectural theory, his radical transformation of Lemberg's oldest medieval churches into what he saw as appropriate "Western" neo-Romanesque buildings served similar purposes. Coupled with the disproportionately modest attention paid by national conservators to Lemberg's "Eastern"-style monuments and with the Central Commission's reluctance to value neoclassical and nineteenth-century architecture, these restoration examples suggest the existence of a larger project. This endeavor was the transformation of Lemberg – seen as a modern capital that lacked historic monuments – into an ostensibly "civilized," "Western," and heritage-rich town. In such a project, those buildings that did not fit the contemporary historic canon would be neglected or forcibly transformed.

Landesausstellungen: Technological and National Display

While architects and conservation activists reshaped historic architecture according to their diverse visions, modern architecture was often used for political purposes – to legitimate universal progress and national economic achievement, and to foster lagging business or industrial development, or, alternatively, to emphasize cultural peculiarity – at diverse world exhibitions and fairs, of which world and provincial exhibitions (*Landesausstellungen*) held in Austria-Hungary were an integral part.[199] Although an enterprise of the late nineteenth century, provincial exhibitions had an immediate Vormärz precedent; this was the annual fairs, both the traditional ones and those organized by the new Municipality in the early nineteenth century.[200] Few of these fairs were held for mere economic reasons, however, as seen in the example of the failure of the "woolen fair" held in Lemberg in July 1837 and 1838. The underlying interest behind the fair can be found in the Municipality's wish to marginalize the activity of Jewish peddlers.[201] Hoping for greater profits, the city built sheds next to the Municipal Park for the storage of wool, spending over three thousand crowns without taxing any of the future participants in the fair. Unprofessionally organized and not sufficiently advertised, however, the fair failed to bring in profits in 1837, failed completely in 1838, and continued only from 1855 on in the town of Brody. Other fairs enjoyed more symbolic significance, mostly that of serving as an occasion for socialization among the landed gentry and aristocracy. This happened with the

Figure 59. St. George Market (before 1844). Lithograph by Anton Lange. L'viv
Stefanyk Scientific Library.

fair of St. Agnes and the famous Lemberg Contracts (*Kontrakty lwowskie*, see
Fig. 60). Popular histories of early nineteenth-century Lemberg are replete with
descriptions of the aristocratic show of fashion that took place in the city during
these events.

The idea of exhibiting agricultural achievements was first put forth in 1847,
during discussions in the Agricultural Society on its plans to organize annual provincial agricultural exhibitions, beginning in June 1848. Because of subsequent
political and military turbulence, the proposal was put into action only in 1877.
By that time, a general consensus had emerged that the main emphasis would
fall on technology, and that the provincial exhibitions would display industrial,
as well as agricultural, achievements. Galicia's economic backwardness of the
time made the organizers' task difficult because substitutes for the nearly nonexistent Galician industry needed to be found. Patrice Dabrowski has covered the
celebrations associated with provincial exhibitions in Galicia, especially the 1894
exhibition and the 1910 Grunwald anniversary, in detail in her recent book.[202] In
an attempt to complement her research, this section will consider Lemberg's provincial exhibitions through the lens of the Lemberg Polytechnic Society's activity
as a window into the local architectural community.

Figure 60. Kontrakty Fair in Lemberg. Lithograph after Franz Gerstenberger. Opałek, *Obrazki z przesłości Lwowa.*

Figure 61. Agricultural-Industrial Exhibition of 1877. Photograph by Edward Trzemeski, 1877. Ľviv Historical Museum.

1877: The Exhibition of Agriculture and Industry and the Emergence of Technicians

Provincial exhibitions had long functioned as local statements of achievement and pride. The architects and the general educated public in Lemberg had been deeply impressed by foreign exhibitions of technology and industry. It is therefore not surprising that when the first exhibition of its kind was organized in Lemberg – the Provincial Exhibition of Agriculture and Industry (*Landwirtschaftliche und industrielle Ausstellung*) in 1877, in Jabłonowski Park,[203] – local aspirations were high. It consisted of eight sections: agriculture; industry and crafts; graphic arts and tools; building and engineering; women's work; technical school students' work; science and education; and foreign participants. The exhibition hoped to display general progress in the Crown Land that would call to mind other model exhibitions. Most of the exhibited material was grouped into 33 sections in the two main pavilions, with the exhibition of machinery laid out under the open sky.[204] Because it was organized by landed aristocracy – Count Włodzimierz Dzieduszycki as the committee's head, Count Adam Sapieha and Count Józef Badeni as vice presidents – and because it was held on military grounds, the exhibition was bound to take on a tone other than an industrial one (Fig. 62). Its invented character may have been one of the reasons that Cracow architects disapproved so strongly of what they thought was parochial.[205]

Several events helped legitimize the predominant local view that the exhibition had been a great success and a demonstration of what was termed Galicia's industrial progress. One was the establishment of the Polytechnic Society, which was followed by its active commentary on the exhibition. A second event was the inauguration of a new building for the Polytechnic University:

> The buildings designed by our present senior professor, Julian Zachariewicz, were opened in October 1877, and the technical academy simultaneously acquired the title '*technische Hochschule*' ....This was yet again an unusually important moment in the history of the institution, connected coincidentally with an equally important moment in our *kraj*'s [Crown Land's] economic development, this being the first provincial exhibition in Lemberg.[206]

Zachariewicz's building thus became a symbol of Galicia's technological advancement.[207] The technical committee that had been responsible for working out the exhibition plans consisted exclusively of members from the newly founded Polytechnic Society, and from this first exhibit until the monarchy's demise, the exhibition was linked with the society's activities.[208] For the reviewers of the society's periodical, *Dźwignia* [Lever], later known as *Czasopismo techniczne* [Technical Journal], the exhibition had lived up to all expectations. The

Figure 62. Agricultural-Industrial Exhibition of 1877, School section. Photograph
by Edward Trzemeski, 1877. Ľviv Historical Museum.

display was of products and goods that had a modern character, quite representative of improvement and progress in the Crown Land over the previous years:
"The exhibition has been a full success; it demonstrated the birth of industrial
development in Galicia."[209]

While providing a detailed account of the exhibition's planning and the participating companies, *Dźwignia* did not mention the style in which the temporary buildings of the exhibition had been built. Commenting on it was difficult,
however, because the 1877 exhibition site consisted of the rococo Jabłonowski
palace and several temporary pavilions typical for the time. Constructed for a
short existence, the pavilions were simple wooden structures built in a highly
economical manner and to which a description of "style" was inapplicable. It was
not, therefore, a particular architectural mode, but the mere fact of the exhibition architecture's erection that became an argument for its success. Regardless
of appearance, this temporary architecture was by its very existence mediating
"progress." Even here, however, an aesthetic and symbolic charge to the major
architectural details was noticeable. According to a university professor, Józef
Jägermann, the decoration of the entrance gate with flags, with the provincial
and Municipal coats-of-arms, and with fir garlands – a clear appropriation of

the temporary triumphal arch from the royal ceremony – made the entrance look magnificent.[210]

The significance of descriptions of the aesthetic appearance and symbolism of temporary architecture becomes clearer through an analysis of the actual content of the exhibit itself. Despite the emphasis on industry, technology, and progress, the list of the exhibition prize winners primarily named artists and local craftsmen, rather than factory owners.[211] Apart from a rather booming production of building materials – much in demand as a result of Lemberg's being an administrative capital – industry was visibly missing.[212] Industrial ventures were awarded prizes not for their high-quality, contemporary products, but instead for having introduced local materials into industry. This was so, for example, with the First Association of Mechanized Brick and Clay Works in Lemberg (*Spółka pierwsza wyroby maszynowych cęgiel i towarów glinianych we Lwowie*). Further, Leopold Schimser's sculptural works had made contributions to Galicia's industry, and Schimser was awarded a prize for "accurate works cut in simple stone (*ciosy zwykłe*)...and above all for the introduction of *krajowy* [regional] materials to the stone industry."[213] Clearly, when industry was insufficient, art – and especially art from the region – had to compensate. In 1877 the first attempt to introduce the arts as an achievement of progress, replacing nonexistent industry, came in the form of the introduction of the "graphic arts" and "crafts industry" to the annual exhibition. [214]

1894 and the Third Congress of Polish Technicians

Although the provincial exhibition of 1877 was influenced by earlier foreign models, 1894 was a locally symbolic year. It was not only the year that marked the centenary of the Racławice Battle of 4 April 1794, an anniversary associated with Kościuszko, but it was also the 50th anniversary of the Polytechnic University's foundation. As in 1877, 1878, and 1892, Galicia's most celebrated provincial exhibition in 1894 was linked with the activities of the Polytechnic Society. Although the site had been developed before 1894 into a prestigious, bourgeois residential quarter, the idea of a comprehensive provincial exhibition emerged in connection with the anniversary of the Kościuszko insurrection.[215] Moreover, other architectural activities, such as the Third Congress of Polish Technicians, were also organized in conjunction with the exhibition.[216]

In comparison to the previous exhibitions, that of 1894 was a large undertaking: 63 pavilions, including 37 private ones, and more than 130 buildings were all situated on the newly established exhibition site.[217] The Stryjski Hills, where the exhibition took place, was one of the showcases that demonstrated strong and continuous Municipal commitment to urban planning, and it was also a presti-

Figure 63. View of the Stryjski Hills and the 1894 exhibition. Unknown photographer, 1894. Private collection of Ihor Kotlobulatov.

Figure 64. The main alley at the 1894 Provincial Exhibition. Photograph by Edward Trzemeski, 1894. Private collection of Ihor Kotlobulatov. The view is dominated by the bottle-shaped pavilion of the Londratowicz & Proux firm.

gious residential area. The first planning measures for the area were undertaken in the late 1830s, when Municipal construction official Underka set up a public park with a restaurant, and in the early 1840s, when the first villa complex, planned by Municipal Building Director Jan Salzmann, was erected there.[218] Developed further a few years before 1894, Stryjski Park was also the terminus of the city's first tramline.

Although the 1894 exhibition boasted a more adequate show of industrial and agricultural progress than previous ones had, culture was advertised as the exhibition's primary attraction: *"Powszechna Wystawa Krajowa 1894 – Allgemeine Landesausstellung 1. Juni - 1. October – Kunst Unterrichtswesen Ethnografie Ackerbau Forstwesen Industrie – Historisches Panorama von W. Kossak und J. Styka."*

Architects participated in the exhibition in a variety of ways. First and foremost, the event represented a prestigious occasion to design pavilions following new trends in architectural fashion and technology. Here the state-employed historicist architects Zygmunt Gorgolewski, Juliusz Hochberger, and Karol Boublik, and – notably, an engineer, Franciszek Skowron – assumed pioneering roles.[219] The exhibition contained a veritable display of architecture representing the entire spectrum of styles and trends in currency. This exhibition may also have been the sole occasion on which public funds were not in short supply. The use of style, however, often appeared as an arbitrary choice made by an architect or owner. This was so with the pavilion of Archduke Albrechs, according to the *Czasopismo techniczne* reviewer, which was built in a *"góral"* (Carpathian) style; with the Skarbek Foundation's pavilion, sporting a "Swiss" style; with the water tower in a "medieval style"; with the Tlumač sugar-refinery in the neo-Gothic; and with a curious pavilion in the shape of a bottle, constructed for the cognac producers Londratowicz & Proux. (Figure 64 shows the main alley of the exhibition dominated by this pavilion.) The traditional association of monumental public architecture with the neoclassicism and neo-Renaissance was noticeable, however: Zygmunt Gorgolewski's triumphal arch was in the neoclassical style, and Franciszek Skowron's Palace of Art (Fig. 65) was neobaroque and his Palace of Architecture neoclassical.[220] Historicism figured as the accepted style for exhibition buildings that represented the state and high culture just as it figured in the permanent structures found in town.

Architects could indulge in greater stylistic freedom and experimentation in their designs for other structures, such as for the exhibition's most visited two pavilions that were full of symbolic national connotations: the Racławice panorama and the Matejko Mausoleum, which were featured on the exhibition poster.[221]

Franciszek Skowron's Matejko Mausoleum housed the works of the renowned academy-trained Polish national painter with appropriate grandeur. Although its architecture was experimental and unusual, its importance stemmed largely from the contents on the inside. The Ruthenian counterpart to these Polish national pavilions was the pavilion of Ukrainian art, designed by Ivan Levynśkyj using Hucul motifs, and the Hucul Church, designed by Alfred Zachariewicz. All

Figure 65. The greeting of an official delegation in front of the Palace of Art at the 1894 Provincial Exhibition. Photograph by Edward Trzemeski. Private collection of Ihor Kotlobulatov.

of these pavilions used advanced technology as a means of promoting a national affiliation.

Various institutions and societies used the occasion to comment on the exhibition's architecture for purposes of self-advertisement. The Society for the City of Lemberg's Development and Beautification (*Towarzystwo dla rozwoju i upiększenia miasta Lwowa*) contributed its own guide to the exhibition, accompanied by its most recent architectural and historical description of Lemberg. Besides information on the exhibition, written by Diet deputy Teofil Merunowicz and architect Michał Kowalczuk, the book included a historical overview of Lemberg by Aleksander Czołowski, a chapter on its development during autonomy, and a general description of the city and its historic monuments.[222]

As in 1877, the Polytechnic University worked to associate itself with the exhibition as the leading Polish educational institution and as a demonstration of technological progress in Galicia. The ministerial approval of a new bill on the status of Polytechnic University was invoked as further proof of the exhibition's significance.[223] The society exhibited its Polish-language publications of 1871 – the year when Polish became the official language of instruction at Polytechnic University – in the pavilion of architecture.[224] It was eager to demonstrate its social role at any event that featured technology and especially architecture. To this end, the society prepared a separate publication on its history, written specifically for the exhibition by Michał Kowalczuk, besides its regular periodical, *Dźwignia*.[225] The clear aim of these efforts was to secure the society's participation in future events of this kind as the only professional technical institution invited. Yet, as illustrated by other events organized in connection with the exhibition, the society's reasons for its actions were social and national. From a deep belief in what it called technicians' social mission, the society argued for the need for the Third Congress of Polish Technicians to be held in Lemberg on 8-12 July 1894.[226]

A congress meeting scheduled precisely at the same time as the provincial exhibition – together with the exhibition itself – was seen as the technicians' duty to further the national cause. In 1894, further legitimization for an explicitly ethnic congress was needed. Curiously, this was found in Galicia's comparative geographic, cultural, and economic backwardness, as well as in the imagined cultural unity of the Polish lands across imperial borders.[227] In this way, a connection was cemented between the Congress of Polish Technicians and the provincial exhibition as two elements that promoted Polish technological advancement. Alexander Pomianowski, the president of the City Casino, formulated it best:

> The present Provincial Exhibition...has shaken to its foundations the outlived building of prejudices.... On this fortunate occasion I greet you in the name of...all of intelligent society: Good luck in your work and let it be of long-term use to our *kraj* [Crown Land] and to the glory of Polish technicians throughout the entire civilized world.[228]

The year 1894 was thus intended to represent the Poles as the only civilizing, progressive force in Galicia as far as the economy and technology were concerned. In the view of both the exhibition and congress organizers, this figured as a particularly challenging task for the unjustly stateless nation.[229] The extent of the seemingly innocent technical congress's far-reaching aims was formulated in other speeches at the official opening. Diet Speaker Count Eustachy Sanguszko opened with the following words: "I greet especially those who came from other regions of Poland (Bravo). I hope that they will feel here as in their motherland. You are united by a common language and by our nation's eternally vital spirit and talent." Lemberg President Edmund Mochnacki echoed these sentiments: "Full of the impression of the view [of the exhibition], I greet you, Gentlemen, as [its] first Polish guests who have arrived here collectively (*gremialnie*) to visit it." And lastly, the exhibition's President Count Sapieha: "If any of you, Gentlemen, could put your fingers on our pulse, you would be assured that our hearts beat in deep gratitude to you who took the initiative for this congress and with your congress have magnified the exhibition. The fact that...you came from all the regions of Poland is the most beautiful prize for those who organized the exhibition. We wanted it, and we wanted it because our *kraj* wanted that it be called Polish. You have blessed it, and for that, in the name of its organizers, I express my gratitude to you (Bravo)."[230]

The exhibition's key buildings and the subsequent press releases on behalf of various societies and institutions notwithstanding, it would be misleading to understand architects' involvement in the exhibition as part of a larger, purely national project. Architects of various backgrounds and affiliations worked on a variety of nationally affiliated architectural projects. Thus, for example, Julian Zachariewicz and Ivan Levynśkyj together drew up the plans for the pavilion of Ukrainian art. In parallel, Zachariewicz also designed the Ruthenian wooden church, another architectural curiosity, and Levynśkyj built the Matejko pavilion.[231] This complicating aspect of the exhibition, as well as all statements from Ruthenian quarters, were curiously left out from the Polytechnic Society's commentary on the exhibition, since these expressions contradicted the representation of the society as an engine of Polish civilization.

The congratulations given by Budapest *Josephineum* representative Emil Asboth to the Polytechnic University upon its 50th anniversary may well have been given to the provincial exhibition, and they illustrated well the common view on technological progress and technicians' duties to their nations:

> We who pursue the same aim and fight for the same ideals as do you, greet you at the conclusion of this, your first epoch, and sincerely wish to you that your institution, which works for the will and prosperity of your motherland, will celebrate many more meaningful epochs in the development of the technical sciences.[232]

Imperial recognition of such undertakings as the 1894 exhibition in Lemberg, taken together with the expression of solidarity on behalf of a more fortunate Hungarian nation, only proved to the Polish technicians of Galicia that they could pursue the national cause further.[233] Yet neither Galicia nor Lemberg – nor, for that matter, Hungary – were monoethnic societies in which the only force preventing the disadvantaged nation from creating a nation-state was the conservative foreign state. Lemberg's Polish technicians insistently refused to see that more than one nation existed in Galicia that could be termed civilized, that there were ways to pursue progress other than with a national focus, and that local technicians could work for more than one national aim. This ensured that in the twentieth century, the paths of Lemberg architects would become increasingly divergent along ethnic lines.[234] The next generation's zeal for the national cause was well expressed by a Polytechnic University student carrying the sound German name of Karol Rübenbauer:

We aim at...working for our Polish society, not as thoughtless imple-
menters of someone's foreign ideas and plans, but as pioneers of civilization...conscious of their goals. We want to work in such a way that
with all our work, and even with the method in which it is carried out,
we draw closer to...our final aim. That aim is the general good of man-
kind, but [especially] the prosperity and happiness of our Polish society.[235]

1910: Polish Art and Polish Technicians

The year 1910 demonstrated that Municipal aspirations exceeded its finances. In
1909, city Vice President Tadeusz Rutowski envisioned an exhibition of Polish
cities (*Ausstellung der polnischen Städte*) that would be held for four-and-a-half
months in Lemberg, beginning in June 1910. We know little about this idea of
an exhibition or, for that matter, what and how exactly were the "Polish cities"
supposed to be "exhibited," but we do know that a related exhibition of Polish
art would be a part of it. In contrast to the exhibitions in 1877 and 1894, this
one would be a purely symbolic affair, one that "was not aimed at profit."[236] The
initial idea was very ambitious: a letter from the Viennese manufacturer of exhibition buildings Elsinger & Stromeyer (*Österreichisch-Ungarische Zelt-&-Hal-
len-Bau-& Liefanstalt*) addressed to Rutowski informs us that the exhibition was
to contain several larger halls and pavilions.[237] Lemberg's vice president clearly
realized what appeal the new structures might have. In January 1910, the organizing committee, headed by Rutowski, imagined a highly ornate (*zdobny*) new
exhibition palace, built in reinforced concrete and planned to cover 800 square
meters to serve as a future exhibition hall, a fair pavilion, and a restaurant.[238] Although intended to surpass the grandeur of 1894, the exhibition was ultimately to
limit itself to a much more modest project.[239]

   We do not know the degree of effort put into the proposed exhibition of cities because none of the buildings was built as a result of financial limitations. As
early as July 1909, Rutowski issued invitations to a meeting in his office, in the
Town Hall, to discuss a much smaller project. The title of the organizing body
reveals the endeavor's focus: the Committee for the Organization of an Exhibition of Polish Art.[240] Once again, the choice of year was not accidental: the 500th
anniversary of the battle of Grunwald, another important event in Polish national
historiography.[241] The brochure printed by the organizing committee advertised
the event in the following manner:

   For several years we have heard voices from all spheres of Polish art,
   from the circles of art critics and intelligent society, on the need for

a great review of Polish art at the threshold of the twentieth century. When the year of great historical memories, the 500th anniversary of the year of glory and strength, was drawing closer, a feeling of necessity was born (*budziło się ... poczucie konieczności*) that the nation (*naród*) should...organize...a review of national work and of its achievements, its vitality and capability (*zywotność i zdolność*) for a better tomorrow. Then the thought came to the fore: let us organize a great review of Polish art![242]

However, Rutowski did not immediately abandon the idea of the new exhibition palace, rather turning his attention to the realization of a dream, the establishment of a picture gallery. He launched this idea, which sparked heated discussion in Lemberg academic circles and the press, as connected to the commemoration of the Grunwald anniversary. An anonymous document in the Municipal file on the exhibition of 1910 linked the idea of a palace with the commemoration of the Grunwald battle in the following way:

> The anniversary of the "field of glory" is drawing near. We all feel that the city of Lwów, that Lwów itself, owes so many advantages to the heroes of Grunwald, that it must celebrate its and [our] nation's anniversary adequately, to commemorate it with an...institution important for all time. Public opinion has already pointed out once that the construction of the Palace of Art could be such an institution. Every educated inhabitant of Lwów (*inteligentny mieszkaniec*) recognizes and feels its need.[243]

The city, the author argued, "simply must build the Palace of Art in the near future" because of the amount of work in the City Gallery's collection, another great personal achievement of Rutowski. That the construction of such a building would be an expensive affair – as an institution of culture, it would need an elaborate and sophisticated architectural design – did not escape attention in the discussion. Yet this did not seem to trouble the proposal's supporters; because the building would house the Municipal art collection, a new building would be "not a loss, but rather a generally recognized city need, simply a necessity."[244] The construction of a permanent exhibition palace to mark the anniversary of Grunwald was to lend to the proposal of a picture gallery further legitimization.

If we are to believe the accuracy of *Czasopismo techniczne*'s commentary, local architects began to take part in the project as early as 1909. In 1910, the journal published a project for the exhibition pavilion by W. Derdacki and W. Mińkiewicz, which the authors claimed had been created the previous year, "when the issue of the unrealized Grunwald exhibition was still current."[245] Since the authors argued that because Lemberg had no adequate building in which to house a large exhibition, and the Palace of Art, built by Franciszek Skowron in 1894 on the exhibition grounds, was not entirely suitable, a need existed for a larger pavilion. The proposed project would not only host cities, architecture, and art displays at the time of the 1910 exhibition, but it would also serve later as a summer theater, concert venue, and dance hall.[246]

In the end, local aspirations were again stymied by a lack of funds. Instead of being held in a newly built exhibition hall, obtained from Elsinger & Stromeyer or Derdacki & Mińkiewicz, the exhibition was to be held in the existing Palace of Art, and the organization of the architectural exhibition was delegated to the Polytechnic Society. Committed to realizing an exhibition, regardless of how small, Rutowski remained at the helm of the ever-changing organizing committees.[247] The Palace of Art, a historicist building that received little symbolic attention at the provincial exhibition in 1894, was to host the exhibition of national art in 1910.

The city no longer concerned itself with expensive architectural endeavors. The idea of the architectural exhibition – titled the First Exhibition of Polish Architects – was additionally promoted by the Polytechnic Society as part of greater celebrations of Grunwald. The exhibition was to display projects, photos of monuments, and images of realized buildings by Polish architects, both deceased and living, and it would also feature Polish-language architectural publications.[248] Even the poster for the exhibition required a competition – as it turned out, an unsuccessful one[249] – in which Polish artists and architects "irrespective of their place of residence" took part.[250]

The need to appeal to the general public and the belief in a kind of architectural *Zeitgeist* figured as primary motives for the organizers:

> The very fact that the exhibition was organized testifies that our architects have arrived at a belief that they not only can, but also should, interest the society, since architecture originates not only from the individual work of the artist, but also from the environment, for which it is created. This very fact one needs to acknowledge as a positive one for the development of architecture.[251]

After time-consuming and senseless negotiations with Rutowski concerning the exhibition's place and date and also for the joint exhibition of architecture and arts, the city proposed that the Architects' Circle launch the two exhibitions together and share the pavilion with them. While obviously Rutowski saw his own project as the priority, he did not want to turn down the architectural exhibition altogether.[252] Numerous difficulties and bitter disagreements stemmed from this agreement. One concerned the need to reconcile in a single space very large pieces of art — such as Kowalski's "The Wolves" and a model of the monument to Puławski, which apparently reached the ceiling of the pavilion – with small-scale architectural drawings and models[253] (Fig. 66).

By late July 1910, the commitment on the part of architects was not impressive.[254] In the end, Lemberg architects predominated at the exhibit, followed by a group from Cracow; the much-desired attendance from Russian Poland, St. Petersburg, and Moscow was minimal.[255] Thus when the Polytechnic Society wrote a report on the architectural exhibition, national value was added to professional quality: "The architectural exhibition...stepped into the foreground not only by virtue of the fact that it was *the first* such exhibition in Poland, but also through the works displayed there."

Figure 66. Interior of the 1910 Exhibition. *CzT* (1910).

As in 1894, the architectural exhibition figured as part of a larger project: at the same time the exhibit was scheduled to take place, Lemberg was to host the Fifth Congress of Polish Technicians. Although it was the technicians' ambition to hold this all-Polish congress in Warsaw rather than again in Lemberg,[256] the organizers had to compensate for a substitute location with a representation of Polish unity across borders. Given the congress's general atmosphere, this was not difficult: instead of offering purely professional technical help, the participants were expecting to socialize in ethnic technical circles.[257]

The head of the organizing committee, Professor L. Syroczyński, made this clear when he pinpointed the overarching ideas behind the congress's organization:

> The present congress is one of the further proofs of our society's vitality. As before, the Poles had acquired a place for themselves in a political world and became the bulwark of Christianity with the use of plough and sword. We remain on the same cultural plane with other nations today through our work and knowledge."[258]

The national value of the exhibition required promoting for yet another reason: the general public proved to be ignorant of narrowly defined architectural matters and appreciated the exhibition largely as a *Polish* affair. Witold Mińkiewicz lamented in his review in *Czasopismo techniczne* that despite a general popularity with the public, despite the numerous articles in daily newspapers, and despite a large attendance, the exhibition demonstrated how distant architecture was to the general public. Most of the reviews simply lacked the criteria necessary for evaluating architectural work. [259] By mentioning that "incompetence in architecture belonged among the public's privileges"[260] and by further explaining that architectural drawings employed a highly specific language understood by only professional architects, Mińkiewicz unintentionally recognized the irrelevance of the professional quality of the exhibition. Contrary to the professional rhetoric of scientific progress and Mińkiewicz's outdated belief in the need to educate the public, the exhibition was organized and primarily served as a means for promoting the architects' work. For these purposes, architecture was advanced for its imagined national qualities, rather than its technical excellence.

Mińkiewicz sharply criticized the exhibition as a means of self-advertisement. He primarily regretted that Wiesław Grzymalski's initial project for the exhibition interior, based on "fantastic old Slavic wooden motifs" and noteworthy for its "originality and great magnitude" (*rozmach*), had not been implemented. He lambasted the organizers' decision to group works by designers, which, in his view, resulted in a greater chaos. For him, the exhibition was to serve educational purposes, rather than be "an institution of advertisement." He then commented on the positive impact that Alfred Wierusz-Kowalski's enormous national-Romantic painting, "The Wolves," had on the general effect of the interior exhibition space.[261] It was obvious that the wolves he portrayed helped the architects' professional drawings appeal to the public in an emotional manner: visitors needed to feel the verve and the fantastic quality (*fantastyczność*) of architecture. This held especially true for the newer modernist trends that Mińkiewicz defined as "often uncrystallized, yet promising a new period in national (*rodzima*) archi-tecture."[262] The representatives of historicism, notably Julian Zachariewicz, Te-odor Talowski, and Wincenty Rawski, similarly "did not possess that connection to the human soul, that charm of sincerity that often radiates from a primitive roadside chapel, though a magnificent cathedral sometimes does not appeal with anything." Even for Art Nouveau architecture, Mińkiewicz did not anticipate that there could be local attempts to create more than one style termed national. Thus Levynśkyj's "*Ruśka besida*" Theater project – exhibited at the First Exhibition of Polish Architects in 1910 – was no more than yet another attempt to merge folk motifs with a historic style, here Romanesque, and fell into the same category as Edgar Kovats's combination of the Zakopane style with Renaissance motifs, namely, the search for *the* national style. [263] Whether an institution of advertise-ment or a means to educate the public, architecture was no longer exclusively judged for its professional characteristics; rather, its main quality became its ap-peal to emotions, and thus its connection with the human spirit.

Provincial exhibitions of the late nineteenth and early twentieth centuries were infamous for their failure to make successful use of the rhetoric of science and technology. As with the Racławice panorama in 1894, creative approaches to exhibition pavilions often became emblematic of the exhibition as a whole. In similar fashion, the opening of Zachariewicz's Polytechnic University was closely linked with the provincial exhibition of 1877, and discussions of the new Palace of Art became connected with the art and architectural exhibition of 1910. The need to associate large exhibition enterprises with their monumental, sym-bolically charged architecture had existed even earlier. This had been the case in 1877 when, in the context of little clear evidence of technological and industrial progress, the exhibition's architectural complex was used to argue for the provin-cial exhibition's success. In this case, technicians' appreciation of the decorations on the entrance gate illustrated the profound significance that architectural sym-bolism held for the technical professions. By 1894, when there was much more in the exhibition's style and aesthetics that deserved commentary, the symbolic con-notation between modernity and Polish nationalism became even more explicit. On that occasion, the exhibition's most-visited "national" pavilions combined technologically advanced construction with nationalist content, thus attempting to demonstrate the advancement of what was viewed as the Polish civilization. The exhibitions' initial association with various symbolic dates in Polish national history, as well as their interpretation by the Polytechnic Society as important national projects, helped to further legitimize this claim. The exhibition, enjoying legitimacy from imperial approval and recognition, in turn helped to advance the Polish nation's political project. Thus in 1910 the grand idea of erecting a large Palace of Art in Lemberg to host an exhibition of Polish cities, arts, architecture, and ethnography was – for lack of funds – limited to the exhibitions of *Polish* art and architecture, in which Levynśkyj's architectural innovation was seen as another experiment in search of the modern Polish style.

◆

For the purposes of small, symbolic, indoor events, such as a theater performance or an art exhibition, it proved simple and affordable to use existing buildings or to erect temporary structures specifically for the event. Architecture was, however, a too-powerful vehicle for conveying ideas for it to be ignored during important anniversaries. This fact dictated the adaptation of traditional royal ceremonies, the pan-European concept of heritage, and the late nineteenth-century fashion of provincial exhibitions as specific, symbolic uses of Lemberg's historic and modern architecture. In the Vormärz, the overarching tone had been a joyfulness and loyalty to the royal court, but in the second half of the nineteenth century this was increasingly replaced with demonstrations of technological, cultural, and national progress. The uses of architecture at Lemberg's public ceremonies, together with preservation practices and provincial exhibitions, demonstrated that these overarching concepts were transformed in the local context to fit the increasing national aspirations of the Polish elite. Royal ceremonies were gradually "nationalized," and new national celebrations were invented, but preservation practices envisioned Lemberg as an ostensibly Western – meaning Catholic and Polish – historic town. Provincial exhibitions failed to represent technological modernity, but they nevertheless succeeded in creating an impression of Polish cultural progress in which the Ruthenian population existed as an integral part of the multiethnic, yet nominally Polish nation. This, by definition, suggested that even at the fin de siècle, Polish nationalism did not derive from ethnicity, but remained inclusive for other groups that wished to join the project. The portrayal of the Polish nation as civilizing, inclusive, and democratic was further instrumental in this endeavor, while divergent visions, such as those expressed in the 1905 Ruthenian protests against the commemorative anniversary of Chmeľnyćkyj's siege, experienced marginalization. The wider public's involvement in the Pawulski celebration of 1874, however, raises questions about the success of the work carried out by the state, diverse kinds of nationalists, and professional architects.

Notes

1   See Bucur and Wingfield, *Staging the past*. Unowsky's work focuses on imperial inspection tours of Galicia in 1851 and 1868 and on the imperial visits of 1880 and 1894 (Unowsky, *The Pomp and Politics of Patriotism* 33-76, 139-41), as well as on the imperial celebrations in Vienna, with a special interest in Karl Lueger's politics (145-74). His and Dabrowski's books cover the Lemberg 1894 provincial exhibition in detail, covering – yet not focusing on – its most interesting architectural aspects (Dabrowski,

Commemorations, 114-15). For a global overview of celebrations as part of the invention of tradition in the nineteenth century, see Hobsbawm and Ranger, *The Invention of Tradition*; Sean Wilentz, ed., *Rites of Power: Symbolism, Ritual, and Politics since the Middle Ages* (Philadelphia: University of Pennsylvania Press, 1985), 177-325.

2 Bronislaw Pawłowski, *Lwów w 1809 r.*, 24.

3 Signed by Lewandowski, Sietnicki, Czerszawski, Sochocki, and Zarzycki (CDIAU F. 146, Op. 7, Sp. 1877, L. 1).

4 Similar expressions of loyalty are present in other provincial documents, such as the Crown Land order of 20 June 1856 (CDIAU F. 146, Op. 7, Sp. 1877, L. 9; CDIAU F. 146, Op. 7, Sp. 3431, L.16-17).

5 CDIAU F. 146, Op. 7, Sp. 1877, L. 1.

6 "Lemberg den 14ten Februar 1828," *Lemberger Zeitung* (20 February 1828).

7 Ibid.

8 CDIAU F. 165, Op. 5, Sp. 230, L. 17.

9 On Galician *Kaiserreise* in 1851, the plans for the eventually canceled 1868 Galician tour of Galicia, and the emperor's 1880 and 1894 visits, and on the 1898 jubilee in Lemberg, see Unowsky, 33-76, 139-41. For the 1791 Constitution anniversary in 1891 and 1894, the Grunwald 1910 celebrations, and the January insurrection anniversary in 1913, see Dabrowski, *Commemorations*, 105-07, 114-15, 118-26, 161-64, 194-98.

10 Ibid., 66-73.

11 Ibid.

12 Schnür-Pepłowski, *Obrazy z przeszłości*, 25-26.

13 Bronisław Pawłowski, *Lwów w 1809 r.*, 43-52.

14 On an earlier ceremony, though not very different in scale and program, marking Stefan Czarniecki's entry into Lemberg in 1656, see Franciszek Jaworski, *Lwów stary*, 137-43. On a much more bizarre celebration of the coronation of the Marian icon at the Dominican Church in 1757, see Jaworski, *Ratusz lwowski*.

15 CDIAU F. 146, Op. 7, Sp. 633.

16 Schnür-Pepłowski, *Obrazy z przeszłości*, 24.

17 Ibid., 33-34.

18 CDIAU F. 146, Op. 7, Sp., 1877, L. 7.

19 CDIAU F. 146, Op. 7, Sp. 2867.

20 Because of the Crown Land and municipal administration's enthusiasm, this resulted in one of the most pompous celebrations in Lemberg and was topped with the donations to the institutes of the poor (CDIAU F. 146, Op. 7, Sp. 3431, L. 6; 8; 16-17; 19-20; 24-25; 52-55.) On the burial ceremony for Governor Hauer, see CDIAU F. 146, Op. 7, Sp. 1230, L. 3-19.

21 On a recent analysis of late nineteenth-century imperial celebrations throughout the Habsburg Monarchy, see Unowsky, *The Pomp and Politics of Patriotism*.

22 Lane, "Szlachta Outside the Commonwealth."

23 Kajetan Ignacy (Gozdawa) Kicki (ca. 1746-1812) was the Roman Catholic archbishop and metropolitan of Lemberg from 1797 to 1812.

24 One of the first orders of the new state requested the population's expression of its loyalty and divided the population by category between "native Poles" and "foreigners" (Pawłowski, *Lwów w 1809 r.*, 59).

25 Franciszek Jaworski, *Lwów stary*, 137.

26 Schnür-Pepłowski, *Obrazy z przeszłości*, 24.

27   Despite having clear pagan roots, the ritual figured as an Easter celebration on Franciscan Square at the start of Kurkowa Street; yet it was imbued with a humorous and erotic urban oral ethos (Jaworski, *Lwów stary*, 95-97).

28   One such site, the pub "*Veteranische Höhle*," a place of socialization for low-ranking members of the military and state bureaucracy, was notorious for the fights that regularly broke out (Jaworski, *Lwów stary*, 97-98).

29   Jaworski, *Lwów stary*, 280-81.

30   Jaworski, *Lwów stary*, 280-81.

31   First mentioned in 1407, the "king" was honored with the right to wear a crown and, importantly, was released from all taxes, this latter measure being found absolutely unacceptable by the Austrian government. From 1546 on, the confraternity organized yearly shooting competitions. After the Swiss invasion of 1704, however, the ceremony was forgotten until its resuscitation under Austria in 1796, when it recruited *bürgerliches Scharfschützenkorps* from among the city restaurant owners and brewery proprietors (Czołowski "Z przeszłości dziejowej Lwowa," in Janusz, *Lwów stary i dzisiejszy*, 3; Jaworki, *Lwów stary*, 278-82, Schnür-Pepłowski, *Obrazy z przeszłości*, 90-94).

32   Schnür-Pepłowski, *Obrazy z przeszłości*, 93.

33   Jaworki, *Lwów stary*, 281.

34   "Lemberg den 14ᵗᵉⁿ Februar 1828," [Lemberg on 14 February 1828] *Lemberger Zeitung* (20 February 1828).

35   The park by the shooting range was laid out by the confraternity in 1775 and renovated by the state in 1823 (Stanislaw Majka, Bohdan Posadśkyj, 105).

36   The shooting range building was designed and built by municipal master builder (*budowniczy*) Franz Trescher in 1825-29 with funding from the local pharmacist Zietkiewicz. Zietkiewicz also paid for the portrait of Emperor Franz I that traditionally hung on the wall of the main hall of the building (Jaworki, *Lwów stary*, 281).

37   This phrase is Jaworski's ironic description of the confraternity's clothing, supported by the fact that a more contemporary military cap (*pieróg*) replaced the traditional hat (*kapelusz*) (Jaworki, *Lwów stary*, 281).

38   Jaworski, 282. Yet even according to the writers of national history, 1830-48 were the confraternity's greatest years, comparable only with the period following its reinvention confraternity in the 1880s (Schnür-Pepłowski, *Obrazy z przeszłości*, 94).

39   On 9 September 1894, the inauguration of the new banner took place during the Congress of Polish Riflemen Societies, organized by the Cracow and Poznań Confraternities (Schnür-Pepłowski, *Obrazy z przeszłości*, 94).

40   See note 1, Introduction.

41   CDIAU F. 146, Op. 7, Sp. 3979, L. 1-11; also see CDIAU F. 146, Op. 7, Sp. 4531; F. 146, Op. 7, Sp. 4514..

42   We do not know how Smolka came to the idea of commemorating the Union of Lublin in exactly this way. The availability of the Cracow model, where the mound to Tadeusz Kościuszko was added to the city's two prehistoric artificial mounds in 1820-23 to honor the leader of the 1794 insurrection who died in 1817, is one likely explanation.

43   Anonymous (Dr. B.), "Wzorki lwowskie,*" Czas* (1852) (CDIAU F. 52, Op. 1, Sp. 950, L. 11)

44   The capitals of the Commonwealth were the Polish cities of Cracow (until 1596) and Warsaw and Grodno (from 1673). The official languages of the Commonwealth were Polish and Latin (in the Kingdom of Poland), and Ruthenian, Latin, and Lithuanian (in the Grand Duchy of Lithuania).

45   CDIAU F. 165, Op. 5, Sp. 110, L. 8-10.

46   CDIAU F. 165, Op. 5, Sp. 110, L. 8-11; see also Schnür-Pepłowski, *Obrazy z przeszłości*, 79-85.

47   For more on the Jagiellonian idea, see Dabrowski, *Commemorations*, 171-75.

48   CDIAU F. 165, Op. 5, Sp. 110, L. 11.

49   "Should we draw parallels between that celebration, which revives a truly commendable idea – yet one from which benefits will be derived only by Austria and by purely German lands – and the celebration that has recently been forbidden by the [local] police, which aimed to commemorate a commendable historical truth?!...And yet [in the former case] the government...had contributed to the event..., and even the ministers took part in it, moreover, exactly in the spirit in which the event was understood!" (ibid., L. 31).

50   Ibid., L. 32.

51   The Ruthenians (*die jungruthenische Partei*, i.e., Ukrainophiles) printed a brochure in June 1869, in which they explicitly positioned themselves against the celebration ("Doniesienie zastępcy Dyrektora policyi we Lwowie 1. sierpnia 1869," ibid., L. 37).

52   Ibid., L. 20-25.

53   The city made a few concessions to the commemoration organizers; the usual daily market on *Rynek* Square was moved to *Castrum* Square, and from 10 a.m. that day the shops on *Rynek* and the street leading to the Dominican church – where the procession would head – were closed.

54   "Bericht des Polizeidirektorats Stellvertreters an das Presidium des Ministeriums für Landesvertheidigung in offentlicher Sicherheit, Lemberg den 12. August 1869," (ibid., L. 48-50); the latter brochure, printed by the Viennese Ruthenian periodical *Zoria Slovjańska*, was followed by an article in the local Russophile *Slovo,* which Polish historiography labeled as false and tendentious (see Schnür-Pepłowski, *Obrazy z przeszłości*, 79-85).

55   CDIAU F. 165, Op. 5, Sp. 110, L. 50.

56   CDIAU F. 165, Op. 5, Sp. 110, L. 50.

57   Schnür-Pepłowski, *Obrazy z przeszłości*, 80.

58   Schnür-Pepłowski, *Obrazy z przeszłości*, 80.

59   On that occasion, Smolka also appealed to the public to refrain from anything that might have been interpreted as a violation of the government's prohibition of the public celebration of the anniversary and, though the celebration would not be held as was wished and as would have been appropriate, to nevertheless mark the occasion with dignified participation (Schnür-Pepłowski, *Obrazy z przeszłości*, 80).

60   Schnür-Pepłowski, *Obrazy z przeszłości*, 80.

61   Polish historian Joachim Lelewel (1786-1861) was one of the most radical figures in the November Uprising (1830-31) in the Congress Kingdom and a political émigré. Karol Otto Kniaziewicz (1762-1842) was a Polish general and political activist. He was active in the Polish-Russian War in 1792, and in the Kosciuszko Uprising in 1794, in the Napoleonic Wars as part of the Polish Legions and of the "Danube Legions" (*Legia Naddunajska*). An émigré in Paris who lived close to "Hotel Lambert," he served as a representative of the "Polish National Government" during the November Uprising in Paris. Juliusz Słowacki (1809–49) was one of the most famous Polish Romantic poets to date and had dedicated much of his verse to the November Uprising; Count Antoni Jan Ostrowski (1782-1845), a member of the Diet in the Kingdom of Poland (1815-30), was appointed general and commander of the National Guards (*Gwardia Narodowa*) in Warsaw during the November Uprising of 1830-31.

62   The Tomb of the Five Victims (*Pogrzeb pięciu poległych*) is the burial place of the victims of the political demonstrations of 27 February 1861, held in Warsaw's Cracow district against Russian rule. It was organized by students of the Art Academy and the Medical Academy in Warsaw. Powązki Cemetery (*Cmentarz Powązkowski*), the oldest and most famous cemetery in Warsaw, is situated in the western part of the city and is Poland's greatest national necropolis.

63   According to Jaworski, *Lwów stary,* 308. According to Schnür-Pepłowski, soil from the tombs of Kościuszko, Krakus, and Wanda, from the Siberian tombs, the Tomb of the Five Victims in Powązki, and the Racławice and Radziwiłłów battles were thrown on the founding stone on 13 August 1871 (Schnür-Pepłowski, *Obrazy z przeszłości*, 83).

64   According to the police report, 120 persons belonging to the Democratic Party were invited to the afternoon dinner and subsequent concert at the restaurant. Three speakers were also invited: Platon Kostecki, a member of *Gazeta narodowa*'s editorial board, as well as two other persons whom the police informer did not know and whose speeches produced no effect on the invited public (CDIAU F. 165, Op. 5, Sp. 110, L. 48-50). According to Schnür-Pepłowski, the speakers were the poet Krystyn Ostrowski, who had also brought soil from the tombs of Mickiewicz, Słowacki, and Kniaziewicz; Father Chromecki; Platon Kostecki; Tadeusz Romanowicz; and Karol Groman (Schnür-Pepłowski, *Obrazy z przeszłości*, 79-85. Also see Jaworski, *Lwów stary,* 308-9).

65   The first scene depicted the Lithuanian wilderness where pagan gods reigned and destroyed altarpieces, the second featured the Christian marriage of Jagiello and Jadwiga, and the final scene portrayed the act of the Lublin Union at the throne of Zygmunt August. In this final act, the king spoke the following words: "Ruthenia, Poland, and Lithuania, with all their towns and villages, / This is our inseparable motherland! /...Let the three brotherly symbols, / Archangel, Pogoń, and our white Eagle / Breathe with the Cross!" (Schnür-Pepłowski, *Obrazy z przeszłości*, 81).

66   During indoor performances such as that at the Skarbek Theater, the organizers did not envision the participation of actual Ruthenians on stage: *ruśka duma* was sung by the Polish actors Kuncewicz and Kwiecińska (Schnür-Pepłowski, *Obrazy z przeszłości*, 81).

67   CDIAU F. 165, Op. 5, Sp. 110, L. 48-50.

68   CDIAU F. 165, Op. 5, Sp. 110, L. 48-50.

69   Smolka had this idea in mind when he suggested that numerous foreign guests from the Polish lands across imperial borders attend the commemoration he planned in 1869.

70   Schnür-Pepłowski, *Obrazy z przeszłości*, 83-84. Yet another source of information is Stanisław Kunasiewicz, *Wzmianka krytyczna o przewodniku po mieście Lwowie wydanym staraniem komitetu zawiązanego na przyjęcie gości z Wielkopolski, Prus, Szlązka i Krakowa, przybyłych na zjazd do Lwowa dnia 13 sierpnia 1871* [A Critical Note to the City Guide issued by the Committee for the Welcome of Guests from Greater Poland, Prussia, Silezia, and Cracow in Lwów, 13 August 1871] (Cracow, 1873). Kunasiewicz is also the author of several other pieces, including *Lwów w roku 1809* [Lwów in 1809] (Lemberg: Wild, 1878) and *Przechadzki archeologiczne po Lwowie* [Archaeological Walks through Lwów] (Lemberg, Przeg. Arch, 1874 and 1876).

71   Schnür-Pepłowski, *Obrazy z przeszłości*, 83-84.

72   Ibid., 83.

73   It was Pawulski who informed Juliusz Hochberger, the head of the Municipal Building Department, in March 1872 about the intention of the committee to demolish part of the historic castle fortifications (CDIAU F. 165, Op. 5, Sp. 110, L. 97).

74   Franciszek Jaworski used the term "*tromtadracja*" to describe the organizers of the 1874 celebration, notably in regard to a popular celebration in the summer of 1874 on Castle Hill and the related installation of a historic sculpture of a lion there (Jaworski, 309).

75   This quote is a curious mixture of Polish and German (Jaworski, 309).

76   From this self-identification, one can speculate that he might have been a regular customer at the "*Veteranische Höhle*" (CDIAU F. 165, Op. 5, Sp. 110, L. 106).

77   CDIAU F. 165, Op. 5, Sp. 110, L. 106, 110.

78   CDIAU F. 165, Op. 5, Sp. 110, L. 110-11.

79   For more on the approval granted on 15 August 1874, see CDIAU F. 165, Op. 5, Sp. 110, L. 112.

80   The Town Hall signaled the start of the ceremony at 2 p.m., and salutations came from the mound at 4 p.m. and ended at 8 p.m. (ibid., L. 111).

81   Ibid., L. 38.

82   Apart from Smolka himself, the committee included Henryk Schmidt, Julian Szemolowski, Karol Widman, Władysław Smolka, Platon Kostecki, Dr. Ignacy Czemerzyński, Alfred Bojarski, Antoni Bogdanowicz, Antoni Halski, Feliks Piatkowski, Wincenty Zaak, and Tadeusz Romanowicz (*Dziennik lwowski* 199 [17 August 1869]. See also CDIAU F. 165, Op. 5, Sp. 110, L. 53).

83   CDIAU F. 165, Op. 5, Sp. 110, L. 76-77.

84   Ibid., L. 59-60.

85   The *Statthalterei's* decision was negative: the committee was not allowed to collect public donations (ibid., L. 55).

86   "*Do sypania Kopca zyskałem pozwolenie właściciela gruntu*" (ibid., L. 46).

87   Thirty to forty prisoners from the provincial prison were employed in that work (ibid., L. 39). The inquiry went down to the Municipality, which reported that the prisoners "belong among those who are being lent (*wynajmowany bywają*) from the local criminal office to the Municipality for use in public works. Those [prisoners] were assigned by the Municipality to its Building Department for the aforementioned works ("Odezwa od Prezydium Sądu krajowego karnego do Prezydium Dyrekcyi policyi we Lwowie," ibid., L. 44).

88   Ibid., L. 40, 43.

89   Bojarski's duty was to catalogue and store in one place all the excavated relics until they would be delivered to heritage specialists (ibid., L. 69).

90   "Sprawozdanie c. k. Dyrektora policyi z dnia 21. wześnia 1869," (ibid., L. 62-63).

91   Ibid., L. 97. When Hochberger repeated his twofold argument in a letter addressed to the committee nine months later, on 19 November 1872, he wrote of the preservation of the ruins as "national monuments" (*pamiatki narodowe*), and by this he clearly meant that the ruins should be under state protection (ibid., L. 102).

92   Ibid., L. 102.

93   When it was reported in June of 1875 that the ruins were still being used as a foundation for the artificial mound, Hochberger noted, "The Building Department has informed the Municipality [about this], while at the same time it has not suggested any technical solution, since it is not at all clear to what extent, from an administrative point of view, the city's intervention would be desired" (ibid., L. 119).

94   Ibid..

95   CDIAU F. 165, Op. 5, Sp. 110, L. 115.

96 "Do Prezydium Rady miasta i Magistratu kr. stól. miasta Lwowa, Stanislaw Kunasze-
wicz, zastępca konservatora budowli i pomników krajowych Galicyi Wschodniej, 17.
Sierpnia 1869," (ibid., L. 65).

97 Ibid., L. 65-66.

98 Ibid., L. 72-73; 82-83. Potocki's tone became even more harsh on 15 March 1872 when
he wrote that "the ruins of the old castle will be completely demolished as well as covered with soil" (ibid., L. 96-97).

99 By 28 June 1875, there existed a separate municipal commission (Baumgarten, Gost-
kowski, Horwath, Spalke, and Zbrożko), though municipal involvement was not yet
clear. On 23 August 1875, the Municipality assigned a sum (200 zlr) for the engineering
work. It turned out that a plan for the construction of the mound did not yet even exist
(ibid., L. 121).

100 Smolka continued to receive his yearly payment for work on the mound at least as late
as 1886. (ibid., L. 133, 142).

101 Ibid., L. 128-33.

102 Ibid., L. 150.

103 Merunowicz was the first Galician politician to attempt to establish an anti-Semitic
political party and advocated anti-Jewish legislation in the Galician Diet in the 1880s.

104 See ibid., L. 152.

105 Teofil Merunowicz, "List otwarty do JWPana Stanislawa Ciuchcińskiego prezydenta
Lwowa," *Gazeta narodowa* 138 (19 June 1907), also see CDIAU F. 165, Op. 5, Sp. 110,
L. 152.

106 The mound's condition sparked fears in the interwar period and was finally stabilized,
using modern technology under socialism in the 1970s and 1980s.

107 "Krysztof Arciszewski. Obrazek historyczny z dawnej przeszłości Lwowa," [Krysztof
Arciszewski. A Historical Image from the ancient history of Lwów] *Przyjaciel domowy*
1-16 (1857); "Tereza Jadwiga. Wspómnienie z dni minionych 26. Września r. 1848,"
[Tereza Jadwiga. Memories from days passed] *Zorza* 7 (1902), 105-7.

108 Mychajlo Hruševśkyj, *Istorija Ukrajiny-Rusy* [History of Ukraine-Ruthenia] (Kyiv:
Naukova Dumka, 1991), Vol. 4, 282; "Osada Lvova Bohdanom Chmelnickim v 1655
r.," [The Lvov Siege by Bohdan Chmelnicki] *Galichanin* 213-16 (1905).

109 CDIAU F. 146, Op. 8, Sp. 448, L. 56; CDIAU F. 101, Op. 1, Sp. 5, L. 35.

110 *Karta pamiatkowa obchodu rocznicy oblezenia miasta Lwowa przez hetmana kozaków
Chmielnickiego i walecznej obrony mieszkańców w roku 1655* [Memory card of the anniversary celebration of the 1655 siege of Lwów by the Cossack hetman Chmielnicki
and the armed resistance against it] (Izraelicka Gmina Wyznaniowa we Lwowie, Lemberg: nakl. A. Goldmana, 1905).

111 "Polskaja demonstracyia v godovshchinu osady gor. Lvova Chmelnickim," [The Polish demonstration on the anniversary of siege of Lvov by Chmielnicki] *Galichanin* 213,
(1905).

112 Semen Wityk, *Pokoj ludziom dobrej woli!* [Peace to people of good will!] (Lemberg:
Drukarnia Udziałowa, 1905). Wityk, a parliament deputy from 1907 to 1914, was one
of the founders of a marginal Social Democratic Party and one of the prominent agita-
tors for socialism in Galician politics. During the short-lived Western Ukrainian Peo-
ples Republic (ZUNR, November 1918 to June 1919), Wityk was a president in chief
of the legislative body of the Ukrainian People's Council (Ukraińska Rada Narodowa)
and the president of the Naphtha Commissariat in Drohobyč. Prior to the booklet *Pokoj
ludziom dobrej woli!*, he was the author of yet another curious publication, *Precz z*

Rusinami! Za San z Polakami! [Away with the Ruthenians! Across the San River with the Poles!] (Lemberg, 1903). After the collapse of ZUNR, he wrote very critically about the Red Army's suppression of Ukrainian socialism. See his article in the newspaper of Hamburg Free Socialists-Anarchists *Alarm* (Nr. 28/1920).

113 CDIAU F. 146, Op. 8, Sp. 448, L. 56.

114 *"Program uroczystości grunwaldskiej"* [Program of the Grunwald Anniversary] (CDIAU F.165, Op. 5, Sp. 50).

115 The use of special costumes was also envisioned (ibid.)

116 See CDIAU F. 146, Op. 7, Sp. 4215; F. 146, Op. 7, Sp. 3685; F. 146, Op. 7, Sp. 4254. On the Lubomirski palace, see CDIAU F. 55, Op. 1, Sp. 191, L. 56-58, 95-96.

117 Under the presidency of Teodor Bohačevśkyj, Diet deputy Levyćkyj lectured on the unfortunate political situation of the Ruthenians under Polish rule and interpreted the siege as an act of national liberation and Chmelnyćkyj as a great hero (CDIAU F.165, Op. 5, Sp. 50, L. 57).

118 CDIAU F.165, Op. 5, Sp. 50, L.57.

119 Ibid., L. 58.

120 Bilous, *Drevniia zdaniia.*

121 See CDIAU F. 52, Op. 1, Sp. 30.

122 Luszczkiewicz, "Katedra," 56.

123 Imperial resolution from 31 December 1850 and 24 June 1853. See *Szematyzm król. Galicyi i Lodomeryi* (Lemberg: Nakł. c. k. Namiesnictwa z druk. Władysława Lozińskiego, 1895), 353.

124 The arena of National Conservators' activity was enlarged by an imperial resolution of 18 July 1873 and by several resolutions of the Ministry of Culture and Education (26 November 1874, l. 16.443; 4 December 1874, l. 7933, and 14 September 1875, l. 9.613). In 1890, the Central Conservation Commission established two conservation offices, one for Western Galicia and one for Eastern Galicia (2 April 1890, l. 368 and 24 August 1890, l. 966), ibid.

125 Further in the text, the Central Commission and honorary curators. Also see CDIAU F. 165, Op. 5, Sp. 110, L. 65-68; T. B. Sprysa. "Pamjatkoochoronne pravo ta dijalnisť Centranoï Komisiï z doslidžennia ta konservaciï pamjatok Halyčyny v dr. pol. XIX st." [Conservation legislation and the activities of the Central Commission for Research and Conservation of Monuments in Galicia in the second half of the 19th c.], *Architektura, Visnyk Hacionaľnoho Universytetu "Ľvivka Politechnika,"* 375 (1999), 86-92.

126 Alois Riegl, "The Modern Cult of Monuments: Its Character and Its Origin," in Kurt Forster, ed., *Oppositions 25: Monument/Monumentality* (New York: Rizzoli, 1982).

127 Art historian Max Dvořák (1874-1921) was one of the main representatives of the Viennese School of art history. On Dvořák's major involvement in Galicia, the restoration of Cracow Wawel Castle, see Jarosław Krawczyk, ed., *Wokół Wawelu. Antologia tekstów z lat 1901-1909* [Around Wawel: Anthology of texts from 1901-1909] (Warsaw and Cracow: Mówią wieki, 2002).

128 See Adolf Markl, "Projekt budowy gmachu na Sejm i bióra Wydzialu krajowego we Lwowie" [Project for the building of Lemberg Sejm and the Crown Land administration], *Dźwignia* 3 (1877), 14-16; 1 (1879), 6-8.

129 In case of excavations, their tasks also included appointing guards and ensuring that the discovered artifacts would be delivered to national collections. Both the Central Commission and the Crown Land's conservators, however, lacked jurisdictional and legal power; although they were supported through imperial protection, they could request help only from state institutions and had no staff at their disposal.

130 The hierarchy among the individuals and official bodies engaging in conservation efforts was not established clearly; before the establishment of the Viennese Committee, the Cracow Academy of Arts had been established as a major site for heritage collections. For example, after being catalogued at the Municipal archive and reported to the Central Commission, the relics that Antoni Schneyder excavated at the Castle Hill and elsewhere in Galicia were delivered directly to the Archaeological Commission within the academy (CDIAU F. 52, Op. 1, Sp. 950, L. 6).

131 CDIAU F. 146, Op. 7, Sp. 3994, L. 18-23.

132 Ibid., L. 47-50.

133 Ibid., L. 25-29.

134 Ibid., L. 52.

135 CDIAU F. 55, Op. 1, Sp. 191, L. 55.

136 CDIAU F. 52, Op. 1. Sp. 950, L. 5.

137 "Memoryal w sprawie konkursu na plany restauracyi zamku krolewskiego na Wawelu" [Report on the issue of the competition for restoration of the royal Wawel Castle] *Dźwignia* 9 (1881), 90-92.

138 See Luszczkiewicz, 72.

139 Using the rhetoric of scientific and technological progress, the society was able to serve as a lobby for preferential treatment of local architects in local building projects (see "3.5. Architects and the state: the Polytechnic Society [1877-1918] and the Polish language").

140 "Sprawozdania ze zgromadzeń tygodniowych" [Report from weekly meetings], *Dźwignia* 3 (1880), 18; 5 (1880), 34.

141 "Sprawozdanie z posiedzeń Zarządu" [Report from board meetings], *Dźwignia* 6 (1880), 41.

142 On this, see Wojciech Bałus, *Krakau zwischen Traditionen und Wegen in die Moderne: Zur Geschichte der Architektur und der öffentlichen Grünanlagen im 19. Jahrhundert. Forschungen zur Geschichte und Kultur des östlichen Mitteleuropa* (Stuttgart: Steiner, 2003).

143 "Sprawozdanie z 10. posiedzenia Zarządu odbytego na dniu 2. stycznia 1882" [Report from a board meeting on 2 January 1882] *Dźwignia* 2 (1882), 18.

144 For more on the Wawel restoration, see Jarosław Krawczyk, ed., *Wokół Wawelu.*

145 Welcome dear Master, / [...We] love you deeply! / Since we have our freedom, / Since we are in our own house, / And if we love each other, / That is no one else's business! / Our ancient Wawel / Sparkles revived. / The hymn of faith from Lwów, / Bells ring loud (Pepłowski, 407).

146 "Memoryal," 90. The Memorial was delivered to the Galician Diet's speaker, Dr. Zyblikiewicz, by a delegation from the Polytechnic Society by August 1881.

147 Ibid.

148 Professor Lindguist, "Plany Zamku na Wawelu," [Plans of the Wawel Castle], *CzT* 3 (1883), 24-26. On a concise summary of the three congresses, see "Zjazd techników polskich," [Congress of Polish Technicians], *CzT* 13 (1894), 99-100.

149 Glorified by Henryk Sienkiewicz's historic novel, the period was particularly unfortunate because of the physical destruction of Lemberg that took place during that time.

150 Austrian parliament deputy Romančuk emphasized that in the previous year, Ruthenians had enjoyed no economic or cultural achievements and consequently argued for their greater political representation and for universal suffrage. (CDIAU F. 146, Op. 8, Sp. 448, L. 78-84).

151   Others, such as the *Dilo* editor, Eugen Levyćkyj, spoke of electoral reform (ibid.).

152   Parliament deputies Karol and Vladysovski, Diet deputy Alexius Barabash, and the *Galichanin* editor, Josef Monchalowski, participated in the meeting (ibid., 83-84).

153   On repeated warnings and reminders to the owners of historic buildings about damage during the renovation, see, for example, CDIAU F. 165, Op. 5, Sp. 110, L.19.

154   Ibid., L. 66.

155   CDIAU F. 55, Op. 1, Sp. 190, L. 15.

156   The Municipal Archive also dealt with much more mundane matters concerning the overall city appearance. A good example is its permission of 8 March 1910 to install electrically lit advertisement boards (*lampy reklamove*) modeled on ones already used in Vienna and Budapest (CDIAU F. 55. Op. 1, Sp. 191, L. 61.)

157   CDIAU F. 55, Op. 1, Sp. 190, L. 19-20; 27. Also see CDIAU F. 55, Op. 1, Sp. 199.

158   Izydor Šaranevyč, a Ruthenian scholar famous for his discovery of the ruins of medieval Halicz, against the predictions of Jan Bołoz Antoniewicz, was asked by the Municipality for his opinion on historic architecture and especially on medieval Ruthenian architecture (CDIAU F. 55, Op. 1, Sp. 191, L. 51-54, 56-59, 91-92, 95-96).

159   "The aforementioned house is a valuable historic and architectural monument....I stress, however, that the house had been renovated several times, and in many places [it] departs from its original style.... In this respect it is very damaged....If, in the light of the great sums needed for restoration, it would be impossible to save it,...I would suggest the extraction of several architectural details, for example, the portal, and for their adequate installation [elsewhere]" (CDIAU F. 55, Op. 1, Sp. 190, L. 21-22).

160   The municipal archivists' commitment to conservation often caused bitter conflicts with owners of historic buildings. On the conflict with tradesman Gabriel Stark concerning an advertisement on his house on Halicka Square, see CDIAU F. 55, Op. 1, Sp. 191, L. 77.

161   For a recent study on the history of the *Stavropigija* building, see Marjana Dolynśka, "Deščo pro kamjanyci Stavropigiï" [About the Stavropigija Buildings] *HB* 15 (May 1996) "Architekturna spadščyna," 8-9.

162   The issue was that the institute's printing and lithography house was situated in an overly small and dark location, and the institute therefore decided to demolish the middle part of the 15th century buildings in its possession, a courtyard, in order to "enlarge the courtyard and therefore to let air and light into the [remaining] buildings" (CDIAU F. 129, Op. 2, Sp. 1600, L. 6-8).

163   Ibid., L. 14-15.

164   Ibid., L. 16-22.

165   On a recent study of the design of Lemberg's medieval churches, see Alla Martyniuk, "Chramy davnioho Lvova" [Churches of Old Ľviv] *HB* 15 (May 1996) "*Architekturna spadščyna*," 14-15.

166   All four restorations, except that of 1868, have been treated extensively in Bohdan Janusz's article "Zabytki architektury Lwowa," (in Janusz, *Lwów stary i dzisiejszy*, 7-49). On the restoration of 1868-69, see CDIAU F. 197, Op. 1, Sp. 1303.

167   This was Julian Zachariewicz's first full-scale restoration project in Lemberg. Previously, in the 1870s he had participated in the renovation of the Viennese cathedral of St. Stephen. Outside Lemberg, Zachariewicz re-interpreted the parish churches in Tarnów (western Galicia, 1889-91) and Stryj (eastern Galicia, c. 1890) into neo-Gothic forms (Žuk, *Julian Zachariewicz*, 8).

168 See, for example, J. Sadovska, "Julian Oktawian Zacharievyč – restavrator kostio-
liv," [J. Z., a restorer of churches] *Architektura, Visnyk Hacional'noho Universytetu
"L'vivka Politechnika"* 439 (2002), 122-27; T. B. "Restavracijni projekty u profesijnij
dijaľnosti Juliana Zacharievyča" [Restoration projects in Julian Zachariewicz's professional career], *Architektura, Visnyk Hacional'noho Universytetu "L'vivka Politechnika"*
410 (2000), 146-51.

169 "Najwieksza, ale też i najniesumienniejsza" Tadeusz Münnich, *CzT* 15-16 (1888).

170 Janusz, *Lwów stary i dzisiejszy*, 11.

171 CDIAU F. 52, Op. 1, Sp. 208, L. 1-2. Janusz thought that the pilasters were "unneces-
sarily added" and the column capitals "poorly made"; the addition was, in his view,
lamentable, given that its foundations had been laid in the church cemetery (Janusz,
Lwów stary i dzisiejszy, 11).

172 During the restoration of St. Mary of Snow, similarly, the facade and the sidewalls were
stylistically upgraded in 1858, and a small up-to-date bell tower was erected (CDIAU F.
197, Op. 1, Sp. 1303, L. 7).

173 Ibid., L. 1-2.

174 Ibid.

175 Cathedral Chapter (*Kapituła*) refers to the governing body of canons for a Catholic
cathedral and a diocese.

176 Because it was not a parish church, St. John the Baptist did not qualify for any state
conservation funds. The Municipality implied that the contemporary cracks were due to
the installation of a large organ in the building's fragile old walls (ibid., L. 5-6.).

177 Ibid., L. 9-10.

178 Ibid., L. 11-19.

179 On the earlier restoration of St. Mary of Snow, see CDIAU F. 52, Op. 1, Sp. 208.

180 Nevertheless, Zachariewicz's pioneering role in the establishment of the local restoration circle in Lemberg must be acknowledged (Žuk, *Julian Zachariewicz*, 8).

181 The earliest source available to the scholars of the late nineteenth century was an instruction (*instrukcja*), compiled by the Dominican convent, to which St. John the Baptist Church initially belonged, that mentioned Constancia, the French wife of King Leo,
who founded a chapel to the left of the church and where she was later buried (CDIAU
F. 197, Op. 1, Sp. 1303, L. 12).

182 In the interwar period, Janusz engaged in a lengthy analysis of the building's structure
to prove that the church was indeed initially built of stone and that its original style
could only be Romanesque (by excluding one by one the possibilities of the Gothic and
subsequent Renaissance)" (Janusz, *Lwów stary i dzisiejszy*, 14).

183 Janusz, *Lwów stary i dzisiejszy*, 15.

184 Anonymous (D. K.), *Odnowienie i rekonstrukcya Katedry Ormiańskiej we Lwowie*
[The renovation and the reconstruction of the Armenian Cathedral in Lwów] (Lemberg:
Wiek Nowy 1908), 3.

185 In this case, as in many others, the building's value was expressed with a particular
term, "monumental": "*Der Zentralbau ist ein Bau von äusserst monumentalen architektonischen Wirkung*" (Anonymous [D. K.], 7).

186 Józef Piotrowski (Dr.), *Katedra Ormiańska we Lwowie w świetle restauracji i ostatnich odkryć* [Armenian Cathedral in Lwów in the light of restoration and the latest
discoveries] (Lwow: Nakl. Kurji Metropolitalnej obradku orm.-kt. we Lwowie, 1925),
29. Also see Jurij Smirnov, "Restavracija Virmenśkoï katedry u L'vovi u 1905-1914

rokach" [The Restoration of the Armenian Cathedral in L'viv in 1905-1914], *HB* 5 (February, March, April 1995) "Krajeznavstvo Halyčyny," 12-14.

187 Per Piotrowski's modernist, iconoclastic assumptions on the ideal Gothic temple: "All the walls were completely empty, there were no chairs…there was no pulpit, and the priest addressed the people from the altar" (Piotrowski, *Katedra ormiańska*, 20-21).

188 Ibid.

189 Piotrowski called it "though not of first-class value, yet good, stylistic baroque altarpieces, the bishop's chair, and the very well-proportioned, successful (*zgrabna, udatna*) pulpit from the eighteenth century" (ibid., 18).

190 This was made under the initiative of Archbishop Józef Teodorowicz, who bought them personally at auction (ibid.).

191 Ibid., 18-19.

192 Anonymous (D. K.), 7.

193 The committee consisted of university professors Leon Piliński and Jan Boloz Antoniewicz and conservators Władysław Łoziński, Seferowicz, and Krzeczurowicz. (Ibid.)

194 The pilasters "in the style of old ornaments" were borrowed from the antique Evangelium that was owned by the Armenian Metropolitan Curia. Piotrowski, perhaps because of his generous publisher, the Curia itself, made no negative comments on either this detail, or more broadly on the plastering in the interior, or especially on the mosaics by Józef Mehoffer, which by that time covered half of the interior that had known no mosaic before. The new mosaics largely replaced old frescoes, along with an 1862 painting by a local theater decorator, Dulla (Piotrowski, *Katedra ormiańska*, 11).

195 "*Sie ist äusserst mittlemässig*" (ibid.).

196 Anonymous (D. K.), 13.

197 Ibid., 16.

198 Ibid.

199 To cover the vast and growing literature on museum and exhibition practices throughout history as well as on exhibition theory and world exhibitions today would require a much longer footnote than is possible here. However, several books that deal directly with nineteenth- and early twentieth-century exhibitions in Europe and the United States deserve specific note. See especially John R. Gold and Margaret M. Gold, *Cities of Culture: Staging International Festivals and the Urban Agenda, 1851-2000* (Burlington: Ashgate Publishing, 2005). The politics behind the Great Exhibition of 1851 in London has already been revisited by Jeffrey A. Auerbach (*The Great Exhibition of 1851: A Nation on Display* [New Haven and London: Yale University Press, 1999]), who demonstrated that contrary to a common assumption, the exhibition was designed to foster local economic development rather than to show British economic superiority; that the machinery was often handcrafted; and that large segments of the public were either indifferent or openly opposed to the exhibition. Also, see Michael Leapman, *The World for a Shilling: How the Great Exhibition of 1851 Shaped a Nation* (London: Headline Books, 2001); Paul Greenhalgh, *Ephemeral Vistas: The Expositions Universelles, Great Exhibition and World's Fairs, 1851-1939* (Manchester: Manchester University Press, 1990); On the World's Expositions in the U.S., see Robert W. Rydell, *All the World's a Fair: Visions of Empire at American International Expositions, 1876-1916* (Chicago: University of Chicago Press, 1984); also see idem, *World of Fairs: The Century-of-Progress Expositions* (Chicago: University of Chicago Press, 1993); Ivan Karp and Steven D. Lavine, eds., *Exhibiting Cultures: The Poetics and Politics of Museum Display* (Washington, D. C.: Smithsonian Institution Press, 1991), 344-65;

Julie K. Brown, *Making Culture Visible: The Public Display of Photography at Fairs, Expositions, and Exhibitions in the United States, 1847-1900* (Amsterdam: Harwood Academic Publishers, 2001). For the World Exhibition in Vienna in 1873, on which the Galician exhibition was modeled, see Jutta Pemsel, *Die Wiener Weltausstellung. Das gründerzeitliche Wien am Wendepunkt* (Vienna and Cologne: Böhlau, 1989). On the Lemberg 1894 exhibition, see On Galician *Kaiserreise* in 1851, the plans for the eventually canceled 1868 Galician tour of Galicia, and the emperor's 1880 and 1894 visits, and on the 1898 jubilee in Lemberg, see Unowsky, *The Pomp and Politics of Patriotism* 72-75; Dabrowski, *Commemorations*, 118-26.

200 The number of fairs gradually rose in Galicia during the Vormärz period, from 121 in 1803 to 313 in 1829, and to around 750 in the 1850s (Ivanočko, "Urbanistyčni procesy Halyčyny," 218).

201 It had been reported that the Jews bought wool directly from the landowners for a very low price and therefore "exploited" (*wyzyskowali*) the city population (Schnür-Pepłowski, *Obrazy z przeszłości*, 43).

202 Dabrowski, *Commemorations*, 118-32, 160-83.

203 For plans of the Jabłonowski palace, one of the traditional places the emperor regularly visited, see CDIAU F. 146, Op. 7, Sp. 1920. For plans of the exhibition, see J. Jägermann (Professor), "Wystawa krajowa rolniczo-przemysłowa we Lwowie w roku 1877 (z rysunkiem na tab. II)" [Provincial Agricultural-Industrial Exhibition in Lwów in 1877]. *Dźwignia* 2 (1877), 12-14.

204 For a concise overview, see "Powszechna Wystawa krajowa we Lwowie otwarta uroczyście dnia 5 czerwca b. r." [The Provincial Exhibition in Lwów opened solemnly on 5 June 1894], *CzT* 11 (1894), 87.

205 Jägermann, 12.

206 "Zjazd techników polskich," 104.

207 Revealingly, it was for this building that the architect was honored with noble status and the self-chosen title of Julian Oktawian von Lwigrod (*z Lwigrodu*) Zachariewicz (ibid.).

208 The resulting plans were declared the society's great achievement (ibid.).

209 Ibid.

210 Jägermann, ibid., 12-14.

211 Sculptures by Leopold Schimser, folk ceramics from Kosów (Kosiv), and linen works from Tarnopol (Ternopil') are but a few examples from a long list. (CDIAU F. 146, Op. 7, Sp. 4154, L. 16-33).

212 The building industry as a "success story" was a narrative forwarded by the organizers of the Exhibition of the Building Industry in 1892 at the Lemberg Polytechnic University; the exhibition was initiated by the Polytechnic Society and personally supported by Julian Zachariewicz.

213 CDIAU F. 146, Op. 7, Sp. 4154, L. 19.

214 This situation was even more explicit at the Cracow 1887 Provincial Agricultural-Industrial Exhibition (*Wystawa krajowa rolniczo-przemysłowa i maszyn pomocniczych dla rolnictva i przemysłu*): the Exhibition of Polish Art (*Wystawa sztuki polskiej*), where "the works of Polish art as well as historical monuments" were exhibited ("Powszechna Wystawa," 87; "Wystawa krajowa w Krakowie," [Provincial Exhibition in Cracow], *CzT* [1887], 13).

215 Because of the ten-year span between the provincial exhibitions, initial plans were to hold the next event in Lemberg in 1897, the previous provincial exhibition having been

held in Cracow in 1887. See "Powszechna Wystawa krajowa we Lwowie otwarta," 87-89; *Powszechna Wystawa krajowa we Lwowie w 1894 r.* (Cracow 1896); Dabrowski, *Commemorations*, 118-22.

216　The Polytechnic University decided to commemorate its 50th anniversary on 10 July, and the Polytechnic Society decided to organize the III Congress of Polish Technicians in the same month. See "Sprawozdanie z czynności Zarządu Towarzystwa za czas od 15. marca 1893 do 7. marca 1894" [Report of the Society's Board for 15 March 1893 - 7 March 1894], *CzT* 4 (1894), 28.

217　The exhibition consisted of 34 special groups, each with a separate organizing committee and jury. For this event, ethnography, women's work, arts, architecture, and music constituted separate sections ("Powszechna Wystawa krajowa we Lwowie otwarta...," 88).

218　Jaworski, *Lwów stary,* 346.

219　Gorgolewski, for example, had designed the triumphal entry arch, all governmental, school, and university pavilions, the Scholz confectionery pavilion, and the Krzeszowice pavilion. Hochberger had designed the Lemberg municipal building, and Skowron designed the main pavilion of industry, the palaces of arts and architecture (the former of which was built in stone), and the Matejko mausoleum. With Karol Boublik, he codesigned the concert hall.

220　For the original drawings of the pavilions of architecture, the city of Lemberg, and the companies of Sosnowski & Co. and Jan Okocim, see DALO F. 2, Op. 4, Sp. 1097; F. 2, Op. 4, Sp. 1098.

221　The idea for panorama of the battle is believed to have come from the painter Jan Styka who, as early as January 1893, had set up an organization called the Committee for the Racławice Panorama to collect the necessary funds for the painting. Styka also involved other renowned individuals such as Wojciech Kossak, Tadeusz Popiel, Zygmunt Rozwadowski, Tadeusz Aksentowicz, Włodzimierz Tetmajer, Michał Sozański, and Wincenty Wodzinowski in the Committee. This glass-roofed rotunda, 40 meters in diameter and 18 meters high, which was an iron construction decorated on the outside with neo-Renaissance plaster details, was erected under the supervision of Ludwik Ramułt. Inside the rotunda, Styka's 114 meters long and 15 meters wide canvas was hung, thus connecting the anniversary associated with Kościuszko and the Galician provincial exhibition in canvas and stone. For more on the Racławice panorama, see Dabrowski, *Commemorations*, 122-26.

222　*Ilustrowany przewodnik po Lwowie i powszechnej wystawie krajowej, z planem i widokami miasta, wystawy i 18 rycinami ważniejszych budynków* [Illustrated Guide to Lwów and the General Provincial Exhibition with a plan, views of the city, and 18 drawings of the most important buildings attached] (Lemberg: Towarzystwo dla rozwoju i upiększenia miasta, 1894).

223　"Sprawozdanie z uroczystego obchodu zakończenia 50-letniego roku istnienia Politechniki we Lwowie" [Report from the Solemn Celebration of the 50th Anniversary of the Lwów Polytechnic University], *CzT* 13 (1894), 104.

224　In the end, and probably because of the sad amount of Polish technical publications, the decision was made to not limit the display of printed material to any language or date. The collective exhibition of Polish technical achievements and the preparation of the exhibition catalogue also fell among the Society's responsibilities ("Rozmaitości" [Miscellaneous], *CzT* 4 [1894], 34).

225　Ibid.

226 "Odezwa," [Appeal], *CzT* 5 (1894), 35.

227 "Our *kraj,* Galicia...belongs to the Austrian state; yet its natural and climatic conditions and its population's thinking and morality result in its economic and social environment being different from other, especially western, Austrian provinces. [It is] much closer to the neighboring provinces in Russia and Prussia where mostly Polish technicians work. With no political intention in mind, the Congress of Polish technicians has therefore its legitimization." E. L., "Zjazd techników polskich," 99.

228 "Zjazd techników polskich,"100.

229 "The [national] work...has for us Poles, more importance than for other, more fortunate nations because they are politically independent. Circumstances have changed and with them the tactics of the struggle: [now] work will be our weapon, and it will accomplish what we could not accomplish with the use of arms" ("Zjazd techników polskich," 101).

230 Ibid.

231 Noha, 22-28.

232 "Sprawozdanie z uroczystego obchodu," 105.

233 The emperor rewarded the organizers of the exhibition with various titles and decorations: Lemberg President Edmund Mochnacki and engineer Franciszek Skowron were awarded the Franz Joseph Cross, and a Municipal Building Department official, Juliusz Hochberger, and others received the order of the Iron Cross. For a full list of imperially bestowed awards, see, for example, "Rozmaitości," *CzT* 22 (1894), 178).

234 The World Exhibition of 1900 in Paris, for example, had a Galician section, curiously divided into two parts: the Zakopane Hall and the Hucul Hall ("Wystawa w Paryżu" [Paris Exhibition], *CzT* 1900, 119). The Ruthenian delegation is reported to have arrived with a Ukrainian national blue and yellow flag (Noha, 35-36).

235 "Sprawozdanie z obchodu," 106.

236 *CzT* 10 (1910), 141.

237 Elsinger & Stromeyer attached their catalogue and a photo of the façade of their pavilion in Hamburg, suggesting that size and architectural appearance could be adapted to the organizers' wishes (CDIAU F. 165, Op. 5, Sp. 1163, L. 2-3; 23).

238 Also, a railway station in the Zakopane style, to be used further as a park pavilion and a music pavilion, was planned (ibid., L. 36-37).

239 Ibid., L. 11.

240 Ibid., L. 4.

241 The battle resulted not only in the Great Duchy of Lithuania – an entity appropriated by Polish historiography as an integral part of Polish history – becoming the most powerful state in Eastern Europe, but it also characteristically symbolized Polish national strength against a German offensive in its halting of the Teutonic Knights' eastward expansion. For more on Grunwald celebrations throughout Poland, see Dabrowski, *Commemorations*, 159-83.

242 Ibid., L. 9.

243 Anonymous (Dr. M. Sz.), *"Pamiatka rocznicy grunwaldskiej,"* (ibid., 30-35).

244 Ibid.

245 "Projekt pawilonu wystawowego dla krol. stol. M. Lwowa (podali inz.-arch. by W. Derdacki i W. Mińkiewicz)" [Plans for the Exhibition Pavilion for the Capital City of Lwów, by W. Derdacki and W. Mińkiewicz], *CzT* 10 (1910), 141-43.

246 Ibid.

247 Rutowski was a vice president of the *Städteausstellung* and also of the committee for the organization of the general exhibition of Polish art (CDIAU F. 165, Op. 5, Sp. 1163, L. 2; 9; 11).

248 "I-sza Wystawa Architektów Polskich" [First Exhibition of Polish Architects], *CzT* 8 (1910), 114.

249 On 10 July 1910, the board decided that of the nineteen submitted works, none was adequate to use for the exhibition poster, and neither was any of outstanding artistic value ("Rozmaitości," *CzT* 14 [1910], 207). In the end, the jury decided to ask the famous Polish Art Noveau-Expressionist painter Kazimir Sichulski to make a drawing for the poster. See Kazimierz Sichulski, *Powszechna Polska Wystawa architektury, rzeźby i malarstwa, Lwów 1910* [General Polish Exhibition of Architecture, Sculpture and Painting, Lwów 1910] (Lemberg: Piller-Neumann, 1910).

250 "Rozmaitości," *CzT* 11 (1910), 163-64.

251 Witold Mińkiewicz, "Z powodu I wystawy Architektury we Lwowie," [On the Occasion of the First Exhibition of Architecture in Lwów], *CzT* 23 (1910), 355.

252 The exhibition committee applied for financial support from both the Diet and the City Council. Although the former refused its support altogether, the latter granted a concession of 10,000 crowns as well as the use of the Palace of Art, which apparently was in its possession, from 1 September on. The city first extended the run of the arts exhibition to the end of August, thus leaving only 10 days to set up the architectural exhibition. Because this seemed very unrealistic, the city extended the time of the arts exhibition further into the autumn ("Sprawozdanie Komitetu Wystawy Architektów polskich," 386).

253 Mińkiewicz, 355.

254 The organizing committee desperately appealed to the architects' conscious in *Czasopismo techniczne, (CzT* 14 [1910], 193).

255 Mińkiewicz sadly commented on this fact in his article quoted above (ibid., 357). To compensate somehow for this, *Czasopismo techniczne* deliberately illustrated his critical review of the exhibition primarily with the works of non-Galician architects, and most notably with their architectural projects for Roman Catholic (Polish) churches. "V Zjazd Techników Polskich we Lwowie w czasie od 8-11 września b. r.," [Fifth Congress of Polish Technicians in Lwów on 8-11 September 1910], *CzT* 18 (1910), 264.

256 Ibid., 263-65. Also see *Architect*, no. 10 (September), Cracow (1910).

257 "V Zjazd," 263-65.

258 Ibid., 265.

259 Mińkiewicz, 355-56.

260 Ibid.

261 Ibid.

262 Ibid., 358.

263 Ibid., 358-59.

CONCLUSIONS

The tendency to write history along the narrow lines of national narratives and professional architectural/art history – themselves often written from nationalist perspectives – has led to overly simplistic understandings of Habsburg Lemberg's architecture. To successfully portray the complexity of its historical development and categories of architecture, as well as the associated politics of culture and nationalism, requires thorough and careful reformulation of terminology. Contrary to conventional national histories, the officials in the Galician governor's office did not single-handedly shape the city's architecture and its use of public space from the annexation of the city to Austria in 1772 until its autonomy almost a century later in 1870. Rather, a variety of groups, including important local figures, interacted in the creation of Habsburg Lemberg during this period. The diverse uses that these individuals placed on architecture highlight the ways in which both imperial and national projects were staged in the Galician capital from the early nineteenth century on. Following 1848, the official policy of restricting public space to imperial symbolic uses was maintained, and further reinforced by much more severe legal measures against those who broke the law. After the *Ausgleich*, the authorities, now Polish-speaking though politically segregated, under increasing pressure from different groups in the city that demanded public presence, gradually arrived at a vision of the city that was both Habsburg and Polish. In this vision, the city center was understood as no place for dilapidated areas, political disturbances, or public nuisances, though the outer districts were left undisturbed and where an appropriate location for Ruthenian meetings was inside cultural institutions, not on the street.

This post-1867 official project of creating a Habsburg Lemberg, yet a Polish Lwów, failed for several reasons. First, the building authorities were continually short of the finances and other resources needed to realize their aspirations.

Second, in a situation where old hierarchies were breaking down and "citizens' rights" were being invoked to support diverse uses of public space, it was no longer possible to control the continuous, semantically ever-shifting staging and reinvention of architectural visions and the local use of space. And third, modern nationalists' attempts to integrate the masses into new ideologies underestimated the vitality of imperial legacies among various social, national, and professional strata that continued to exist as late as the last years immediately preceding World War I.

Throughout the nineteenth century, newly constructed buildings and monuments transmitted values that far exceeded the preoccupation with style and building techniques found in standard architectural histories. These values became most visible during street celebrations, restoration practices, and provincial exhibitions. In this way, streets, banners, inscriptions, and evening illumination became statements of identity on display. When the architectural surroundings would not have corresponded to an individual ceremony's meaning, temporary architecture was constructed and existing structures appropriately decorated. Façades became arenas for the public display of beliefs, and building interiors, perhaps publicly accessible but restricted to select audiences, delivered particular views of private values.

Polish and Ukrainian writings on architecture have long linked the quality and aesthetic values of buildings, as well as of monuments, to the politics of the era in which they were constructed. This practice was shaped in large measure by the Marxist-Leninist views of history, but it was hardly new in historiographies of architecture. Almost from the moment that Austrian officials, such as the theater director, Franz Kratter, and Police Director Joseph Rohrer, arrived in Lemberg with the mission of making it the capital of the newly acquired Crown Land of Galicia in the early nineteenth century, they viewed architecture in political terms. For such men, the architecture they found in the city reflected Polish culture's perceived backwardness, and they emphasized this by describing it as ugly and "baroque" in contrast to the neoclassical and enlightened aesthetics then current in Austria.

From Austria's acquisition of Galicia in 1772 on, Lemberg's architecture was seen as – and used for – the symbolic coding of public values. These values changed with the actors involved and with the passage of time. In the early nineteenth century, Austrian high officials such as Kratter and Rohrer strove for architecture that represented good government, worthy of the Habsburg capital of Galicia and of esteemed visits from Vienna. This view extended into the Vormärz, as exemplified by Governor Ludwig Taaffe's understanding of public space in 1824. Numerous employees of the Crown Land Building Department executed this vision in practice over the course of Habsburg rule in Galicia. The physical expression of good government implied architecture of an austere neoclassicism: restrained ornamentation, cleanliness, greenery, proportionately sized buildings, and a straightness to the streets. During the time this vision prevailed, the new Town Hall building (1827) and several other key public buildings emerged.

Most of the major planning projects realized in nineteenth-century Lemberg began as initiatives made by state authorities. From the early nineteenth century until 1870, in the period of the Vormärz and neoabsolutism, such proposals came from the Gubernium, the arm of state power at the time. The Municipal government, deprived of its autonomy and drastically diminished in size, merely executed the Crown Land administration's projects that were closely monitored from Vienna. The grand project of the Vormärz, the ring road built on the location of the former fortifications and only partially executed by the Crown Land Building Department, involved the architectural reshaping and greening of the city. This was accompanied by what was termed the cleaning of the city, which in practice included as many social "nuisances," such as prostitutes, beggars, and Jews, as actual filth. During the Vormärz, the grandeur of this project failed largely because of a lack of resources, these having been redirected toward the symbolic expression of the state – that is, toward buildings of power and culture – in the city center. Thus prostitution remained a problem in the historic center, where it was constrained to the limits of the Jewish quarter, while the plan of relocating the Jewish population residing outside the ghetto was fully implemented.

The nature of such culturally specific urban policies was shaped by changing concepts of public space and public order. The staffing of an increasingly bureaucratized *Gubernium* with large numbers of Austrian officials, per late eighteenth century Josephinian reforms of centralization, and the use of public spaces being restricted exclusively to imperial events led to the eventual contestation of those spaces in the Galician capital from the 1830s onward.

The idea of introducing greenery into public areas transformed the garden, traditionally associated with notions of privacy and later with *Biedermeier*-era aesthetics of natural beauty and solitude, into such a contested space. The impetus to bring more plantings into public spaces came from the late eighteenth-century Crown Land building authorities who aimed to design gardens according to newly emerging notions of beauty and to legitimize their authority over Lemberg's physical appearance. Working with the goal of persuading themselves – and distinguished visitors from Vienna – that Galicia was well ruled, officials from the Building Department (*Landesbaudirection*) embarked on the grand ring road project, which involved the demolition of historic fortifications and the creation of stately boulevards, embellished by cleanly planted greenery and lined with beautiful, meaning neoclassical, buildings. In its aim to leave its mark on urban life, the German-speaking administrative elite initiated ambitious projects that far exceeded the financial resources of the Gubernium and that were received with caution in Vienna. Once portions of this project were concluded, Theater Director Kratter and Police Director Rohrer wrote of them as examples of benefits of the Austrian rule in Galicia and contrasted them with the previous conditions, which they and others termed as times of ruin.

Yet by becoming involved in much symbolic work, such as the renaming of streets with German names, the Crown Land *Landesbaudirection* created a false vision of reality, because it simultaneously neglected areas not associated with state power, most especially the Jewish quarter in the city center and the outer districts and all their problems. By limiting redevelopment to a few sites within the historic center, the building authorities transformed the city center into a Potemkin village of sorts, surrounded by outer districts that remained unimproved. When copies of Galician *Schematismus* were presented to members of an exclusive public at the inauguration of the new Town Hall in 1835, whose renovation was intended to symbolize recent successes at urbanization as well as the benevolence of Austrian rule, no mention was made of the condition of the outlying districts or the Jewish ghetto.[1]

Vormärz society – segregated as it was into the gentry, bureaucracy, and the greater public and further segregated along religious and ethnic lines – understood particular buildings and complexes as sites for exclusive socializing and increasingly as sites for the free expression of sentiments. Here again, the characteristics associated with the audiences at public performances, versus private ones, came to the fore. The German Theater, its neoclassical *Redoute,* and, to a lesser extent and later, the Skarbek Theater became associated with bureaucratic German-speaking circles, though these also included a large segment of local Polish gentry loyal to the empire. Although the Roman Catholic cathedral represented the larger Polish-speaking society, traditional districts associated with specific nationalities – notably the Jewish quarter, Ruthenian Street, and Armenian Street – retained their ethnic dimensions. In parallel, the lower strata also had their places of representation, such as the area around Kurkowa Street, where the Ruthenian *haïvky* celebration was annually held.

Besides its inherent limitations, the imperial project suffered from inconsistency on the part of the authorities toward local cultures and their place in imperial representation. Following the Congress of Vienna in 1815, Crown Land's cultural concessions to national parties that were perceived as troublesome were intended to ensure their loyalty, but placed yet another limitation on the unilateral reconfiguration of public space by state authorities and on the grand imperial project. In reality, most of these pronational figures of the early nineteenth century and of the Vormärz period, such as Józef Maksymilian Ossoliński and Stanisław Skarbek, respectively, were deeply loyal to Vienna, and the national cultural institutions they championed received only modest popular support. Yet the transformation of public space from a site of formal imperial presence, imported from Vienna, to a more heterogeneous space where local sentiments could find expression marked a significant shift.

In the nineteenth century, "nations" were undergoing great change in size and self-identification. At the beginning of the century, the Galician Polish nation" seen in the public sphere was largely limited to wealthy noblemen, such as Ossoliński, who saw themselves as the only legitimate representatives of Galician society. The bureaucratic stratum, understood as German, was very heterogeneous: although Franz Kratter, Joseph Rohrer, and one of the very few architects of the period to leave an account, Ignac Chambrez, might have subscribed to the notion of the German culture's civilizing mission, they differed in their understandings of "motherland" and "nation," which were at times blurry. Kratter expressed admiration only for Vienna; for Rohrer, Prague remained a good model to follow in general urban affairs, in addition to Vienna. And for Chambrez, Moravia and Bohemia elicited only deep emotional sentiment; the universalist, neoclassicist principle remained his professional motto. The Ruthenian nation – a minority in Lemberg and yet to be "invented" politically – consisted of various followers of the Eastern Christian faith, besides the individuals who spoke the Ruthenian vernacular.

Ossoliński's conception of the Galician nation as the Polish-speaking aristocracy, revealed him as very distant from later Polish nationalists such as Franciszek Smolka, who was a proponent of a liberal, democratic, and inclusive Polish nation that stretched across imperial borders. Similarly, Skarbek's preferences in both the design for his theater and in its repertoire clarifies that he shared the "commonly expressed wish of the local public" irrespective of ethnic sentiment and that despite the great aspirations of Lemberg's Polish stage, he continued to maintain the theater's popular, mixed, and international repertoire. The size of the theater that Skarbek provided to the Galician capital was arguably excessive, but it did accommodate German and Polish troops alike in a tense, yet workable coexistence.

Although definitions and identities were in constant flux, historical evidence reveals that locals did not view negatively the new aesthetic that the Austrian administration imposed on Lemberg. This stands in contrast to later historiographies written in the late nineteenth and early twentieth centuries by Polish historians that included a range of theories on what were called the national features of late neoclassicism in the local context and that remain influential to this day. In fact, when Polish leaders were in a position to construct buildings in the Vormärz, they demonstrated quite similar tastes to those of the Austrian administration, as demonstrated by the *Ossolineum* (1827-50s) and the Skarbek Theater (1837-43).

Moreover, the intentions of the founders of these two cultural institutions – later known as national bastions – did not lie in a national mission, as generally presented in national histories. That Ossoliński and Skarbek wished to encourage Polish culture was largely viewed as unproblematic by all concerned at the time. The emergence of cultural institutions came about thanks to connections with Vienna and was largely made possible by imperial approval. Ossoliński's insistence on commissioning Viennese Court architect Pietro Nobile as the prime designer of his institution revealed him as an admirer of the Viennese neoclassicist school.

The Vormärz-era use of streets and local cultural institutions for local celebrations further expressed the Austrian rule's flexibility and the local population's honest appreciation of the Austrian state. The unusual celebration of the Riflemen Confraternity, derived from medieval roots, was transformed to fit within official state culture, only to be revived as a part of the Polish national movement half a century later. Although for Hobsbawm the invention of tradition is linked quite specifically to nationalism, the case of the Rifleman's ceremony demonstrates that the tradition was quite flexible, even before national identity was a serious concern. Indeed, the celebration was first reinvented to accommodate the political realities of the early nineteenth century, at which time it was transformed into a vehicle for expressions of loyalty to Lemberg's new Austrian emperor.

The formal street ceremonies traditionally held during royal visits survived largely unchanged in a rationalized form that dated from the late eighteenth century, finding use on occasions as different as imperial visits and the arrival of Polish Napoleonic troops in 1809. Banners declaring statements of loyalty to the emperor hung from the façades of public buildings, private homes, and cultural institutions, such as a standard glorifying the emperor that was displayed on the *Ossolineum* in 1828. Temporary triumphal arches additionally greeted every Austrian emperor during royal visits to Lemberg. Although the *Ossolineum* became a site of illegal printing activity in the early 1840s, just a decade earlier the institution had taken the initiative to make special changes to its interior to accommodate symbols of loyalty, as well as depictions of heroes and historic events. During the 1828 imperial visit, the portrait of the emperor decorated the theater hall during the singing of the Habsburg anthem "*Gott erhalte*" during imperial celebrations, which was articulated in both German and Polish.

With the civil disturbances of 1809 that figured within a pompous welcome for the Polish Napoleonic troops short-lived and quickly forgotten, Lemberg remained a peaceful city well into the late 1840s, as documented by police reports of the time. Thus the imperial project of transforming the Galician capital into a city boasting a Habsburg appearance unfolded simultaneously and smoothly with the establishment of several cultural institutions of local significance. Even though the local effects of the events of 1848 are often exaggerated, a significant split existed between small national revolutionary parties and the broader population that remained loyal to Austria during the revolutionary turbulence. Yet the events of 1848 seriously undermined the legitimacy of the Vormärz concept of public order, as understood by the authorities. Keeping the streets clean and empty and public space limited to official uses and imperial symbols was no longer possible, even after the revolution had been suppressed.

While neoabsolutist building authorities continued the symbolically charged activities of their Vormärz predecessor in the 1850s and 1860s – the grand beautification plan, with stylistic changes to state buildings and the establishment of new medical and sanitary institutions – they were obliged to undertake these efforts through different means. Strict disciplinary measures were introduced against persons who disrupted the public order, such as paupers and individuals obstructing traffic. The drastic and arbitrary interventions in problematic districts, especially the Jewish outer districts, that aimed to eliminate disorderly persons and paupers completely did not yield the desired results. The lack of a comprehensive policy and the continuing lack of financial resources for projects other than renovations to the symbolically significant central areas delayed the consideration of these other issues as serious concerns. The subsequent neoabsolutist tightening of restrictions on assembly in public places only further restricted crowds to diverse public and private gardens and interior spaces, but it could not altogether eliminate the public demand for key buildings and the street.

The policy of *divide et impera* that Governor Franz Stadion introduced into Lemberg in 1848 subsequently yielded fruit with the establishment of the Ruthenian National Institute in the 1850s and 1860s, an event associated with the political invention of the Ruthenians during the same period. The site of the institute – the former location of the university and one of the major places of earlier revolutionary resistance – had been chosen based on an imperial gift aimed to counter Polish presence in the city, rather than from a desire to increase Ruthenian cultural activities. This *Rundbogenstyl* building, matching in style the military barracks on Wronowski Berg, the *Citadel* (built 1852-54), and Theophil Hansen's *Invalidenhaus* (built 1855-63), has remained the location for Ruthenian regular meetings ever since. Yet the *divide et impera* policy revealed an inadequacy in its lack of commitment to the Ruthenian elite, with both the older clerical elite and a young populist movement having interests in the countryside rather than the Galician capital. Variously divided Ruthenian groups and parties socialized at the National Institute, though they failed to articulate a unified political agenda. The Ruthenian architectural enclave around the National Institute, which notably included the Preobraženska Church, completed in 1892, largely emerged in spite of the Ruthenian institutional board's inaction and as a result of the Polish Municipality's efforts.

Significant political changes initiated by the 1860 adoption of the local autonomy law by the *Reichsrat* allowed the Polish conservative aristocratic elite to gradually gain control of Galician affairs. This in turn culminated in the establishment of Galician autonomy in 1867 and in Lemberg's Municipal self-government in 1870. Subsequently the composition and authority of the Municipal Building Department changed, becoming increasingly Polish dominated and empowered with decision-making rights. But with all these political changes notwithstanding, the Municipal Building Department continued to focus on architecturally significant projects in prestigious areas and on symbolic changes, such as the renaming of streets – this time, with Polish appellations. Interest in public green spaces and infrastructural improvements also continued as a part of the policies that involved street cleaning and the establishment of medical institutions, as they had previously. In a new turn, these policies were expanded to include disciplinary institutions. In short, the existing official beliefs about social hierarchies did not disappear, though the new, autonomous administration proved abler to intervene in Lemberg's public sphere than the former centralized bureaucracy had.

In the new political atmosphere that followed the *Ausgleich*, Polish writers began to assess negatively the cumulative impact of the previous century's architecture, thus creating the metaphor of "barrack classicism" that has survived until today. In parallel, the great historicist buildings that the newly autonomous, local Galician authorities constructed during the last third of the century continued to reflect pan-Austrian aesthetic values. The new public buildings of the Galician Parliament (*Sejm*) and the viceroy's office that were built in the 1870s, together with major banks and hotels along Lemberg's main boulevard, would arguably not have appeared out of place in any major Austrian city of the time.

Lemberg's political and intellectual elite, whose ranks were increasingly joined by the professional elite of architects and engineers, figured as the most influential forces shaping the city during the era of autonomy that followed 1870. Although initially having quite disparate interests, these groups over time developed a common view of Lemberg as a city that was simultaneously Polish and pro-Habsburg; this they achieved through the restoration of historic buildings, the construction of modern monuments, and the erection of buildings in a way that reconciled local styles with wider architectural trends. However, even as these elite groups made the city's Polishness more visible, the intent underlying their actions was quite different from the later nationalists' project of making a cult out of the city's Polishness. Rather, these late nineteenth-century individuals sought to elevate the Galician Polish elite to the position of the dominant social force in the city and Crown Land, while preserving traditional social hierarchies. This focus represents the significant difference between these efforts and the Polish national project carried out in Lwów in the interwar period.

This group of Lemberg's decision makers, to whom we owe the city's fin de siècle architectural appearance, was hardly homogenous. The neoabsolutist political elite that survived well into the era of the Dual Monarchy, represented by the likes of Governor Agenor Gołuchowski, and the older generation of Ruthenian intellectuals close to the National Institute understood public space as a realm exclusively intended for imperial symbols. At the same time, the interiors of public cultural institutions could for these same individuals curiously represent "inner" national endeavors. Thus public meetings held *inside* the Ruthenian National Institute in the late 1860s and 1870s became a Ruthenian private matter; concurrently the Polish liberal politicians were making much more radical claims to public space, and this to the consternation of the former national group.

The increasingly Polish-dominated Crown Land and Municipal authorities could no longer make unilateral decisions on the reconfiguration and maintenance of public space. The authorities needed not only to legitimize their symbolic domination of the streets, but also to position themselves in relation to the increasing demands by Polish – and later Ruthenian – intellectuals for alternate national commemorations. Most important, the liberal Polish elite, the main opponent to the views shared by Gołuchowski and the like, understood the use of public space and architecture for the symbolic expression of national self as a "citizen's right." This concept was first formulated in 1869 by Franciszek Smolka, the leading local democratic politician, an advocate for commemorations and future "master of street ceremonies." In this understanding, the use of the Town Hall bell tower, processions through the city center, and passing through the permanent triumphal arch at the entrance to Castle Hill became matters to contest with the authorities.

The Union of Lublin Mound, a man-made structure erected on Lemberg's highest hill to commemorate the establishment of the historic Polish-Lithuanian Commonwealth, came to represent Polish presence in the city, as well as the liberal, inclusive, and democratic claims of Polish nationalism. The 1869 conflict over the Union of Lublin Mound serves as a fine example of several key political changes that were taking place in the late 1870s. The mound was proposed by Democrats who opposed the central state administration, a political stance that would have been unthinkable a few years earlier. Just as significant, however, was the split that emerged within the government on how to respond to Smolka's project for this monument. Predictably, the viceroy's administration and the police reacted negatively to the idea of the mound, even though many of the officials in these institutions were now of Polish nationality. The Municipal government, however, was supportive and eventually assumed responsibility for the project, a move illustrating the shift in power from the central administration to Municipal authorities that was reflected in the local autonomy law of 1870.

Franciszek Smolka appropriated Lemberg's traditional street royal greeting ceremony – previously adapted to welcome visits by the Habsburgs – for a different, national celebration. The double reinvention of a medieval practice, its first reconfiguration having been its transformation for official use in the late eighteenth century, made the new celebration appear much more natural in the local context of 1869, and it was gradually adopted by the broader public. Key elements of this street-based event, such as the signaling of its start from the Town Hall tower, the street procession, the illumination of Castle Hill and public buildings, and the gala performance in the theater, have remained integral to Polish celebrations in the city ever since.

Thus shaped by a variety of individuals and institutions, Lemberg's public space lost the homogeneity previously imparted to it by official uses and imperial symbols. Various celebrations were reinvented in the local context and surrounded with their particular *butaforia*. It is quite telling, for example, that the Rifleman's ceremony was in fact also reinvented twice; first, during the Vormärz era, it was adapted to fit the imperial project, and then again in the 1880s – by which time the Galician Poles had regained political control of Lemberg – the pre-Austrian ceremony was rediscovered and used as the basis for openly celebrating the Polish nation.

Nationalist narratives about the Lemberg's development, however, often overlook a significant aspect of this heterogeneous public space, namely, the attitudes of the wider public during such commemorative practices. On several occasions, such as the 1874 celebration initiated by war veteran and supposed Democratic Party member Jan Pawulski, various local, national, and imperial symbols were employed in a manner even more creative and inclusive than in celebrations organized by the professional, political, and ethnic elites. The general public appears to have remained elusive to the nationalist historians who stood alone in their view that architecture's symbolism exclusively referenced national histories.

As the use of public space became increasingly flexible, the decision-making processes on further Municipal beautification and the installation of commemorative markers in Lemberg's public spaces followed an established pattern, with slight modifications. When the Galician conservative elite were joined by their former main opponents, the Democrats, in a decision on Municipal matters after 1870, their national programs needed to conform to official (meaning imperial) historic interpretation. Further, this group continued to regard some citizens as more equal than others in their right to spatial representation. This move on their part demonstrates that they too had not broken with the previously existing understanding of hierarchical social order to the degree that is often supposed. This continuity became most apparent during the various planning and commemorative projects of the 1880s and 1890s.

Officials in the Vormärz and later neoabsolutist period could only have dreamed of the complete removal of paupers and prostitutes from the town center that the autonomous Municipal administration was able to realize in the late nineteenth century. This measure was legitimized as the rational management of Lemberg's built environment, green spaces, and stately architecture along the ring road, as evident in Mayor Edmund Mochnacki's report of 1889. This type of legitimization was at the top of the Municipal agenda, as various individuals and institutions increasingly challenged the scope of Municipal activity in public spaces.

Municipal decisions in the 1890s regarding national monuments granted representation to some great Poles, notably those who could be interpreted as great defenders of the Habsburg state, such as King Jan III Sobieski, and Governor Agenor Gołuchowski. These figures in fact represented long-standing, common Polish-Austrian interests that reached their apex under the Badeni government in Vienna. Others, such as Polish heroes who had distinguished themselves by attempting to revive independent Poland, like Tadeusz Kościuszko, and figures from the Russian Ukraine popular among the Ruthenians, such as Taras Ševčenko, received a much more marginal recognition.

Like the sweeping theories of local neoclassicism, the period of Lemberg's historicist and Art Nouveau architecture has been hailed as a "national school." These characterizations have disregarded the complex identity of the architects involved and the stylistic similarity of the buildings to the ones erected in the other parts of the monarchy. Thus these interpretations have neglected not only significant portions of leading architects' built legacies – which followed architectural fashions, rather than foreshadowing national revival – but also the architects' own writings on their works. A fresh view of these writings reveals that they were not keen to understand their work as part of a national endeavor, but rather remained confined to the established canons of their profession. These canons in turn had been shaped by previously existing professional architectural theories, especially neoclassicism, and newly emerging information that architects chose to incorporate into their beliefs. The latter especially concerned the archaeological discoveries in 1881 of Galicia's medieval architecture in the town of Halicz.

In the late nineteenth century, heated national contests for public space were taking place, and architects' identities were shifting to accommodate the fact that the old guild hierarchies had broken down and that architects had now become independent geniuses and artists. Therefore Julian Zachariewicz and other local historicist architects were put in the position of integrating the national dimension of architecture both theoretically and in practice. These efforts resulted in Zacha-riewicz's theory on what he called architectural civilizations and in subsequent restoration practices that, intentionally or otherwise, reshaped Lemberg's historic architecture into boasting an ostensibly Western, or neo-Romanesque appear-ance, and thus an implicitly Polish one.

With new, contemporary architecture, neither Zachariewicz nor Julius Hoch-berger, another leading historicist architect and director of the Municipal Build-ing Department, would compromise on the strictly set system of orders used for historicist facades. To please the national public, they employed leading, acad-emy-trained, national painters to work on the interior and to impart nationally acceptable designs for an exclusive public in the buildings' semiprivate realm. Yet until well into the early twentieth century, despite official policies and public activists' efforts to transform Lemberg into a national bastion and to memorialize its spaces with national monuments, architectural facades expressed the cosmo-politan language of historicism, one that many would term Viennese. Diverse views on architecture coexisted in this diverse setting, where people could be divided by ethnic, social, and professional affiliation and still be united in a larger group that transcended these divisions. The city's architecture, deeply rooted in neoclassicist thinking, followed fashion closely. This culminated in a search for a local, Art Nouveau style derived from vernacular practices by several architects, especially Ruthenian Ivan Levynśkyj, resulting in something similar to what in Poland is known as the Zakopane style and in Hungary as Ödön Lechner's school of architecture.

The unfulfilled nationalizing restoration of the Town Hall in 1908 according to an invented, historicizing design illustrates that even in the 1910s the prevail-ing belief supporting most Municipal building practices was to express impe-rial loyalty rather than political nationalism. The gradual shift toward policies that favored national architecture occurred only with the election of Tadeusz Ru-towski as Lemberg's vice mayor in 1905. Rutowski's actions, highly reminiscent of Vormärz-era beliefs that architecture represented certain ethical values, such as being good, healthy, and practical, as well as civilizational values, aimed to place architecture on a national path. Yet while the pathos of the debate raging in the press – strongly influenced by Rutowski – demonstrated how deeply emotional architectural issues had become, the local attitude wavered between reluctance and ignorance, as demonstrated by the Union of Lublin Mound's unchecked de-terioration after every rain by the late 1900s.

In the 1900s, diverse cultural and professional societies, such as the Society of the Admirers of Lemberg's Past and the Polytechnic Society, became active in promoting their projects on Lemberg's past and its architecture. The year 1901 saw the inauguration of the monument to Agenor Gołuchowski, and 1904 the dedication of one to Adam Mickiewicz. In parallel, national visions predominated in the celebration of the Chmeľnyćkyj siege anniversary in 1905 and the Grunwald battle in 1910. Gradually, the Ruthenian population became a serious threat to the public peace in the eyes of Municipal employees. By the 1910s, even the Greek Catholic clergy, one of the most loyal and nationalism-resistant social groups, embraced a national vision of architecture, as expressed in a speech by Andrej Šeptyćkyj, the archbishop and metropolitan of the Greek Catholic church, at the opening of the Ruthenian National Museum in 1914. As old hierarchies were gradually collapsing, the bonds of loyalty to Austria were loosened further with the outbreak of war.

◆

It is ironic that the national historians who constructed Lemberg's divergent pasts and who routinely disregarded the achievements of the Vormärz administration in architectural and urban planning projects fell victim to many preconceptions about architecture established by this administration itself. The Vormärz political elite of both Lemberg and Vienna wished to leave its mark on the local environment and legitimize its rule through architecture and through the reshaping of public space. It further viewed these efforts as an integral part of a much more complex set of cultural policies dealing with the restriction, beautification, and cleaning up of public space. The post-1870 Galician rulers modified this approach to fit a very different political arrangement, that of Galician autonomy combined with Polish nationalism still loyal to the Habsburg throne. From serving as the metaphor of Austrian progress, order, and neatness, architecture came to be a metaphor of Polishness, though the precise definition of the nation remained in flux. Yet existing buildings and sites figured as powerful mediums in their own right, exuding diverse, heavily coded messages that often were in friction with arbitrary political intrusions.

Writings on architecture – in memoirs, official correspondence, and the press – reflected on and even created particular views of history. The construction process and uses found for architecture figured centrally in the staging of grand imperial and national projects. Lemberg's ring road that ran around the city center was embellished with stately, historicist buildings in a fashion reminiscent of the Viennese *Ringstrasse*, though rounded out with monuments to loyal, noble Poles. Provincial exhibitions aimed to demonstrate the great technological progress of the loyal Galician Crown Land, but in the absence of any evidence of such progress they promoted Polish history instead, as expressed in 1894 in the Racławice Panorama and the Matejko Pavilion, and in 1910 with the Grunwald Anniversary and Palace of Art.

Nations and empires were easily imagined through buildings, including those of cultural institutions, through monuments that memorialized historical events, and through the mass attendance of national celebrations. The commemoration of events in Polish and Ruthenian history in the public space of the streets became a matter of local politics in the Autonomy era. However, these national projects employed the very same buildings, monuments, streets, and celebrations that had been used to invent a local version of the empire and monarchy throughout Habsburg rule in Galicia.

By permitting national claims to space at different times throughout the nineteenth century, such as the *Ossolineum*, the Ruthenian National Institute, and the Union Mound, the authorities actually created specific places of socialization for Lemberg's diverse urban groups. They thus further stimulated the emergence of alternate public spheres where political nationalism was seriously discussed. These sites were not used effectively by all concerned, however. Manipulating the understanding of public space and taking advantage of cultural concessions, the Polish elite gradually established their own divergent, though national, sites of reference in the physical landscape of the city. In contrast, the Ruthenian elite did not use their National Institute nearly as effectively as they might have during the 1850s, when instead of convincing the Ruthenian public of their nationalist cause, they continued socializing exclusively among themselves in the style typical of *Biedermeier*-era practices. In this context, when the street became the greatest stage for the expression of nationalism in the early twentieth century, Polish claims appeared to have greater legitimacy than Ruthenian ones, given the physical presence of Polish buildings and the constructed, ostensibly historic Polishness of the city.

Consequently, the Municipal government and independent organizations increasingly competed over the memorializing of public space, rather than over its rationalization. These tensions resulted in a hybrid version of imperial symbolism that was infused with select national and even local heroes and events. None of the national parties – or the societies that claimed to represent them – fully realized its aspirations, with Ruthenian hopes finding the least success. Yet the only entity truly vanquished in the long run was the Vormärz-era German culture of enjoyable *Biedermeier* privacy, centered on the German theater and restricted Metternichian public space, that ceased to exist following the events of 1848.

Even though the elites would only occasionally unite forces, as with Polish conservative and democratic elites in the 1880s, Lemberg's general public participated indiscriminately in all public ceremonies, turning out in great numbers for imperial visits, commemorations, and national celebrations. Various testimonies suggest that until the outbreak of the First World War, a sense of loyalty to the empire coexisted with ethnic and religious sentiments for most of Lemberg's inhabitants. Well into the twentieth century, strong social boundaries separated small national parties of educated Poles and Ruthenians from the general public, as well as professionals sharing group affiliations. Enduring loyalties to the empire provided that Lemberg's heterogeneous national actors had much more in common with their local national foes than with their conationals outside of Austria-Hungary. At the same time, most of these actors shared a sense of imperial loyalty with Municipal and Crown Land officials. As a consequence, different strands of nationalism in Lemberg heavily borrowed from one another and from the imperial project in the invention of historic pasts and in their claims on public space. The resulting intensification in contests for public, spatial representation at the fin de siècle and the early twentieth century bears evidence of national groups sharing greater similarities in their claims and tactics than differences. Although sometimes overlapping, diverse small groups of committed individuals were engaged in particular symbolic projects, such as Julian Zachariewicz's restoration practices that Westernized Lemberg's oldest church, but that were based on the architectural theory influenced by Ruthenian scholar Šaranevyč. Another such project was Franciszek Mączyński's "renovation" of the Armenian Cathedral in response to the Ruthenian Preobraženska Church's domination in the area. Individuals as diverse as Tadeusz Rutowski, with his politically loaded arts gallery project, and the participants of the 1910 Congress of Technicians often shared the system of values inherited from their Vormärz predecessors, a system that was in itself an adaptation of European aesthetic theories to the local context. Within this system of values, the parks and greenery were beautiful and healing, as opposed to the ugly city center; one's own "backward" city was compared with "better" cities, and the Jewish quarters were seen as places of filth and stench. Even the opposing Polish and Ruthenian sides, as during the 1905 Chmelnyćkyj siege anniversary, saw a particular building, the Town Hall, as a symbol of Polishness and shared the tactics of attempting to symbolically take over the city from their competing group.

Perhaps the reason Lemberg's population accepted invented traditions so readily lay in the new traditions' remaining open to reinterpretation in ways not initially anticipated. In Lemberg's case, popular enthusiasm for public street events stemmed in part from the city's long-standing tradition of holding public celebrations during which the public's unrestrained enjoyment of public space – the streets – was routinely reported. With the severe restriction of public spaces to imperial representation during the Vormärz and even further restriction during neoabsolutism, such popular enjoyment became a rarity. In the Autonomy era, public space turned into an area of contested architectural and historical visions and encompassed other comprehensive political programs that pursued goals beyond national representation. Thus the meaning of traditions invented in the early nineteenth century or revived in the 1870s, 1880s, and 1890s underwent subsequent reinterpretation as political thinking changed, and these semantic shifts became increasingly possible as the existing social hierarchies broke down. Yet how far these diverse stagings actually influenced the larger public is a different matter. As in a popular celebration that involved the moving of the statue of a lion to Castle Hill, the idea of veteran and Democrat Jan Pawulski, the general public was able to integrate contradictory "invented traditions" into what appeared to be an attractive combination of loyalties and sentiments. Rather than being necessarily confined within the limits of public order or, conversely, political nationalism, the public remained ready to socialize and be entertained either within the national seminars of theaters, cultural institutions, and gardens or on the streets.

This tendency within a general public has further implications for the understanding of the general affairs of the late monarchy. Although there are recent studies that see the monarchy as having been unable to adapt to and deal with local nationalisms and consequently to view these movements as the primary cause of the monarchy's demise,[2] others have shown that not only did the dynasty reinvent itself after 1848, but also that it proved adept at change and transformation in the constitutional era. Further, it proved its strength on the eve of World War I.[3] Moreover, for various actors in local political and cultural scenes, nationalism neither became an overarching ideology nor prevented them from cooperating with Vienna. This book is a contribution to those works that argue this broad theme. Nationalism, as Robin Okey has recently argued, became inextricably entangled with socioeconomic issues, and the Habsburg state successfully transformed itself "from the 'baroque court-oriented society' to the nineteenth century *Rechtsstaat*, a unique fusion of Josephinist bureaucratism with the bourgeois spirit of the age, tingeing its largely conservative masses. That this society showed few signs of developing further into a democratic federation of equal nations is neither surprising nor discreditable, because such an association still nowhere exists."[4]

The overlapping multiplicity of loyalties appears to be true not only for the general public, but also for nationalist fin-de-siècle Polish and Ruthenian intellectuals who blurred the terms "citizen," "nation," "homeland," and "region," and in so doing served as part of the audience for – and as the actors behind – the staging of national and imperial projects. Even as Lemberg increasingly became a focal point of nationalist divisions, the Habsburg context allowed its inhabitants to avoid making a final decision on their national loyalties. Despite an increasingly tense political environment, most people could continue to consider themselves and their neighbors as Lembergers, first and foremost, most of the time. Thus contrary to Polish and Ukrainian national historiographies that emphasize either the city's historical Polishness or the Ukrainians' increasing prominence in the city, Lemberg remained a Habsburg city where individuals held multiple identities until the outbreak of World War I.

Notes

1   *Schematisma* were administrative handbooks issued by the Galician Crown Land administration, which covered the administrative structure of the Crown Land of Galicia. See *Schematismus der Königreiche Galizien und Lodomerien* (Lemberg: Piller, 1835). *Schematisma* were later renamed *Provinzial-Handbuch der Königreiche Galizien und Lodomerien* (Lemberg: Piller, 1844-84); *Handbuch der Lemberger Statthalterei-Gebietes in Galizien* (Lemberg: Piller, 1855-69); and *Szematyzm Królewstwa Galicyi i Lodomeryi z Wielkim Ks. Krakowskim* (Lemberg: Piller, 1870-1914).

2   See especially Solomon Wank, "The Nationalities question in the Habsburg Monarchy: reflections on the historical record," *Working Papers in Austrian Studies* 93 (April 1993) 3; Steven Beller, *Vienna and the Jews, 1867-1938: A Cultural History* (Cambridge: Cambridge University Press, 1989); idem, "Reinventing Central Europe," *Working Papers in Austrian Studies* 91 (October 1991) 5. On an example of the orthodox argument that the dissolution of the Dual Monarchy was due to the emergence of nationalisms and the lack of imperial identity, see, for example, Oscar Jászi, *The Dissolution of the Habsburg Monarchy* (Chicago and London: The University of Chicago Press, 1929), 447-55.

3   John W. Boyer, *Culture and Political Crisis in Vienna: Christian Socialism in Power, 1897-1918* (Chicago: University of Chicago Press, 1995); On the economic rise of the Habsburg Monarchy, see David F. Good, *The Economic Rise of the Habsburg Empire, 1750-1914* (Berkeley: University of California Press, 1984); idem, "The economic lag of Central and Eastern Europe: evidence from the late nineteenth-century Habsburg Empire," *Working Papers in Austrian Studies* 93 (December 1993) 7. On flexibility and the situational character of the political conflict along the national lines of politics in late imperial Austria, see Lothar Höbelt, "Parliamentaty politics in a multinational setting: late imperial Austria," *Working Papers in Austrian Studies* 92 (March 1993) 6. Also see Jean Bérenger, *A History of the Habsburg Empire 1700-1918*, trans. by C. A. Simpson (London and New York: Longman, 1990), 272-89; Robin Okey, *The Habsburg Monarchy ca. 1765-1918. Enlightenment to Eclipse* (Houndmills, Basignstoke, Hampshire, and London: Macmillan Press, 2000), 369-401; Alan Sked, *The Decline and Fall of the Habsburg Empire, 1815-1918* (London and New York: Longman, 1989): 264-69.

4   Okey, 401.

Figure 67. Map of Lemberg, "Plan de la Ville de Leopole Capitale de la Russi
Rouge avec les Feauxbourgs," by Charles de Scheffer, ca. 1780. Center for
Urban History of East Central Europe, L'viv.

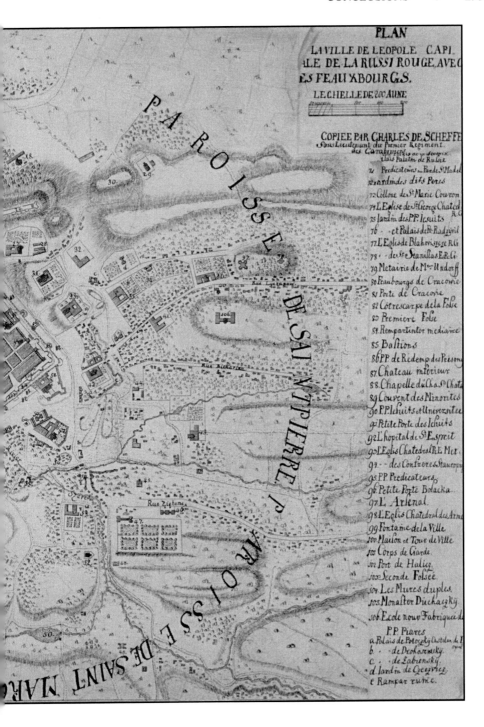

PLAN

LA VILLE DE LEOPOLE CAPI.
ALE DE LA RUSSI ROUGE, AVEC
ES FEAUXBOURGS.

LE CHELLE DE 200 AUNE

COPIEE PAR CHARLES DE SCHEFFE
Sous Lieutenant du Premier Regiment
des Carabiniers au service
Sous Palatin de Ruluz.

71 Predicateurs au Ponde S.t Madel
72 Iardindes dits Portes
72 Collone des S.t Marie Couron
74 L'Eglise de S.t George Chated
75 Iardin des P.P. Iesuits A.G
76 - et Palais de R. Radziwil
77 L'Eglisde Blahoviziege R.G
78 - de S.te Stanislas E.R.G.
79 Metairie de M.r Urdorff
80 Faubourgs de Cracovie
81 Porte de Cracovie
82 Cotrescarpe de la Fosse
83 Premiere Fosse
84 Rempartinter mediance
85 Bastions
86 P.P. de Redemp des Peison
87 Chateau interieur
88 Chapelle du Cha. S.t Chat
89 Couvent des Minorites
90 P.P. Ieuits et Universitee
91 Ptite Porte des Ieuits
92 L'hopital de S.t Esprit
93 L'Eglis Chatedral R.L. Mer
94 - des Confreres Stauropin
95 P.P. Predicateurs
96 Petite Porte Bolacka
97 L' Arsenal
98 L'Eglis Chatedral des Arme
99 Fontame de la Ville
100 Maison et Tour de Ville
101 Corps de Garde
101 Port de Halicz
102 Seconde Fossee
103 Les Mures duples
103 Monaster Duchaczky
104 Ecole noun Fabriquee du
P.P. Piares
a Palais de Potoczky Castelan de P
b - de Drohoivisky
c - de Labrensky
d Iardin de Geezpricz
e Rampar ruine.

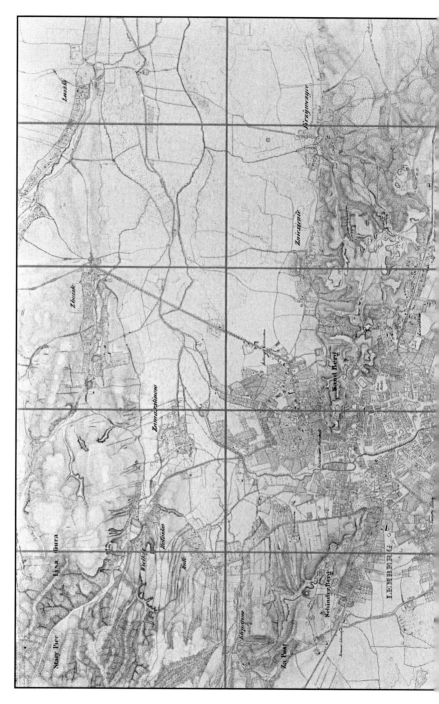

Figure 68. Map, "Lemberg mit seinen Umgebungen nach der Original Aufname des k.k. General-Quartiermeister-Stabes; auf Stein graviert im Jahre 1836." Center for Urban History of East Central Europe, Lʹviv.

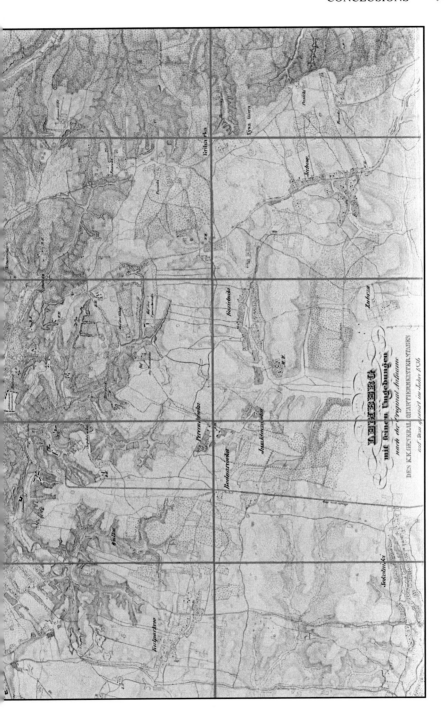

Figure 69. Map, "Lemberg mit seinen Vorstädten im Jahre 1844," by Kratochwill, Radoicsich, and Brankowich, 1844. Center for Urban History of East Central Europe, L'viv.

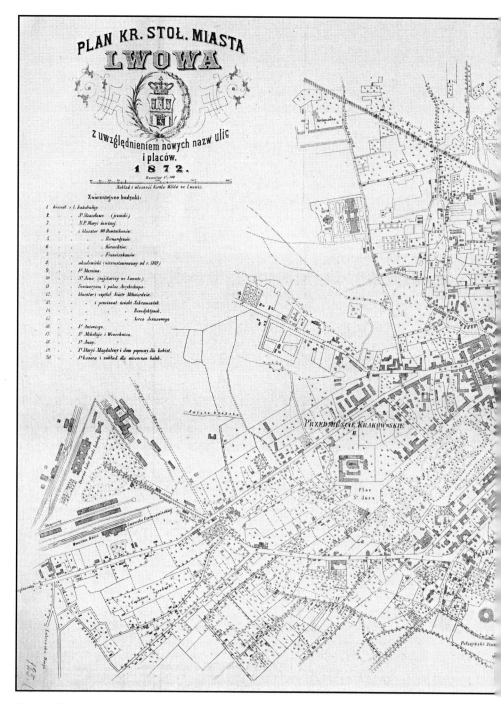

Figure 70. Map, "Plan kr. stoł. miasta Lwowa, 1872." Center for Urban History of East Central Europe, L'viv.

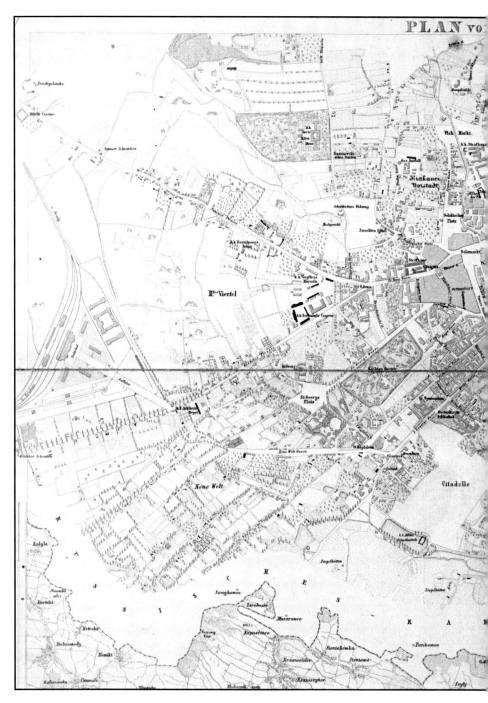

Figure 71. Map, "Plan von Lemberg, 1910." Center for Urban History of East
Central Europe, Ľviv.

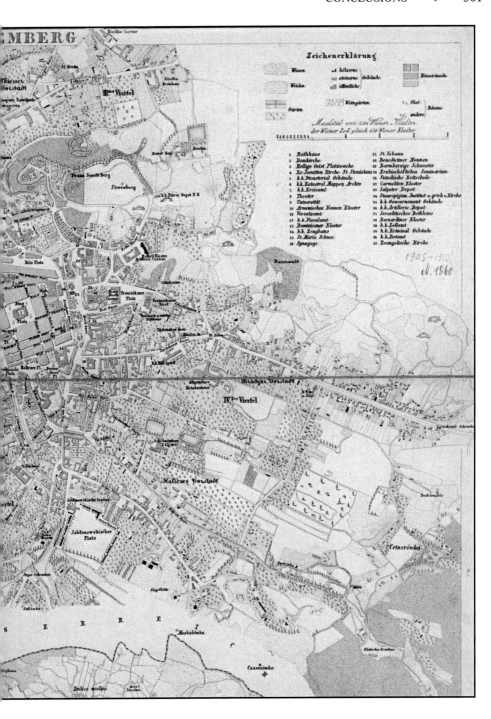

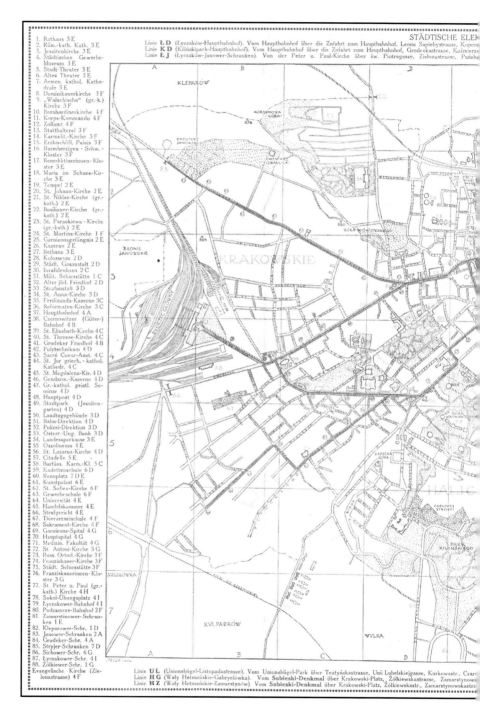

Figure 72. Map, "Plan miasta Lwowa, 1916." Center for Urban History of East Central Europe, L'viv.

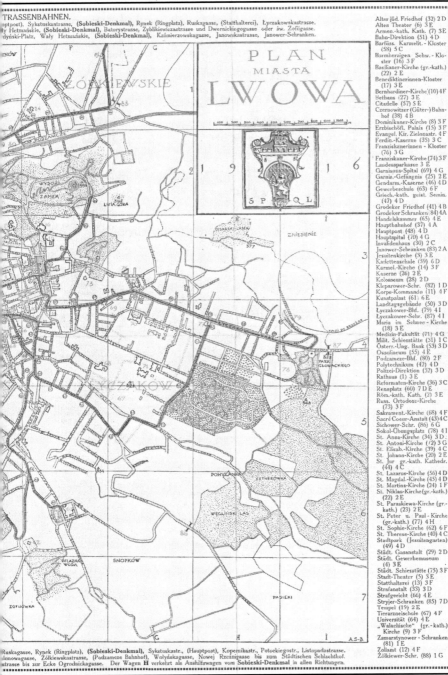

TRASSENBAHNEN.

...uptpost), Sykstuskastrasse, **(Sobieski-Denkmal)**, Rynek (Ringplatz), Ruskagasse, (Statthalterei), Łyczakowskastrasse.
...y Hetmańskie, **(Sobieski-Denkmal)**, Batorystrasse, Zyblikiewiczastrasse und Dwernickiegogasse oder św. Zofligasse.
...dyński-Platz, Wały Hetmańskie, **(Sobieski-Denkmal)**, Kazimierzowaskastrasse, Janowskastrasse, Janower-Schranken.

Ruskagasse, Rynek (Ringplatz), **(Sobieski-Denkmal)**, Sykstuskastr., (Hauptpost), Kopernikastr., Potockiegostr., Listopadastrasse.
...donowagasse, Żółkiewskastrasse, (Podzamcze Bahnhof), Wołyńskagasse, Nowej Rzeżniagasse bis zum Städtischen Schlachthof.
...strasse bis zur Ecke Ogrodnickagasse. Der Wagen **H** verkehrt als Aushilfswagen vom **Sobieski-Denkmal** in allen Richtungen.

PLAN MIASTA LWOWA

S P Q L

1916

Alter jüd. Friedhof (32) 2 D
Altes Theater (6) 3 E
Armen.-kath. Kath. (7) 3 E
Bahn-Direktion (51) 4 D
Barfüss. Karmelit. - Kloster (58) 5 C
Barmherzigen Schw. - Kloster (16) 3 F
Basilianer-Kirche (gr.-kath.) (22) 2 E
Benediktinerinnen-Kloster (17) 3 E
Bernhardiner-Kirche (10) 4 F
Bethaus (27) 3 E
Citadelle (57) 5 E
Czernowitzer (Güter-) Bahnhof (38) 4 B
Dominikaner-Kirche (8) 3 F
Erzbischöfl. Palais (15) 3 F
Evangel. Kir. Zielonastr. 4 F
Ferdin.-Kaserne (35) 3 C
Franziskanerinnen - Kloster (76) 3 G
Franziskaner-Kirche (74) 3 F
Landessparkasse 3 E
Garnisons-Spital (69) 4 G
Garnis.-Gefängnis (25) 2 E
Gendarm.-Kaserne (46) 4 D
Gewerbeschule (63) 6 F
Griech.-kath. geist. Semin. (47) 4 D
Grodeker Friedhof (41) 4 B
Grodeker Schranken (84) 4 A
Handelskammer (65) 4 E
Hauptbahnhof (37) 4 A
Hauptspital (48) 4 D
Hauptspital (20) 4 G
Invalidenhaus (30) 2 C
Janower-Schranken (83) 2 A
Jesuitenkirche (3) 3 E
Kadettenschule (59) 6 D
Karmel.-Kirche (14) 3 F
Kaserne (26) 2 E
Kolosseum (28) 2 D
Kleparower-Schr. (82) 1 D
Korps-Kommando (11) 4 F
Kunstpalast (61) 6 E
Landtagsgebäude (50) 3 D
Łyczakower-Bhf. (79) 4 I
Łyczakower-Schr. (87) 4 I
Maria im Schnee - Kirche (18) 3 E
Medizin-Fakultät (71) 4 G
Milit. Schiesstätte (31) 1 C
Österr.-Ung. Bank (53) 3 D
Ossolineum (55) 4 E
Podzamcze-Bhf. (80) 2 F
Polytechnikum (42) 4 D
Polizei-Direktion (52) 3 D
Rathaus (1) 3 E
Reformaten-Kirche (36) 3 C
Rennplatz (60) 7 D E
Röm.-knth. Kath. (2) 3 E
Russ. Ortodoxe-Kirche (73) 3 F
Sakrament.-Kirche (68) 4 F
Sacré Coeur-Anstalt (43) 4 C
Sichower-Schr. (86) 6 G
Sokol-Übungsplatz (78) 4 I
St. Anna-Kirche (34) 3 D
St. Antoni-Kirche (12) 3 G
St. Elisab.-Kirche (39) 4 C
St. Johann-Kirche (20) 2 E
St. Jur gr.-kath. Kathedr. (44) 4 C
St. Lazarus-Kirche (56) 4 D
St. Magdal.-Kirche (45) 4 D
St. Martins-Kirche (24) 1 F
St. Niklas-Kirche (gr.-kath.) (22) 2 E
St. Paraskiewa-Kirche (gr.-kath.) (23) 2 E
St. Peter u. Paul - Kirche (gr.-kath.) (77) 4 H
St. Sophie-Kirche (62) 6 F
St. Therese-Kirche (40) 4 C
Stadtpark (Jesuitengarten) (49) 4 D
Städt. Gasanstalt (29) 2 D
Städt. Gewerbemuseum (4) 3 E
Städt. Schiesstätte (75) 3 F
Stadt-Theater (5) 3 E
Statthalterei (13) 3 F
Strafanstalt (33) 3 D
Strafgericht (66) 4 E
Stryjer-Schranken (85) 7 D
Tempel (19) 2 E
Tierarzneischule (67) 4 F
Universität (64) 4 E
„Walachische" (gr.-kath.) Kirche (9) 3 F
Zasmarztynower - Schranken (81) 1 E
Zollamt (12) 4 F
Żółkiewer-Schr. (88) 1 G

ABBREVIATIONS

CDIAU   Centraľnyj Deržavnyj Istoryčnyj Archiv Ukraïny,
                      [Central State Historical Archive of the Ukraine]

CzT   Czasopismo techniczne [Technical Journal]

DALO   Deržavnyj Archiv Ľvivśkoji Oblasti [Ľviv Regional Archive]

HB   Halyćka Brama [Galician Gate]

NTŠ   Naukove Tovarystvo imeny Tarasa Ševchenka [Scientific
                      Society in the name of Taras Ševchenko]

F.   Fond [Larger collection of archival documents]

Op.   Opys [register/inventory of archival documents]

Sv.   Sviazka [folder, outdated unit of archival documents]

Sp.   Sprava [file of archival documents]

L.   Lyst [sheet, in archival documents]

BIBLIOGRAPHY

PRIMARY SOURCES

Archival Material

Centraľnyj Deržavnyj Istoryčnyj Archiv Ukraïny, (CDIAU, Central State Historical Archive of Ukraine)

<u>F. 52</u> (Magistrat mista Lvova 1772-1918)

Op. 1, Sp. 15: "Materialy pro vyrišennia sporiv Radoju mista i vlasnykamy ta orendatoramy starych znyščenych kamjanyć, tak zvanych 'ruder'" (1735-1774)

Op. 1, Sp. 17: "Projekty rekonstrukciï mista Ľvova skladeni architektorom Defilles-om i dyrektorom proektno-budiveľnoho viddilu Casparini Caspar-om (1774-1784)"

Op. 1, Sp. 30: "Protokoly, plany, schemy, dohovory ta in. dokumenty pro restavraciju Ľvivśkoï ratuši pislia bombarduvannia" (1849-50)

Op. 1, Sp. 32: "Nakazy, rozporiadžennia, plany ta in. materialy pro sporudžennia Budynku vojennych invalidiv u Ľvovi" (1855-57)

Op. 1, Sp. 172: "Opys architekturnoho ozdoblennia miśkoho teatru u Ľvovi ta perelik teatraľnoho repertuaru"

Op. 1, Sp. 208: "Koštorys na restavraciju kostiola Mariji Snižnoji u Ľvovi ta lystuvannia Budiveľnoho upravlinnia z Ľvivśkym Magistratom u ciomu pytanni (1857-1858)"

Op. 1, Sp. 950: "Čornovi zamitky, vyrizky z nimećkych gazet, žurnaliv ta in. materialy do statti A. Šnajdera 'Vysokyj Zamok' u Ľvovi (1845-1873)"

Op. 1, Sp. 953: "Geschichtliches über Lemberg' – Narys istoriï mista Ľvova nevidomoho avtora (litografija - 1901)"

F. 55 "Archiv davnich aktiv"

Op. 1, Sp. 23: "Zvit pro archeologični rozkopky na pl. St. Ducha u Ľvovi"

Op. 1, Sp. 75: "Materialy pro vydannia putivnyka po Ľvovu ta planu mista" (1886-97)

Op.1, Sp. 86: "Naukovi praci pracivnykiv archivu"

Op. 1, Sp. 190: "Lystuvannia Magistratu Ľvova z riznymy ustanovamy ta pryvatnymy osobamy v spravi konservaciï ta remontu architekturnych pamjatok (1881-1906)"

Op. 1, Sp. 191: "Materialy pro dijaľnisť archivu po restavraciï ta ochoroni pam'jatnykiv starovyny (koštorysy, lystuvannia ta in. 1896-1919)"

Op. 1, Sp. 199: "Lystuvannia ustanov ta pryvatnych osib z chranytelem pam'jatok starovyny Oleksandrom Čolovśkym v spravi restavraciï ta konservaciï pam'jatok architektury (1907-10)"

Op. 1, Sp. 217: "Stattia D. Didušyćkoho pro ikonostasy v Halyčyni (fragment)" (1880s-1890s)

F. 101 "Javorśkyj Franz – archivarius miśkoho archivu u Ľvovi, istoryk"

Op. 1, Sp. 5: "Gazetni povidomlennia ta žurnaľni statti pro istoryčni podiï u Ľvovi ta Halyčyni"

Op. 1, Sp. 22: "Gazetni povidomlennia pro sviatkuvannia oblohy Ľvova" (1905)

Op. 1, Sp. 23: "Gazetni i žurnaľni publikaciï pro novobudovy m. Ľvova ta sociaľno-ekonomičnu specyfiku zachidnohalyckych mist" (1866-1901)

F. 129 (Stavropigijśkyj instytut u Ľvovi), Op. 2, Sp. 1600: "Lystuvannia z magistratom i konservatorom Janom Antonovyčem pro rekonstrukciju bud. No. 189 – 193 (1902-1906)"

F. 137 "Kovalyšyn Franz: Istoryk, kolekcioner, služboveć Ľvivśkoho Magistratu"

Op. 1, Sp. 1-2: "Notatky do istoriï mist i mistečok Halyčyny i mista Ľvova"

F. 146 (Halyćke namisnytstvo [Galician Viceroy office - Statthalterei], 1772-1918)

Op. 1. Sv. 76 (Besondere Akten), Sp. 1426: "Sprava pro vydannia dozvolu grafu Skarbeku na budivnyctvo teatru u Ľvovi" (1834-37)

Op. 1. Sv. 76, Sp. 1427: "Perepiska s nadvornoi kantseliariiei, gubernskim prezidiumom po vopr. stroilelstva i vosstanovlieniia zdamii, mostov, tserkvei i dr. obyektov" (1834-35)

Op. 1. Sv. 76, Sp. 1429: "Perepiska s nadvornoi kantseliariiei, gubernskim prezidiumom i dr. po vopr. vydachi dotacyi i assignovaniia sredstv na otkrytiie i soderzhaniie konventov, shkol i dr. uchebnych i religioznych zavedienii" (1839-46)

Op. 53, Sp. 1163: "Rozporiadžennia Ministerstva virospovidań ta osvity pro vžyttia zachodiv po ochoroni pamjatnykiv pryrody" (1903)

Op. 6 ("Geheime"), Sp. 51 (1807)

Op. 6, Sp. 218-23 (1813)

Op. 6, Sp. 312-13 (1823)

Op. 6, Sp. 319 (1824)

Op. 6, Sp. 322-24 (1824)

Op. 6, Sp. 573-782 (1846)

Op. 6, Sp. 787-93 (1846)

Op. 6, Sp. 869-83 (1846)

Op. 65, Sp. 958: "Lystuvannia z Administracijeju deržavnych majetkiv ta solianych kopaleń pro samoviľnu reorganizaciju rozvažaľnoho zakladu v Jezuïtśkomu parku u Ľvovi"

Op. 7 (Namisnyctvo), Sp. 258: "Perepyska z Nadvirnoju Kanceliarijeju, Apeliacijnym Sudom i Upravlinniam herbovych zboriv pro nadannia zakladam pomiščeň v deržavnych budynkach i arendovanych budynkach" (1807)

Op. 7, Sp. 300: "Perepyska z Ľvivskoju Dyrekcijeju Policiï i Provincijnoju Buchhalterijeju pro blahoustrij m. Ľvova (1808-1809)"

Op. 7, Sp. 436: "Perepyska z Nadvirnoju Kanceliarijeju, okružnymy upravlinniamy i Provincijnoju deržavnoju buchhalterijeju po zachodach z pidhotovky do pryjizdu v Halyčynu vpovnovaženoho Imperatora erzhezoga Karla (1809)"

Op. 7, Sp. 445: "Perepyska z Štabom Korpusu pro zrujnuvannia vijśkovych forteć v Brodach i Stanislavi (1811)"

Op. 7, Sp. 512: "Perepyska z Nadvirnoju Kanceliarijeju, Ministerstvom Policiï ta in. pro pokraščennia sanitarnoho stanu i vporiadkuvanniu dijaľnosti administratyvnych vlastej m. Ľvova (1810)"

Op. 7, Sp. 576: "Perepyska z Ľvivskoju Dyrekcijeju Policiï i Provincijnoju buchhalterijeju pro blahoustrij m. Ľvova (1811-1816)"

Op. 7, Sp. 611: "Perepyska z Nadvirnoju Kanceliarijeju, okružnymy upravlinniamy ta in. pro nadannia prymiščeń dlia deržavnych ustanov. (V niomu je poverchovi plany budivli pry kosteli Jezuïtiv u Ľvovi (1811-1814)"

Op. 7, Sp. 633: "Perepyska z Ľvivśkym magistratom pro provedennia sviata v zv. z imenynamy Imperatora i zakinčennia vijny (1814)"

Op. 7, Sp. 661: "Lystuvannia z Nadvirnoju Kanceliarijeju, Ľvivśkym Magi-stratom pro nahorodžennia Ľvova portretom imperatora"

Op. 7, Sp. 662: "Perepyska z Žytomyrśkym Gubernatorom i Černivećkym okružnym upravlinniam pro zachody, povjazani z pereïzdom osib imperśkoho dvoru" (1812)

Op. 7, Sp. 840: "Materialy pro poïzdku imperatora Franza I v Halyčynu (dozvil, povidomlennia, perepyska, 1817-1818)"

Op. 7, Sp. 860: "Perepyska z Ministerstvom vnutrišnich sprav pro zasnuvan-nia budynku Ossolinśkych i chudožnioï vystavky u Ľvovi (1818)"

Op. 7, Sp. 894: "Perepyska z policijnymy vladamy pro blahoustrij Ľvova" (1819-20)

Op. 7, Sp. 970: "Perepyska z Nadvirnoju kanceliarijeju, Upravlinniam pošty ta in. po zachodach v zv'jazku z obïzdom Halyčyny erzhezogom Karlom i pereïzdom velykoho kniazia Mychajla (1819)"

Op. 7, Sp. 1094: "Perepyska z Administracijeju Deržmajetkiv i soliareń, Dy-rekcijeju v spravach navigaciï i budivnyctva z pynań skladannia geo-kart i planiv miscevosti z dodanymy vytratamy" (1821)

Op. 7, Sp. 1230: "Sprava pro organizaciju pochoronu halyćkoho gubernatora barona Hauera Franzyška (1822)"

Op. 7, Sp. 1430: "Perepyska z Nadvirnoju Kanceliarijeju, okružnymy upra-vlinniamy, z pytań sviatkuvannia juvilejnych dat Avstrijśkoho imperatora" (1824)

Op. 7, Sp. 1573: "Perepyska z okružnymy upravlinniamy, budiveľnoju dy-rekcijeju Ľvova ta in. z pytań budivnyctva, vidnovlennia i remontu budiveľ, dorih ta in. objektiv i asyhnuvannia hrošej na ci cili (1826)"

Op. 7, Sp. 1577: "Sprava pro vidnovlennia budivli Kasy Holovnoï pošty u Ľvovi (1823-1826)"

Op. 7, Sp. 1615: "Materialy pro organizaciju dijaľnosti biblioteky Ossolinśkych u Ľvovi (1826)"

Op. 7, Sp. 1663: "Perepyska z okružnymy upravlinniamy, Holovnym Poštovym upravlinniam ta in. z pytań spryjannia v poïzdkach imperatora, gubernatora ta in. vysokoposadovych osib" (1826)

Op. 7, Sp. 1744: "Perepyska z Nadvirnoju Policijeju, Dyrekcijeju Ľvivśkoï Biblioteky ta in. pro organizaciju publičnych mitynhiv i pošyrenni knyh" (1827-28)

Op. 7, Sp. 1805: "Perepyska z Nadvirnoju Kanceliarijeju, Ľvivśkym Burgomistrom ta in. pro vstanovlennia pam'jatnyka grafovi Gaisruk ta in. pytań (1827-1828)"

Op. 7, Sp. 1877: "Perepiska s Ministerstvom vnutrennich del, okruzhnymi upravelijami i dr. o prazdnovanii dnia rodzennia imperatora i dr. dat (1828)"

Op. 7, Sp. 1834: "Perepyska z Ľvivśkym Magistratom, Administracijeju Deržmajetkiv ta in. pro miśke budivnyctvo u Ľvovi, zvedennia mostiv čerez p. Poprad ta in. pytań" (1826-28)

Op. 7, Sp. 1877: "Perepyska z Ministerstvom Vnutra, okružnymy upravlinniamy ta in. pro sviatkuvania dnia narodžennia imperatora ta in. dat" (1828)

Op. 7, Sp. 1884: "Perepyska z Ministerstvom Vnutrisnich Sprav, okružnymy upravlinniamy ta in. pro vporiadkuvannia prodažu otrujnych rečovyn, poriadok organizaciï hromadśkych sviatkuvań ta in. z pytań hromadśkoho poriadku (1829-1830)"

Op. 7, Sp. 1889: "Perepyska z Nadvirnoju Kanceliarijeju, okružnymy upravlinniamy ta in. z pytań budivnyctva administratyvnych budiveľ i dyslokaciï deržavnych ustanov" (1829-30)

Op. 7, Sp. 1920: "Perepyska z Nadvirnoju Kanceliarijeju pro vidnovlennia palacu Jablonovśkych u Ľvovi (dokladeni plany... 1830)"

Op. 7, Sp. 1950: "Rozporiadennia Prezydenta Nadvirnoï policiï i donesennia cenzurnoho upravlinnia na prydbannia seriï portretiv poľśkych koroliv" (1831)

Op. 7, Sp. 2243: "Perepyska z Bochnianśkym i Novo-Sončśkym okružnymy upravlinniamy ta in. pro zbir zasobiv na vstanovlennia pam'jatnykiv imperatoru Franzu I i erzherzogu Franzu Karlu u Ľvovi (1838-1840)"

Op. 7, Sp. 2468: "Perepyska z Nadvirnoju Kanceliarijeju i Stanislavśkym Okruhom z pytań vidkryttia pamjatnyka imperatoru Francu I v Stanislavi" (1844)

Op. 7, Sp. 2480: "Perepyska z objednanoju Nadvirnoju Kanceliarijeju pro otrymannia zajmu na budivnyctvo bud. Ossolinśkoho Instytutu" (1845)

Op. 7, Sp. 2633: "Rozporiadžennia Ministerstva vnutrišnich sprav, perepyska z Finansovoju Prokuratorijeju ta okružnymy upravlinniamy z pytań budivnyctva i remontu žytlovych i deržavnych budiveľ, cerkov, dorih i t. p." (1847-51)

Op. 7, Sp. 2867: "Rasporiazheniya Ministerstva vnutrennich del i Tsyrkuliar Gubernskogo upravleniya o provedenii torzhestv v sv. z provozglahseniyem Avstrij'koy Konstitucii (1849)"

Op. 7, Sp. 3104: "Lyst-zvernennia Komintetu z budivnyctva pamjatnyka Kopaľ Karlu, ščo vidznačyvsia pry prydušenni italijśkych povstanciv v r. 1848 i cyrkuliar pro zbir zasobiv dlia budivnyctva pamjatnyka" (1851)

Op. 7, Sp. 3107: "Materialy pro prykrašennia i osnaščennia zaliv administratyvnych ustanov i vydilennia zasobiv na ïch vykonannia (rozporiadžennia, protokoly, donesennia)" (1851-53)

Op. 7, Sp. 3117: "Materialy pro provedennia zboru zasobiv Ukraïnśkym Nacionaľnym Sobranijem na utvorennia Ukraïnśkoho Nacionaľnoho Instytutu i vidkryttia ukraïnśkoï cerkvy" (1851)

Op. 7, Sp. 3365: "Perepyska z Ľvivśkym Magistratom, Ľvivśkoju Dyrekcijeju Policiji ta in. pro blahoustrij m. Ľvova (1854-1855)"

Op. 7, Sp. 3431: "Perepyska z Ministerstvom vnutrišnich sprav z pytań organizaciï religijnych ta suspiľnych toržestv v česť družyny Franca Josypa v zvjazku z narodženniam prynca" (1856)

Op. 7, Sp. 3457: "Perepyska z Ministerstvom vnutrišnich sprav po pryjniatti zachodiv po remontu i pokraščenniu stanu vulyć i dorih" (1857)

Op. 7, Sp. 3685: "Perepyska z Ministerstvom Policiï, Staatsministerium ta in. pro utvorennia ukraïnśkych teatriv i dramatyčnoï školy i poriadok vydannia dozvolu na postanovky (1860-1864)"

Op. 7, Sp. 3979: "Perepyska z Ministerstvom vnutrišnich sprav, starostvamy i dyrekcijeju Policiï pro pidhotovku i provedennia traurnych dniv 100-litnioji ričnyci I Podilu Polšči pols'kymy deržavnymy organizacijamy"

Op. 7, Sp. 3989, "Donesennia Dyrekciï Policiï pro kraži, publični budynky ta inši kryminaľni porušennia"

Op. 7, Sp. 3994: "Perepyska z ministerstvamy, Krajovym komitetom ta in. pro nadannia dotacij dlia restavraciï pam'jatok architektury, pryznačenni členiv Komisiï z ochorony pam'jatok, t. p." (1871-79)

Op. 7, Sp. 4154: "Perepyska z Miniserstvamy, Komitetom z organizaciï vys-tavok i halyćkym hospodarśkym tovarystvom pro vidpovidnisť i dozvil na organizaciju promyslovych i siľśkohospodarśkych vystavok a takož vystavok poľśkoho mystectva (1877-1888)"

Op. 7, Sp. 4215: "Donesennia Dyrekciï Policiï, starostv i pepepyska z Min-isterstvom vnutrišnich sprav pro provedennia miropryjemstv v 100-ričnyciu vstupu na prestol Jozefa II (1880-1881)"

Op. 7, Sp. 4254: "Perepyska z Dyrekcijeju Policiï u Ľvovi pro provedennia juvilejnych večoriv v česť Ševčenka i M. Kačovśkoho (1882-1883)"

Op. 7, Sp. 4255: "Perepyska z ministerstvamy, starosvamy ta in. pro ob'javlennia konkursu na vstanovlennia pam'jatnykiv 200-riccia oborony Vidnia, Mickievyču, Bemu Juzefu (1882-1883)"

Op. 7, Sp. 4340: "Perepyska z Ministerstvom virospovidannia i osvity, Centraľnoju Komisijeju pro ochoronu pamjatok i nedostatnij nahliad za sta-nom starodrukiv ta in. pamjatok" (1886)

Op. 7, Sp. 4365-66: "Donesennia Dyrekciï Policiï i Starostv pro provedennia zachodiv v dni ricnyć poľśkych Povstań 1863 i 1831 poľśkymy tovarystvamy, polityčnymy organizacijamy i naselenniam, (1885-1890)"

Op. 7, Sp. 4437: "Perepiska s Ministerstvom vnutrennikh del, direkcyiei poli-cyi i dr. ob ustanovlenii polskim naseleniiem pamiatnika Kilinskomu Janu vo Lvovie" (1888-95)

Op. 7, Sp. 4471: "Perepyska z Ľvivskoju Dyrekcijeju Policiï pro projekt vid-kryttia narodnoho teatru u Ľvovi (1889-1890)"

Op. 7, Sp. 4472: "Raport Ľvivskoï Dyrekciï Policiï pro provedennia redakci-jeju gazety 'Pravda' i studentamy Universytetu večora pamjati pyśmennyka Osypa Jurija Feďkovyča" (1890)

Op. 7, Sp. 4513: "Donesennia Dyrekciï Policiï pro provedennia zachodiv poľśkymy suspiľnymy i polityčnymy organizacijamy i naselenniam v dni ričnyć povstań 1831- i 1863 p." (1891-99)

Op. 7, Sp. 4514: "Donesennia Dyrekciï Policiï pro provedennia poľśkym naselenniam trauru v dni rokovyn II Rozdilu Poľšči (1891-1893)"

Op. 7, Sp. 4531: "Donesennia Dyrekciï Policiï pro provedennia zachodiv poľśkymy syspiľnymy i polityčnymy organizacijamy i naselenniam v dni ricnyć poľśkych povstań 1831 i 1863 rokiv (1891-1899)"

Op. 7, Sp. 4600: "Donesennia Dyrekciï Policiï, starostv i perepyska z Minis-terstvom vnutrišnich sprav pro provedennia naselenniam demonstracij, zibrań i mityngiv z pryvodu juvilejnych dat (Mickevyča, t. p. 1893-1899)"

Op. 78, Sp. 338-40: "Lystuvannia Dyrekciï Policiï u Ľvovi z Ľvivśkym okružnym upravlinniam pro vstanovlennia nahliadu miśkoï policiï nad selamy Znesinnia, Kryvčyci, Lysynyči z zvjazku z pošyrenniam v cych selach vypad-kiv porušennia pravyl budivnyctva, spekuliaciï i t. p." (1826-50)

Op. 79 (Militaria), Sp. 210: "Lystuvannia z Nadvirnoju Kancelarijeju pro zasypannia oboronnych roviv u zvjazku z rozšyrenniam Ľvova" (1782-83)

Op. 8 (Prezydiaľnyj Viddil), Sp. 448: "Doneseniia L'vovskoj Direkcyi poli-cyi, starostv v g. Lvov, Peremyshl', Rohatyn, Borshchev i dr. o sostojavshy-chsia sobraniyach, sozvannych ukrainskoi sotsyal-demokraticheskoi partiei i drugimi politicheskimi organizatsyiami (1 March – 31 December 1905)"

Op. 8, Sp. 448: "Donesennia dyrektora policiï Prezydiï Halyćkoho Namisnyctva pro mitynh i demonstraciju na česť 250-ričča oblohy Chmeľnyćkoho" (1905)

Op. 85 (Publico-Politica), Sp. 2768: "Lystuvannia z Ľvivśkym Magistratom pro vydilennia plošči dlia rozvah" (1823)

Op. 85, Sp. 2792: "Perepiska s lvovskim magistratom, provintsyalnoi buchgalteriiei i dr. po vopr. rekonstruktsyi ulits, arende zemelnych uchastkov i snabzhenii toplivom naseleniia gor. Lvova" (1801-5)

Op. 109, Sp. 101: "Zvity, protokoly, lystuvannia pro projekt blahoustroju Vysokoho Zamku u Ľvovi" (1840-58)

F. 165 (Krajovyj komitet – Komitet krajowy, [Crown Land Administration, 1861-1920])

Op. 5, Sp. 103: "Plan pojezuïtśkoho horodu" (1876)

Op. 5, Sp. 110: "Sprava pro budivnyctvo i remont nasypnoho pahorba Ľublinśkoï Unïi Kopiec Unji Lubelskiej na Zamkovij hori u Ľvovi" (1869-1919)

Op. 5, Sp. 230-232: "Delo o sbore deneg z naselenija Galicii na stroitelstvo pamiatnika grafu Goluchowskomu Agenoru (1875-1898)"

Op. 5, Sp. 1163: Sprava pro organizaciju Zahaľoï krajovoï vystavky poľśkoho mystectva u Ľvovi 1910. Plany"

F. 197, Op. 1, Sp. 1303: "Kostorys vydatkiv na restavraciju kostela Jana Chrestytelia u Ľvovi (1868-1869)"

F. 358 "Šeptyćkyj Andrij, Okeksandr, graf, mytropolyt greko-katolyćkoji cerkvy (1865-1944)"

Op. 2, Sp. 22: "Dopoviď pro ochoronu pamjatnykiv kuľtury i nauky" (1914).

F. 720 (Kolekcija planiv i kart naselenych punktiv, zemel'nych dilianok i shliachiv spoluchennia na terytoriji Ukrajiny [land parcels, highways, and water roots])

Op. 1, Sp. 623: "Sytuacijnyj plan Jezuïtśkoho sadu u Ľvovi (plany zemeľnych dilianok)" (1786-1844)

F. 726 (Kolektsija planiv budynkiv [collection of building plans, 1780-1861])

Op. 1, Sp. 12: "Plany budynku Gubernśkoho Upravlinnia u Ľvovi" (1781)

Op. 1, Sp. 1616: "Plany prymiščeń kvartyry Gubernatora i prezydiaľnoho budynku u Ľvovi"

F. 739, Op. 1, Sp. 130: "Hramota Miśkoï Rady m. Ľvova z nahody vidkryttia pamjatmyka poľśkomu koroliu Janu III Sobieskomu" (1897)

Deržavnyj Archiv Ľvivśkoji Oblasti (DALO, Ľviv Regional Archive)

F. 2 ("Magistrat mista Ľvova")

Op. 1, Sp. 5428: "Delo po stroitelstvu doma No. 3 po ul. Kopernika"

Op. 1, Sp. 5451: "Delo po stroitelstvu doma No. 20 po ul. Kopernika"

Op. 2, Sp. 3455: "Delo po stroitelstvu doma No. 24 po ul. Radianskoi"

Op. 2, Sp. 3456: "Delo po stroitelstvu doma No. 26 po ul. Radianskoi"

Op. 4, Sp. 829: "Delo po stroitelstvu pamiatnika Kostiushko vo Lvove"

Op. 4, Sp. 847: "Delo po uregulirovaniiu goroda Lvova"

Op. 4, Sp. 939: "Eskizy Vysokogo Zamka, Gubernatorskikh valov"

Op. 4, Sp. 1092: "Delo po stroitelstvu i remonte zdaniia teatra im. Zankovetskoi"

Op. 4, Sp. 1097: "Plany i chertezhy paviliona arkhitektury na vseobshchej vystavkie vo Lvovie"

Op. 4, Sp. 1098: "Proekty planov paviliona arkhitektury na vseobshchej vystavkie vo Lvovie"

Op. 4, Sp. 1146: "Plany i chertezhy doma invalidov vo Lvove"

Op. 4, Sp. 1221: "Plany i chertezhy kostela sv. Ielzhbety po ul. Gorodetskoi vo Lvove"

Op. 4, Sp. 1260: "Plany i chertezhy pamiatnika Smolki na pl. Pobedy"

Op. 4, Sp. 1261: "Plany i chertezhy pamiatnika Iana Sobieskogo po ul. 1 Maia"

Op. 4, Sp. 1266-70: "Plany i chertezhy grobnits, sklepov i pamiatnikov na Lychakovskom kladbishche"

F. 27, Op. 4, Sp. 363: "Lichnoie delo prepodavatelia Levinskogo Iana" (1921-39)

PRINTED PRIMARY SOURCES

Periodicals

Architect. Cracow: 10 (1910).

Auf der Höhe. Leipzig: 1880-82.

Czas. Cracow: 282 (1852).

Czasopismo techniczne. Lemberg: 1883-1918.

Dilo. Lemberg: 157 (1894).

Dziennik lwowski. Lemberg: 181 and 199 (1869).

Dziennik polski. Lemberg: 2 (1902).

Dźwignia. Lemberg: 1877-82.

Galichanin. Lemberg: 213-16 (1905).

Gazeta narodowa. Lemberg: 138 (1907).

Kółko rodzinne. 7 and 25 (1860).

Lemberger Zeitung. Lemberg: 20 February 1828.

Mnemosyne. Lemberg: 52 (1845).

Przyjaciel domowy. Lemberg: 1-16 (1857).

Tygodnik powszechny. Warsaw: 15-30 (1882).

Zoria. Lemberg: 1882-90.

Zorza. Warsaw: 7 (1902).

Memoirs

Haquet, Baltasar. *Haquets neueste physikalisch- politische Reisen in den Jahren 1788 und 1789 durch die Dacischen und Sarmatischen oder Nördischen Karpaten.* Nürnberg: Verlag der Raspischen Buchhaltund, 1790-91.

Kratter, Franz. *Briefe über die itzigen Zustand von Galizien, Ein Beytrag zur Statistik und Menschenkenntniss.* 2 Vols., Leipzig, 1786.

Rohrer, Joseph. *Bemerkungen auf einer Reise von der türkischen Grenze über die Bukowina durch Ost- und Westgalizien, Schlesien und Mähren nach Wien.* Wien, 1804, Berlin, 1989.

Sacher-Masoch, Leopold. "Memorien des k. k. Hofraths v. Sacher-Masoch (1809-1874)." *Auf der Höhe*: internat. Revue/hrsg. von Leopold von Sacher-Masoch, Leipzig, 1880-82.

City Guides

Ilustrowany przewodnik po Lwowie i powszechnej wystawie krajowej, z planem i widokami miasta, wystawy i 18 rycinami ważniejszych budynków. Lemberg: Towarzystwo dla rozwoju i upiększenia miasta, 1894.

Jaworski, Franciszek. *Przewodnik po Lwowie i okolicy z Żółkwi i Podgorcami.* Lemberg: B. Poloniecki, 1907.

Kronika Lwowa, jego zabytki, osobliwoci z przewodnikiem oraz planem Lwowa. Lemberg: Nakl. Lwowskiego Biura Adresowego, 1909.

Piotrowski, Józef. *Lemberg und Umgebung (Żołkiew, Podhorce, Brzerzany und and.).* Handbuch für Kunstliebhaber und Reisende. Lemberg: Hotel George; Leipzig: F. A. Brockhaus; Wien: Moritz Perles, after 1915.

Plan kr. st. m. Lwowa ze skorowidzem dawnych i nowych nazw, placow i ulic. Lemberg: Nakl. K. Widla, 1872.

Przewodnik po mieście Lwowie. Lemberg: Druk. i lit. K. Pillera, 1871.

Tschischka, Franz. *Kunst und Alterthum in den oesterreichischen Kaiserstaate.* Georgaphisch dargestellt von. Vienna, 1836.

Wilczkowski, Józef. *Lwów: jego rozwój i stan kulturalny oraz przewodnik po mieście.* Lemberg: Wydział Gospodarczy X. Zjazdu Lekarzy i Przyrodników Polskich, 1907.

Zipper, Albert. *Führer durch die Allgemeine Landes-Austellung sowie durch die Königl. Haubstadt Lemberg.* Lemberg: Verlag der Ausstellungs-Direction, 1894.

Government Publications

Dziubiński, Leon Gustaw. *Poczet prezydentów, wizeprezydentów i obywateli honorowych miasta Lwowa. Odbitka z "Księgi pamiątkowej," wydanej w 25-letni jubileusz autonomii krolewskiego stołecznego miasta Lwowa.* Lemberg: Nakl. Gminy m. Lwowa, 1896.

Handbuch Statthalterei-Gebietes in Galizien. Lemberg: k.k. galizische Aerarial Druckerei, 1859, 1860.

Miasto Lwów w okresie samorządu, 1870-1985, Introduction by Edmund Mochnacki. Lemberg: Nakł. Gminy król. Stoł. Miasta Lwowa, 1896.

Papeé, Fryderyk. *Historya miasta Lwowa w zarysie z 24 illustracyami.* Lemberg: Nakł. Gminy król. Stoł. Miasta Lwowa, 1894.

Schematismus der Königreiche Galizien und Lodomerien für das Jahr 1842. Lemberg: k.k. galizische Aerarial Druckerei, 1842.

Szematyzm król. Galicji i Lodomerji. Lemberg: Nakł. c.k. Namiestnictwa z druk. W. Lozińskiego, 1895.

Mochnacki, Edmund. *Sprawozdanie Prezydenta k. st. miasta Lwowa z trzechletniej czynności Reprezentacyi miasta i Magistratu (1886, 1887 i 1888) wygłoszone na posiędzeniu pełnej Rady dnia 19. Stycznia 1889.* Lemberg, 1889.

Papée, Fryderyk. *Historia m. Lwowa w zarysie.* Lemberg: Gmina Król. Stoł. Miasta Lwowa, 1894.

Rutowski, Tadeusz (Dr.). *Galerya miejska w swietle polskiej i obcej krytyki.* Lemberg: Nakł. Gminy miasta z drukarni W. A. Szyjkowskiego, 1908.

Other Primary Sources

Antoniewicz, Jan Bołoz. *Nasz Rafael.* Lemberg, 1908.

Bilous, F. *Drevniia zdaniia v sravnienii z nynishnimi.* Lemberg: Stauropigija, 1856.

Czołowski, Aleksander (Dr.). *W sprawie Galeryi miejskiej. Odpowiedź prof. Dr. Janowi Bołoz Antoniewiczowi.* Lemberg, 1907.

Karta pamiatkowa obchodu rocznicy oblezenia miasta Lwowa przez hetmana kozaków Chmielnickiego i walecznej obrony mieszkańcow w roku 1655. Lemberg: Izraelicka Gmina Wyznaniowa we Lwowie, nakł. A. Goldmana, 1905.

Konkurs na projekt rekonstrukcyi gmachu ratuszowego we Lwowie (z 10-ma tablicami), Odbitka z Czasopisma technicznego. Lemberg, 1908.

Lukomskii, G. K. *Galitsiia v ieia starinie. Ocherki po istorii arkhitektury XII-XVIII vv. i risunki*. St. Petersburg: T-vo R. Golike I A. Vilborg, 1915.

Kroupa, Petr. "Odkaz moravského umělce k poučení svých synů (umělecký cestopis z konce 18. stoleti)," "Nachlass eines mährischen Künstlers zur Belehrung seiner Söhne, Zweites Heft Worinnen die in Prag Gesehenen Arbeiten der alten Mahler, Bildhauer, und anderer Künstler Böhmens beschrieben stehn," *Studie Muzea kroměřižska* 83 (1983), 123-31.

Miasto Lwów w okresie samorządu 1870-95. Lemberg, 1896.

Mowa Dr. Tadeusza Rutowskiego na zgromadzeniu wyborców m. Tarnowa dnia 19. Maja 1883. Cracow: Nakł. Autora, Drukarnia Związkowa, 1883.

Rutowski, Tadeusz (Dr.) "W sprawie Galeryi miejskiej," *Słowo polskie* (5 June – 4 August 1907).

_____. *W sprawie Galeryi miejskiej z planem "Pałacu Sztuki"*. Lemberg: Księgarnia H. Altenberga, Drukarnia i litografja Pillera, Neumanna i sp., 1907.

Stachiewicz, Piotr. *Plakat der Landesausstellung 1894*. Lemberg: P. Stachiewicz, 1894.

Wityk, Semon. *Pokój ludziom dobrej woli!* Lemberg: Drukarnia Udzialowa, 1905.

Zachariewicz, Julian. *Odczyt o architekturze, wygłoszony 19.Marca 1877*. Lemberg: Nakł. Księgarni polskiej, 1877.

SECONDARY SOURCES

Compendia

Bucko, Mykola. *Vidomi včeni deržavnoho universytetu "Ľvivka Politechnika" 1844-1994. Biografičnyj dovidnyk*. Ľviv: Ľvivka Politechnika, 1994.

Garkavy Aleksandr and L. Katzenelson, eds. *Evreiskaia entsiklopediia, Svod zna-nii o evreistvie i ego kulture v proshlom i nastoiashchem.* St. Petersburg: Brock-haus-Efron, 1906-13; The Hague: Mouton, 1969-71), vol. 10.

Kennedy Grimsted, Patricia. "Ukraine," *Austrian History Yearbook,* vol. XXIX (1998: part 2): 171-200.

Łoza, Stanisław. *Architekci i budowniczowie w Polsce.* Warsaw: Budownictwo i Architektura, 1954.

Magocsi, Paul Robert. *Galicia: A historical Survey and Bibliographical Guide.* Toronto: University of Toronto Press, 1983.

Neue österreichische Biografie ab 1815: grosse Österreicher. Vol. XVI, Zurich, Leipzig, and Vienna: Amalthea Vlg., 1960.

Popławski, Zbysław. *Wykaz pracowników naukowych Politechniki lwowskiej w latach 1844-1945.* Cracow: Politechnika krakowska im. Tadeusza Kościuszki, Seria Historyczno-techniczna, Bind 2, Monograph 175, 1994.

Szolginia, Witold. *Historiografia architektury i urbanistyki dawnego Lwowa.* Warsaw: PAN Instytut Sztuki, 1989.

Topinka, Jevhen, ed. *Čechy v Halycyni: Biograficnyj dovidnyk.* Ľviv: Centr Je-vropy, 1998.

Wandruszka, Adam and Peter Urbanitsch, eds. *Die Habsburgermonarchie 1848-1918.* vol. 2 "Verwaltung und Rechtswesen," Vienna: verlad der Österreichischen Akademie der Wissenschaften, 1975.

Wurzbach, Constantin Ritter von -Tannenberg, *Biographisches Lexikon.* vol. 26, Vienna 1874.

Periodicals

Architektura, Visnyk Hacionaľnoho Universytetu "Ľvivka Politechnika" 310 (1996); 358 (1998); 375 (1999); 410 (2000); 429 (2001); 439 (2002).

Architekturna spadščyna Ukraïny, Issue 1 (Kyiv, 1994) "Malovyvčeni problemy istoriï architektury ta mistobuduvannia"; Issue 3, Par 1-2 (1996) "Pytannia istoriografiï ta džereloznavstva urkaïńśkoï architektury."

Budujemo inakše 1 (1998); 1, 3, 4, 5, 6 (2000), 1, 2 (2001).
Krytyka 7-8: 57-58 (July - August 2002) "Strasti za Ľvovom."

Istoryko-architekturnyj atlas Ľvova, Series II: "Vyznačni budivli,"
   Bind 1, "Budynok tovarystva 'Dnister'" (1996);
   Bind 2, "Preobraženska Cerkva" (1997);
   Bind 3, "Torhovo-promyslova palata" (1998).

Halyćka Brama (*HB*) 4 (December 1994 - January 1995) "Prochody po vovu";
   5 (February, March, April 1995) "Krajeznavstvo Halyčyny";
   6 (June and July 1995) "Dvadciať rokiv";
   7 (August, September, and October 1995) "Promyslovist";
   8 (November 1995) "Teatr";
   9 (December 1995) "Ukraïnśki rodovody";
   11 (January 1996) "Ľvivśki poliaky";
   15 (May 1996) "Architekturna spadščyna";
   16 (June 1996) "Čechy v Halyčyni";
   20 (October 1996) "Koledž imeni Ivana Truša";
   9: 33 (September 1997) "Plošča Mickevyča";
   10-11: 34-35 (October November 1997) "Jevreï ľvova";
   1: 37 (January 1998) "Ľvivśkyj nekropoľ";
   2: 38 (February 1998) "Prospekt Svobody";
   3: 39 (March 1998) "Fortyfikaciï Ľvova";
   10: 46 (October 1998) "Vesna narodiv";
   11: 47 (November 1998) "Vulycia Kopernyka";
   7: 55 (July 1999) "Lyčakiv-Pohulianka";
   9-10: 57-58 (1999) "P'jať rokiv";
   2-3: 74-75 (February March 2001) "Ľviv i ľvivjany";
   11-12: 59-60 (November December 2001) "Ľviv i ľvivjany."

Ukrzachidprojektrestavracija. Visnyk 9 (1998), Special issue "Synagogy Ukraïny."

Visnyk Ukraïnoznavstva. Visnyk Deržavnoho universytetu "Ľvivka Politechnika" 296 (1995), 309 (1996).

Visnyk Deržavnoho universytetu "Ľvivka Politechnika" 287 (1995) "Rezervy progresu v architekturi i budivnyctvi."

Žovteň 2, 12, (1983) 7, 11 (1984) 11 (1987).

Habsburg History

Barany, George. *Stephen Szechenyi and the Awakening of Hungarian Nationalism, 1791-1841*. Princeton: Princeton University Press, 1968.

Beales, Derek. *Joseph II*. Cambridge: Cambridge University Press, 1987.

Beller, Steven. *Vienna and the Jews, 1867-1938: A Cultural History*. Cambridge: Cambridge University Press, 1989.

_____. "Reintenting Central Europe." *Working Papers in Austrian Studies* 91 (October 1991) 5.

Bérenger, Jean. *A History of the Habsburg Empire 1700-1918*. Trans. by C. A. Simpson. London and New York: Longman, 1990.

Bernard, Paul P. *From the Enlightenment to the Police State: The Public Life of Johann Anton Pergen*. Urbana and Chicago: University of Illinois Press, 1991.

Blanning, T.C.W. *Joseph II*. London: Longman, 1994.

Bradley, John F. N. *Czech Nationalism in the Nineteenth Century*. Boulder: East European Monographs, 1984.

Boyer, John W. *Political Radicalism in Late Imperial Vienna: Origins of the Christian Social Movement, 1848-97*. Chicago: University of Chicago Press, 1981.

_____. *Culture and Political Crisis in Vienna: Christian Socialism in Power, 1897-1918*. Chicago: University of Chicago Press, 1995.

Cohen, Gary B. *The Politics of Ethnic Survival: Germans in Prague, 1861-1914*. Princeton: Princeton University Press, 1981.

Glassheim, Eagle. *Noble Nationalists: The Transformation of the Bohemian Aristocracy*. Cambridge, Massachusetts: Harvard University Press, 2005.

Gerő, András, ed. *Hungarian Liberals*. Budapest: Uj Mandatum Konyvkiado, 1999.

Gneisse, Bettina. *Istvan Szechenyis Kasinobewegung im ungarischen Reformzeitalter (1825-48): ein Beitrag zur Erforschung der Anfange der nationalliberalen Organisation im vormarzlichen Ungarn*. Frankfurt am Main: Peter Lang, 1990.

Good, David F. *The Economic Rise of the Habsburg Empire, 1750-1914*. Berkeley: University of California Press, 1984.

_____. "The economic lag of Central and Eastern Europe: evidence from the late nineteenth-century Habsburg Empire." *Working Papers in Austrian Studies* 93 (December 1993), 7.

Gutkas, Karl, et al., ed. *Osterreich zur Zeit Kaiser Josephs II: Mitregent Kaiserin Maria Theresias, Kaiser und Landesfurst*. Vienna: Amt der Niederösterreichichen Landesregierung, 1980.

Höbelt, Lothar. "Parliamentary politics in a multinational setting: late imperial Austria." *Working Papers in Austrian Studies* 92 (March 1993), 6.

Jászi, Oscar. *The Dissolution of the Habsburg Monarchy*. Chicago and London: The University of Chicago Press, 1929.

Kann, Robert A. *Multinational empire: nationalism and national reform in the Habsburg monarchy, 1848-1918*. New York: Octagon Books, 1983.

King, Jeremy. *Budweisers into Czechs and Germans: A Local History of Bohemian Politics, 1848-1948*. Princeton, N.J.: Princeton University Press, 2003.

Macartney, Carlile Aylmer. *The Habsburg Empire, 1790-1918*. New York: Macmillan, 1969.

Okey, Robin. *The Habsburg Monarchy: 1765-1918. Enlightenment to Eclipse*. Houndmills, Basignstoke, Hampshire and London: Macmillan Press, 2000.

Oplatka, Andreas. *Graf Stephan Szechenyi: Der Mann, der Ungarn schuf*. Vienna: Paul Zsolnay Verlag, 2004.

Padover, Saul K. *The Revolutionary Emperor: Joseph II of Austria*. London: Eyre and Spottiswoode, 1934, 1967.

Palmer, Alan. *Metternich*. London: History Book Club, 1972.

Sayer, Derek. *The Coasts of Bohemia: A Czech History*. Princeton: Princeton University Press, 1998.

Sked, Alan. *The Decline and Fall of the Habsburg Empire, 1815-1918*. London and New York: Longman, 1989.

Unowsky, Daniel. *The Pomp and Politics of Patriotism: Imperial Celebrations in Habsburg Austria, 1848-1916*. West Lafayette, Indiana: Purdue University Press, 2005.

Varga, Janos. *A Hungarian Quo Vadis: Political Trends and Theories of the Early 1840s*. Budapest: Akademiai Kiado, 1993.

Walker, Mack, ed. *Metternich's Europe*. New York: Harper and Row, 1968.

Wank, Solomon. "The Nationalities question in the Habsburg monarchy: reflections on the historical record." *Working Papers in Austrian Studies* 93 (April 1993), 3.

Zacek, Joseph Frederick. *Palacky: The Historian as Scholar and Nationalist*. The Hague: Mouton, 1970.

Architectural and Urban History and Theory, Urban Planning

Alberti, Leon Battista. *On the art of building in ten books*. Trans. Joseph Rykwert, Neil Leach, and Robert Tavernor. Cambridge, Massachusetts: MIT Press, 1994, 1988.

Alofsin, Anthony. *When Buildings Speak: Architecture as Language in the Habsburg Empire and Its Aftermath, 1867-1933*. Chicago: The University of Chicago Press, 2006.

Babejova, Eleonora. *Fin-de-siècle Pressburg: Conflict and Cultural Coexistence in Bratislava 1897-1914*. Boulder: East European Monographs, 2003.

Ballinger, Pamela. "Imperial nostalgia: mythologizing Habsburg Trieste." *Journal of Modern Italian Studies* 8 (2003), 1: 84–101.

Bałus, Wojciech. *Krakau zwischen Traditionen und Wegen in die Moderne: Zur Geschichte der Architektur und der öffenlichen Grünanlagen im 19. Jahrhundert.* Stuttgart: Franz Steiner Verlag, 2003.

Bairoch, Paul, Jean Batou, and Pierre Chevre. *La population des villes européennes, 800-1850: banque de donnees et analyse sommaire des resultats*. Geneve: Droz, 1988.

Beckova, Katerina. *Wenceslas Square in the Course of Bygone Centuries*. Prague: Schola Ludus Pragensia, 1993.

Benjamin, Walter. *The Arcades Project*. Cambridge, Massachusetts: Belknap Press of Harvard University Press, 1999.

Bilećkyj, Platon Oleksandrovyč, Dmytro Omelianovyč Horbačov, Eduard Oleksandrovyč Dymšyć, eds. *Ukraïnśke mystectvo ta architektura kincia XIX – počatku XX st*. Kyiv: Naukova Dumka, afer 1990.

Blau, Eve and Monika Platzer, eds. *Shaping the Great City: Modern Architecture in Central Europe, 1890 – 1937*. Munich, London and New York: Prestel, 1999.

Borden, Iain and David Dunster. *Architecture and the Sites of History: Interpretations of Buildings and Cities*. New York: Whitney Library of Design, 1995.

Brandstätter, Christian, ed. *Vienna 1900 and the Heroes of Modernism*. London: Thames and Hudson, 2006.

Brown, Karin Brinkmann. *Karl Lueger, the Liberal Years: Democracy, Municipal Reform, and the Struggle for Power in the Vienna City Council, 1875-82*. New York: Garland Publishing, 1987.

Cannadine, David and David Reeder, eds. *Exploring the Urban Past, Essays in Urban History, by H. J. Dyos*. Cambridge: Cambridge University Press, 1982.

Choay, Francoise. *The invention of the historic monument.* Trans. Lauren M. O'Connell, Cambridge: Cambridge University Press, 2001.

_____. *The Modern City: Planning in the 19th century.* New York: George Braziller; 1969.

Davies, Norman and Roger Moorhouse. *Microcosm: Portrait of a Central European City.* London: Jonathan Cape, 2002.

Dedijer, Vladimir. *The Road to Sarajevo.* New York: MacGibbon and Kee, 1967.

Demetz, Peter. *Prague in Black and Gold: Scenes from the Life of a European City.* New York: Hill and Wang, 1997.

Diomin, M. et al. *Teorija ta istorija architektury.* Kyiv: Deržkolegija Ukraïny v spravi mistobuduvannia, 1995.

Dubin, Lois C. *The Port Jews of Habsburg Trieste: Absolutist Politics and Enlightenment Culture.* Stanford, CA: Stanford University Press, 1999.

Frycz, Jerzy. *Restauracja i konserwacja zabytków architektury w Polsce w latach 1795-1918.* Warsaw: Państwowe Wydawnictwo Naukowe, 1975.

Geehr, Richard S. *Karl Lueger: Mayor of Fin-de-Siècle Vienna.* Detroit: Wayne State University Press, 1990.

Gerle, János, Attila Kovács, and Imre Makovecz. *A századforduló magyar építészete.* Budapest: Szépirodalmi Könyvkiadó, 1990.

Gerő, András and János Poór, eds. *Budapest: A History from Its Beginnings to 1996.* Boulder: East European Monographs, 1997.

Giustino, Cathleen M. *Tearing down Prague's Jewish town: ghetto clearance and the legacy of middle-class ethnic politics around 1900.* Boulder: East European Monographs, 2003.

Hall, Thomas. *Planning Europe's Capital Cities: Aspects of Nineteenth Century Urban Development.* London: Studies in History, Planning, and the Environment 21, 1997.

Hametz, Maura. *Making Trieste Italian, 1918-1954*. Woodbridge: Boydell Press, 2005.

Herrmann, Wolfgang, *Gottfried Semper: in search of architecture*. Cambridge, MA.: MIT Press, 1984.

Hohenberg, Paul M. and Lynn Hollen Lees, eds. *The Making of Urban Europe, 1000-1950*. Cambridge, MA: Harvard University Press, 1985.

Hrůza, Jiří. *Město Praha*. Prague: Odeon, 1989.

Hübsch, Heinrich, *In what style should we build? The German debate on archi-tectural style*. Introduction and trans. Wolfgang Herrmann. Santa Monica, CA: Getty Research Institute for the History of Art and the Humanities, 1992.

Jaroszewski, Tadeusz S. *Od klasycyzmu do nowoczesności. O architekturzre pol-skiej XVIII, XIX I XX wieku*. Warsaw: Wydawnictwo Naukowe PWN, 1996.

Kohout, Jiří and Jiří Vancura. *Praha 19. a 20. stoleti: technicke promeny*. Prague: SNTL-Nakl. technicke literatury, 1986.

Kostof, Spiro. *The City Shaped: Urban Patterns and Meanings Through History*. London: Thames and Hudson, 1991.

Mallgrave, Harry Francis. *Gottfried Semper: architect of the nineteenth century*. New Haven, CT: Yale University Press, 1996.

Mazower, Mark. *Salonica, City of Ghosts: Christians, Muslims, and Jews, 1430–1950*. New York: Alfred A. Knopf, 2005.

Melinz, Gerhard and Susan Zimmermann, eds. *Über die Grenzen der Armenhilfe: Kommunale und staatliche Sozialpolitik in Wien und Budapest in der Doppel-monarchie*. Vienna and Zürich: Europaverlag, 1991.

Michalski, Sergiusz. *Public Monuments. Art in Political Bondage 1870-1997*. London: Reaction Books, 1998.

Mieszkowski, Zygmunt. *Polscy teoretycy architektury (XVI-XIX w.)*. Cracow: P.A.N., 1972.

Moravánszky, Ákos. *Competing visions: aesthetic invention and social imagination in Central European architecture, 1867-1918.* Cambridge, MA: MIT Press, 1998.

Mumford, Lewis. *The City in History.* New York: Harvest and HBJ, 1961.

Olsen, Donald. *The Growth of Victorian London.* New York: Holmes & Meier, 1979.

_____. *The City as a Work of Art: London, Paris, Vienna.* New Haven: Yale University Press, 1986.

Pohanka, Reinhard. *Eine kurze Geschichte der Stadt Wien.* Vienna, Cologne and Weimar: Böhlau, 1998.

Prokopovych, Markian, et al., eds. "Editorial Introduction," *East Central Europe/ l'Europe du Centre-Est: Eine wissenschaftliche Zeitschrift* 33 (2006) 1–2, thematic issue "Urban History in East Central Europe," 1-4; http://www.ece.hu/files/pdf/volume/33/introduction.pdf.

_____. "New Monumentality and Capital Cities. A Discursive Analysis of Berlin, Vienna, Budapest and Prague Around 1900." Peter Stachel and Cornelia Szabo-Knotik, eds. *Urbane Kulturen in Zentraleuropa um 1900.* Wien: Passagen, 2004 (Studien zur Moderne 19).

_____. "Staging Empires and Nations: Politics in the Public Space of Habsburg Lemberg." Rudolf Jawoski and Peter Stachel, eds. *Die Besetzung des öffentlichen Raumes. Politische Codierungen von Plätzen, Denkmälern und Straßennamen im europäischen Vergleich (19.u. 20. Jhd.).* Berlin: Frank & Timme, 2007.

_____. "The Lemberg Garden: Political Representation in Public Greenery under the Habsburg Rule," in Maciej Janowski, Balazs Trenscenyi, Constantin Iordachi, and Markian Prokopovych, eds., *East Central Europe - l'Europe du centre-est - eine wissenschaftliche Zeutschrift,* 33 (2006) 1-2, 73-99.

_____. "Lemberg (Lwów, L'viv), 1772-1918: "Little Vienna of the East," National Bastion or Else?" *East Central Europe/l'Europe du Centre-Est: Eine wissenschaftliche Zeitschrift* (2008), thematic issue "Reframing the European Pasts: National Discourses and Regional Comparisons" (forthcoming).

_____. *"Kopiec Unii Lubelskiej:* Imperial Politics and National Celebration in *fin-de-siècle* Lemberg." ece-urban - The online publication series of the Center for Urban History of East Central Europe (forthcoming) www.lvivcenter.org/en/ publications.

Schwarzer, Mitchell. *German Architectural Theory and the Search for Modern Identity.* Cambridge, New York, and Melbourne: Cambridge University Press, 1995.

Semper, Gottfried. *The four elements of architecture and other writings.* Trans. Harry Francis Mallgrave and Wolfgang Herrmann. Cambridge: Cambridge University Press, 1989.

Sičynśkyj, Volodymyr. *Architektura v starodrukach.* Ľviv: Zbirky Nacionaľnoho Muzeja u Ľvovi, 1925.

_____. *Naše narodne budivnyctvo. Za svij narodnyj styľ v budivnyctvi.* Užhorod: Svoboda, 1937.

Spector, Scott. *Prague Territories: National Conflict and Cultural Innovation in Kafka's Fin de Siècle.* Berkeley: University of California Press, 2000.

Tymofijenko. V. I. and V. Ju. Jerošev. *Ukraïnśka sadybna architektura druhoï polovyny XVIII – peršoï polovyny XIX st.* Kyiv: NDITIAM, 1993.

van Pelt, Robert and Carroll William Westfall, *Architectural Principles in the Age of Historicism.* New Haven and London: Yale University Press, 1991.

Varnedoe, Kirk. *Vienna 1900: Art, Architecture & Design.* Boston, 1986.

Vergo, Peter. *Art in Vienna 1898-1918: Klimt, Kokoschka, Schiele and Their Contemporaries.* Ithaca: Cornell University Press, 1975.

Vitochova, Marie, Jindrich Kejr, and Jiri Vsetecka. *Prague and Art Nouveau.* Prague: Vraji, 1995.

Vitruvius, Pollio. *On architecture.* Ed. and trans. Frank Granger. London: W. Heinemann, 1931-34, Cambridge, Massachusetts: Harvard University Press, 1985.

Waissenberger, Robert, ed. *Vienna in the Biedermeier Era, 1815-48*. London: Alpine Fine Arts Collection, 1986.

_____. et. al., *Vienna, 1890-1920*. New York : Tabard Press, 1984

Watkin, David and Tilman Mellinghoff. *German Architecture and the Classical Ideal: 1740-1840*. London: Thames and Hudson 1987.

Weber, Max. *The City*. New York: Free Press, 1966.

Wiebenson, Dora and József Sisa, eds. *Architecture of Historic Hungary*. Cambridge, Massachusetts: MIT Press, 1998.

Wittlich, Petr. *Prague: fin de siècle*. Paris: Flammarion, 1992.

Zimmermann, Susan. *Prächtige Armut: Fürsorge, Kinderschutz und Sozialreform in Budapest: Das „sozialpolitische Laboratorium" der Doppelmonarchie im Vergleich zu Wien, 1873-1914*. Sigmaringen: J. Thorbecke, 1997.

General Methodological Approaches

Anderson, Benedict. *Imagined Communities: reflections on the origin and spread of nationalism*. London: Verso, 1991.

_____. *The spectre of comparisons: nationalism, Southeast Asia, and the world*. London: Verso, 1998.

Auerbach, Jeffrey A. *The Great Exhibition of 1851: A Nation on Display*. New Haven and London: Yale University Press, 1999.

Boris, Eileen and Angélique Janssens, eds. *Complicating Categories: Gender, Class, Race and Ethnicity. International Review of Social History, Supplement 7*. New York: Cambridge University Press, 1999.

Brown, Julie K. *Making Culture Visible: The Public Display of Photography at Fairs, Expositions, and Exhibitions in the United States, 1847-1900*. Amsterdam: Harwood Academic Publishers, 2001.

Bucur, Maria and Nancy M. Wingfield, eds. *Staging the past: the politics of commemoration in Habsburg Central Europe, 1848 to the present.* West Lafayette, IN: Purdue University Press, 2001.

Colomina, Beatriz. *Privacy and Publicity: Modern Architecture as Mass Media.* Cambridge MA and London: The MIT Press, 1994.

Connor, Walker. *Ethnonationalism: the quest for understanding.* Princeton, N.J.: Princeton University Press, 1994.

Evans, Richard J. "Introduction. Redesigning the Past: History in Political Transition," Evans, Richard J. ed., *Journal of Contemporary History, Special Issue: Redesigning the Past,* vol. 38, 1 (January 2003).

Freifeld, Alice. *Nationalism and the Crowd in Liberal Hungary, 1848-1914.* Baltimore and Washington, D.C.: Johns Hopkins University Press and Woodrow Wilson Center Press, 2000.

Fritzsche, Peter. *Reading Berlin 1900.* Cambridge, MA: Harvard University Press, 1996.

Gellner, Ernest. *Nations and Nationalism.* Oxford: Blackwell, 1983.

Gold, John R. and Margaret M. Gold. *Cities of Culture: Staging International Festivals and the Urban Agenda, 1851-2000.* Burlington: Ashgate Publishing, 2005.

Greenhalgh, Paul. *Ephemeral Vistas: The Expositions Universelles, Great Exhibition and World's Fairs, 1851-1939.* Manchester: Manchester University Press, 1990.

Gyáni, Gábor. *Identity and the urban experience*: fin-de-siécle Budapest (Boulder: Social Science Monograph 2004).

Hall, Catherine, Keith McClelland, and Jane Rendall, eds. *Defining the Victorian Nation: Class, Race, Gender and the British Reform Act of 1867.* Cambridge: Cambridge Univesity Press, 2000.

Hanák, Péter. *The Garden and the Workshop: essays on the cultural history of Vienna and Budapest.* Princeton, N. J.: Princeton University Press, 1998.

Hobsbawm, Eric and Terence Ranger (eds.), *The Invention of Tradition*. Cambridge University Press, 1992.

Hroch, Miroslav. *Social Preconditions of National Revival in Europe: a Comparative Analysis of the Social Composition of Patriotic Groups Among the Smaller European Nations*. Cambridge, Cambridgeshire: Cambridge University Press, 1985.

Hutchinson, John and Anthony D. Smith, eds. *Nationalism*. Oxford and New York: Oxford University Press, 1994.

Jedlicki, Jerzy. *A Suburb of Europe: Nineteenth-century Polish Approaches to Western Civilization*. Budapest: Central European University Press, 1999.

Karp, Ivan and Steven D. Lavine, eds. *Exhibiting Cultures: The Poetics and Politics of Museum Display*. Washington D C: Smithsonian Institution Press, 1991.

Kłańska, Maria. *Daleko od Wiednia. Galicja w oczach pisarzy niemieckojęzycznych 1772-1918*. Cracow: Universitas, 1991.

_____. *Problemfeld Galizien in deutschsprachiger Prosa 1846-1914*. Vienna: Böhlau, 1992.

Leapman, Michael. *The World for a Shilling: How the Great Exhibition of 1851 Shaped a Nation*. London: Headline Books, 2001.

Paces, Cynthia. "The Battle for Prague's Old Town Square: Symbolic Space and the Birth of the Republic," in Blair Ruble and John Czaplicka, eds. *Composing Urban History and the Constitution of Civic Identities*. Washington, D.C., and Baltimore: Woodrow Wilson Press, Johns Hopkins University Press, 2003.

Pemsel, Jutta. *Die Wiener Weltausstellung. Das gründerzeitliche Wien am Wendepunkt*. Vienna and Cologne: Böhlau, 1989.

Rydell, Robert W. *All the World's a Fair: Visions of Empire at American International Expositions, 1876-1916*. Chicago: University of Chicago Press, 1984.

_____. *World of Fairs: The Century-of-Progress Expositions*. Chicago: University of Chicago Press, 1993.

Schorske, Carl E. *Fin-de-siècle Vienna: politics and culture*. New York: Vintage Books, 1981.

Sherman, Daniel J. *Worthy Monuments: Art Museums and the Politics of Culture in Nineteenth-Century France*. Cambridge, MA: Harvard University Press, 1989.

Smith, Anthony D. *Nationalism and Modernism: A critical survey of recent histories of nations and nationalism*. London and New York: Routledge, 1998.

Stauter-Halsted, Keely. *The Nation in the Village: The Genesis of Rural National Identity in Austrian Poland, 1848-1900*. Cornell University Press, 2001.

Walicki, Andzej. *Poland between East and West: the controversies over self-definition and modernization in partitioned Poland*. Cambridge, Harvard University Press, 1994.

Wilentz, Sean, ed. *Rites of Power: Symbolism, Ritual, and Politics Since the Middle Ages*. Philadelphia: University of Pennsylvania Press, 1985.

Historiography on Lemberg and Galicia

Binder, Harald. "Making and Defending a Polish Town: Lwow (Lemberg), 1848-1914," *Austrian History Yearbook*, 34 (2003), 57-82.

Bisanz, Hans, ed., *Lemberg / Lviv 1772-1918. Wiederbegegnung mit einer Landeshaupstadt der Donaumonarchie*. Vienna: Historisches Museum der Stadt Wien, Katalog der 179. Sonderausstellung, 1993.

Bałaban, Majer. *Dzielnica żydowska we Lwowie*. Lemberg, 1909.

_____. *Historya lwowskiej synagogi postępowej*. Lwów, 1937.

_____. *Żydzi Lwowscy na przelomie XVI i XVII wieku*. Lemberg,1909.

Chodyniecki, Ignacy. *Historja stólecznego Królewstw Galicyi i Lodomeryi Miasta Lwowa od założenia jego aż do czasów terazniejszych w r. 1829 wydana. Wydanie wznowione tanie*. Lemberg: Karol Wild, 1865.

Chołodecki, Józef Białynia. *Franciszek Smolka*. Lemberg: Komitet budowy pomnika Franciszka Smolki, 1913.

Czaplicka, John J., ed. *Lviv: a City in the Crosscurrents of Culture*. Cambridge, MA: Distributed by Harvard University Press for the Harvard Ukrainian Research Institute, 2005.

Czołowski, Aleksander. *Wysoki zamek z 19 rycinami w tekscie*. Lemberg: Towarzystwo Miłośników Przeszłości Lwowa, 1910.

Dabrowski, Patrice M. *Commemorations and the shaping of modern Poland*. Bloomington, IN: Indiana University Press, 2004.

Fässler, Peter, Thomas Held, and Dirk Sawicki, eds. *Lemberg, Lwow, Lviv: eine Stadt im Schnittpunkt europaischer Kulturen*. Cologne: Bohlau, 1993.

Finkel, Ludwik and Stanisaw Starzyski. *Historya uniwersytetu lwowskiego*. 2 vols., Lemberg: Senat Akademicki c.k. Uniwersytetu lwowskiego, 1894.

Glassl, Horst. *Das österreichische Einrichtungswerk in Galizien (1772-1790)*. Wiesbaden: Otto Harrasowitz, 1975.

Got, Jerzy. *Das österreichische Theater in Lemberg im 18. und 19. Jahrhundert*. Wien: Verlag. der Österreichischen Akademie der Wissenschaften, Wien 1997.

Grzębski, Edmund Bronisław. *Towarzystwo Politechniczne we Lwowie. 1877-1902. Pamiętnik jubilejuszowy*. Lemberg: Towarzystwo Politechniczne, 1902.

Himka, John-Paul. "The Greek-Catholic Church in Nineteenth-Century Galicia," Geoffrey Hosking, ed., *Church, Nation and State in Russia and Ukraine*. London: Macmillan, 1991, 52-64.

_____. *Religion and Nationality in Western Ukraine: The Greek Catholic Church and the Ruthenian National Movement in Galicia, 1867-1900*. Montreal and Kingston, London, Ithaca: McGill-Queen's University Press, 1999.

_____. "German Culture and National Awakening in Western Ukraine before the Revolution of 1848." Hans-Joachim Torke and John-Paul Himka, eds. *German-Ukrainian Relations in Historical Perspective*. Edmonton and Toronto: Canadian Institute of Ukrainian Studies Press, 1994, 29-44.

_____. "The Construction of Nationality in Galician Ruś: Icarian Flights in Almost All Directions." Ronald Grigor Suny and Michael D. Kennedy, eds. *Intellectuals and the Articulation of the Nation.* Ann Arbor: University of Michigan Press, 1999, 109-64.

Hoczowski, Stanisław. *Ekonomiczny rozwój Lwowa w latach 1772- 1918.* Lwów, 1935.

Hrytsak, Yaroslav and Viktor Susak. "Constructing a National City: The Case, of Ľviv," in John J. Czaplicka, Blair A. Ruble, and Lauren Crabtree, eds. *Composing Urban History and the Constitution of Civic Identities.* Washington DC and Baltimore MD: Woodrow Wilson Press, Johns Hopkins University Press, 2003.

Isajevyč, Jaroslav et al., ed. *Istorija Lvova v trioch tomach.* Lviv: Centr Jevropy, 2007.

Janowski, Maciej. *Intelligencja wóbec wyzwań nowoczesności. Dylematy ideowe polskey demokracji liberalnej w Galicji w l. 1889-1914.* Warsaw: Instytut Historii P.A.N., 1996.

Janusz, Bohdan, ed. *Lwów stary i dzisiejszy. Praca zbiorowa pod redakcyą.* Lwów: Nakl. Wyd. "M.A.R." (Malop. Ajencja Reklamowa), 1928.

Jaworski, Franciszek. *Ratusz lwowski z 21 rycinami w tekście.* Lemberg: Towarzystwo miłośników przeszłości Lwowa, 1907.

_____. *Lwów stary i wczorajszy (szkice i opowiadania) z illustracyami, Wydanie drugie poprawione.* Lemberg: Nakl. Tow. Wydawniczego, 1911.

Kostiuk, S. P. ed. *Katalog graviur XVII-XX st. z fondiv Ľvivśkoï Naukovoï Biblioteky im. V. Stefanyka AN URSR (Architektura Ľvova).* Kyiv: Naukova Dumka, 1989.

Kozik, Jan. *The Ukrainian National Movement in Galicia, 1815-49.* Edmonton: Canadian Institute of Ukrainian Studies Press, 1986.

Krypjiakevyč, Ivan P. *Istoryčni próhody po Ľvovi.* Lwów: Vyd. TP, no. 771, 1932, reprinted in Ľviv: Kameniar, 1991.

Kramarz, Henryka. *Tadeusz Rutowski. Portret pozytywisty i demokraty gali-cyjskiego.* Cracow: Wydawnictwo Naukowe AP, 2001.

Kalinka, Walerian. *Galicya i Kraków pod panowaniem austryackiem.* Paris: W komisie Księgarni polskiej, 1853.

Lane, Hugo Viktor. *State Culture and National Identity in a Multi-Ethnic Context: Lemberg 1772-1914.* Ph.D. dissertation, University of Michigan, Ann Arbor: 1999.

_____, *Nationalizing Identity: Culture and Politics in Austrian Galicia, 1772-1918.* Unpublished book manuscript.

_____, "Szlachta Outside the Commonwealth. The Case of Polish Nobles in Galicia," *Zeitschrift für Ostmitteleuropa-Forschung* 52/4 (2003).

Lityński, Michał. *Gmach Skarbkowski na tle architektury lwowskiej w pierwszej połowie XIX wieku.* Lemberg: Nakl. Fundacyi Skarbkowskiej, 1912.

Loziński, Bronislaw (Dr.). *Agenor Hrabia Głuchowski w pierwszym okresie rządów swoich (1848 - 1859).* Lemberg: Nakl. Księgarni H. Altenberga, 1901.

Majka, Stanislaw and Bohdan Posadśkyj, *Lviv u staromu i novomu obrazi.* Rzeszowski Odzial Stowaryszenia "Wspolnota Polska," Rzeszow 1990.

Mahler, Raphael. *Hasidism and the Jewish Enlightenment: Their Confrontation in Galicia and Poland in the First Half of the Nineteenth Century.* Philadelphia: Jewish Publication Society of America, 1985.

Maleć, Sofija. *Za časiv Markijana Šaškevycha.* Lviv: Centr Jevropy, 2001.
Maleczyński, T., Mańkowski, F. Pohorecki i M. Tyrowicz, *Lwów i ziemia czerweńska.* Lwów: Państwowe Wydawnictwo Ksiązek Szkolskich we Lwowie, 1931.

Markovits, Andrei S. and Frank E. Sysyn, eds. *Nationbuilding and the Politics of Nationalism: Essays on Austrian Galicia.* Cambridge MA: Harvard University Press, 1982.

Melamed, Vladimir. *Yevrei vo Lvove (XIII - pervaja polovina XX veka): sobytija, obshchestvo, liudi.* L'viv: TEKOP, 1994.

Mick, Christoph. "War and Conflicting Memories – Poles, Ukrainians and Jews in Lvov 1914–1939." *Simon Dubnow Institute Yearbook,* 4 (2005), 257-78.

_____. "Ethnische Gewalt und Pogrome in Lemberg 1914 – 1941." *Osteuropa,* 53 (2003), 1810-29.

_____. "Wer verteidigte Lemberg? Totengedenken, Kriegsdeutungen und nationale Identität in einer multiethnischen Stadt." Dietrich Beyrau, ed., *Der Krieg in religiösen und nationalen Deutungen der Neuzeit.* Tübingen: 2000, 189-216.

_____. "Nationalisierung in einer multiethnischen Stadt. Interethnische Konflikte in Lemberg 1890–1920." *Archiv für Sozialgeschichte,* 40 (2000), 113-46.

Mudryj, Marjan, ed. *L'viv: misto-suspiľstvo-kultura: Zbirnyk naukovych prać.* 3 Vols, L'viv: Vydavnyctvo L'vivśkoho Universytetu, Serija Istoryčna, Special'nyj vypusk, 1999.

Pawłowski, Bronisław. *Lwów w 1809 r. z 20 rycinami w tekście.* Lemberg: Towarzystwo Miłośnikow Przeszłości Lwowa, 1909.

Pepłowski, Stanisław. *Teatr polski we Lwowie, 1780-1881.* Lemberg: Gubrynowicz i Schmidt, z drukarni "Dziennika polskiego," 1889.

Podgorecki, Leszek. *Dzieje Lwowa.* Warsaw: Oficyna Wydawnicza Volumen, 1993.

Proskuriakov, Viktor. *Architektura ukraïnśoho teatru: prostir i dija.* L'viv "L'vivska Politechnika," 2001.

_____ and Jurij Jamaš. *L'vivśki teatry: Čas i architektura.* L'viv: Centr Jevropy, 1997.

Rudnytsky, Ivan L., ed. *Rethinking Ukrainian History.* Edmonton: Canadian Institute of Ukrainian Studies Press, 1981.

Schneider, Ludwig. *Das Kolonisationswerk Josefs II in Galizien. Darstellung und Namenlisten*. [book online] Leipzig, 1939, Berlin, 1989, available from http://feefhs.org/gal/ggd/gkjg/dkjg-idx.html; Internet, accessed 31 May 2004.

Schneyder, Antoni. *Encyklopedia do krajoznawstwa Galicji pod względem historycznym, statystycznym, topograficznym, orograficznym, hidrograficznym, geograficznym, etnograficznym, handlowym, przemysłowym etc.* Vols. 1-2, Lemberg, 1869.

Schnür-Pepłowski, Stanisław. *Obrazy z przeszłości Galicyi i Krakowa (1772-1858)*. Lemberg: Gubrynowicz & Schmidt 1896.

Stauter-Halsted, Keely. *The Nation in the Village: The Genesis of Rural National Identity in Austrian Poland, 1848-1900*. Ithaca: Cornell University Press, 2001.

Steblij, Feodosij. *L'viv: istoryčni narysy*. L'viv, 1996.

Šyška, Oleksandr. *Naše misto – L'viv*. L'viv: Centr Jevropy, 2002.

_____. "Tragična dolia Antonija Šnajdera,"*HB* 5-6 (May, June, and July 1995) "Dvadciať rokiv."

Ther, Philipp. "Die Bühne als Schauplatz der Politik. Das Polnische Theater in Lemberg 1842-1914," *Zeitschrift für Ostmitteleuropa-Forschung* 52 (2003), 543-71.

Walicki, Henryk W. and Kazimierz Karolczak, eds. *Lwów: miasto, społeczeństwo, kultura*. 2 vols., Cracow: Studia z dziejów Lwowa, 1998.

Wendland, Anna Veronika. *Die Russophilen in Galizien: ukrainische Konservativen zwischen Österreich und Russland, 1848-1915*. Vienna: Verlag der Österreichischen Akademie der Wissenschaften, 2001.

_____. "Russophilie: Auch ein ukrainisches Projekt?" *Ї* 18 (2000).

Wolff, Larry. "Inventing Galicia: Messianic Josephinism and the Recasting of Partitioned Poland." *Slavic Review* 63 (Winter, 2004) 4, 818-40.

Yaremko, Michael. *Galicia – Halychyna (A Part of Ukraine): From Separation to Unity*. Ukrainian Studies, vol. XVIII: English section, vol. III, Toronto. New York and Paris: NTSh, 1967.

Zajączkowski, Wladyslaw. *C. k. Szkola Politechniczna we Lwowie. Rys historyczny jej założenia i rozwoju, tudzież stan jej obecny*. Lemberg, 1894.

Studies in Lemberg Architecture, Architects, Planning, and Restoration

Anonymous (D. K.). *Odnowienie i rekonstrukcya Katedry Ormiańskiej we Lwowie*. Lemberg: Wiek Nowy, 1908.

Biruliov, Jurij. *Ĺvivka secesija. Katalog vystavky*. Lviv, 1986.

_____. *Secesja we Lwowie*. Trans. Janusz Derwojed. Warsaw: Krupski i S-ka, 1995.

Czerner, Olgierd. *Lwów na dawnej rycinie i planie*. Wroclaw, Warsaw and Cracow: Zakad Naukowy imienie Ossolińskich, 1997.

Grankin, Pavlo. "Žebraky, čenci, jepyskopy." *HB* 9-10: 57-58 (1999) "P'jat' rokiv," 22-23.

_____. "Ĺvivśkyj opernyj teatr: istorija budovy i restavraciï." *Budujemo inakše* 6 (2000), 1 (2001).

Kučeriavyj, V., Olejniuk, O., Lukjanuk, N. *Sady i parky Ĺvova*. Ĺviv: Misioner, 2001.

Lewicki, Jakub. *Między tradycyją a nowoczesnością: architektura Lwowa lat 1893-1918*. Warsaw: Nevison, 2005.

Linda, Svitlana. "Stylistyčni ta architekturno-kompozytsijni aspekty rozvytku architektury Ĺvova periodu istoryzmu XIX – poch. XX st." Candidate dissertation, Ĺviv, 1999.

Mańkowski, Tadeusz. *Dawny Lwów: jego sztuka i kultura artystyczna*. London 1974.

_____. *Dzieje gmachu Zakładu Narodowego imienia Ossolińskich*. Lwów, 1927.

_____. *Lwów przez laty osiemdziesięciu w współczesnych litografijach Zakladów Pillera*. Lwów: Piller and Neumann, 1928.

_____. *O poglądach na sztukę w czasach Stanisława Augusta. Prace Sekcyi historyi sztuki i kultury Towarzystwa Naukowego we Lwowie*. vol. 2, Bind 1. Lwów: Nakł. Towarzystwa Naukowego, Drukarnia Uniwersytetu Jagielloskiego, 1929.

_____. *Początki nowożytnego Lwowa w architekturze*. Lwów: Drukarnia Uniwersytetu Jagiellońskiego w Krakowie, 1923.

Noha, Oleś. *Ivan Levynśkyj: Chudožnyk, Architektor, Promysloveć, Pedagog, Hromadśkyj Dijač*. Ľviv: Osnova, 1993.

Oleksyn, Ivan. "Žyttia i dijaľnisť Ivana Levynśkoho," in *Ivan Levynśkyj, Joho žyttia ta pracia*. Lwów: Nakl. Agronomino-techninoho tovarystva "Pracia" imeny Ivana Levynśkoho, 1934, 9-22.

Opałek, Mieczysław. *Obrazki z przesłości Lwowa*. Lwów: Towarzystwo Miłośników Przeszłości Lwowa, 1931.

Opalińska, Stanislawa. "Kraków i Lwów," in Tabkowski, J.S., ed. *Widoki dawnego Lwowa i Krakowa. Wspólna wystawa Muzeum Historycznego miasta Krakowa i Lwowskiego Muzeum Historycznego*. Cracow: Museum historiczne miasta Krakowa, 1996.

Ovsijčuk, Volodymyr. *Klasycyzm i romantyzm v ukraïnkomu mystectvi*. Kyiv: Dnipro, 2001.
_____. *Architekturni pamjatky Ľvova*. Ľviv: Kameniar, 1969.

Piotrowski, Józef (Dr.). *Katedra Ormiańska we Lwowie w świetle restauracji i ostatnich odkryć*. Lwów: Nakł. Kurji Metropolitalnej obradku orm.-kt. we Lwowie, 1925.

Purchla, Jacek, ed. *Architektura Lwowa XIX wieku*. Cracow: International Cultural Centre, 1997.

Trehubova Tetiana and Roman Mych. *Ľviv. Architekturno-istoryčnyj narys.* Kyiv, 1989.

Tscherkes, Bohdan, Martin Kubelik, and Elizabeth Hofer, eds. *Architektura Halyčyny XIX-XX st. Vybrani materialy mižnarodnoho sympoziumu 24-27 travnia 1994 r. prysviačenoho 150-ričča zasnuvannia Deržavnoho universytetu "Ľvivśka Politechnika" – Baukunst in Galizien XIX-XX Jh.* Ľviv: Ľvivśka Politechnika, 1996.

Thullie, Czeslaw (Dr.) *O kościolach lwowskich z czasów Odrodzenia.* Lemberg: Ksiegarnia W. Gubrynowicza i syna, 1913.

Vujcyk, Volodymyr. *Deržavnyj istoryko-architekturnyj zapovidnyk u Ľvovi.* Ľviv: Kameniar, 1979, reprinted in 1991.

_____. "Do istoriï budynkiv Naukovoho Tovarystva im. Ševčenka. Budynok na vul. Vynnyčenka 24," in *Visnyk NTŠ* 16-17 (spring-summer 1997).

_____. "Do istoriï budynkiv Naukovoho Tovarystva im. Ševčenka. Budynok na vul. Vynnychenka 26." in *Visnyk NTŠ* 18 (winter, 1997).

_____. "Do istoriï teatraľnych budynkiv u Ľvovi." in *Narodoznavči Zošyty* 2 (32), 2000.

_____. "Fontany staroho Ľvova," in *Ratuša*, no. 67 (625) 9.4-10.6.1997.

_____. "Istorija odnoho fontana" in *Express* (1-9.3.1997).

_____. "Narodnyj Dim u Lvovi." in *Viľna Ukrajina* (30.7.1988).

_____. "Vulycia Halyćka u Ľvovi," in *Visnyk instytutu Ukrzachidproektrestavracija* 10 (1999).

_____. and Roman Lypka, *Zustrič zi Ľvovom.* Ľviv: Kameniar, 1987.

Žuk, Ihor. "Ivan Levynśkyj, architektor-budivnyčyj Lvova." in *Architektura Ukraïny* (Kyiv, 1992)

_____. ed. *Julian Zachariewicz 1837-98. Alfred Zachariewicz 1871-1937– wielcy architekci szkoly lwowskiej*, Wystawa Tworczosci. exh. cat. Warsaw: Stowarzyszenie Architektow Polskich Oddzial Warszawski, 1996.

INDEX